© 2007 Brepols Publishers n.v., Turnhout, Belgium
All rights reserved. No part of this book may be reproduced, stored
in a retrieval system, or transmitted, in any form or by any means,
electronic, mechanical, photocopying, recording, or otherwise, without the prior permission of the publisher.

D/2007/0095/10
ISBN 978-2-503-51985-2

When the potato failed

Causes and effects of the 'last' European
subsistence crisis, 1845–1850

Edited by Cormac Ó Gráda, Richard Paping
& Eric Vanhaute

BREPOLS

CONTENTS

LIST OF CONTRIBUTORS

HANS H. BASS — Bremen University of Applied Science, Germany

JEAN-MICHEL CHEVET — Institut National de la Recherche Agronomique – CORELA, France

MARY E. DALY — University College Dublin, Ireland

TOM M. DEVINE — University of Aberdeen, United Kingdom

PEDRO DÍAZ MARÍN — University of Alicante, Spain

CARL-JOHAN GADD — Göteborg University, Sweden

INGRID HENRIKSEN — University of Copenhagen, Denmark

GUNTER MAHLERWEIN — Gimbsheim, Germany

CORMAC Ó GRÁDA — University College Dublin, Ireland

PETER GRAY — Queen's University Belfast, United Kingdom

RICHARD PAPING — University of Groningen, The Netherlands

PETER M. SOLAR — Vesalius College, Vrije Universiteit Brussel, Belgium

VINCENT TASSENAAR — University of Groningen, The Netherlands

ERIC VANHAUTE — Ghent University, Belgium

NADINE VIVIER — Université du Maine, France

LIST OF FIGURES

LIST OF TABLES

Preface

Earlier versions of most of the papers published here were first presented at a conference on 'The mid 19th century subsistence crisis. A comparative analysis of the causes and effects of the 'last' European hunger crisis', held in University College Dublin on 11–12 December 2003. All have been significantly revised in the interim. The papers by Gunter Mahlerwein (on southern Germany) and Cormac Ó Gráda (on Ireland) were commissioned subsequent to the conference, while those by Pedro Díaz Marín (on Spain) and Tom Devine (on Scotland) are slightly revised versions of papers previously published elsewhere.[1]

The initial impetus for the conference came from the CORN (Comparative Rural History of the North Sea Area) research network. Its starting point was the perceived need for a scholarly volume that would offer a broad and comparative perspective on what may be truly deemed Europe's last extensive peacetime subsistence crisis (or crises).

We begin accordingly with an extensive introduction that treats the topic in comparative perspective. The subsistence crisis had its most catastrophic impact in Ireland, and three chapters in the current volume (those by Peter Gray, Mary Daly, and Cormac Ó Gráda) are concerned mainly with that country. A fourth chapter by Peter Solar uses price data to shed comparative perspective on the crisis, while the remaining nine chapters are case studies covering countries ranging from Sweden to Spain, and from Scotland to Prussia. In planning the volume, the editors encouraged contributors to focus on a range of common themes.

The conference was funded mainly by CORN and hosted by the Humanities Institute of Ireland (HII), University College Dublin. The editors are grateful to the discussants and referees, and to Mary Daly, then acting director of the HII, for facilitating the location of the conference in Dublin. They also wish to thank the secretarial staff of NIAS (Netherlands Institute for Advanced Study in the Humanities and Social Sciences) for their technical support, Koen de Scheemaeker for technical editing, and Torsten Wiedemann for making end re-editing the maps.

October 2006

Eric Vanhaute, Gent
Richard Paping, Groningen
Cormac Ó Grada, Dublin

---

[1] Pedro Díaz Marín, 'Crisis de subsistencia y protesta popular: los motines de 1847', *Historia Agraria*, 30, 2003, pp. 31-62; Tom Devine, 'Why the Highlands did not starve', in S.J. Connolly, R.A. Houston and R.J. Morris (eds.), *Conflict, Identity and Economic Development: Ireland and Scotland, 1600-1939* (Preston, 1995), pp. 77-88. A slightly different version of Ó Gráda's chapter also appears in his *Ireland's Great Famine: Interdisciplinary Essays* (Dublin, 2006).

1 The European subsistence crisis of 1845–1850: a comparative perspective[1]

Eric VANHAUTE, Ghent University
Richard PAPING, University of Groningen
Cormac Ó GRÁDA, University College Dublin

I. Introduction

The decade that gave rise to the term 'the Hungry Forties' in Europe is often regarded, and rightly so, as one of deprivation, unrest, and revolution. Two events – the Great Irish Famine and the various political events of '1848' – stand out. Poor harvests and political unrest were widespread across the continent, however, and the connection between the two has been widely discussed. The subsistence crises of the second half of the 1840s may be divided into two rather distinct sorts. On the one hand, the failure of the potato caused by the new, unfamiliar fungus, *phytophthera infestans*, which first struck Europe in mid-1845, resulted in a catastrophe in Ireland that killed about one million people, and radically transformed its landscape and the economy. Ireland's disaster puts the impact on the potato harvest elsewhere in the shade, but poor potato crops in 1845 and after resulted in significant excess mortality in other parts of Europe also. On the other hand, this period, and 1846 in particular, was also one of poor wheat and rye harvests throughout much of Europe. Failure of the grain harvest alone rarely resulted in a subsistence crisis, but the combination of poor potato and grain harvests in a single place was a lethal one.

Outside Ireland the 1840s are primarily associated with '1848', the 'Year of Revolutions'. When Karl Marx and Friedrich Engels forged their *Communist Manifesto* in London at the end of 1847 (the *Manifesto* was first printed in German shortly before the February Revolution a few months later), they made no mention of harvest crises. Later, though, Marx would interpret the crisis as a delayed reaction to the failure of the potato and the high price of cotton. The crisis that began in England, where it was delayed for a year or more by repeal of the Corn Laws, and 'gradually... affected the whole world, from the giants of the City of London down to the smallest German shopkeeper...finally broke out in September 1847'. There followed several hectic months of revolutionary ferment when (in the words of English historian G.M. Trevelyan) 'history failed to turn' (see also Boyer, 1998).

Helge Berger and Mark Spoerer have argued recently, much in the spirit of Marx, that '1848' was the product of 'economic misery and the fear thereof', claiming that in most of Europe's shortfalls in agricultural output led to 'a decline in manufacturing activity after a certain lag'. Ironically, however, in their findings one of the few countries

---

[1] An earlier version of this chapter was presented at the International Economic History Association Conference in Helsinki in August 2006. We are grateful to Peter Solar for his extensive comments both on that occasion and in subsequent correspondence.

where agricultural distress did not impact much on the rest of the economy is industrial Britain. Their case for British exceptionalism finds support in C.N. Ward-Perkins' classic 'The Commercial Crisis of 1847', which claims that in Britain in 1847 the downturn in production applied only to cotton, and that this was due to an exogenous factor – the shortage of raw cotton in the U.S. South. On the other hand, macroeconomists Rudiger Dornbusch and Jacob Frenkel blame the British banking crisis of 1847 on the 'massive real shock' of a harvest failure that gave rise to 'commercial distress and financial panic'. The Bank of England dealt with this crisis by suspending the Bank Charter Act of 1844, which prohibited the Bank from issuing banknotes without full gold backing (Berger and Spoerer, 2001; Ward-Perkins, 1950; Dornbusch and Frenkel, 1984).

Connections between the local and the global, between the economic and the political, and between the rural and the industrial, make the crisis of the late 1840s a multi-layered one. Indeed, contemporaries frequently discussed the causes and effects of the Irish Famine in a broader, European perspective, mostly from very ideological presumptions concerning, for example, the pros and cons of a peasant-based society. Whether the Irish story was an example of or an exception to the European 'model' is a question always lurking in the background. Recently several contributions have sought to put the Irish Famine in a broader perspective (Mokyr, 1989; Gray, 1997; Solar, 1989, 1997; Ó Gráda, 1999: 226–227), but much more work needs to be done in this respect.

Figure 1.1   Map of Europe in the 1840s, indicating the countries and regions mentioned in the book

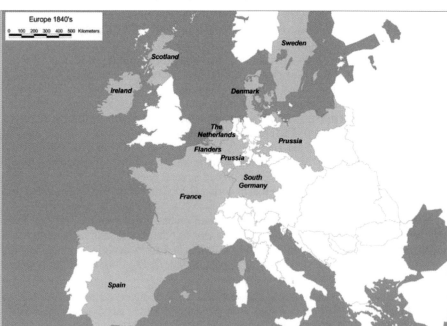

This book is the first to offer a truly comparative perspective on the causes and the effects of what is sometimes considered as the 'last' European subsistence crisis. This introductory chapter summarises and attempts to distil some of the most important findings of the book's dozen case studies. It begins with a review of economic and demographic trends in the century or so preceding the 1840s (Part II) and c. 1850 (Part III). This is followed by an account of the role of the potato and its impact on the subsistence crisis in different regions (Part IV), and of economic trends during the 1840s (Part V). Part VI summarises the demographic impact of the crisis. There follow sections on social unrest (Part VII) and the range of relief policies pursued (Part VIII). The impact (if any) on commercial policy is discussed in Part IX, while Part X points to some long-run effects of the crisis. Part XI stresses the importance of the regional dimension to the crisis within individual countries, and discusses the crisis as a set of regional crises. Finally, Part XII notes that both 'traditional' and 'modern' elements characterized the crisis of the 1840s.

II. Economic growth, social polarisation and food availability: Western Europe before 1845

After a century of stagnation, population began to grow almost everywhere in Western Europe around the middle of the eighteenth century. The origins of this population growth are still not completely clear. A fall in the age of marriage and a general rise in fertility because of higher living standards, an attenuation or even disappearance of predatory epidemics, and a general fall in mortality because of a qualitatively improved diet, all seem to have contributed to this development to a greater or less extent. Compared with earlier centuries, at first glance Western Europe seems a very different place in economic terms at the start of the nineteenth century. Growth, not stagnation, was the keyword. A significant rise in industrial production especially in England (though less revolutionary than formerly believed) but also to a lesser extent elsewhere in Western Europe, and widespread agrarian improvements accompanied population growth. At the end of the eighteenth century growth of population even accelerated. Nonetheless, recent estimates of GDP suggest that the second quarter of the nineteenth century still saw sound economic growth per capita in most Western European countries (Table 1.1). Growth was considerably less in Northern Europe (e.g. Sweden) and Southern Europe (e.g. Spain). However, even in these more peripheral countries of Europe GDP per capita rose slightly between 1820 and 1850. In heavily agrarian Ireland, for which GDP estimates are lacking, evaluating living standards before the 1840s is problematic. Different proxies offer different signals. Real wages seem to have risen somewhat between 1820 and 1835, after which date they fell again, though they were still above their pre-1820 level on the eve of the crisis. Other indicators imply a gloomier picture (Mokyr and Ó Gráda, 1988; Geary and Stark, 2004).

Rising urbanisation resulted in a higher general production per capita because people were moving from low productivity agriculture to high productivity industry and services. The rising share of labour input of industry and services made fast growth of these sectors possible, a growth which was stimulated even further by technological improvements. Despite all these positive developments, however, Western Europe in the first

Table 1.1   Estimates of growth of GDP per capita in Western European countries, 1820–1850

	1820/1850
Belgium	+1.1%
Denmark	+1.2%
Sweden	+0.2%
France	+1.1%
Germany	+0.9%
Netherlands	+0.9%
Spain	+0.2%
United Kingdom	+1.0%

Source: Calculated from: Maddison, 2003: 58–59, 66–67; Tortella, 2000: 4. United Kingdom includes Ireland.

half of the nineteenth century still had not completely freed itself from old Malthusian restrictions. Food intake per capita, in particular, remained a problem. Although national production figures were rising nearly everywhere at an unprecedented rate, caloric intake for large parts of the population lagged behind or even fell for shorter periods. Especially in the second quarter of the century anthropometric measures imply deterioration in the 'biological' standard of living (Komlos, 1998). The food intake of large parts of the Western Europeans had diminished enough to reduce the mean height of adolescents between 1830 and 1860. These are clear signs that Western European agriculture in the decades before 1860, despite economic growth in other sectors, was proving incapable of producing enough to improve significantly the diet of a majority of its inhabitants. Agricultural production between 1750 and 1850 rose (Glennie, 1999: 26–27), but no more than, and possibly even less than population growth.

In this respect, the contemporary ideas of Marx and Engels about the *Verelendung* (impoverished condition) of the working class around 1850 have some empirical basis. But they miss the point that labourers' consumption of non-food goods and services was rising. Before 1800, food availability in the countryside had been quite good in normal years, but non-food products were scarce and expensive. There were two ways of getting hold of them: (1) producing them at home in an unspecialised way; (2) producing a considerable agricultural (or proto-industrial) surplus to secure – after the deduction of taxes and land rents – the money to buy such products. After 1800 many opted for the latter. Trends over these decades thus highlight the 'index number problem' presented by anthropometric measures of the standard of living: other, more comprehensive measures as real wages (taking into account non-food products too) show more favourable outcomes.

In the century before the potato blight, despite the different socio-economic settings, nearly all rural parts of Europe experienced severe social polarisation. Between 1750 and 1850 a growing part of the rural population was no longer able to fall back on even a small family holding. The result was increasing dependence on (a combination of) uncertain forms of wage labour. In this respect we see for example a rising share of small peasants and cottagers in Ireland, of near-landless peasants dependent on proto-industrial activities in parts of Flanders, and of a specialized farm labour force in Dutch and Danish commercial agriculture (Klep, 1981; Vanhaute, 1992; Paping, 1995; Henriksen, Ch. 14).

In all regions the combination of the rise of a relatively large and well-to-do class of commercial farmers with the expansion of the group of part time rural labourers and cottagers experiencing poor and deteriorating food conditions may be noted. In Sweden, for example, the share of landless and semi-landless rural dwellers rose from one fifth to about one half of the population between 1750 and 1870 (Gadd, Ch. 15). These social consequences of population growth resulted in the mid-19th century in about one-fourth to one-third of the European rural population (the share differing from region to region) being extremely vulnerable to large price increases.

Agricultural production did rise due to land reclamations and minor technical and organisational improvements, but it was hardly enough to escape from the law of diminishing marginal returns to labour. Agricultural labour productivity was stagnant or possibly even slowly deteriorating as a result of a falling land-labour ratio. Although rural population grew fast, urban population grew even faster in the period 1750–1850 (De Vries, 1984). Urbanisation was inevitably accompanied by a diminishing share of agriculture in labour input and this contributed to stagnant or even falling food availability per capita in the first half of the nineteenth century. Rising prosperity of parts of the urban population also resulted in a large demand for livestock products, the consumption of which was distributed very unevenly over the population. Increased production of livestock decreased the land available for the production of agricultural products with a higher calorific yield per hectare (cereals and potatoes). As a result large imports of cereals remained crucial for meeting Western Europe's food requirements, especially for the richer and more urbanised parts, such as in the Netherlands and increasingly England and Belgium.

It can be concluded that food availability remained a weak point in Western European economic prosperity and growth around 1840. Growth in real income of most groups in society in the previous years resulted mainly in a rising consumption of industrial goods and services, due to their high price and income elasticities. Technological change meant that the supply of these products was rising quickly and their prices falling relative to food. On the other hand the demand for food for large parts of the population was not completely price inelastic, so relative price increases resulted in a falling demand, insofar as the income elasticity of food products was very low.

Securing a larger money surplus to buy more non-food products meant for a lot of rural people selling more agricultural products to the market, reducing their self-provisioning (Komlos, 1998). This became an increasingly attractive strategy considering the relative rise of agricultural prices, and the relative fall in price of industrial products after 1830, especially on the European continent. Because of an enormous improvement in the terms of trade of the agricultural countryside, limited (or even zero) rises in productivity were accompanied by large increases in real income, but also by a fall in food consumption (Paping, 1995; Komlos, 1998). In this way relative price trends delivered more food from the countryside to the growing numbers of city dwellers. However, the price rises meant that the lower classes in the cities were unable – or unprepared – to buy much more food, even more so when the amount of bread one could buy for one's daily wage did not rise or even fell. Economizing on food on the other hand brought new cheap products within reach.

In general, the potato's track record as a staple food prior to 1845 was good and Europe had been spared major subsistence crises since the late 1810s. However, European economic progress before the 1840s was insufficient to prevent the unprecedented ecological shock of the potato blight from 1845 onwards and the failure of the harvest of the most important cereals, rye and wheat, in 1846 from causing severe problems for large parts of the population. In particular, the continuing failure of the potato harvests formed an enormous shock, because the widespread appearance of potatoes in the fields was one of the main positive agricultural developments in the period 1750–1850. The tuber showed very high yields per hectare compared to other crops, even taking into account that the calorific intake per kilo was far less than cereals. Potatoes had some further advantages. First, because they were rich in vitamin C, they enriched the diet. Second, they could be grown easily on tiny pieces of relatively infertile land, with no need for horse power, making them very suitable as garden vegetable for those with little or no land, who formed a rising part of the rural population. In this way it could replace cereals in the diet to a considerable extent. Even in cities the potato found its way to numerous gardens.

In the previous pages a general picture has been painted of the economic developments in Western Europe in the century before 1850. However, in reality large differences existed in economic development and structure between countries and also within countries. These differences help explain why the impact of the potato blight and the failure of the harvest of 1846 differed so much within Western Europe. In this volume most of the articles will focus on the consequences of the potato blight in a certain country or region. In the rest of this introductory article we will try to draw some comparisons between the different countries and regions in order to explain the differences.

III. The economic structure of Western Europe around 1850

This paragraph focuses on regional differences around the middle of the century. As Table 1.2 shows the Dutch were still producing the highest GDP per capita, an inheritance of their extremely wealthy 17th and 18th century past. The difference with the more industrialised United Kingdom, however, was only small. If one takes into account that the figures for the United Kingdom include populous though backward Ireland, the level on the main British island will even have been around 2,700–2,800 Geary-Khamis 1990 dollars per capita, considerably more than the Netherlands. Belgium as the second European country experiencing industrialisation and Denmark with its relatively modern capitalistic agriculture were next in line. The economies of France and Germany lagged behind. GDP per capita around 1850 was lowest in peripheral Spain and Sweden, which experienced as already noted only very modest economic growth in the previous decades. Assuming that Irish GDP per head was 40–50% of the British average implies that it was roughly on a par with that of Sweden and higher than that of Spain.

Important features of the high levels of economic development in Great Britain and the Netherlands were a relatively high urbanisation rate and a low share of agriculture. Belgium followed at a clear distance. Differences between the other countries were small with a share of agriculture still fluctuating between 49% and 54% in 1870, while urbanisation ran in 1850 from 6% in Scandinavia to a comparatively high 17% for Spain. It may be concluded that except for the Netherlands and the British mainland the major part of the Western European population was rural, living on farms, in villages or in small cities. About half of the population was dependent directly on agriculture for its living. Clearly, however, a considerable part of the rural population was active outside agriculture, pointing at the fact that even outside large cities specialisation was becoming of importance. Rural activities outside agriculture ranged from artisans and salesmen working for the local markets to families working in proto-industry supplementing their income with small agricultural activities mainly directed at self-provision. Differences between regions within countries however could be large.

Table 1.2   Some key data for Western European economies around 1850

	Population in 1850 (thousands)	GDP per capita in 1850	employment in agriculture in 1870	Urbanisation cities of 10,000
Belgium	4,449	1,847	43%	21%
Denmark	1,499	1,767	52%	6%*
Sweden	3,483	1,289	54%	
France	36,350	1,597	49%	15%
Germany	33,746	1,428	49%	11%
Netherlands	3,098	2,371	37%	30%
Spain	14,894	1,079	67%	17%
United Kingdom excluding Ireland	20,303	2,330	23%	40%
Ireland (1851)	6,552			10%

Note: * = Scandinavia

Source: Maddison, 2003: 34–35, 42, 58–59, 66; Maddison, 1991: 248; de Vries, 1984: 45; Tortella, 2000: 68. GDP per capita is in 1990 international Geary-Khamis dollars.

Concerning food supply, Bass (Ch. 9) makes a very useful division between four kinds of regions within Prussia: 1. Long-distance export regions (large farms and many labourers/cottagers); 2. Short-distance export regions (middle-sized farms); 3. Self-supplying regions (mainly peasant agriculture); 4. Food import regions (urbanised; proto-industrial regions). Taking into account that large internal differences existed, we can extend this division to the other European Countries. Ireland – apart from the northeast and parts of the remote west – was typically a long-distance export region, which supplied England with cereals and meat. France and Spain seeme to have been dominated by short-distance export regions producing for the few cities. Belgium, at least Flanders, was a combination of self-sufficient regions with heavy proto-industrialisation and some urbanised food importing regions. For the Netherlands food imports were of more importance (especially in the coastal area), although large parts can be considered as short-distance export regions. However, the very modern, market-oriented and specialised economy of the coastal Netherlands combined food exports (livestock, oats, cole-seed) with food imports (bread cereals and barley). Denmark can be best characterised as a long-distance export region, while in Sweden self-supplying regions seem to have been in the majority. However, it has to be stressed, that there were large differences in social-economic structure within all countries.

IV. The significance of the potato and the impact of the crisis

Unfortunately, nineteenth century national figures are scarce, and if available they are not completely comparable. This makes it difficult to compare the consequences of the potato blight and the accompanying failure of the rye harvest for different Western European countries. However, in several chapters in this book some clues are given to make a rough comparison viable. Table 1.3 implies that the role of the potato differed enormously between countries. Within-country differences were also large as – among others – the contributions on France (Vivier), South Germany (Mahlerwein), and the Netherlands (Paping and Tassenaar) in this volume show.

Table 1.3   Potato production and consumption and the fall in yields in 1845 and 1846 compared to 'normal' years

	Pre blight % arable land Potatoes	Pre blight daily potato consumption per capita (kilo)	1845 decline in potato yields	1846 decline in potato yields	1846 decline in rye/ wheat yields
Belgium	14%	0.5/0.6	−87%	−43%	−50%/−10%
Denmark	3%	0.2/0.3	App. −50%		App. −20%
Sweden	5%	0.5/0.6	App. −20/25%		App. −10%
France	App. 6%	0.5	−20%	−19%	−20%/−25%
Württemberg	3%–8%	n.a.	−55%	−51%	−15%/−24%
Prussia	11%	1.0/1.1	n.a.	−47%	−43%
Netherlands	11%	0.7	−71%	−56%	−47%/−6%
Spain	2%	low	n.a.	n.a.	n.a.
Highlands of Scotland	n.a.	high	n.a.	App. −80%	n.a.
Ireland	App. 32%	2.1	App. −30%	App. −88%	App. −33%

Source: Figures mainly estimated from the different chapters in this book, with spe-cial thanks to Hans-Heinrich Bass, Carl-Johan Gadd and Peter Solar; Tortella, 2000: 60 (Spain 1857); Von Reden,1853/54: 87–95; Hellstenius, 1871: 106; Gadd, 1983: 248; *Emigrationsutredningen* (1913: 91); *Statistisch en staathuishoudkundig Jaar-boekje* (1850: 232); Ó Gráda, 1999: 24. See also: Bourke, 1993: 53.

Clearly the position of potatoes in Irish diet had no parallel in Western Europe. Irish population growth in the century before 1845 depended heavily on the increasing availability of potatoes. Nearly comparable amounts of potatoes were eaten in the Scottish Highlands, with Prussia (according to Bass's estimates) as the next largest consumer following at great distance. In food-importing Netherlands and in Belgian Flanders the potato played a somewhat larger role in agriculture and diet relative to most of the rest of continental Europe, although the differences were rather small. On average, potatoes delivered between 10 and 30 percent of the necessary daily calories. However, averages do not tell the complete story. For families in specific conditions and regions, the proportionate share of potatoes in the diet could have been a lot higher. Vanhaute (Ch. 7), for instance, suggests that Flemish peasants and rural labourers consumed 1 to 1.5 kilos potatoes daily on average. Ó Gráda (Ch. 2: table 2.1) shows that Irish labourers comprising two-fifths of the population consumed about one and a half as much potatoes than the average Irishman.

The potato blight appeared in the United States in 1843, possibly having come from Mexico or South America. In Europe it was first noticed in June 1845 near Courtrai in Belgium (Bourke, 1993: 140–144) from were it spread in the next weeks through the Netherlands, parts of northern France and the neighbouring English coast. Within weeks after the middle of August the disease also appeared in western Germany, southern Denmark, the rest of England and eastern Ireland. Only after the middle of September the whole of Ireland, and parts of Scotland, eastern Germany, south Norway and south Sweden were touched.

Because of its rather small share in the average diet, the failure of the potato harvest in 1845, though causing hardship, could quite easily be overcome in most of continental Western Europe. In France the potato blight only appeared in certain areas. The potato harvests in the Netherlands and Belgium were hit hardest in 1845. In Denmark the consumption of potatoes was very low and in Sweden, as Gadd (Ch. 15) clearly shows, the problems were restricted to parts of the country, while the north for climatic reasons remained untouched by the potato blight. In Ireland (where the blight showed up only in September and October) and in France (the south remained untouched in 1845) the loss of potatoes in 1845 was – about 30% and 20%, respectively – significant, but still not dramatic.

The harvest of 1846 was a different story. In Ireland and the Scottish Highlands the potato yields were barely enough or insufficient to provide for the next year's seed. On the other hand, in 1846 potato yields improved in Belgium and The Netherlands. However, in these countries and also in Prussia about half the potato harvest was lost. In much of northwestern Europe the problems caused by the potato were exacerbated by the loss in 1846 of almost half of the rye harvest, while the wheat harvest was considerably below normal. This was disastrous, with bread from rye or wheat being even more important than potatoes in continental European diets. It bears emphasis that the failure of the Dutch, Belgian and Prussian rye harvest of 40–50% in 1846 was extreme by nineteenth century standards. For example, in the Netherlands in the period 1852–1913 the rye harvest was never more than 34% below normal, and in France in the period 1815–1835 it never fell by more than 13% below average (see Solar, 1989: 116).

Although in the years after 1846 the potato blight still depressed yields in specific years (e.g. 1848), this didn't result in grave problems outside Ireland inasmuch as the production of food alternatives remained nearly untouched those years. In fact, judging by the very low levels of cereal prices, supplies of wheat and rye may have been particularly abundant in these years.

V. Economy and population during the blight

Tables 1.1 and 1.4 present Angus Maddison's most recent estimates of the development of GDP per capita in most of the countries surveyed in this volume. Because of the difficulties in reconstructing national accounts, the annual fluctuations in the estimates of GDP per capita only give a rough idea of what is happening in national economies. For the 1840s annual data are available only for five countries in Western Europe, and these do not seem very much in line with each other. Excluding the Netherlands, in all other countries enormous yearly fluctuations seem to have taken place, which, however, can only partly be linked to the potato blight in 1845–1846 and the disastrous rye harvest in 1846. In the first half of the 1840s a process of catching-up seems to have been taking place. The very wealthy Netherlands and United Kingdom experienced a slow deterioration of the economy, while more backward countries like France, Denmark and Sweden showed quite healthy growth figures.

In the specific years of the potato blight GDP figures developed rather opposite. In the United Kingdom were agriculture played only a relatively minor role in economy, the national product increased very fast in 1845 and 1846. In the Netherlands which were in quite the same situation, no important fall in the overall economic figures can be traced. In the other three countries agriculture played a far more important role in economy. In France and especially in Sweden there were clear signs of a depression in 1845 and 1846. Denmark on the other hand remained remarkably untouched, possibly because of its specialisation in livestock farming.

Table 1.4   Annual growth of GDP per capita in Western Europe (percentages)

	1840/44	1845	1846	1847	1848	1849	1850/60
Belgium	n.a.	n.a.	n.a	+4.0%	−0.5%	+2.1%	+2.3%
Denmark	+1.8%	+1.6%	+1.2%	−1.4%	+4.2%	+4.9%	+0.3%
Sweden	+1.3%	−6.6%	−3.0%	+5.6%	+4.9%	+2.2%	+1.0%
France	+2.8%	−3.5%	−0.1%	+10.6%	−6.5%	+2.8%	+1.7%
Germany	n.a.	n.a.	n.a.	n.a.	n.a.	n.a.	+1.7%
Netherlands	−0.4%	+0.1%	−0.3%	+0.4%	+1.1%	+2.3%	+0.2%
Spain	n.a.	n.a.	n.a.	n.a.	n.a.	n.a.	+1.4%
United Kingdom*	−0.9%	+4.3%	+5.7%	+1.3%	+2.7%	+2.7%	+1.8%

Note: *United Kingdom is including Ireland.
Source: Maddison, 2003: 58–59, 66–67.

Countries such as France and Sweden, which were affected mainly by the 1845–1846 crisis, returned to normal or near-normal in the following year 1847. Trends in Belgium, for which GDP figures are available from 1846 onwards, seem in line with these two. On the other hand, in 1847 growth in the Netherlands and the United Kingdom[2] was quite low, while the economy of Denmark even experienced a setback after growth in the previous three years.

This is not the place to consider short-run economic developments in the following years; however, some remarks can be made. From 1848 onwards, although annual economic fluctuations differed enormously between countries, in the long-run developments were quite in line, with the Netherlands and to a lesser extent Denmark growing con-

---

[2] However, as noted above, the British financial crisis of 1846–1847 is hardly reflected in the macro figures, suggesting that this crisis did not have much impact on output in most sectors and for the employment of Irish moving to England. However, the figures for industrial growth alone were far worse in 1848: France −11%, Prussia −24%, and the Netherlands −4% (Berger and Spoerer, 2001: 313).

siderably more slowly than the other countries in the period 1848–1860. Interesting is also the fall in production in France during the year of revolution (1848).

Table 1.5   Estimated annual population growth rates in some Western European countries (percentages)

	1840/45	1845/6	1846/7	1847/8	1848/9	1849/50	1850/60
Belgium	+1.1%	+0.9%	+0.9%	+0.0%	+0.5%	+0.2%	+0.7%
Denmark	+1.1%	+1.0%	+0.8%	+1.0%	+1.0%	+1.0%	+1.2%
Sweden	+1.1%	+0.8%	+0.6%	+1.0%	+1.3%	+1.2%	+1.0%
France	+0.5%	+0.7%	+0.4%	+0.1%	+0.3%	+0.0%	+0.5%
Germany (total)	+1.0%	+1.0%	+0.5%	+0.2%	+0.1%	+0.9%	+0.7%
Prussia	+1.3%	+1.4%	+0.8%	+0.5%	+0.4%	+0.9%	+1.0%
Netherlands	+1.1%	+1.1%	+0.3%	−0.2%	+0.1%	+0.3%	+0.7%
United Kingdom*	+1.2%	+1.2%	+0.7%	+0.7%	+0.7%	+0,7%	+1.3%
Ireland	+0.4%	−0.2%	−4.0%	−4.0%	−4.0%	−4.0%	−1.7%

Note: * United Kingdom is excluding Ireland, and the result of interpolation between 5-year estimates. The figures for Ireland are only very rough estimates, and must not be taken literally.
Source: Denmark, Sweden and United Kingdom: Maddison (2003: 34–35, 42–43), mid-year numbers have been compared. France: 'Recensement' (1966); Prussia: www.learn-line.nrw.de/angebote/eda/medio/preussen; the Netherlands: Smits et al (2000: 109–110); Belgium: *Population* (1843–1851); *Documents* (1857–1869). For these countries 1845/46 relates to the development from 1 January 1845 to 1 January 1846. For Spain and Ireland annual figures are lacking.

Clearly, a genuine subsistence crisis has to show up in demographic data. During the first half of the 1840s there were very few differences in population growth between the different countries (Table 1.5). Only Ireland stands out, showing some signs of adjustment to the enormous economic and demographic problems that it faced in this period. The deceleration in Irish population growth before 1845 was mainly the result of a reduction in nuptiality and heavy emigration (Ó Gráda, 1999: 25–26). The rest of Western Europe experienced a considerable annual growth of around 1% already since the first half of the 19th century.

The demographic effects in other countries were dwarfed by what happened in Ireland. Maddison's figures imply, probably correctly, that Irish population fell marginally between mid-1845 and mid-1846. Over the following four years famine Ireland lost about one-fifth of its population, especially because of starvation and emigration, but also because of falling birth rates. It seems logical that during the actual potato blight mortality was the prime mover in this process of depopulation, while at the end of the 1840s emigration to North America and England was of most importance, death and birth figures returning to more normal values. Emigration continued to reduce the Irish population in the 1850s. In the Scottish Highlands, having a somewhat comparable potato-dependent structure as Ireland, a similar process of depopulation was taking place. However, Devine (Ch. 6) argues that because the Highlands were less overpopulated thanks to heavy emigration before 1845, and because it was easier for Highlanders to escape starvation by moving to the industrialised Lowlands, adjustment was less dramatic in the late 1840s.

Population trends in the rest of Western Europe during the Irish disaster are of interest. Two groups of countries show up in the figures. A first group comprises of Great Britain, Sweden, and Denmark who all experienced only very minor setbacks in population growth. The consequences in Sweden are clearest, while in Denmark they were negligible. In the United Kingdom population growth slowed down in the period 1847–1850, however the figures are the result of interpolation between 5-year periods so they are not really suitable for a year-to-year analysis.

The figures for Germany, the Netherlands, France and Belgium, however, suggest that the potato blight had relatively more distinct general demographic effects on the Western European mainland. A closer look makes clear that in 1846 and 1847 the Netherlands were hit more than Germany, France and Belgium, which had to do with a malaria epidemic raging the Dutch coastal provinces. In 1847 population growth in all four countries was nearly zero. In Prussia population growth was a little bit higher, suggesting a fall in population in other parts of Germany. However, in 1848–1849, after the worst of the blight was over, population growth remained remarkably low in these Western European countries. Paping and Tassenaar (Ch. 8) attribute this continuing stagnation in the Netherlands to cholera and possibly to an influenza epidemic.

VI. Deaths, births, and migration

The Irish Famine killed about 1 million people, or one-eighth of the total population. This makes it one of the major human disasters in the last centuries, even on a world scale. Mortality started to rise steeply only in the autumn of 1846, after the second harvest failure. In 1847, the mortality rate was more than three times higher than its pre-Famine norm (first half of the 1840s). The famine struck hardest in the west and southwest. Most of the victims were the rural poor. Even in the Irish case, local 'triggers' seem to have been important, such as the spread of infectious fevers, the health situation in over-populated workhouses and the labour conditions (certainly in the winter months) in public works. As in other famine-affected regions few people died directly of starvation. Most of them succumbed to hunger-related diseases such as typhoid fever, typhus and dysentery (Mokyr and Ó Gráda, 2002).

Relative to Ireland, the death toll of the famine years 1845–1847 in the rest of Europe was small, a few hundred thousands at most. But figures are not easy to compare and interpret. What are famine-related deaths? We should exclude excess mortality in 1849, an infamous cholera year. What are normal ratios? In practice our comparison refers to average rates in the first half of the 1840s.

In Scotland, 'people did survive' as Devine (Ch. 6) notes. Surplus mortality was limited in time, from late 1846 to early 1847. Contrary to Ireland, excess mortality was highest in the cities. In Belgium mortality figures in 1847 were 30% higher than in the preceding years. Total excess mortality in 1846–1848 may have been as much as 40,000–50,000 deaths. Mortality was highest in the linenregions in East- and West-Flanders with excess death rates rising from two-fifths to double or more in certain locations. Most died from typhus and other hunger-related diseases. Dutch excess mortality was comparable to that in Belgium, an increase of 32% in 1847, with regional peaks of up to

50–60%. The highest numbers were not recorded in inland sandy regions such as Flanders, but in the coastal clay provinces and in the densely urbanised province of North-Holland. In Prussia mortality rose in 1847 by two-fifths relative to earlier years, resulting in an excess mortality of about 42,000 people. Surplus mortality was highest in long-distance exporting regions with a large-scale commercial agriculture such as East Elbia, followed by proto-industrial regions such as Upper Silesia.

In the rest of Europe, crisis-related mortality seems to have been very light. In South Germany and Switzerland only some regions such as the canton of Bern were confronted with surplus mortality. The same seems to be true for France. On average, in France mortality in 1847 was only 4–5% higher than in the years 1841–45, resulting in some 10,000s crisis-related excess deaths. However, regional differences were marked. Chevet and Ó Gráda (Ch. 12) claim that these differences were related to 'local epidemics, and not, at least directly, to the problems of subsistence'. In Denmark and Sweden mortality in 1847 was about one-tenth higher than normal. Mortality in Copenhagen rose by up to one-fifth due to typhus and other epidemics seemingly unrelated to famine.

Little is known about the gender and age differentiated impact of the 1840s famine. Sparse figures from Ireland and other regions suggest that slightly more men than women became victims of the famine. The Flemish and Dutch case studies indicate that surplus mortality was highest in the groups of adults and elderly people (40–69 years old). In case surplus mortality was not related to privation and famine related diseases, young children seem to have been much more the prime victims, for example, during the cholera epidemic of 1849 (compare Dyson and Ó Gráda, 2002).

It must be stressed that most people faced by famine conditions did not die, but they did suffer. An indication is the slowing down of the body growth of adolescents in crisis years. In Flanders the group of undersized recruits of 18–21 years old increased from less than 20% to more than 25% after 1847. A similar decrease in heights took place in the Netherlands, where the group of small recruits under 1.57 m increased by 20% in the years after 1847. Here the rise was strongest in the cities, as against Flanders in the villages in the linen districts.

The demographic impact of sudden economic shocks such as famines becomes not only visible in a sudden rise in mortality, but also in a decline in fertility and natality. Typically, the decline in births started about a year after the local outbreak of the blight. In Ireland births fell back by a third, resulting in about 0.5 million averted conceptions. Declines were lower but still remarkable in Flanders (one-fifth to one-third in 1847), the Netherlands (one-tenth to one-fifth), and Prussia (one-eighth). In France the decline was only one-sixteenth, but that nevertheless represented the sharpest decline in the period 1810–1870. Compared to the preceding years, nuptiality in 1847 declined by 30–40% in Flanders and by 11% in France. In Denmark and Sweden the impact of the crisis on natality and nuptiality was negligible.

As in the case of excess mortality, Ireland in the 1840s and 1850s was the classic case of a famine-driven wave of mass-emigration. In 1855 one quarter of native Irish men and women lived abroad. Most moved to North America, but the famine also greatly increased the number of Irish-born in Great Britain (Neal 1997). As in Ireland, Scottish collective memory of the famine is closely related to transatlantic mass migration. Mainly as a result of mass clearances and manifold schemes of assisted passage across the

Atlantic, some Scottish regions lost, between 1841 and 1861, one-third to one-half of their population. Moreover, movements of temporary migrants from the Highlands to the Lowlands and to England helped to relieve the impact of the famine. The situation on the continent was strikingly different. Even in the worst affected regions such as inland Flanders or East Elbia, the crisis generated no movements of mass migration, neither to the cities nor overseas. As a result, most rural dwellers stayed in the region of origin. Rural Flanders, much affected by a subsistence and industrial crisis, lost only 9% of its population between 1846 and 1850.

The information provided in the contributions in the book suggest that the demographic effects of the subsistence crisis of the 1840s were most pronounced on a west-east axis from Ireland over the British Islands, the Northern and Southern Netherlands and further to East Prussia. The further north and south of this line, the weaker the demographic impact of the crisis. Comparative analysis of the demographic effects of the subsistence crisis of the 1840s confirms the necessity of a regional approach. A fortiori the same is true for national correlations, for example between demographic and price data. It is not surprising that most contributors in this book stress that explanations for these regional differences must be sought within the organisation of the regional and local economy and society, and not in national comparisons.

As a crisis indicator, mortality is a very incomplete benchmark. More direct indicators of human crisis behaviour are nuptiality, natality and migration. The case studies in the book show clearly that in the most affected regions (British Isles, Belgium, The Netherlands, Prussia, but also in France), the shock of the blight was followed by a strong decline in conceptions (births) and (presumably) marriages. This implies that regions such as Denmark and Sweden which produced no meaningful reaction in fertility behaviour witnessed no crisis shock comparable with the other regions mentioned. The effects on migration behaviour correlates not with that of nuptiality and fertility. Only the devastated 'British' regions of Ireland and Scotland were the scenes of a dramatic wave of mass migration. On the continent, the crisis was often harsh, but not in the sense that it wiped away completely the basics of rural survival relations.

VII. Social unrest

In a recent publication Berger and Spoerer (2001) explored the correlation between grain price shocks in the years 1845–1847 and political turmoil in 1848 for 21 European regional economies. They concluded that if a country was subjected to a grain price shock between 1845 and 1847, then it was more likely to experience a political revolution in 1848. They found only a few exceptions, such as Denmark (a revolution without price shocks). Berger and Spoerer's research brought back to the fore the argument that political unrest and revolutions were very closely linked with short-term economic disturbances. This argument was particularly popular in French historiography about the revolutions of 1848, as both Vivier (Ch. 11) and Chevet and Ó Gráda (Ch. 12) have underlined in their contributions. At the same time these authors warn against blowing up the crisis-factor as a main explanation for the revolutionary waves. Social unrest as a political protest of poor against rich only appeared in the aftermath of the crisis, as Vivier notes (e.g., the forest riots in 1848). Moreover, as Solar's contribution (Ch. 4) implies, grain markets in Europe were quite well integrated during the crisis, and tended to move in broad tandem. As for the Danish case, Henriksen (Ch. 14) concludes that the political revolution of 1848 was triggered by matters other than food prices.

The other cases presented in the book confirm the opinion that social unrest resulting from the famine crisis was not related to national protest movements, but rooted in local and regional social relations. This is most clear in case of 'classic' market riots. A real wave of market disturbances surged over Europe in 1846–1847, with a peak in the spring of 1847, when grain prices peaked. It is striking that regions with market-oriented agriculture and a substantial number of wage labourers were by far most affected by market disturbances. In France riots were heaviest in cities and in grain exporting regions. This resulted in different forms of protest, from blockades and forced sales to local riots arising from rumours of speculation. According to Diaz Marin (Ch. 13) the pattern in Spain is very similar: a huge wave of short time market riots, mostly lasting one or two days, in the first half of 1847, all instigated by a rise in grain and bread prices and by suspected instances of speculation and export. Unrest was most intense in regions such as Andalucia with a significant number of workers relying mainly on wage income and where access to relief was very limited. In Prussia, riots were almost exclusively restricted to the long-distance grain exporting regions. Although price rises were as high, market disturbances were much less common in more self-supplying counties. As Bass (Ch. 9) suggests, a combination of three sets of causes is necessary to trigger collective social unrest in a period of high bread prices: a) an assumed threat of food deprivation and of uncertainty on the food markets by a large group of market-dependent families, b) strong group formation and 'horizontal' communication (on market supply and prices) in the lower (labouring) classes and c) the reaction of the authorities ('vertical' information). In other regions, such as South Germany, Flanders and The Netherlands, riots were almost exclusively urban events, mostly directed against the symbols of (perceived) speculation, such as millers, bakers and traders.

Some contributors to this volume stress the double nature of the massive wave of local riots: first, the older, more traditional reactions against higher food prices, against alleged injustices in the working of the markets; second, more modern reactions against new contingencies resulting from proletarianisation, job uncertainty, wage instability, and a growing dependency on insecure forms of wage labour.

The case studies in the book suggest that market riots triggered by actual or expected shortages and price rises were almost exclusively restricted to regions with commercial, grain-exporting agriculture and to cities. In peasant-based economies with a lower dependency on purchased grain and bread consumption, collective actions were scarce, even in the darkest days of the crisis. Social unrest in peasant economies was mostly limited to small, often individual actions of resistance and law-breaking. Even in famine-devastated Ireland, food riots were limited to the first period of the crisis (Eiríksson, 1997). Rising unrest was reflected in higher numbers of registered criminality (such as theft, cattle- and sheep rustling, burglaries and robberies). In Flanders small food riots were confined to the cities. On the other hand, petty criminality (notably mendicancy and vagrancy, petty theft, pillage, stealing crops) rose by 50% in the crisis years 1846–1847. In these crisis-related actions, women and children were overrepresented, as Vanhaute (Ch. 7) showed. The same pattern can be seen in Sweden, where crimes against property as theft and pilfering rose most in the crisis years. As expected, the correlation with (grain) prices was weak, in contrast with crop failure in general, as Gadd (Ch. 15) convincingly argues.

VIII. Local social policy

Both the impact of famine and the range of social unrest were mostly absorbed within the structures of local society, at least on the continent. Village structures had two major components, the village institutions and the actions of the local elites, whether or not through the local institutions.

In most crisis-affected areas there was a strong increase in municipal activities at different levels: (a) local relief policy (through structural institutional relief and food aid), (b) market regulation by protective rules, price subsidies, the purchase of grain, potatoes and other food products, export prohibitions, and so on, (c) employment actions either in charity workshops and workhouses or by projects of public work, and (d) repression such as prohibitions against begging and vagrancy.

Flanders is a typical case where local communities carried the heaviest burden in organising and financing relief, control and repression activities. In the crisis years about two-fifths of the people in the most affected areas received some form of communal aid. In the Netherlands in 1847 18% of the people were supported by local relief boards, against 13% in 1840–1844. In some regions the numbers supported doubled. In France expenditures of the local relief boards doubled between 1843 and 1847, often financed by an extra 'poor tax'. The same pattern is seen in South Germany.

Such timely village actions are less clear in regions with large-scale export agriculture, as in East Elbia. In Prussia local poor institutions were strongest in the west and weakest in the most affected regions in the east. In Spain local authorities only intervened after the riots of spring 1847 with a combination of aid actions and employment programmes such as public works and coercive employment of the poor by farmer-proprietors. In Scandinavian countries pressure on local communities remained limited. Nonetheless on average one-fifth of the population was temporarily dependent on poor relief.

The situation in the British Isles was very different. As Gray (Ch. 4) shows, there was considerable interest in the London epicentre in the 'continental response' to the crisis, but that interest mainly fed an ingrained scepticism. Supported by the axiom of Irish and Highland economic backwardness, the main focus was not on amelioration, but on the need for a radical transformation of rural society. That is why London elites 'tended to pathologize Irish difference from British social, economic and cultural norms' (Ch. 4). As a consequence British policy in Ireland was rooted in the idea that the local structures were the cause and not the solution of the problem. The 1847 reform of the poor relief system drastically reduced relief entitlements of rural smallholders when the Famine was still raging. The workhouse system, initiated in 1838, was not designed to cope with a major famine crisis. As Daly (Ch. 3) states, 'famine relief policies were designed, not simply to bring about short-term assistance, but to transform Irish rural society'.

A major explanation for the resilience of local communities is the interests and actions of local elites. Such elites played a decisive role through their control of local policy, relief and police institutions, through their financing (via poor rates and other forms of taxation) of extra expenditure, and through their organising of private relief and protection actions. The role of private initiative is very clear in the case of Denmark, where the relief actions in 1845–1847 were organised by local merchants and exclusively funded by private charity. This exceptional situation was a result of the mild nature of the late 1840s crisis in Denmark. During the harsher crisis of 1853–1856 local institutions were much more active.

In Ireland local elites could not fill in the gap that the weakness of local village structures left. The often absentee Anglo-Irish landlords were mostly preoccupied by their own survival, often resulting in campaigns of mass eviction and weak support for local relief structures. As Devine (Ch. 6) remarks, this is in contrast with the Scottish case, also part of the United Kingdom. In Scotland, the landlord response was much more pro-active and aimed at support and help (food aid, job creation, rent remissions). Evictions were one of the responses, as in Ireland. But here, they involved more assisted emigration to North America and Australia (Norton, 2005). Devine regards the stronger financial position of the Scottish landlords, due in large part to their concentration on sheep-farming, as the main explanation (compare Éiríksson and Ó Gráda, 2006).

In his contribution Vanhaute (Ch. 7) argues that one of the main differences in the effects of the crisis in Flanders and Ireland is that in Flanders local institutions and the strategies of local elites absorbed much of the tension provoked by the subsistence crisis. It seems that this reasoning can be extended to all regions where peasant agriculture was still strong. Conversely, regional economies based on export agriculture and with elites with only small interests in the local village communities tended to have only small-to-minimal shock absorbing mechanisms. As a result the lower classes were much more vulnerable to simple price shocks.

IX. National trade policy

The debate about the relationship between famine and government has always been a very emotional and even ideological one. As Daly (Ch. 3) and Gray (Ch. 5) point out both the contemporary debate about and the subsequent assessment of the impact of the mid 19th century famine have been very much biased by the 'Irish example'. Those stressing the disastrous English 'colonial' policy in Ireland claim that the rejection of 'food entitlements' is by far the main cause of the mass starvation. The firm belief in the need to breakdown Irish peasant society and the ideological adherence to the principal of free trade prevented a coherent interventionist policy. Others claim that the absolute level of food shortage ('food availability') was so immense, that no contemporary government could ever have prevented the destructive impact of the Irish famine. But even in the last case, the British authorities could and did make choices, and those were all dictated by the ideologically-based conviction that centralisation of the Irish relief institutions and an open border policy was the best option to achieve the intertwined goals of ending the famine, restructuring the Irish society and making the Irish people pay for what was regarded as 'their' crisis.

The British did not act in an international vacuum. On the contrary, as Gray makes clear, they where very much interested in how continental authorities coped with the crisis. In each country active policy measures were accompanied by sometimes vivid debates about the merits of free trade versus protection. But all in all, in contrast to Britain, actions taken by the continental governments were mostly dictated by very practical motivations. The Dutch government was, after the British, probably the one most dedicated to the ideology of open borders and undisturbed market mechanisms. Although the Dutch government did take actions to stimulate imports and to discourage exports, both imports and exports increased in the crisis years, highlighting the role of the Netherlands as a centre of international trade. The same 'intermediary' attitude is seen in internal policy, as famine relief was considered to be primarily a matter for private initiative. Also firmly attached to free trade ideology was Denmark. Although as early as September 1845 some anti-crisis measures were taken, such as the installation of a 'potato commission', the Danish government did not ban food exports or raise export duties. They even started in 1846 with the phasing out of their own Corn Laws, bringing into practice in the middle of the crisis the rules of free trade. Spanish trade policy was also directed towards stimulating exports. Proposals to limit exports of grain and potatoes in 1847 generated animated discussions but ultimately did not pass parliament. Only some regional regulations protected internal consumption, but this was according Diaz Marin (Ch. 13) too little and too late. Liberal orthodoxy was only occasionally deviated from when public order was at stake (e.g. with the repressive Vagrancy Law).

Belgian policy was characterized by a much more interventionist stance. From as early as September 1845 exports of food products were prohibited and imports were stimulated. As a result of an active purchase policy, bread grain imports doubled, then trebled in 1845–1847. Direct subsidies were voted to support the flax industry and to finance public works. This prompt reaction was consistent with the country's protectionist policy since the founding of the Belgian state in 1830. This is most clear in the protection of the 'old' proto-industrial flax industry (trade conventions, subsidies etc.). This example of pragmatic, short run 'crisis management' was not accompanied by a more fund-amental, long-term interventionist policy (emigration, internal colonization, and structural support of industrial activities). On the contrary, after 1850 Belgium became one of the best pupils in the classroom of free trade.

In France too, the 'liberal state' of the 1840s intervened in adjusting customs tariffs, in reducing transport costs, and in purchasing large quantities of Russian wheat. Compared to the pre-crisis norm, imports (in nominal terms) rose by tenfold in 1846 and 1847. Prussia is also regarded as a non-interventionist liberal state, at least insofar as exports are concerned. In order to protect producers east of the Elbe, until the mid 1850s high tariffs on grain imports were the rule. Nonetheless, the Prussian government took several anti-crisis initiatives between December 1846 and September 1847, including the financing of public works and the massive purchase of rye. Even tariffs on grain exports were raised temporarily in spring 1847, but in the East only in the month of May, after most of the harvest was already exported. As Mahlerwein (Ch. 10) shows, the authorities in southern Germany followed 'old patterns', such as the prohibition of distillation and 'attempts' at market regulation.

Although in relative terms the crisis in Sweden was very moderate, the national government issued a ban on the export of potatoes in 1846 and on all sorts of grains, bread and potatoes in August 1847. Concerning internal relief, the authorities also brought into application traditional methods based on temporary trade regulations in support of regions with bad harvests (so-called 'relief grain'). Moreover the national government invested substantial amounts of money in subsidies and loans for public works and for interest-free loans for local and regional authorities. This regionally diversified support could be very substantial. As Gadd (Ch. 15) points out, this interventionist policy is motivated by the fact that the Swedish government was until then extremely dependent on incomes from rural areas, and thus on the fiscal and political significance of peasant farmers.

Strategies and actions taken by national governments differed considerably in the crisis-affected zone. Variables that can explain these differences are the structure of the regional economy (commercial versus peasant), the impact of the subsistence crisis (strong versus mild), and the ideological orientation (strong versus weak free-traders). There is however one constant in the analyses in this volume, the doubt about the impact and effectiveness of the measures taken by the national authorities. In what way were national governments of the mid 19th century able to master economic shocks such as the harvest crisis of 1845–1847? It seems clear that everywhere locally based institutions were best positioned to cope with the also locally very diversified effects of the subsistence crisis. Everywhere, except in Ireland, where such institutions were effectively lacking.

X.   Long term effects

As Gray points out in his contribution, the key premise underlying the contemporary British debate on the origins and effects of the Irish famine, was the desirability of and/ or the need for a 'social revolution' within Irish society. Arguments pro and con often pointed at the vices and virtues of the 'continental model' based on peasant farming. According to the ideological presumptions of the debater, the so-called 'European peasantry model' was the cause of or, on the contrary, the safety net for the agricultural crisis. Comparisons with the continent (and especially with France and Flanders) were popular because the Irish tragedy was so difficult to analyse and understand. Was it due to the peasant structure of the society or, on the contrary, to the fact that the British had broken down the pillars under the former rural society? Was the famine an 'eternal' slur on Irish history, or did it, eventually, transform and modernize society? Supporters of the first view stress the surprising slow demographic recovery of the island and the permanent emigration flow until well in the 20th century. Others argue that living standards did rise after the famine and life for survivors was better before than after the famine.

The picture of the long-term effects of the crisis of the 1840s on the continent is not unambiguous either. The contributions on Flanders and the Netherlands draw a rather gloomy picture. In Flanders, the crisis of the 1840s broke down the resilience of the mixed family farm. The disappearance of old proto-industrial activities further reduced the household income position. Lace-making, small industrial activities, and commuting (e.g. to mines in Wallonia and Northern France) provided alternative survival chances for the majority of the Flemish rural population. In the Netherlands, the subsistence crisis of the 1840s marked the start of a long-term deterioration of living standards as reflected in mean height as an indicator of physical well-being (aggravated by the high food prices during the Crimean war 1853–1856). Only after 1860s did things begin to ameliorate.

Regions and countries dependent on or shifting to agricultural exports seem to have profited from the aftermath of the subsistence crisis. This is most clear in Denmark. Henriksen (Ch. 14) speaks of 'favourable effects', not only for the commercial farmer, but also for the peasantry. 'Wheat was an important element in the Danish gain from the grain crisis'. Similar effects are noted for Sweden and Spain. In Sweden, grain exports grew after 1847 (with a push during the years of the Crimean War). Spain shows the same accelerating process, where according to Diaz Marin (Ch. 13) 'the crisis was inscribed in a process of expansion of agrarian capitalism'. This process, however, increased in the short run social inequality and reduced living standards.

XI. A regional crisis

Famines are regional crises (e.g. Mokyr, 1985; Lachiver, 1991: 144–153; Maharatna, 1996: 179–195). One might go further and claim that famines are regional crises which only can be understood by the 'local story'. Thus the marked differences between the east and west of Ireland, between the Scottish Highlands and Lowlands, between Inner-Flanders and South Belgium, between clay and sandy regions in the Netherlands, and between East and West Prussia show that national averages are often meaningless. Although this book brings together ten 'national' cases, the bottom line in the different stories is that the causes and effects of the subsistence crisis of the 1840s cannot be evaluated on a national scale. Regional differences are a key feature. Only in Ireland did the famine grow into a national disaster, and even then its incidence varied considerably by region. In the rest of Europe, the crisis was examined and handled as a regional event. As Bass (Ch. 9) puts it clearly: 'There was not a single subsistence crisis, but instead a bundle of economic and demographic crises in the late 1840s, only partly tied together by causal chains'.

This means that famines such as the potato famines of the 1840s have to be analysed on different spatial levels: international (the dispersion of the blight, international trade, market integration etc.), national (national policy), regional (regional agro-systems) and local (local communities, local elites, households). However, the regional level seems to be the central scale. All contributions in this book show how differences in the regional economic and social organisation determine the impact of the harvest failures. By summarizing the arguments for the regional differences, we bring together the basic elements for a comparative interpretation scheme.

Devine (Ch. 6) gives four explanations why mortality in Highland Scotland was much lower than in Ireland: a) in Scotland, the 'population at risk' was much smaller, and as a result the famine struck only some well defined regions; b) Scottish peasant society was more diversified and less dependent on one crop; c) Scottish peasants had more income alternatives because temporary migration was possible to the industrialising regions in the lowlands; d) relief systems in Scotland were more diverse, with a central role for landlords and for private networks as organised by the Free Church of Scotland. Local communities such as parishes remained important in Scotland. Therefore, as Devine concludes, aid in Scotland was 'immediate, generous and vigorous'. Vanhaute (Ch. 7) draws an extensive comparison between Flanders and Ireland. Like Devine, he stresses some similarities (peasant agriculture, demographic growth, structural tensions between population and income, peripheral position towards the political centre). According to Vanhaute the main reasons why Flanders did not starve were: a more differentiated peasant economy, stronger village structures (resulting in more effective poor relief), the strong position of local elites and the church, and a prompt and protective state reaction.

In his contribution on Prussia Bass (Ch. 9) argues that vulnerability was much more marked in commercial agricultural regions with high numbers of wage labourers. In this setting, aggregate food availability is not the central explanatory factor; much more important are distribution and food entitlements, as reflected in purchasing power and market access, price setting and the relief regime. Typically, wage labour means greater vulnerability. Paping and Tassenaar (Ch. 8) make the same point for the Netherlands.

The regions at risk were not the inland peasant villages, but the market-oriented regions near the big rivers and the sea. The correlation between food shortage, high prices and hunger is also stressed in the contribution of Mahlerwein (Ch. 10) on southern Germany.

In an analysis based in part on a comparison with earlier French subsistence crises, Chevet and Ó Gráda (Ch. 12) label the French crisis of 1846–1847 'not a genuine subsistence crisis'. This is not to deny the presence of a 'crisis' associated with the political revolution of 1848 and the severe social turmoil associated with it. Vivier (Ch. 11) refines the Labrousse thesis, labelling the 1840s as a 'transitional crisis', a combination of a 'traditional' subsistence crisis and a 'modern' capitalistic crisis. She describes the period as a 'mixed crisis', a crisis with many dimensions: a regional harvest and supply crisis, an industrial and credit crisis and a social and political crisis. The case of Spain is partly comparable with France, because of the political and constitutional turmoil of the late 1840s. As an example of a 'crisis without potatoes', Diaz Marin (Ch. 13) stresses the impact of high grain and bread prices (reaching a peak in spring 1847). Declining real wages caused distress, starvation and higher infant mortality among the social group of wage labourers.

Henriksen (Ch. 14) evaluates the crisis in Denmark as mild. Main reasons are the gains, also for the peasantry, from growing export of wheat, the small role of the potato in consumption and production, the absence of cottage industries. Gadd in his essay on Sweden (Ch. 15) concurs in this evaluation by stating that the years 1845–1850 'can hardly be considered a crisis period'. The country as a whole escaped, because Sweden became in this period a net grain exporter, the potato blight had a limited impact on production and consumption, the grain crisis was regionally limited. Hardship in these countries was limited to people dependent on wage labour and/or benefits.

XII. A traditional and a modern crisis?

The main focus of this book is on the agricultural sector, and on the contrasting impacts of a series of harvest failures in different parts of Europe. Some regions and countries escaped largely unscathed; in others, the harvest failures led to serious famines.

In his famous account of the conditions producing 'gigantic inevitable famine', Thomas Malthus differentiated Europe from the rest of the world; indeed, he erred on the side of complacency when he conceded that 'perhaps in some of [Europe] an absolute famine may never have been known' (1992: 42). Yet by the time the crisis described in this book struck in the mid-1840s, the impact of famine on Europe had already been diminishing for several centuries. Northern Italy, for example, had been virtually free of famines since the seventeenth century; England's last had been in the then remote northwest in the 1620s; and in France after *le grand hiver* of 1708–09 famine-related mortality was modest relative to the disasters of the previous century. Even in Ireland it is claimed that there was a 'gap in famines' between the great famines of the 1740s and 1840s (Dickson, 1989).

Of course, this is not to deny outbreaks of famine or near-famine in the half-century or so before the crisis of the 1840s. France (and surrounding regions) had suffered excess mortality in 1794–1795 in the wake of a poor harvest and a bitterly cold winter; Ireland suffered a whole series of mini-famines before the cataclysm that struck it in 1846; the severe hardship facing the poor in England in 1790s prompted both Edmund Burke's *Thoughts and Details on Scarcity* (1795) and T.R. Malthus's *Essay on the High*

Cost of Provisions (1800); and war-torn Finland endured significant famine-related excess mortality in 1808–09. Yet even the well-known famine of 1816–1817, famously dubbed 'the last great subsistence crisis in the western world' by John D. Post (1977), pales into insignificance when compared to the slaughter wrought by famine in 1690s in France, Scotland, or Finland. In the 1830s and 1840s it would have been reasonable to assume that Western Europe at least had escaped from the clutches of what Malthus called 'gigantic, inevitable famine'.

It seems plausible to link this apparent reduction in the risk of famine in Western Europe to gradual improvements in agricultural productivity and to better communications. The previous two centuries had seen the introduction of new crops, better rotations, and better livestock. There were signs of improved road networks and the development of inland waterways leading to increasing regional specialization. It must be said, however, that there is no consensus among scholars regarding trends in productivity and living standards in Europe in the pre-industrial era. Most recent assessments suggest very modest productivity growth in agriculture before 1800 and downward pressure on real wages. The anthropometric evidence from military archives and skeletal remains, albeit spotty, tends to corroborate (Steckel, 2001). Angus Maddison, it is true, reckons that real GDP per head in Western Europe rose by almost three-fifths between 1500 and 1820, but that increase is deemed far too high by Jan Luiten van Zanden and Giovanni Federico (Maddison, 2001: Table B-21; van Zanden, 2001; Federico, 2002).

Although the declining frequency and gravity of famines suggests that life was gradually becoming less precarious in Europe, estimates of average nutritional intake in France and England c. 1800 imply – on plausible assumptions about the distribution of calories across the whole population – that even in those relatively developed economies the bottom tenth or so were still endemically malnourished. The situation a century earlier was even worse: Robert Fogel, author of these exercises in energy accounting, reckons that average calorie consumption per male adult equivalent c. 1800 (2,933 kcals) was over two hundred kcals more than a century previously. It seems reasonable to link the decline in crisis mortality in England since Tudor times to improved calorific intake. However, Ireland's higher average daily intake (of about 3,150 kcals) on the eve of the Great Famine did not shield it against the catastrophe (Fogel, 1992; Ó Gráda, 1994: 85–86).

In parts of Europe the gradual attenuation of subsistence crises and associated 'moral economy' protests made it easier for central and local governments to pursue the economic policies of the Enlightenment and liberalize the trade in foodstuffs (Persson, 1999). The liberalization tended to apply to internal rather than foreign trade, however. In France all restrictions on the internal grain trade were finally removed with the Revolution. Significantly, during the crisis of 1816–1817 most governments throughout northwestern Europe – though not the British – maintained free trade in corn.

The crisis, or crises, described in this book can be put down to four proximate or immediate factors:
[1] In most of the case studies the most important factor was the failure of the 1846 wheat and rye harvests. Those failures stretched from Andalusia to Prussia, and grain prices everywhere were affected, as Solar shows (Ch. 4). The price increases led to panic, popular unrest, and privation.
[2] However, grain harvest failures alone did not lead to excess mortality (except to

a minor extent in Spain). Most of the excess mortality in this period was due to the failure of the potato crop, either alone or in combination with the failure of grain crops. The mysterious blight responsible, *phytophthera infestans*, reached Belgium first, where it inflicted most damage in 1845. The timing and size of its impact on crops varied across countries. In 1845 Belgium (Flanders) was worst hit. In 1846 the blight wiped out most of the potato harvests in Belgium and in Ireland, but its ravages in France were no worse in 1846 than in 1845. In 1847 *phytophthera* was less evident, but in Ireland the crop failures of 1845–1846 had reduced the area under potatoes in 1847, so that the harvest was again only a fraction of its pre-famine norm (see again Table 1.3 above).

[3] Wherever the potato bulked large in the people's diet, its failure resulted in severe hardship and in excess mortality (Ireland, Flanders, the Scottish Highlands, the Netherlands, Prussia). In some of these areas (the west of Ireland, Flanders, the Scottish Highlands) the potato was accompanied by extreme fragmentation of holdings, although the degree of dependence on the potato reached in Ireland was matched nowhere else. In such places, the potato was associated with population pressure, with output pressing at the margins, and the very unbalanced agrarian regime that it underpinned had more or less reached its limits by the 1840s. However, in the Netherlands, East Prussia and much of eastern and southern Ireland the potato was associated with large farms and export-oriented capitalist agriculture. The connection between agrarian structure and vulnerability to famine is thus not straightforward, although in all cases the entitlements status of the poor was paramount.

[4] The crisis in agriculture coincided with the rapid diffusion of mechanization in the spinning of flax. In the north of Ireland the numbers of (mainly female) spinners plummeted in the 1840s for much the same reasons they collapsed in western Flanders. In Ireland, the famine was not the main cause of the collapse, although it may have exacerbated it in some areas. By contrast with Flanders, in Ireland the famine was most intense where dependence on the linen industry was lowest.

These years also saw a financial crisis that spanned the continent, and which in England resulted in the suspension of the recently legislated Banking Act. Some blamed the crisis on the bursting of a bubble in railway shares (though not a halt to railway construction) but, as noted above, the link with poor grain and potato harvests is more plausible. In Britain the Bank Act of 1844 placed an unnecessary straitjacket on the money supply, with the result that one of its main provisions had to be suspended in late 1847. In some countries, this crisis resulted in bankruptcies and factory closures.

When the costs of this crisis in total lives lost are reckoned, Ireland clearly counted for the major part. Excess mortality in Spain was modest, and evidence of excess mortality in France is elusive. In Scandinavia, too, there was no excess mortality. However, famine-related deaths in Germany and the Low Countries in 1846–1848 totalled perhaps one-fifth of the Irish toll of about one million. The unfolding famine in Ireland was responsible for both the repeal of the controversial Corn Laws and the ensuing demise of Sir Robert Peel's Tory administration. For Great Britain the crisis of 1846–1847 was more of an 'externality' in another sense: immigration from Ireland was responsible for far more deaths than the failure of English harvests per se (Neal, 1998). Similarly, the modest excess mortality in Scotland in 1847 occurred mainly in the towns and cities, and was mainly the product of immigration from the Highlands, where the potato failure resulted in severe privation but little if any excess mortality (Ch. 6).

The crisis exhibited some common features across most of the countries examined here. Rioting and petty theft rose sharply almost everywhere. And judging by the evidence of Flanders and in Ireland, as described in Chapters 1 and 6, the character of crime changed too. The pattern follows that described by Pitirim Sorokin (1975 [1922]: 236) and Ancel Keys *et al.* (1950: 785) over half a century ago. According to these scholars, food riots – as distinct from individual acts of thieving and cheating – are more likely to be the product of 'minor hunger and deprivation' rather than 'real starvation'. When the latter strikes, '[t]hough moral and social standards may be lost, lethargy and weakness are powerful deterrents against strong action.' In Sorokin's version, 'we must expect the strongest reactions from the starving masses at the time when hunger is great but not excessive'. It is surely telling that in Ireland, which suffered more than anywhere else in the 1840s, the 'revolution' of 1848 was confined to the one-day siege of a farmhouse in Tipperary (compare Eiríksson, 1997).

In Ireland the apocalyptic character and the demographic dimensions of the crisis recalled famines of earlier era. Nothing comparable had happened in Ireland itself since 1740–1741, and in relative terms the Irish famine surpassed the disasters of the 1690s and 1700s in France and of the 1690s in Scotland. At the same time, the crisis was a 'modern' one in that it took place in a context of considerable market integration and food movements across national borders. In Ireland the crisis prompted the opening up of the country to foreign grain, and prompted mass long-distance migration on an unprecedented scale. Indeed, without such migration the crisis would have been even worse (Ó Gráda and O'Rourke, 1997). Such was the degree of market integration that the relative gravity of the crisis in different countries cannot be inferred by price increases. As Solar shows in Ch. 4, prices across Europe rose and fell more or less in tandem. Such would hardly have been the case in earlier centuries.

Bibliography

Berger, H. and Spoerer, M. (2001) 'Economic Crisis and the European Revolutions of 1848', *Journal of Economic History*, 61, pp. 293–326.

Bourke, A. (1993) *'The visitation of God'? The potato and the great Irish famine*, Dublin.

Boyer, G.R. (1998) 'The historical background of the Communist Manifesto', *Journal of Economic Perspectives*, 12, pp. 151–174.

Dickson, D. (1989) 'The gap in famines: a useful myth?', in E.M. Crawford (ed.) *Famine: the Irish Experience,* Edinburgh, pp. 96–111.

Dornbusch, R. and Frenkel, J.A. (1984) 'The Gold Standard and the Bank of England in the Crisis of 1847', in M.D. Bordo and A. J. Schwartz (eds), *A Retrospective on the Classical Gold Standard, 1880–1913*, Chicago, pp. 233–264.

Documents Statistiques, 1851–1869 (1857–1869), Bruxelles.

Dyson, T. and Ó Gráda, C. (2002) *Famine Demography: Perspectives from Past and Present*, Oxford.

Eiríksson, A. (1997) 'Food supply and food riots', in C. Ó Gráda (ed.), *Famine 150. Commemorative Lecture Series*, Dublin, pp. 67–93.

Eiríksson, A. and Ó Gráda, C. (2006) 'Bankrupt landlords and the Irish famine', in C. Ó Gráda, *Ireland's Great Famine*, Dublin, pp. 48–62.

Emigrationsutredningen. Betänkande i utvandingsfrågan (1913), Stockholm.

Fogel, R.W. (1992) 'Second Thoughts on the European Escape from Hunger: Famines, Chronic Malnutrition, and Mortality Rates,' in S.R. Osmani (ed.). *Nutrition and Poverty*, Oxford, pp. 243–286.

Gadd, C.-J. (1983) *Järn och potatis. Jordbruk, teknik och social omvandling i Skaraborgs län 1750–1860*, Goteborg.

Geary, F. and Stark, T. (2004) 'Trends in real wages during the industrial revolution: a view from across the Irish Sea', *Economic History Review*, 57, pp. 362–395.

Glennie, P. (1999) 'Introduction to part I', in B.J.P. van Bavel and E. Thoen (eds), *Land productivity and agro-systems in the North Sea area (Middle Ages – 20th century) Elements for comparison*, Turnhout, pp. 22–29. (CORN Publication Series; 2).

Gray, P. (1997) 'Famine relief in comparative perspective: Ireland, Scotland and North-West Europe, 1845–49, *Éire-Ireland*, 37, pp. 86–108.

Hellstenius, J. (1871) 'Skördarna i Sverige och deras verkningar', *Statistik tidskrift*, 20, pp. 77–120.

Keys, Ancel, J.B., Henschel, A., Mickelsen, O. and Taylor, H.L. (1950) *The Biology of Human Starvation*, vol. I, Minneapolis.

Klep, P.M.M. (1981) *Bevolking en arbeid in transformatie. Een onderzoek in Brabant 1700–1900*, Nijmegen.

Komlos, J. (1998) 'Shrinking in a Growing Economy? The Mystery of Physical Stature during the Industrial Revolution', *Journal of Economic History*, 58, pp. 779–802.

Lachiver, M. (1991) *Les années de misère: la famine au temps du Grand Roi*, Paris.

Maddison, A. (1991) *Dynamic Forces in Capitalist Development*, Oxford and New York.

Maddison, A. (2003) *The World Economy. Historical Statistics*, Paris.

Maharatna, A. (1996) *The Demography of Famines*, Delhi.

Malthus, T.R. (1992) *An Essay on the Principle of Population*, Cambridge. [The original version was published in London in 1798].

Mokyr, J. (1985) *Why Ireland Starved: A Quantitative and Analytical History of the Irish Economy 1800–1850*, London.

Mokyr, J. (1989) 'Industrialisation and Poverty in Ireland and the Netherlands: Some Notes Toward a Comparative Study', *Journal of Interdisciplinary History*, 10, pp. 429–459.

Mokyr, J. and Ó Gráda, C. (1988) 'Poor and getting poorer? Irish living standards before the Famine', *Economic History Review*, 41, pp. 209–235.

Mokyr, J. and Ó Gráda, C. (2002) 'Famine disease and famine mortality: lessons from the Irish experience, 1845–50', in T. Dyson and C. Ó Gráda, *Famine Demography: Perspectives from Past and Present*, Oxford, pp. 19–43.

Neal, F. (1998) *Black '47: Britain and the Famine Irish*, London.

Norton, D. (2005) 'On landlord-assisted emigration from some Irish estates in the 1840s', *Agricultural History Review*, 53, pp. 24–40.

Ó Gráda, C. (1994) *Ireland: A New Economic History 1780–1939*, Oxford.

Ó Gráda, C. (1999) *Black '47 and beyond. The Great Irish Famine in History, Economy, and Memory*, Princeton.

Ó Gráda, C. (2006). *Ireland's Great Famine: Interdisciplinary Perspectives*, Dublin.

Ó Gráda, C. and O'Rourke, K.H. (1997) 'Mass migration as disaster relief: lessons from the Great Irish Famine', *European Review of Economic History*, 1, pp. 3–26.

Paping, R.F.J. (1995) *Voor een handvol stuivers. Werken, verdienen en besteden: de levens-standaard van boeren, arbeiders en middenstanders in de Groninger kleigebieden, 1770–1860*, Groningen.

Persson, K.G. (1999) *Grain Markets in Europe, 1500–1900: Integration and Deregulation*, Cambridge.

Population. Mouvement de l'etat civil, 1841–1850 (1843–1851), Bruxelles.

Post, J.D. (1977) *The Last Great Subsistence Crisis in the Western World*, Baltimore.

'Recensement de la population, 1846, 1851' (1966), *Annuaire statistique de la France*.

Smits, J.-P., Horlings, E. and Zanden, J.L. van (2000) *Dutch GNP and its components, 1800–1913*, Groningen.

Solar, P.M. (1989) 'The Great Famine was no ordinary subsistence crisis', in E.M. Crawford (ed.) *Famine: The Irish Experience, 900–1900*, Edinburgh, pp. 112–131.

Solar, P.M. (1997) 'The potato famine in Europe', in C. Ó Gráda (ed.), *Famine 150. Commemorative Lecture Series*, Dublin, pp. 113–128.

Sorokin, P.A. (1975) *Hunger as a Factor in Human Affairs*, Gainesville. [The original Russian version was published in St. Petersburg in 1922].

Statistisch en staathuishoudkundig Jaarboekje, 2 (1850).

Steckel, R. (2001) 'Health and nutrition in the pre-industrial era: insights from a millennium of average heights in northern Europe', *NBER Working Paper No. 8542*.

Tortella, G. (2000) *The Development of Modern Spain. An Economic History of the Nineteenth and Twentieh Centuries*, Cambridge, Massachusetts and London.

Traugott, M. (1983) 'The mid-nineteenth-century crisis in France and England', *Theory and Society*, 12, pp. 455–468.

Vanhaute, E. (1992) *Heiboeren. Bevolking, arbeid en inkomen in de 19de-eeuwse Kempen*, Brussel.

Vries, J. de (1984) *European Urbanization 1500–1800*, London.

Von Reden, F.W. (1853/54) *Erwerbs- und Verkehrs-Statistik des Köningstaats Preussen. In vergleichender Darstellung*, 3 Teile, Darmstadt, http://www.digitalis.uni-koeln.de.

Ward-Perkins, C.N. (1950) 'The Commercial Crisis of 1847', *Oxford Economics Papers*, 2, pp. 75–94.

Zanden, J.L. van (2001) 'A survey of the European economy 1500–2000', in M.R. Prak (ed.), *Early Modern Capitalism: Economic and Social Change in Europe 1400–1800*, London, pp. 69–87.

Zanden, J.L. van (1985) *De economische ontwikkeling van de Nederlandse landbouw in de negentiende eeuw 1800–1914*, Utrecht.

PART I

THE IRISH FAMINE IN AN INTERNATIONAL PERSPECTIVE

2 Ireland's Great Famine. An overview

Cormac Ó Gráda, University College Dublin

I. The potato famine

The proximate cause of the Great Irish Famine (1846–1852) was the fungus *phythophtera infestans* (or potato blight), which reached Ireland in the fall of 1845. The fungus destroyed about one-third of that year's crop, and nearly all that of 1846. After a season's remission, it also ruined most of the 1848 harvest. These repeated attacks made the Irish famine more protracted than most. Partial failures of the potato crop were nothing new in Ireland before 1845, but damage on the scale wrought by the ecological shock of potato blight was utterly unprecedented (Solar, 1989; Bourke, 1993; Clarkson and Crawford, 2001). However, the famine would not have been nearly so lethal had Ireland's dependence on the potato been less. The experience of other European econo-mies in the 1840s is telling in this respect. In Ireland the daily intake of the third or so of the population mainly reliant on the potato was enormous: 4–5 kilos daily per adult male equivalent for most of the year. After allowing for non-human consumption and provision for seed, the 2.1 million acres (or 0.8 million hectares) under potatoes in the early 1840s produced 6.2 million metric tons for human consumption. That amounted to an average daily intake of 4.6 lbs (or over two kilos) per man, woman, and child. In France, by comparison, the average daily intake of potatoes was only 165 grams in 1852; in Norway in the early 1870s, 540 grams; in the Netherlands about 800 grams in the 1840s; in Belgium 640 grams. A few European regions – Belgian Flanders, parts of Prussia, and Alsace – came closer to the Irish norm, however (for sources see Ó Gráda, 1999: 18, 237). Table 2.1 (based on Bourke, 1993: 90–113; Mokyr, 1981) gives a sense of the potato's importance in the Irish rural economy.

In Ireland the potato's initial impact was as a seasonal garden crop, complementing a diet based mainly on oatmeal and dairy products, in the seventeenth century. The precise contours of its subsequent diffusion are controversial, but its consumption rose over time, and by the 1840s poverty had reduced the bottom one-third or so of the population to almost exclusive dependence on it for sustenance. Before the potato assumed such dominance, it arguably lessened the risks of severe famine in a country where earlier famines (in 1649–1652 and 1740–1741) had wrought devastation that was probably at least on a par, relatively speaking, with that of the 1840s.

Human consumption accounted for only half of Irish potato production: this meant that in the event of failure the portion normally reserved for pigs and hens acted as a crude buffer-stock. Ireland's moist climate, moreover, gave it a comparative advantage in potato cultivation, and potato yields were high: about fifteen metric tons per hectare. The potato tended to alternate with grain in the crop rotation, and played a useful role in preparing the soil for grain crops, of which oats was the most important. However, the potato's low yield-to-seed ratio exacerbated the impact of repeated shortfalls. Its importance in the Irish diet, coupled with an inadequate policy response from the

Figure 2.1 Map of 32-county Ireland

Table 2.1   Allocation of the potato in the early 1840s

A. Human Consumption in Ireland

Occupation	Population (millions)	Annual consumption (million metric tons)
Labourers	3.30	3.9
Cottiers	1.40	0.8
Small farmers	0.50	0.3
Large farmers	0.25	0.1
Textile workers	0.75	0.4
Other workers	0.85	0.4
Professional et al.	0.95	0.3
Total	8.20	6.2

B. Other Uses (million metric tons)

Animal consumption: pigs	2.6
Animal consumption: cattle	1.8
Animal consumption: horses and other	0.3
Exports	0.2
Seed and wastage	2.5

authorities, made the consequences of repeated shortfalls in the 1840s devastating (Bourke, 1993; Mokyr, 1981; Rosen, 1999).

Ireland was a poor country in 1845, income per head being about half that in the rest of the United Kingdom. The regional contrast between the northeast, which was undergoing rapid industrialization at this time, and the west and the south was marked. Moreover, while there were some signs of a rise in urban and middle-class living standards, the half-century or so before the famine was a period of increasing impoverishment for the landless poor (Mokyr and Ó Gráda, 1988). Population rose from about five million in 1800 to seven million in 1820 and 8.5 million in 1845. A rising emigration rate and a falling birth rate offered only partial relief to increasing population pressure (Boyle and Ó Gráda, 1986). Moreover, demographic adjustment was weakest in the western and southern areas most at risk. The collapse of a largely home-based textile industry exacerbated the situation in some rural areas, particularly in north Connacht and south Ulster; the result was increasing dependence on the potato and increasing recourse to seasonal migration during the summer months. The nutritional content of the potato and widespread access to heating fuel in the form of turf eased somewhat the poverty of Ireland's three million 'potato people', who were healthier and lived longer than the poor in other parts of Europe at the time. One indication of this, based on evidence from military and prison archives, is that adult Irish males from the lower end of the socio-economic scale on the eve of the famine were at least as tall as, if not taller than, their English peers (Ó Gráda, 1991; Mokyr and Ó Gráda, 1996). However, their poverty meant that when the potato failed, there was no trading down to a cheaper alternative food (Ó Gráda, 1994a: 80–97). Nowhere else in Europe had the potato, like tobacco a gift from the New World, made such inroads into the diet of the poor. It bears noting that the potato also failed throughout Europe in the 1840s. This brought hardship in many places, and excess mortality in the Low Countries and in parts of Germany. Yet nowhere was Ireland's cataclysm repeated (Solar, 1997; other articles in this volume).

The first attack of potato blight inflicted considerable hardship on rural Ireland, though no significant excess mortality. The catastrophe of the Great Irish Famine really dates from the autumn of 1846, when the first deaths from starvation were recorded. By mid-October 1846 four of the country's 130 workhouses were already full, and three months later the workhouses – established under the Irish Poor Law of 1838 – held nearly one hundred thousand people. By the end of 1846 three in five already contained more inmates than they had accommodation for, and many were turning away would-be inmates (Ó Gráda, 1999: 50–52). Of those still with spare capacity, a third or so were in less affected areas in the northeast and east. Ominously, however, several more were located in areas already threatened with disaster, but lacking the resources and the political will to cope. Good examples are the workhouses of Ballina, Ballinrobe, Ennistymon, Gort, Kilrush, Swinford, and Westport.

At first there were the food riots and 'moral economy' protests often associated with famines, but these subsided as hope and anger gave way to despair (Eiríksson, 1997b; see too Ó Murchadha, 1998: 98–99, 170–175). The numbers of crime reported by the police force peaked in 1847, at more than three times the pre-famine (1844) level. However, the nature of crime shifted: incidents of cattle- and sheep-rustling rose eleven-fold, and burglaries and robberies quintupled, while the number of reported rapes dropped by two-thirds. Inmates with no previous conviction formed a rising proportion of the prison population and, in Dublin, proportion of inmates from the distant provinces of Connacht and Munster rose sharply. A further indication of the changing nature of crime is that the mean height of both male and female prisoners in Dublin's Newgate prison rose during the famine. Some prison inmates, it is claimed, committed petty crimes in order to gain access to prisoners' rations; and that much of famine-era crime was driven by desperation is also suggested by the deaths of some of the perpetrators in prison from famine-related causes (Ó Gráda, 1994a: 202–204; 1999: 188–191).

The famine did not impact much on Irish politics. The aging leader of Catholic Ireland, Daniel O'Connell, was in poor health at the height of the crisis and died in Genoa in May 1847. An electorate restricted to middle- and upper-class voters increased the representation of O'Connellites in Westminster in the general election of July 1847, but the Irish M.P.s exerted little pressure on Lord John Russell's weak and divided Whig administration. Nor did extra-parliamentary opposition achieve much: the 'rising' of 1848 was an improvised, tragic-comic affair that lasted less than a week.

Ireland's representatives in Westminster were beholden to a tiny, economically-privileged electorate. In June 1847 only two of them opposed a clause inserted into the Poor Law Amendment Act (1847), which drastically reduced the relief entitlements of rural smallholders. Henceforth households occupying more than about 0.1 hectare of land were excluded from public relief. Given the attachment of the poor to their mini-holdings, this clause is usually deemed to have exacerbated mortality. Nor was there much political solidarity within Ireland: in 1849–1850 the so-called 'rate-in-aid', a property tax imposed by the authorities in London on richer Irish regions in support of the poorer, provoked strong resentment from political spokesmen in loyalist Ulster (Grant, 1990).

The human carnage reached its peak during the winter and spring of 1846–1847, but the crisis continued to cost lives for another three or four years. Like all major famines, the Irish potato famine produced many instances of roadside deaths, of neglect of the very young and the elderly, of heroism and of anti-social behavior, of evictions, and of a rise in crimes against property. Like all famines, it produced its grotesque cameos of life turned upside down and of bonds of friendship and kinship sundered:

– In May 1847 two teenage girls sold their hair for 2s 3d (about three times the daily wage of an unskilled worker) to a hairdresser in Clonmel, County Tipperary, 'an original and extraordinary mode of seeking relief' (Ó Gráda, 1999: 40).

– In west Kerry a local poet described how young women might venture out at night without fear of harassment from the young blades of the neighbourhood (Ó Gráda, 1994b: 73).

– In Ballykilcline in County Roscommon an entire family succumbed to famine fever and was not discovered for a week: the men who carried the corpses 'got weak and had to be given whiskey' (Ó Gráda, 1999: 40).

– In May 1847 a mail car traveler sought to help a seventeen-year old girl whose child had died on the roadside between Glin and Tarbert. Unwilling to leave the body with nobody to watch over it, the girl too died 'under the broad canopy of Heaven' (Curtin, 2000: 111).

– In Cork Denis Lane was found dead in his prison cell after being brought in for 'forcibly taking meal from carmen' (Ó Gráda, 1994a: 204; 1999: 40).

– Deaths on the highway gave rise to the term 'road sickness'. In Ballydehob in west Cork in January 1847 'a poor man named John Coughlan from Kilbronoge...was on his way to one of these new roads, that lead to nothing save death, when he fell from exhaustion and...was numbered with the other victims of the Board of Works' (Hickey, 2002: 169).

– In May 1847 Thomas Mahon of Ennis relief committee received a letter from 'Captain Starlight', accusing him of inflicting 'lingering death by starvation' on the poor of the town. 'Starlight' berated Mahon and his committee for their meager dole of 'a quart of a pint of porridge and a penny brown loaf for a poor creature for 24 hours'. 'Tempt your dogs with it', he added, 'and in a month you'll have no dogs' (Ó Murchadha, 1998: 118–119).

– There were even rumours of cannibalism, at least in the more restricted sense of the flesh of victims being eaten by survivors: in Mayo a starving man was reported to have 'extracted the heart and liver... [of] a shipwrecked human body...cast on shore' (*The Times*, May 23rd 1849).

The famine was widely reported in the contemporary press at first, both in Ireland and abroad. It elicited a massive response in terms of private donations for a time, especially through the agency of the Roman Catholic Church worldwide and the Society of Friends. Philanthropists in Britain were also moved by Irish suffering, until compassion fatigue set in. Even the Choctaw Nation in faraway Oklahoma subscribed $170 for famine relief. Accessible narrative accounts of the tragedy include Edwards and Williams (1956), Woodham-Smith (1962), Ó Gráda (1994a, ch. 8; 1999), and Donnelly (2001).

II. Public action

Much of the historiography of the Irish famine addresses this issue. Critics of the stance of British policy-makers during the Irish famine, both in the 1840s and today, castigated them for not doing more. Accusations of tightfistedness were common: for example, the guardians of Fermoy's workhouse in November 1846 pleaded with ministers 'who gave twenty million to emancipate the slaves, who were never so much to be pitied as the people of this country are at present'. In the *Cork Constitution* a month later a correspondent from devastated Skibbereen 'could not help thinking how much better it would be to afford [the poor] some temporary relief in their own homes during this severe weather, than thus sacrifice their lives to carry out a miserable project of political economy' (cited in Ó Gráda, 1996: 104). Influential ideologues such as Nassau Senior in the *Edinburgh Review* and Thomas Wilson in the *Economist* urged ministers to err in the direction of economy: according to Wilson, 'it [was] no man's business to provide for another', and redistribution would only shift resources from 'the more meritorious to the less' (cited in Ó Gráda, 1989: 52). These points anticipate modern critiques of relief policy by the likes of Thomas P. O'Neill (1956) and Christine Kinealy (1994).

Supporters of the same policy-makers, then and now, make the points that: (a) the backward character of Irish agriculture made disaster inevitable; (b) much was done in an era when parsimony and callousness were 'exhibited as much to the English as to the Irish poor'; and (c) given widespread corruption in the areas worst affected, further expenditure would have saved few lives (e.g. Daly 1986: 114). In a classic variant of (a), the late E.R.R. Green (1984: 273–274) described the famine as 'primarily a disaster like a flood or an earth quake ', by way of implying that there was little that state intervention could have done to save lives.

The choice of appropriate relief measures for Ireland was widely debated in the press and in parliament in the 1840s. Some of the debates have quite a modern resonance (compare Drèze and Sen 1989). At first the government opted for reliance on the provision of employment through public works schemes, the cost of which was to be split between local taxpayers and the central government. The schemes consisted for the most part of small-scale infra-structural improvements; relief considerations constrained their size and location. At their height in the spring of 1847 the works employed seven hundred thousand people, or one-in-twelve of the entire population. The public works did not contain the famine, partly because they did not target the neediest, partly because the average wage paid was too low (McGregor, 2003), and partly because the works entailed exposing malnourished and poorly clothed people (mostly men) to the elements during the worst months of the year.

Exasperated by the ineffectiveness and rising cost of 'workfare', and concerned that it was diverting labour from more productive uses in the agricultural sector, early in 1847 the authorities decided to phase out the public works and switch to food aid. The publicly financed soup kitchens, which replaced the public works were designed to target those most at risk directly. The food rations were in effect non-transferable and non-storable. They reached three million people daily at their peak in early 1847, an extraordinary bureaucratic feat. Doubts remain about the effectiveness of a diet of thin meal-based gruel on weakened stomachs, but mortality seemed to fall while the soup kitchens operated.

The drop in food prices during the summer of 1847 prompted the authorities in London to treat the famine henceforth as a manageable, local problem. The main burden of relieving the poor henceforth was placed on the workhouses established under the Irish Poor Law of 1838. Thus the worst hit areas bore the heaviest fiscal burdens. In principal those requiring relief were supposed to pass 'the workhouse test', i.e. refusal to enter the workhouse was deemed evidence of being able to support one's self. In practice, most of the workhouses were poorly equipped to meet the demands placed upon them, and in the event about one-quarter of all excess famine mortality occurred within their walls. Workhouses in the worst affected unions began to fill up in late 1846, and mortality within their walls rose in tandem. Local histories highlight mismanagement and the impossible burden placed on local taxpayers government; and, indeed, the high overall proportion of workhouse deaths due to contagious diseases is an indictment of this form of relief. Several excellent studies of individual workhouses are available. These paint a mainly negative picture of workhouse management, highlighting venality, overcrowding, and incompetence. They also demonstrate, however, how risky employment in the workhouse was: a significant proportion of those so employed perished of famine-related diseases (O'Neill, 1956; Kinealy, 1994; Ó Murchadha, 1997).

Measurable yardsticks of union performance are available: a poorly-managed union might be one that was relatively late to open, or in which mortality from infectious diseases was relatively high, or in which the overall death rate was relatively high (Guinnane and Ó Gráda, 2002). For instance the workhouse in Enniskillen, County Fermanagh, opened on 1 December 1845. Enniskillen, 96th in terms of poor law valuation per head, was only 123rd of 130 to open. The late opening of the workhouse left little time for 'non-crisis' admissions before the famine. Moreover, a high proportion of the Enniskillen dead (about 56–57%) perished from infectious diseases. This meant either that they entered the workhouse in a very bad state, in which case they should have been admitted sooner or catered for elsewhere, or else that they contracted an infectious disease within the workhouse from another inmate. Some workhouse managements sought to segregate the diseased from the healthy; some did not. In July 1847 Enniskillen's guardians voted against building a fever hospital, whereupon its medical officer remarked: 'Now that is all over, I have only to say there are 24 persons lying of fever in the house, and the rain is dripping down on them at this moment'. The percentages succumbing to marasmus and dropsy (what today is called hunger oedema), both famine-related conditions indicating severe malnutrition, were also high in Enniskillen relative to neighbouring and similarly circumstanced unions. Whether inmates succumbing to these diseases acquired them in the workhouse due to inadequate diet, or arrived in a dying state and on the verge of starvation, cannot be known, however. The very high mortality in some workhouses in 1850 and 1851 is evidence of the long-lasting character of the famine in some western areas (Guinnane, McCabe and Ó Gráda, 2004; Eiríksson, 1997a; Ó Murchadha,1998).

Traditional accounts of the famine pit the more humane policies of Sir Robert Peel's Tories against the dogmatic stance of Sir John Russell's Whig administration, which succeeded them. Peel was forced out of office in July 1846 when his party split on the issue of the Corn Laws. The contrast between Peel and Russell oversimplifies. Though Peel was more familiar with Ireland's problems of economic backwardness than Whig ideologues such as Chancellor of the Exchequer Charles Wood, the crisis confronting Peel in 1845–1846 was mild compared to what was to follow. Moreover, Peel broadly supported the Whig line in opposition, and it was left to his former Tory colleagues to mount a parliamentary challenge against Russell and Wood. It was left to Tory leader Lord George Bentinck to accuse the Whigs of 'holding the truth down', and to predict a time 'when we shall know what the amount of mortality has been'; then, Bentinck added, people could judge 'at its proper value [the Whigs'] management of affairs in Ireland'.

Assessment of the public policy response cannot ignore the apocalyptic character of the crisis that it faced. Nonetheless, the government's obsession with parsimony and its determination to make the Irish pay for 'their' crisis cannot but have increased the death rate. The same goes for the insistence on linking relief with structural reform (e.g. by making the surrender of all landholdings a strict condition for relief). At the height of the crisis the policy stance adopted by the Whigs was influenced by Malthusian providentialism, i.e. the conviction that the potato blight was a divinely ordained remedy for Irish overpopulation. The fear that too much kindness would entail a Malthusian lesson not learnt also conditioned both the nature and extent of intervention (Gray, 1999). This stance rationalized caution, circumscribed relief, and shifted the responsibility to Irish property-owners. Compassion on the part of the British elite was in short supply.

Though Ireland was a highly bureaucratized polity by mid-nineteenth century standards, administrators in Dublin and London still faced the challenge of how best to identify and relieve the destitute in remote areas. Critics of relief could point to many instances of red tape, incompetence, and corruption. The case of the workhouses has already been mentioned; cheating and favouritism were also features of the public works and, to a lesser extent, the soup kitchens. On the other hand, the authorities had the benefit of a numerous and able police force and of hard-working and well-informed clergy of all denominations. And relieving officers ensured that many abuses were short-lived (Kerr, 1996; Ó Gráda, 1999: Ch. 2).

III. Demographic consequences

The Irish famine killed about one million people, or one-eighth of the entire population. This made it a major famine, relatively speaking, by world-historical standards. In pre-1845 Ireland famines were by no means unknown – those caused by a combination of war and poor harvests in the early 1650s and arctic weather conditions in 1740–1741 killed as high a share of much smaller populations (Lenihan,1997; Dickson, 1998), but those that struck during the half-century or so before the Great Famine were mini-famines by comparison. The excess death toll of a million is an informed guess, since in the absence of civil registration excess mortality cannot be calculated directly (Mokyr, 1985; Boyle and Ó Gráda, 1986). The record of deaths in the workhouses and other public institutions is nearly complete, but the recording of other deaths depended on the memory of survivors in households where deaths had taken place. In many homes, of course, death and emigration meant that there were no survivors. The estimate does not include averted births, nor does it allow for famine-related deaths in Britain and further afield (Mokyr, 1981; Neal, 1998). On the basis of an analysis of a large sample of surviving baptismal registers, Joel Mokyr put the drop in the birth rate at the height of the crisis at one-third. This was the product of reduced fecundity, reduced libido, and a lower marriage rate.[1]

---

[1] There was also a marked decline in the number of rapes recorded during the famine (Ó Gráda, 1994: 203).

Within Ireland mortality was regionally very uneven. No part of the island escaped entirely, but the toll ranged from one-quarter of the population of some western counties to negligible fractions in Down and Wexford on the east coast. The timing of excess mortality varied too, even in some of the worst hit areas. In west Cork, a notorious black spot, the worst was over by late 1847, but the deadly effects of the famine ranged in Clare until 1850 or even 1851. Infectious diseases – especially typhoid fever, typhus and dysentery/diarrhea – rather than literal starvation were responsible for the bulk of mortality. By and large, the higher the death toll in a county or province, the higher the proportion of starvation deaths. While Karl Marx was almost right to claim that the Irish famine killed 'poor devils only', many which were not abjectly poor and starving died of famine-related diseases. Medical progress, by shielding the rich from infection, has made subsequent famines even more class-specific. As in most famines, the elderly and the young were most likely to succumb, but women proved marginally more resilient than men. The slightly lower excess death rate of women was due to physiological rather than cultural factors (Ó Gráda, 1999: 101–104; Mokyr and Ó Gráda, 2002).

The famine also resulted in emigration on a massive scale. Again precise estimates are impossible. Though the emigrants were also victims of the famine, their departure improved not only their own survival chances, but also those of the majority who remained in Ireland. True, the Atlantic crossing produced its own carnage, particularly in Quebec's Grosse-Isle, but most of those who fled made it safely to the other side. There thus is a sense in which migration was a crude form of disaster relief, and that more public spending on subsidized emigration would have reduced the aggregate famine death toll (Ó Gráda and O'Rourke, 1997). Most of those who emigrated relied on their own resources, though some landlords helped through direct subsidies or by relieving those who left of their unpaid rent bills. For the most part, the landless poor simply could not afford to leave.

While migration saved lives in Ireland, it led to increased mortality across the Irish Sea. In England and Wales mortality was one hundred thousand above trend in the 1846–1848 period: however, its distribution between arrivals from Ireland and natives succumbing to famine diseases is not known. There was also a drop in the birth rate in England and Wales in the late 1840s, indicating that the crisis was not solely an import from John Bull's Other Island. In Scotland, virtually all the excess mortality was in the cities. In Glasgow burials doubled in 1847. This might be seen as the result of the influx of destitute Highlanders, but immigration into Glasgow from Ireland easily exceeded that from the Highlands. So the Irish famine may also have been mainly responsible for the fever deaths causing excess mortality in Scotland (Devine, this volume; Neal, 1997; Ó Gráda, 1999: 112–113).

IV. A hierarchy of suffering

Like all famines, the Irish famine produced its hierarchy of suffering. The rural poor, landless or near landless, were most likely to perish, and the earliest victims were in that category. Farmers found their effective land endowment reduced, since their holdings could no longer yield the same quantity of potatoes as before. They also faced increased labor costs, forcing them to reduce their concentration on tillage. Between 1847 and the early 1850s hundreds of thousands of smallholders and landless or semi-landless labourers were evicted by hard (and sometimes hard-pressed) landlords and by unsentimental land agents. Proprietors employed bailiffs to carry out the evictions and demolish cabins, while the police stood by (O'Neill, 2000). Thus it is hardly surprising that although the recorded labour force fell by nearly one-fifth between 1841 and 1851, the number of bailiffs rose by over one-third (Ó Gráda, 2001: 125).

Landlords' rental income plummeted by as much as one-third while the crisis lasted, while their outlays on poor relief rose. Naturally, historians have linked the high bankruptcy rate of landowners in the wake of the famine to these pressures: in the words of one, 'up to one quarter of all land changed hands as a result of Famine-induced bankruptcy among landowners'. A corollary is that landlords who were spared were too impoverished to buy up the properties that came on the market in the wake of the crisis, leaving the way open to *nouveau riche* shopkeepers and lawyers. These arguments contain a strong element of *post hoc ergo propter hoc*. In reality most of the sales processed through the Incumbered Estates Court from 1849 on were of estates so financially embarrassed that debts accruing from the famine can have accounted but for a small fraction of the total. Alas, the proprietors of such estates were poorly equipped to help their tenants when the famine struck (Ó Gráda, 1999: 128–129).

It is natural to focus on agriculture and on the countryside, but no sector of the economy was unscathed. Banks had to cope with bad debts and massive withdrawals of deposits. Retail sales declined. Pawnbrokers found their pledges being unredeemed as the crisis worsened. Least affected were those businesses and their work forces that relied on foreign markets for their raw materials and their sales. Many clergymen, medical practitioners, poor law officials, and others in contact with the poor paid the ultimate price, dying of infectious diseases.

The relative impact of the famine on different occupational groups may be inferred from comparing the 1841 and 1851 censuses. The overall decline in the labor force was 19.1 per cent. There were 14.4 per cent fewer farmers, and 24.2 per cent fewer farm laborers. Not surprisingly, given their vulnerability, the number of physicians and surgeons dropped by 25.3 per cent. The small number of coffin makers (eight in 1841, twenty-two in 1851) is a reminder that during the famine most coffins were not made by specialist coffin makers. It is difficult to identify any significant class of 'winners' in the 1840s, though the census indicates increases in the numbers of millers and bakers, of barristers and attorneys, and of bailiffs and rate collectors. The huge fall in the numbers of spinners and weavers was partly a consequence of the famine, partly due to other causes (Ó Gráda, 1999: ch. 4; 2001).

The famine was also distributed very uneven regionally. Its impact on Ireland's metropolis is worth brief consideration. Dublin's population of 250,000 people contained a large underclass of desperately poor people, but their diet was more varied and less dependent on the Lumper potato (an inferior, tasteless variety) than that of the rural poor. Yet at the height of the famine Dublin was far from the 'brightly lit, comparatively well fed, slightly neutral country' imagined long ago by economists Patrick Lynch and John Vaizey (1960). Several sources – burial records, censal evidence, religious records, poor law registers – imply excess mortality in Dublin, and not only of unfortunate country people seeking work and relief. Moreover, all creeds were affected: burials in the Society of Friends graveyard in Cork Street rose from an average of fourteen in 1841–1846 to twenty-five in 1847–1851. Yet the excess death rate in Dublin was but a fraction of that in the west coast (Ó Gráda, 1999: ch. 5).

V. Famine and food markets

Berthold Brecht once wrote that famines don't just happen; they are organized by the grain trade. In Ireland in the late 1840s many poor people doubtless believed that the determination of traders or producers to corner markets or to extract higher prices exacerbated the famine. However, an analysis of price data suggests that at least at wholesale level markets worked more or less as normal. Nor does the evidence of sales at Cork's potato markets support the belief that during the famine traders held back a higher-than-normal proportion of output earlier in the season (Ó Gráda, 1999: 134–156). That is not to say that supplies responded to price signals like clockwork: on the contrary, merchants responded cautiously to the challenge of finding substitute foods (mainly maize) for the potato. However, as Amartya Sen (1981: 160) reminds us, 'the law stands between food availability and food entitlement. Starvation deaths can reflect legality with a vengeance'. Alas, for those stripped of subsistence by the blight, the functioning of food markets was somewhat of a red herring.

Table 2.2, based on a table in an important paper by Peter Solar, is a stark reminder of the point that markets worked slowly. Comparing the two periods, 1840–1845 and 1846–1850, captures the fall in production but also suggests that imports largely made up for the shortfall in production. However, this ignores the lag between the failures of the potato in 1845 and 1846 and the arrival of large quantities of imports of Indian corn in the spring of 1847. Treating the 1846–1850 period as a block muffles the serious supply problems in 1846–1847 in particular (Solar, 1989; Ó Gráda, 1994a: 200–201). During the famine Ireland switched from being one of Britain's bread baskets to being a net importer of food-grains. However, in the winter and spring of 1846/47 exports still exceeded imports, presumably because the poor in Ireland lacked the purchasing power to buy the wheat and oats that were being shipped out.

Table 2.2   Aggregate Irish food supplies, 1840–1845 and 1846–1850 (in 1,000 million kcal/day)

	1840-1845	1846-1850
Irish production (less seed and horses)	32.1	15.7
Less exports and non-food uses	–11.8	–3.1
Net domestic supplies	20.3	12.6
Plus imports	+0.2	+5.5
Total consumption	20.5	18.1

Source: Ó Gráda (1994: 2000) after Solar (1989: 123).

VI. Post-famine adjustment

The Great Irish Famine was not just a watershed in Irish history, but also a major event in global history, with far-reaching and enduring economic and political consequences. In the 1840s the Irish cataclysm dwarfed anything occurring elsewhere in Europe. Nothing like it would happen in Ireland again. Individual memories of the famine, coupled with 'collective memory' of the event in later years, influenced the political culture of both Ireland and Irish-America, and indeed still play a role (Cullen, 1997; Donnelly, 2000; Ó Gráda, 2001; Daly, this volume). The blight's damage was long-lasting too: although the introduction of new potato varieties offered some respite against *phythophtera infestans* in the post-famine decades, no reliable defense would be found against it until the 1890s.

The famine brought the era of famines in Ireland to a brutal end. Serious failures of the potato in the early 1860s and late 1870s, also due to potato blight, brought privation in the west of the country, but no significant excess mortality. Ireland thus does not lend much support to the claim advanced by Jane Menken and Susan Watkins that famines typically create a demographic vacuum that is quickly filled. Other famines, it is true, seem to fit such a model, but in Ireland in only a few remote and tiny pockets in the west did population fill the vacuum left by the 'Great Hunger', and then only very briefly (Watkins and Menken, 1985; Ó Gráda, 1994a: 190; Guinnane, 1997).

What of the Irish famine's long-term economic impact? The relative importance of the arable component in agricultural output dropped sharply in its wake. Crops accounted for nearly two-thirds of net output in 1840–1845, but less than a quarter in 1876 and only one-seventh in 1908 (Ó Gráda, 1993: 57, 154). The famine resulted in higher living standards for survivors, since it increased the bargaining power of labor. Any negative impact on landlords' income from a declining population was more than compensated for by the relative increase in the prices of land-intensive output, the disappearance of thousands of uneconomic holdings, and the prompter payment of rents due. Higher emigration was another by-product of the famine, as the huge outflow of the crisis years generated its own 'friends and neighbors' dynamic. The late Raymond Crotty, an agricultural economist, claimed in a classic contribution that most of these changes would have taken place in any case, famine or no famine: the disaster only accelerated structural and demographic shifts already in train. So did the famine 'matter' in the long run? Kevin O'Rourke submitted Crotty's hypothesis to computable general equilibrium analysis in 1991, and found it wanting: the main reason being the profound impact of *phythophtera infestans* on the pasture/tillage balance in Irish agriculture. O'Rourke's simulations suggested that had the potato remained healthy, but allowing for exogenous price shocks and an annual one per cent rise in real wages, by 1870 agricultural employment would have fallen by two per cent instead of the actual forty-five per cent, and potato output would have risen marginally instead of plummeting by four-fifths (Crotty, 1966; O'Rourke, 1991). Thus the famine, far from being a mere catalyst, was a watershed event in nineteenth-century Irish history.

In the early 1980s, one eminent Irish historian claimed that 'even the scale of the great famine was not unique when seen in the context of contemporary European experience'. That was just before a burgeoning historiography began to reassert the cataclysmic dimensions of the Irish famine. Modern research comes closer to supporting instead Amartya Sen's surmise that '[in] no other famine in the world [was] the proportion of people killed...as large as in the Irish famines in the 1840s' (Boyce, 1982: 170; Sen, 1995). During the 1990s research into the Irish famine, prompted in part by sesquicentennial commemorations, reached unprecedented levels. Scores of monographs and articles were published, many of them of high quality (for surveys see Ó Gráda, 1996; Daly, this volume). These included several studies of the crisis at local level (e.g. O'Neill, 1997; Eiríksson, 1997; Ó Murchadha, 1998; Hickey, 2002).

Several issues require further investigation, however. For instance, whether or not the famine led to the decline of certain native industries by reducing the domestic market remains a moot point (Whelan 1999). The long-run impact of the famine on the health of survivors conceived or born during or in the wake of the famine is another un-researched topic (compare Lumey, 1998). Other issues calling for further work are: evictions and their impact on mortality, the evaluation of crisis management at the local level, the extent and consequences of famine-induced internal migration, the functioning of food and credit markets at retail level, and the role of maize as a substitute for the potato.

Bibliography

Bourke, A. (1993) *The Visitation of God? The Potato and the Great Irish Famine*, Dublin.

Boyce, D.G. (1982) *Nationalism in Ireland*, London.

Boyle, P.P. and Ó Gráda, C. (1986) 'Fertility trends, excess mortality, and the Great Irish Famine', *Demography*, 23, pp. 543–562.

Clarkson, L.E. and Crawford, E.M. (2001) *Feast and Famine: Food and Nutrition in Ireland 1500–1920*, Oxford.

Crotty, R.D. (1966) *Irish Agricultural Production*, Cork.

Cullen, L.M. (1997) 'The politics of the famine and famine historiography', *Comhdháil an Chraoibhín 1996* (Roscommon, Ireland), pp. 9–31.

Curtin, G. (2000) *A Pauper Warren: West Limerick 1845–49*, Limerick.

Daly, M.E. (1986) *The Famine in Ireland*, Dundalk.

Dickson, D. (1998) *Arctic Ireland: the Extraordinary Story of the Great Frost and the Forgotten Famine of 1740–41*, Belfast.

Donnelly, J.S. (2000) *The Irish Potato Famine*, London.

Drèze, J. and Sen, A. (1989) *Hunger and Public Action*, Oxford.

Edwards, R.D. and Williams, T.D. (1956) *The Great Famine: Studies in Irish History 1845–52*, Dublin [new edition 1994].

Eiríksson, A. (1997a) *The Great Famine in Ennistymon Poor Law Union*, Dublin.

Eiríksson, A. (1997b) 'Food supply and food riots', in C. Ó Gráda (ed.), *Famine 150: Commemorative Lecture Series*, Dublin, pp. 67–93.

Grant, J. (1990) 'The Great Famine and the poor law in the province of Ulster: the rate-in-aid issue of 1849', *Irish Historical Studies*, 105, pp. 30–47.

Gray, P. (1999) *Famine, Land, and Politics: British Government and Irish Society 1843–50*, Dublin.

Green, E.R.R. (1984) 'The Great Famine', in T.W. Moody and F.X. Martin (eds), *The Course of Irish History*, Cork.

Guinnane, T.W. (1997) *The Vanishing Irish: Households, Migration and the Rural Economy in Ireland, 1850–1914*, Princeton.

Guinnane, T.W. and Ó Gráda, C. (2002a) 'Workhouse mortality and the Great Irish Famine', in T. Dyson and C. Ó Gráda (eds), *Famine Demography*, Oxford, pp. 44–64.

Guinnane, T.W. and Ó Gráda, C. (2002a) 'Mortality in the North Dublin Union during the Great Famine', *Economic History Review*, 55, pp. 487–506.

Guinnane, T.W., McCabe, D. and Ó Gráda, C. (2004) 'Agency and famine relief: Enniskillen workhouse during the Great Irish Famine', downloadable at www.ucd.ie/economic/workingpapers/wp04.15.pdf.

Hickey, P. (2002) *Famine in West Cork: The Mizen Peninsula Land and People, 1800–1852*, Cork.

Kerr, D. (1996) *The Catholic Church and the Famine*, Dublin.

Kinealy, C. (1994) *This Great Calamity: the Irish Famine 1845–52*, Dublin.

Lenihan, P. (1997) 'War and Population, 1649–52', *Irish Economic and Social History*, 24, pp. 1–21.

Lumey, L.H. (1998) 'Reproductive outcomes in women prenatally exposed to undernutrition from the Dutch famine birth cohort', *Proceedings of the Nutrition Society*, 57, pp. 129–135.

Lynch, P. and Vaizey, J. (1960) *Guinness's Brewery in the Irish Economy 1759–1880*, Cambridge.

McGregor, P. (2003) 'The failure of the public works and mortality during the Great Irish Famine', paper presented to the CORN/UCD workshop on the Crises of the 1840s.

Mokyr, J. (1981) 'Irish history with the potato', *Irish Economic and Social History*, 8, pp. 3–29.

Mokyr, J. (1985). *Why Ireland Starved: An analytical and Quantitative History of the Irish Economy 1800–1850* (2nd edition), London.

Mokyr, J. and Ó Gráda, C. (1988) 'Poor and getting poorer ? Irish living standards before the Famine', *Economic History Review*, 51, pp. 209–235.

Mokyr, J. and Ó Gráda, C. (1996) 'Heights and living standards in the United Kingdom, 1815–1860', *Explorations in Economic History*, 34, pp. 1–27.

Mokyr, J. and Ó Gráda, C. (2002) 'What do people die of during famines? The Great Irish Famine in comparative perspective', *European Review of Economic History*, 6, pp. 339–364.

Neal, F. (1998) *Black '47: Britain and the Famine Irish*. London.

Ó Gráda, C. (1989) *The Great Irish Famine*, London.

Ó Gráda, C. (1991) 'The height of Clonmel prisoners, 1840–9', *Irish Economic and Social History*, 18, pp. 38–47.

Ó Gráda, C. (1993) *Ireland before and after the Famine: Explorations in Economic History 1800–1925* (2nd ed.), Manchester.

Ó Gráda, C. (1994a) *Ireland: A New Economic History 1780–1939*, Oxford.

Ó Gráda, C. (1994b) *An Drochshaol: Béaloideas agus Amhráin*, Dublin.

Ó Gráda, C. (1996) 'Making Irish famine history in 1995', *History Workshop Journal*, 42, pp. 87–104.

Ó Gráda, C. (1999) *Black '47 and Beyond: The Great Irish Famine in History, Economy, and Memory*, Princeton.

Ó Gráda, C. (2001) 'Famine, trauma, and memory', *Béaloideas*, 69, pp. 121–143.

Ó Gráda, C. and O'Rourke, K.H. (1997) 'Mass migration as disaster relief: lessons from the Great Irish Famine', *European Review of Economic History*, 1, pp. 3–25.

Ó Murchadha, C. (1998) *Sable Wings over the Sand: Ennis, County Clare, and its Wider Community during the Great Famine*, Ennis.

O'Neill, Th.P. (1956) 'The organization and administration of relief', in Edwards and Williams (1956).

O'Neill, T. P. (1997) 'The famine in Offaly', in T.P. O'Neill and W. Nolan (eds), *Offaly: History & Society*, Dublin.

O'Neill, T.P. (2000) 'Famine evictions', in C. King (ed.), *Famine, Land and Culture in Ireland,* Dublin.

O'Rourke, K. (1991) 'Did the Great Irish Famine matter?', *Journal of Economic History*, 51, pp. 1–22.

Rosen, S. (1999) 'Potato paradoxes', *Journal of Political Economy*, 107, pp. 294–313.

Sen, A.K. (1981) *Poverty and Famines*, Oxford.

Sen, A.K. (1995) 'Starvation and political economy: famines, entitlement, and alienation', address to the NYU/Ireland House Conference on Famine and World Hunger, New York.

Solar, P.M. (1989) 'The Great Famine was no ordinary subsistence crisis', in E.M. Crawford (ed.), *Famine: the Irish Experience, 900–1900*, Edinburgh, pp. 112–131.

Solar, P.M. (1997) 'The potato famine in Europe', in C. Ó Gráda (ed.), *Famine 150: Commemorative Lecture Series*, Dublin, pp. 113–127.

Whelan, K. (1999) 'Economic geography and the long-run effects of the Great Irish Famine', *Economic and Social Review*, 30, pp. 1–20.

Woodham-Smith, C. (1962) *The Great Hunger: Ireland 1845–49*, London.

3 Something old and something new. Recent research on the Great Irish Famine

Mary E. DALY, University College Dublin

In 1989 Peter Solar published a paper about the Irish famine, which he titled, 'The Great Famine was no ordinary subsistence crisis'(Solar, 1989: 112–133). Solar was referring to the question of food deficit, but his title is capable of carrying a much wider meaning. The Irish famine of the mid nineteenth century differs from any other famine of that period, because it continues to arouse strong emotions in some quarters, and it remains a topic for discussion and indeed polemic far beyond the academy. The Irish famine is the only nineteenth century famine that continues to attract popular interest. Irish popstar Sinead O'Connor has released a record about the famine and in 1997 British Prime Minister Tony Blair issued a statement about the role of the British administration during the famine that came close to an apology for the inadequacy of British relief efforts. The then US ambassador Jean Kennedy Smith figured prominently in a rather ill-advised famine concert held in Millstreet, Co. Cork in the summer of 1997 (Kinealy, 2002: 1–30; Toibin and Ferriter, 2001: 34). Two famine ships have been built in recent years, one, the Jeanie Johnston cost approximately €15 million, is now used as a sail training vessel and for corporate entertainment. There are museums and memorials to the Irish famine in Australia, Britain and North America, and Ireland. The Irish famine is included, along with the Holocaust and the Armenian massacres, in a syllabus on genocide studies adopted by the state of New Jersey. An extensive syllabus, of more than 1,000 pages on the Irish famine has been adopted by New York state schools for use with children ranging in age from 6–18 or so. It includes lessons on how to cook potatoes, poems by Seamus Heaney, material on Irish immigration to the USA, contemporary famine in the Third World, and a lot more besides (Murphy and Singer, 2001; Mullin, 2002: 119–129; Archdeacon, 2002: 130–152). While contemporary events and public interest undoubtedly exercise a stronger influence on academic research than we often admit, these influences are much more evident with respect to the Irish famine than perhaps for any other topic in the history of nineteenth century Europe. Some recent contributions to the literature of the Irish famine appear to have been more closely influenced by writings on the Holocaust and by research on contemporary famines in the Third World, than by scholarship relating to food, disease, or governance in mid-nineteenth century Europe.

The volume of material published on the Irish famine during the past ten years has almost certainly been greater than the total number of publications on that subject over the previous 140 years or so. In part this is a reflection of the extraordinary expansion in research and publications on Irish history. In 1980 the Select Bibliography of Writings on Irish Economic and Social History, published in the journal *Irish Economic and Social History*, listing books and articles published in the previous year listed 254 items.[1] By

---

[1] Economic and social history is interpreted in very liberal terms; in practice this bibliography covers all aspects of Irish history. The list also includes items published in previous years that were inadvertently omitted from earlier bibliographies.

1990 this had risen to 371. The bibliography published in the 2001 volume contained over 1,250 items. The increasing tie-in between commemoration and publications or TV documentaries has also boosted publications. Many contemporary accounts of Ireland during the famine years have been published within the past decade, some for the first time, together with local studies, collections of essays, and numerous articles, monographs and more general histories, some geared to the popular market. The impact of the Irish famine in Britain, North America and Australia has also attracted attention.

It is possible to divide publications into those that are primarily addressed to a non-academic audience, whether local, national or international, and those that are directed towards a more scholarly debate, but the distinction is not clear-cut and at times it may be rather artificial. Scholarly interest in the Irish famine is no longer confined to political, social and economic historians; it extends to those who are engaged in cultural and gender studies and postcolonial theorists. The vogue for historicising literary studies has extended to the Irish famine, but this historicising often prefers to privilege literary texts and material relating to twentieth century famines rather than nineteenth century Ireland and Europe, although this practice is not unique to studies of the Irish famine. It has also impacted on the interpretation of topics such as Irish nationalism. Yet at times there would appear to be little sense of any dialogue between writings on the famine by scholars with a background in cultural studies, and those writing from the perspective of a historian (Daly, forthcoming).

Recent research has significantly advanced our understanding of the Irish famine and its impact on Irish society. In the remainder of this paper I propose to examine a number of specific topics: food supplies and markets, aspects of famine relief, landlords and land clearances, and the evidence forthcoming from the local studies carried out by the National Famine Research Project, which is beginning to reveal the diverse local impact of the famine and the factors that accounted for favourable or unfavourable outcomes in particular areas.

I. Food supplies and markets

The central question regarding any famine is whether there was a shortage of food, and if so the extent of the food deficit. A secondary, and closely-related question is whether markets functioned to ease the famine or to exacerbate the shortage, indeed whether the famine was caused by market failure, e.g. hoarding. Solar (1989) shows that the immediate cause of the Irish famine was the failure of the potato crop, and that the food loss resulting from the potato blight was much greater than in other documented crop failures in nineteenth century Europe. He estimated that Irish production of the major crops used for human and animal food (excluding grass and hay), fell by more than 50 per cent during the years 1846–1850 compared with 1840–1845; when distilling, brewing and exports were taken into account net domestic food supplies were only 62 percent, of the 1840–1845 average. The high dependency on the potato, and the fact that in Europe the blight was largely confined to the 1845 and 1846 crops go a considerable way to explaining why no part of northern Europe experienced a subsistence crisis on the scale of the Irish famine (Solar, 1997: 114–117). Irish crisis of the 1840s was much more acute than elsewhere in Europe.

Estimates of potato output before the famine and the consumption of potatoes by humans and by livestock still rely on the work of the late Austen Bourke (Bourke, 1967/8: 72–96).

A later paper by Bourke on the Irish grain trade remains essential to the understanding of pre-famine export and import markets (Bourke, 1976: 156–169). Yet despite the convincing statistical evidence, firstly of the extent of Irish dependence on the potato, and of the food shortfall caused by the potato blight, the recent practice of comparing the Irish famine with recent famines in the Third World has served in some quarters to shift the emphasis away from food scarcity to the question of market failure and entitlements (Sen, 1981). Dyson and Ó Gráda note that most food crises were probably caused by a combination of food shortage and market failure and entitlements, but they suggest that FAD (food availability declines) played a greater role in famines during the nineteenth and the early twentieth century, and a lesser role in more recent famines (Dyson and Ó Gráda, 2002: 14). There is obviously scope for examining the Irish famine from the perspective of entitlements, but not at the expense of ignoring the extent of the food shortage. Yet Amartya Sen's account of the Bengal famine of the 1940s, a famine that apparently occurred, despite there being no shortage of food, has served to reinvigorate a traditional strand in Irish nationalist historiography of the famine, because the central image in the nationalist memory of the Irish famine was that at the height of the famine Ireland was producing more than sufficient food to provide for the entire population, and that a ban on food exports to Britain would have been sufficient to prevent deaths. Nationalist writings denied the existence of famine, or the legitimacy of the word famine, a line of analysis that first appeared in the 1840s and has continued to be repeated throughout the nineteenth century and beyond (Donnelly, 2001: 209–221). The most vocal exponent of this claim in recent years is Christine Kinealy, who has asserted that '[t]he new research which has appeared since 1994 has largely rejected the viewpoint that the Famine was a natural disaster' (…) 'sufficient food was being produced in the country to feed the people' (Kinealy, 2002: 11, 25). Kinealy suggests that the statistics on the Irish grain trade compiled by the late Austin Bourke 'were flawed and provided an underestimation of exports' and that Bourke had admitted this (Kinealy, 2002: 24). In fact what Bourke wrote was that the statistics were 'neither orderly nor complete' – but he did not suggest that they significantly underestimated exports; indeed, he believed 'they are not in major error', because they were consistent with the calculations that he had made of crop yield, grain production, and so on (Bourke, 1976: 156). There is undoubtedly scope for revising Bourke's statistics – and Peter Solar's detailed work on Irish trade is the obvious place to look for this (Solar, 2003: 277–289), but it would be foolhardy to jettison Bourke without providing a superior alternative. Kinealy claims that on the eve of the famine potatoes only accounted for 20 per cent of agricultural output, but she does not indicate the share of human food consumption. To bolster her argument that the famine was a consequence of Britain's failure to ban the export of food from Ireland, she supplies long lists of livestock exports, but whatever about the financial value of these exports, they would not have compensated for the shortage of potatoes (2002: 29). Solar claims that the calorific value, as opposed to the financial value of livestock and dairy produce was quite small, only 9 per cent of the total in pre-famine times (Solar, 1989: 131).

The export of food during the famine remains an emotive topic for many people. Bourke (1976: 165) concluded that at best a ban on exports 'could have served only as a temporary device to win time'; Solar's reconstruction of agricultural trade statistics shows that 'exports in 1846 were sustained almost entirely by a large increase in live animal exports, part of which may have been the forced liquidation of assets by small holders'. During the famine agricultural exports fell by about 30 per cent, with the collapse in exports of cereal, pigmeat, poultry and eggs offset to a large degree by increased exports of cattle and sheepmeat (Solar, 2003: 284). Pigs and poultry were fed almost entirely on potatoes. The increase in livestock exports probably reflects additional sales by farmers who were forced to buy more food than usual and at a higher price or farmers disposing of their stock preparatory to emigrating with their families. Exporting livestock in order to buy grain was a rational response to the circumstances; any case for controlling food exports rests almost entirely on the export of grain.

How well did markets function during the Irish famine? Having examined a number of price series for potatoes during the 1840s, and regional price variations before and during the famine years, Cormac Ó Gráda determined that the evidence was 'more consistent with orderly than segmented markets in the wake of the blight'. Indeed he has suggested that markets worked more smoothly during the Irish famine than during famines in 18th century France or 20th century Africa. The winter of 1846–1847 saw a very sharp rise in food prices throughout Ireland, in marked contrast with what Sen has suggested about famine in Bengal. The Irish food shortage of 1845/46 coincided with a European-wide shortage, and evidence from the records of Cork grain merchants suggests that during the autumn of 1846 Irish merchants were rather cautious in placing orders for imported grain, at a time when prices were rising steadily (Ó Gráda, 1999: 140–146). Their caution presumably reduced the quantity of food available at a critical time. Were merchants elsewhere less cautious, and did their foresight reduce the food deficit? Contemporary accounts in Ireland refer to grain ships being diverted to ports in the Mediterranean.

II.   Government policies for famine relief

Many writers on the Irish famine would not view Ó Gráda's evidence that markets functioned effectively as a good thing, because the critique of British government policy with respect to the Irish famine rests heavily on the determination of British government ministers and senior officials to use the famine to promote free trading conditions, not only with regard to food, but also in land and labour. The key book on this topic is Peter Gray's 1999 study. Earlier writings on the Irish famine tended to distinguish between a relatively benign attitude towards famine relief and positive interventions on the part of the Tory government of Sir Robert Peel, and the much less sympathetic regime adopted by the Liberal government led by Lord George Russell (Edwards and Williams, 1956; Woodham Smith, 1962). However Gray shows conclusively that Peel and Russell had very similar attitudes towards the Irish economy and Irish rural society. Already before the potato blight had appeared, Peel's government was of the opinion that the socio-economic structure of rural Ireland was fundamentally flawed; that potatoes – the bedrock of that system – were a morally inferior foodstuff that enabled the Irish peasantry to survive in indolence and poverty; that conacre – which was based on potato cultivation removed any incentive to improve land or work harder; and that the Irish land system was preventing the emergence of an industrious middle class. For Peel and those who shared his views the solution lay in bringing English-style commercial farming to Ireland; replacing cottiers and small farmers with larger commercial farms and wage-earning farm labourers, with a staple diet of bread rather than potatoes. The famine was seen as confirmation that the potato-based economy was inherently flawed. It also offered an opportunity to implement measures that they regarded as essential to transform rural Ireland into a market economy (Gray, 1999).

The debate over the respective merits of free trade and protection was not confined to Britain and Ireland; in Europe too it became a key issue during the food crisis of the 1840s. The corn laws were also suspended in France, Belgium and the Netherlands – but only the Netherlands followed Britain in adhering to a strict policy of non-intervention in food markets. In France, Belgium and a number of German states governments took steps to manage the internal or external food markets, encouraging imports, preventing exports or managing internal food distribution (Solar, 1997: 123; Gray, 1997: 86–108; Gray, this volume). An assessment of how effective these measures were in containing famine *might* help to enlighten the debate in Ireland with regard to controlling food exports, government grain depots etc., although the scale of the comparative food deficits must be kept in mind.

If the traditional nationalist critique of government policy was directed at the food trade, most attention in recent times has concentrated on relief expenditure. Joel Mokyr contrasted the £69.3 million that Britain spent on the Crimean War with the miserly allocation for Irish famine relief. Jim Donnelly gives the figure as £7 million (Mokyr, 1983: 292; Donnelly, 2001: 118–119). Whatever about the moral argument, this comparison fails to take account of the fact that military spending was acknowledged as a key (perhaps the key) responsibility for central governments during the nineteenth century, whereas relief of poverty or destitution was not. Equally, perhaps more important was the determination to place the cost of famine relief on Irish landlords in order to bring about a major change in the rural economy.

Irish famine relief can be divided into a number of phases. First, the programmes of relief works implemented first by Peel, and then by Russell. There are some distinctions: Peel's was accompanied by the establishment of food depots and the sale of a limited amount of meal which had been stockpiled by the state; Russell placed a greater proportion of the cost of relief works on local taxation. Secondly, from the spring of 1847 when the Liberal government abandoned relief works in favour of the distribution of cooked food, until the autumn of 1847 when the food distribution came to an end. Thirdly, the period after the autumn of 1847 when there was no formal famine relief programme in operation. From the thousands of pages written on this topic, I wish to focus on a limited number of topics.

II.1. Public works and food supplies

Employment on relief works peaked during the winter of 1846/47, almost simultaneously with the peak in food prices, with the result that the wages paid on relief works were not sufficient to support a family, yet offering higher prices on relief works would probably have wrecked existing wage structures and drawn men to the relief works and away from their regular employment. The programme of relief works came to an end in the spring of 1847, at a time when food supplies had improved and prices were falling, yet it is probable that in those circumstances the relief works might actually have proved effective in relieving distress. The winter of 1846/47 was exceptionally severe. Ó Gráda notes that the typical Irish farming cycle meant that Irish labourers and smallholders spent these months indoors, not out in the fields. Even before the famine the Irish poor were described as extremely badly clothed. So relief works in mid-winter probably contributed to deaths (Ó Gráda, 1999: 34–37).

Would alternative relief programmes have been more effective? What of claims that landlords should have been left to their own devices, or that government assistance should have been directed towards aiding landlords in draining their properties etc? Tom Devine's account of the famine in the Highlands shows the contribution made by landlords there. But the landlords in question were newcomers, affluent businessmen, not traditional lairds, and many of the landlords who worked hard to provide relief for their tenants were equally efficient at clearing their estates of the same tenants within a decade (Devine, 1988; Devine, this volume). The very modest contributions made by many Irish landlords towards various relief funds suggest that private efforts did not offer a realistic alternative to state aid (Hickey, 2002: 145). Railway development – as suggested by Sir George Bentinck, would have required a long time to plan and organise. Given the short window of time between the failure of the potatoes and the onset of distress, if public works were to be used as a form of relief, there is no obvious indication that a noticeably better system could have been found. But an effective programme of public works could have helped to ease the later stages of the famine – from the autumn of 1847 until the early 1850s, a time when many famine victims died.

While a lot of contemporary criticism focused on administrative ineptitude, financial waste and/or dishonesty, both on the part of local committees, or government officials, Ó Gráda has claimed that 'the bureaucracy responsible for Irish famine relief was much more honest and probably more sophisticated than its Third World counterparts today' (Ó Gráda, 1999: 58) However, we'll revisit that point later in this article.

II.2.   Local and national responsibilities

The cost of relief, both through public works, and from the autumn of 1847 when the only source of relief was the poor law, fell heavily on local taxes, and therefore on local property, with the result that the poorest areas were saddled with the heaviest taxes and borrowings. On the other hand, policy decisions, whether in the administration of public works, soup kitchens, or the poor law were determined and closely monitored by the authorities in Dublin. The respective shares of relief borne by local and national governments in other parts of Europe during the 1840s would be enlightening. In Ireland the first call was almost invariably made, not on local resources, but on the central administration (by which I mean Dublin). The first response by most catholic priests in the west of Ireland to the potato blight was to write to Dublin Castle seeking assistance. (Swords, 1999: 41; Hickey, 2002: 144–145; Foley, 1997: 55–56). They may have reacted in this fashion because it would appear that during earlier, admittedly much less acute food shortages, the combination of government relief and assistance from British voluntary organizations had proved effective in preventing deaths (O'Neill, 1971).

III. Landlords and the famine

The decision to place much of the cost of relief on local taxes was not accidental, nor was it prompted primarily by financial considerations. The British authorities were of the opinion that responsibility for the subdivision of rural holdings, the heavy reliance on the potato, and therefore for the famine rested with Irish landlords, and that they should bear the consequences of this irresponsible management (or mis-management) of their estates (Gray, this volume). James Donnelly closes a chapter dealing with British famine policy by noting that 'What is remarkable, then, about the discussion of the great famine in Britain in early and mid-1847 is the extremely harsh and almost unanimous verdict given against Irish landlords, to the point of holding them primarily responsible for having allowed the country 'to sink to its present awful state" (Donnelly, 2001: 100).

Did the decisions that the British government made about who should pay for famine relief, force Irish landlords to evict their tenants in order to stave off financial ruin? Should the evictions of the famine years be seen as a desperate survival strategy by landlords facing crippling taxation demands caused by the high cost of relief? Do Irish landlords qualify for inclusion among the victims of the famine? Or did some landlords take advantage of the famine, the breakdown in popular resistance, to carry out a long wished-for rationalization of their estates (landlords were responsible for the entire poor rate on holdings valued at less than £4)?

The Gregory clause plays an important part in this story. Introduced by the Irish landlord and MP for Dublin, Sir William Gregory (whose much younger future wife achieved fame as the founder of the Abbey Theatre and major patron of W.B. Yeats and other writers), as an amendment to the 1847 Irish Poor Law Act, the clause denied relief in the workhouse to those holding in excess of one-quarter acre. Donnelly suggests that the British newspapers were so obsessed with the 'delinquencies' of the Irish landlords that they failed to recognise the significance of the Gregory clause (Donnelly, 2001: 100).

In order to determine if landlords were forced to clear estates because of high tax bills, it is critical to examine when the number of evictions began to rise. Unfortunately there are major statistical difficulties, because the Irish constabulary only began to collect statistics on evictions from 1849, which is too late for our purpose. Fortunately Tim O'Neill has begun to fill the gap, using data on the number of families who were served with eviction notices. In the period 1846 to 1848 inclusive, 140,835 families were served with ejectment proceedings, though not all of these families would have been evicted. O'Neill suggests, that approximately 97,000 households may have been evicted between 1846 and 1848. The constabulary returns of evictions, which may be an underestimate, record 47,511 families permanently evicted between 1849 and 1854. This would suggest that approximately 150,000 families, or 750,000 people (assuming an average household size to be five) were evicted between 1846 and 1854 (O'Neill, 2000: 42–44). He makes a strong case for giving evictions a more central role in the famine story:

'The role of eviction in the creation of the catastrophe of the Great Famine is central. The larger landowners guarded their estates with the same zeal as any Irish farmer protected his field. Impoverished tenants were removed or were threatened with removal and the administration encouraged that development by the introduction of the Gregory clause in 1847, which prohibited any family holding more than a quarter acre from drawing relief. The underestimation of eviction rates and even threats of eviction has led to a distortion of famine studies by a generation of historians.' (O'Neill, 2000: 45; O'Neill, 1998: 681–732).

If O'Neill's figures are correct, not only were the number of evictions significantly higher than often suggested, but evictions begin to rise sharply in 1847, before the full impact of high poor rates would have been evident; previous scholars suggested that evictions peaked in 1850 (Daly, 1986: 110; Kinealy, 1994: 218, Donnelly, 1989: 337–338). Donnelly's chapters in the *New History of Ireland* highlighted the role of evictions, and he has extended that discussion in his 2001 book, with a particular focus on Kilrush

Union, where the clearances on the Vandaleur estate attracted sufficient attention in Westminster to prompt an official inquiry (Donnelly, 1989: 332–349; Donnelly, 2001: 144–156). He highlights the misery, sickness and deaths resulting from mass clearances, but places responsibility for evictions on the high tax bills that landlords faced and their insolvent circumstances, referring to 'the relative poverty of Kilrush landlords'. 'Evict their debtors or be disposed by their creditors, this perceived choice provided a general rationalisation among landlords for the great clearances of defaulting or insolvent tenants' (Donnelly, 2001: 149, 138). Yet the records of the Incumbered Estates Courts, a tribunal established by the British government in 1849 to clear the log-jam of insolvent estates in Ireland, as part of the process of creating a capitalist and commercial farming system in Ireland, show that very few landlords were bankrupted by the famine. Most of the estates that changed hands through the court were already hopelessly incumbered before 1845. The famine did not present a serious threat to the lifestyle of King's County landlords; very few ended up in the Incumbered Estates Court as a consequence. Ó Gráda and Eiriksson concluded that 'the famine, then, might have cost some landlords two or three years' rent, a small fraction of the median debt of the estates sold by the Encumbered Estates Court.' (Ó Gráda and Eiriksson, 1996; Ó Gráda, 1999: 127–134; O'Neill, 1998: 714).

In his essay on 'The potato famine in Europe' Solar indicates that the nature of land holding and the agricultural labour market were factors that helped determine the ability to withstand the subsistence crisis: 'Where smallholders also owned their land, they had additional resources to help surmount the crisis. They could, if necessary, borrow against their property, or even sell out. In the longer term, if they had enough land, they could shift away from potatoes to other intensive crops. Where smallholders were tenants, or only obtained land in exchange for labour, they were more vulnerable'; Agricultural labourers employed by larger farmers were exceptionally vulnerable (Solar, 1997: 121). The essays in this volume by Bass and Vanhaute show that complex factors determined whether individuals survived the subsistence crisis of the mid 1840s, but the most important would appear to have been the level of income and command of economic resources. To those with first-hand experience of the famine in rural Ireland, the secure possession of a sufficiently large farm must have appeared to offer the best chance of survival. Mokyr suggests that the landless and those with less than twenty acres of land were vulnerable to the famine (Mokyr, 1983: 275). Memories of mass evictions of the famine years fuelled Irish nationalist hatred of Irish landlords, and the British government, and they provided the emotional drive behind later campaigns for tenant right and peasant proprietor. When another subsistence crisis loomed in the late 1870s, rural Ireland responded by forming the land league. One of the leaders was Michael Davitt, whose family was evicted from their Mayo holding during the famine (Donnelly, 2001: 221–229).

IV. The local story

'There was little famine in the eastern counties or in the north. In the midlands and south the effects of famine were confined to the labouring population and were never general in the rural community. It was only in the poor regions of the west that the failure of the potato presented whole regions with the threat of starvation. The death rate did, of course, rise across the country. Fever followed famine, and because the desperately poor migrated from west to east, and from country-side to towns, it spread across the country. In the east and north, fever was the cause of death rather than starvation.' (Cullen, 1972: 131).

Although Cullen may have overstated his case, he is correct in emphasizing the regional dimension.[2] The sesquicentenary of the famine prompted a large number of local studies (Cowman and Brady, 1995; Kildare County Council, 1995; Swinford Historical Society, 1995; Marnane, 1996; Cork Archives Institute, 1996; O'Gorman, 1996; Stewartstown and District, 1996; Marnane, 1997; Grant, 1997a and 1997b; Kinealy and Parkhill, 1997; McAtasney, 1997; O'Neill, 1998; Swords, 1999; Hickey, 2002). However the potential offered by local studies has not been fully realized, because of the absence of a common methodology. Furthermore, while the famine had an impact on all parts of Ireland, there is a danger that numerous accounts of local hardship and suffering may give the impression that areas were equally affected.

A comprehensive understanding of the local incidence and impact is one of the major challenges for historians of the Irish famine. Source material is plentiful, but uneven in its quality and rate of survival. There are substantially fewer surviving poor law records from areas worst affected by the famine, such as the west of Ireland, than from Ulster, where the famine had less impact. Most of the surviving records are descriptive: minutes of boards of guardians, letters written by relief committees. Nominal data, such as workhouse registers and catholic parish registers is very sparse. The 1851 census enumeration records do not survive. Comparing data from administrative units such as poor law unions, with data from the 1841 and 1851 census and agricultural statistics is a complex exercise. During the famine period official statistics were collected on the basis of two distinct, and incompatible administrative units. The older system was based on the county, with each county sub-divided into baronies, each comprising several civil parishes. Census data was presented on this basis. The 1838 Irish Poor Law Act divided the country into poor law unions, centred on major market towns, and sub-divided into electoral divisions, which took no account of country boundaries; to further complicate matters the boundaries of some unions and electoral divisions were changed during the famine years (McCabe, 1996: 4). Local newspapers are an invaluable source, but the availability of estate records is patchy, and no local famine study as yet has successfully combined an in-depth study of local administrative and relief records plus estate records. The most comprehensive local study now available is arguably the least representative, Dublin city, where data from the North Dublin Union is augmented by burial records, information from local charities, church records of marriages and births and other sources (Cox, 1996; Ó Gráda, 1999: 157–193). A comprehensive collection of the marriage and burial data to hand for the 1840s and the early 1850s must rank high on the list of further research priorities for local studies.

The National Famine Commemoration Project – the only scholarly research funded by the government's commemoration fund – carried out studies of seven poor law unions, Ballina (Mayo), Dublin North, Enniskillen (Fermanagh), Ennistymon (Clare), Kinsale (Cork), Parsonstown (King's Co.), Rathdrum (Wicklow). They were selected on the basis of the quality of the surviving records (Lindsay and Fitzpatrick, 1993), geographical spread and differing outcomes.[3] This concentration on poor law unions had undoubted

---

[2] For a map of the counties of Ireland, see this volume, chapter 2, Figure 2.1.
[3] The project was directed by David Dickson, David Fitzpatrick, Cormac Ó Gráda and myself.

pluses and minuses. While the poor law had only a peripheral role in famine relief in 1845 – it was responsible for providing fever hospitals – during the winter of 1846/47 workhouses became crowded with starving and desperate people, and from the autumn of 1847 the poor law was the sole source of official relief for famine victims. The story of the famine told from the perspective of the poor law, is therefore weighted towards the later stages of the famine. This is actually a very good thing, since it provides a clear reminder of how long-drawn-out the crisis was in some areas. During the years 1846/47 the famine was undoubtedly a national crisis (pace Cullen); however in later years the regional dimension became more pronounced, and during 1848/49, the greatest distress did not correspond with the areas where potato blight was most acute.

In the following section I shall examine the local evidence under a number of headings: the poor law, agency, mortality.

IV.1. The poor law in famine relief

Irish local authorities had no statutory responsibility for poor relief until 1838, when Ireland adopted a variant of the new English poor law. But whereas the new English poor law continued to provide outdoor relief, in Ireland relief was only provided in the workhouse. The 1838 report, which provided the blue-print for the Irish poor law, specifically stated that it was not designed to cope with a major famine (Daly, 1997: 12–18).

The typical pre-famine workhouse had plenty of spare capacity. Pre-famine admissions followed a seasonal cycle determined by agricultural employment and food scarcities: workhouse numbers were at their lowest in the autumn, rising during the mid-winter as agricultural work became scarce, falling in the spring as work picked up and inmates were discharged, only to rise again in early summer. These were the 'meal months' when the old season's potatoes were generally exhausted, and the new season's food was not yet available. This was also a period when there was little agricultural employment. But as the harvest approached discharges exceeded admissions. The breaking of this cyclical pattern, and the date when it was re-established in the early 1850s may provide an indication of when the famine might be said to have ended in different places.

The profile of workhouse inmates before the famine varied somewhat among the workhouses whose records are to hand, and a systematic comparative analysis is extremely difficult: workhouse registers are fragmentary, the data available and the categories recorded in the registers or minute books change over time. Classification is not consistent from one union to another, and the observations that follow should be read with these caveats in mind. The number and composition of inmates reflects local demand for workhouse places, and the policy of the board of guardians, which was composed of local property-owners. In all workhouses studied except Ballina, women were in the majority, accounting for between 53 and 55 per cent of inmates. Children under 15 formed a major component of the pre-famine workhouse population: 42 per cent in Ballina; 51 per cent in Parsonstown, but only 30 per cent in the North Dublin Union. Pre-famine Parsonstown catered primarily for widows and orphans and the elderly.

The poor law was given no formal role in the early stages of the Irish famine, other than to provide medical care in workhouse hospitals, and during 1845 and the spring and summer of 1846 workhouses continued to have spare capacity. However in the autumn or winter of 1846 most workhouses became full, and perhaps over-crowded, and the composition of the inmates altered. Women continued to account for a majority of workhouse inmates throughout the famine, except in Ballina, where men constituted a majority of admissions at a number of crisis periods: the 2nd and 4th quarters of 1846, and the 2nd quarter of 1847. Almost 60% of the inmates of Ballina workhouse were male in the second quarter of 1846. For the 2nd and 3rd quarters of 1847 the percentages were 56–57%, McCabe suggests that the relaxed regime of the local guardians was responsible for the high proportion of men who were admitted. When the board of guardians was dissolved and replaced by appointed vice-guardians in 1848 the proportion of able-bodied men fell sharply (McCabe, 1997: ch.6).[4] The Union with the second highest proportion of male inmates was the North Dublin Union, where a female majority before the famine (54% 1844/5) became male/ female parity over the years 1845–1849, presumably reflecting an influx of men into Dublin either looking for work or going to or coming from Britain (Cox, 1996: tables 16 (a) i and ii). But on the whole it would appear that women were more readily granted admission to workhouses than men.

The proportion of famine inmates who were children varied quite widely, depending on the rate at which adult males were admitted, and this in turn may reflect either administrative policy, or the severity of the crisis. In Inishowen, a union that escaped relatively lightly, 44% of female inmates and 48% of male inmates during the years 1846–1849 were under 15 years. Children under 15 accounted for 52% of workhouse admissions in Enniskillen during the years 1845–1847, which may be read as an indicator of a stringent admission policy by the guardians, but in Parsonstown in 1849 – a period coinciding with heavy land clearances – only 28% of men and 30% of women were under 15 years, which was considerably below the proportion in the pre-famine period. (Cox, 1997a: Tables 172 and 173; McCabe, 1996: Table 17(b); Eiriksson, 1996, ch 8 and Table 8.2). Data on the inmates of workhouses in Co. Kerry during the famine years, which are presented in a somewhat different fashion, show wide variations in the composition by gender and age, although the 1848–1849 figures for Dingle may well be incorrect.

Information on family admissions is fragmentary, but in Parsonstown in 1849 (during a period of major clearances) there was a significant increase in the proportion of single persons admitted compared with 1842/3; likewise in the North Dublin Union between 1846 and 1849. However in Enniskillen a majority of inmates in the months before the famine arrived alone – many apparently were beggars and tramps – by 1847 only one-fifth of those admitted were not accompanied by family members. From the winter of 1846 onwards there was a substantial increase in family parties seeking admission. It seems probable that families were given preference over solitary applicants. In Parsonstown,

---

[4] Boards of Guardians were responsible for the management of each poor law union, including the determination of the local poor rate. The initial legislation provided for a maximum of one-quarter of the guardians to be *ex officio* members. In 1847 this was increased to one-half, because an amendment introduced in 1843 made landlords responsible for the payment of rates on all properties valued at £4 or less (this would cover most holdings of less than 5 acres and some larger holdings). *Ex officio* guardians were chosen from the local magistrates, and they were invariably landlords. They were also obliged to serve. The electorate consisted of ratepayers with property valued in excess of £4, but a system of multiple votes gave greater weight to larger tenants and landowners.

Table 3.1   Population of Kerry Poor Law Unions (percentages)

	Adults Male	Adults Female	Children under 15 years
Dingle			
1848–1849	29.6	48.3	22.1
1849–1850	20.9	41.7	37.4
Kenmare			
1848–1849	29.2	30.6	40.2
1849–1850	18.4	34.0	47.5
Killarney			
1848–1849	21.6	27.9	40.5
1849–1850	16.4	27.8	55.8
Listowel			
1848–1849	24.1	34.6	41.3
1849–1850	19.6	27.2	53.2

Source: Foley, 1997: 218.

57% of mothers with children admitted in 1842–1843 were widowed and 40% were married. These proportions were reversed in 1849 (54% married, 41% widows) (Eiriksson, 1996: ch. 8; Cox, 1996: ch 16 (a) and (b)). The proportion of orphaned and deserted children seems lower than might have been expected: 5.8% of total admissions in Inishowen (1846–1849), 7.2% in Enniskillen (1845–1847). In both cases just over 14 per cent of inmates were under 15 years. Orphaned and deserted children accounted for 6.8% of admissions in Parsonstown (1849). Eiriksson suggests that abandoned children did not make it to the workhouse. He also claims, contrary to the prevailing image of the workhouse in Irish memory, that workhouses did not break up families, the famine did. Of the 153 inmates who entered Parsonstown in 1849 as members of identifiable family units, 21 died and the remainder were discharged. 58% left as part of a family unit. Most of the remainder were discharged within two weeks (Cox, 1997; McCabe, 1996; Eiriksson, 1996, ch 8).

IV.2.   Agency

Although Ó Gráda suggests, with justification, that administrative standards in Ireland during the 1840s were higher than in many Third World countries suffering from contemporary famines, there is little doubt that administrative standards varied between the different areas. For example, whereas local committees in Limerick and Clare were remarkably active in applying for funds under the government's relief works schemes, more active than unions in more distressed areas such as Mayo, authorities in east Ulster and in Enniskillen Union were less inclined to apply for assistance. O'Neill suggests that this was also true in Offaly, perhaps because there was 'no tradition of this type of local organisation'. As in Ulster the initiative rested with the landlords, whereas in the west, because of the shortage of local gentry, clergy, merchants and agents were more involved, and they may well have been more active in making demands on the government (Daly, 1986: 83; McCabe, 1996: 47–48; O'Neill, 1998: 688; Swords, 1999). It was commonly believed that the famine was less acute in Ulster because of the better relationship that existed between landlords and tenants there, but this point of view has been seriously questioned by recent studies, such as the history of the famine in the Lurgan/Portadown area, which documents the poor standard of administration in Lurgan workhouse (McAtasney, 1997).

There is further scope for investigating how far landlord paternalism, and local pride, or an unwillingness to admit the extent of distress, determined relief efforts in parts of Ulster and perhaps elsewhere in Ireland. Boards of guardians in north-east Ulster asserted that there was no need for outdoor relief in their area. Parsonstown was the only union in Leinster not to grant outdoor relief. The Earl of Rosse bragged of this in the House of Lords (Grant, 1997b: 193; Eiriksson, 1996).

There are numerous contemporary reports of poor attendance by poor law guardians. In Rathdrum many guardians only appeared when the board was appointing a workhouse master, chaplain or porter, awarding contracts, setting the poor rate, or altering boundaries that would determine the incidence of local taxation. In October 1848 only 3 out of 40 members of the Listowel Board of Guardians turned up for a meeting. It would appear that the Cahiriciveen guardians were equally negligent, although their shortcomings were less subject to the scrutiny of local newspapers because of Cahirciveen's isolated location (Cox, 1997b: Rathdrum; Foley, 1997: 222–223). Enniskillen board of guardians is another instance of poor attendance. Moreover some members of the board and their families benefited personally from the awarding of contracts or the filling of jobs. The Earl of Enniskillen, who chaired the board, was directly responsible for a 33% increase in the cost of building the workhouse and was the personal beneficiary of the overrun. At the height of the famine several meetings had to be abandoned for want of a quorum (Guinnane, McCabe and Ó Gráda, 2003). In Ballina – the largest union in Ireland – only 30% of the guardians achieved a 33% attendance record during the years 1846–1848. The best attenders were the ex-officio guardians (local landlords or their agents), and one of these, Edward Howley was present at an impressive 115 out of 150 meetings. Attendance of guardians from Erris was especially low. While their absence may be explained by distance – a journey of approximately 50 miles – their absence adversely affected admissions, because the guardians who were present frequently rejected applications for admission from the Erris area. Although Erris was one of the poorest parts of Ireland, the needy of Erris were effectively excluded from consideration by the local authorities until April 1848, some months after the board of guardians was dissolved and replaced by appointed vice-guardians. This may be an exceptional instance, there is no evidence yet to hand of comparable behaviour in other unions. In Parsonstown union there was no relationship between attendance at meetings and the addresses of those who were admitted to the workhouse. Distance from the workhouse was also less significant than might be expected. The proportion of rates collected or uncollected in an area does not appear to have determined admission from an area, although the non-payment of rates may have determined the overall policy of the workhouse (McCabe, 1997: chs. 15 and 18; Eiriksson, 1996: ch 8).

IV.3. Mortality

One million remains the best estimate for the number of famine deaths, but considerable progress has been made in disaggregating deaths by age, gender, cause of death, and geography. Mokyr and Ó Gráda suggest with due caution that 'the implication that the famine killed roughly twice as many people in proportion in Munster and in Connacht as it did in Ulster and Leinster is perhaps not too far off the mark' (Mokyr and Ó Gráda, 2002: 31). Efforts have been made to distinguish between diseases that are directly attributable to hunger, and those that reflect a greater incidence of infection due to famine-related migration, overcrowding and the break-down of normal life.

Deaths by starvation are almost certainly underreported in the statistical tables by Sir William Wilde that were published as part of the 1851 Census, but Mokyr and Ó Gráda believe that the numbers reported appear to be an accurate indicator of the severity of the crisis in an area. While the traditional accounts of famine deaths lump fever and dysentery together, Mokyr and Ó Gráda classify dysentery and diarrhoea with hunger-related diseases, like starvation, dropsy and marasmus, because they were often caused by eating unusual and unsuitable foods. There are numerous accounts of starving people eating raw shell-fish, grass and other substances (McHugh, 1956: 397–406; Portéir, 1995: 50–67; 85–99). The proportion of deaths from dysentery and diarrhoea was highest in the areas most affected by the famine. Deaths from fever, dysentery, diarrhoea, dropsy and starvation accounted for only 0.6 per cent of deaths in Co. Antrim, but 11 per cent in West Cork and almost 15 per cent in Co. Mayo, which is universally accepted as the poorest county in Ireland at the time (Ó Gráda, 1997: 88). The differential mortality from starvation and associated diseases confirms the traditional belief that the famine was much more acute in the west and south-west of Ireland.

Fever is an infectious disease, not directly caused by hunger. The proportion of famine deaths attributed to fever was very similar across the four provinces, and the incidence of fever rose by a factor of 4–5, compared with a factor of 8–12 for starvation-related diseases. Mokyr and Ó Gráda estimate that two-thirds of famine related diseases were directly attributable to hunger and dietary deficiency, one-third to contagious diseases, such as typhus or other fevers that were caused by factors such as the break-down in personal hygiene, overcrowding, migration, which can be indirectly, but not directly attributable to food scarcity. These were the diseases that brought about the deaths of doctors, clergymen and workhouse officials. Many deaths from fever could have been prevented, especially among the middle class, if there had been a better knowledge of the mechanisms by which fever was transmitted. One incidental consequence however is that the proportion of deaths among the better-off was higher than in contemporary famines. The greatest excess mortality occurred among young children and adolescents. Children and infants were more likely to die from starvation or dysentery and diarrhoea, whereas adults in the active age group were more likely to succumb to fever (Mokyr and Ó Gráda, 2002; 32–33).

Estimates derived from Wilde's statistics suggest that mortality among women was lower than for men, with the greatest advantage among women in child-bearing years. The implied female share of deaths from starvation, dysentery, diarrhea and even fever were significantly less. The female advantage contrasts with excess female mortality over the next century or so (Ó Gráda, 1999; 92, 102; Kennedy, 1973) Biology offers the most convincing explanation for female advantage, although David Fitzpatrick has tried to argue that women's better survival rates reflected the fact that their nurturing skills were especially privileged during the famine (Fitzpatrick, 1997: 50–69). Did other factors play a part, such as the adverse effect on men's health of heavy labour on public works, the fact that poor law admissions consistently favoured women, and the evidence that women may have gained admission to workhouses while they were in a less distressed state than men?

The information to hand from poor law records adds further detail regarding deaths and disease to the statistics published in the 1851 census, and they open up new lines of research regarding agency, although as yet it has not proved possible to relate the administrative records of deaths, disease, and workhouse admissions in a specific area to information on land clearances, incumbered estates and other events beyond the workhouse. It proved impossible, for example, to locate records of incumbered estates in Parsonstown Union, which might have provided information on land clearances and ownership that could be examined in order to see what impact they might have had on workhouse admissions. However an examination of the 1849 indoor registers for Parsonstown in conjunction with agricultural statistics for changes in farm size shows a positive correlation between admissions and the reduction in the number of farms with less than 15 acres. Eiriksson concluded that 'there are signs that the geographical origin of inmates reflected the geographical pattern of evictions and reduction of smallholders' (Eiriksson, 1996: ch. 8).[5] However the eviction of 400 people in a village on the Mullet peninsula, Co. Mayo, in December 1847, was not reflected in admissions to Ballina workhouse, because the guardians refused them relief (McCabe, 1997: ch. 16).

Workhouse mortality is one obvious measure of performance during the famine, but this must be used with caution. A high death-rate might reflect the poor quality of workhouse administration, or conditions in the community, which were beyond the control of the poor law guardians. Likewise a low death-rate might reflect the benign environment outside the workhouse, a very restrictive admissions policy, or good housekeeping. The data generated by the National Famine Research Project have highlighted some possible ways of addressing these questions, by focusing on variables such as causes of death and the length of time spent in a workhouse before death. Our hypothesis is that workhouses could be absolved from responsibility for the deaths of recently-admitted inmates, unless of course by refusing them earlier admission they contributed to these deaths. In Ennistymon workhouse over 2/3rds of those dying from dysentery in 1850–1851 had been in the workhouse for more than four weeks. In Parsonstown 65% of those who died in 1849 had between 3 and 6 weeks in the workhouse, which would appear to indicate that they had contracted an illness after entering the workhouse. In Inishowen, a workhouse with a low mortality, almost 60% of those dying between 1846 and 1849 had spent 11 weeks or more in the workhouse. Minutes of the Inishown board of guardians reveal a preoccupation with white-washing, preventing overcrowding and other measures that apparently reduced infection and mortality (Eiriksson,1996: Table 9.3; Cox, 1997a: 135).

The records of Parsonstown Union testify to appalling maladministration, which was reflected, not just in a high incidence of fever caused by overcrowding and poor housekeeping, but in starving inmates. Almost one-quarter of deaths in Parstonstown workhouse between 1841 and 1851 was attributed to marasmus. This is a non-infectious disease caused by malnutrition, and therefore a condition that should be capable of being cured by proper feeding. Most of the victims were children. There were allegations that temporary staff were stealing the children's food (Eiriksson,1996: ch. 9). In Enniskillen,

---

[5] The conclusion relates only to the 16 divisions in King's County, now Offaly, but not the 6 division in Co. Tipperary, because no agricultural statistics were collected for Tipperary because of the disturbed condition of the county.

12.2% of male deaths and 9.9% of female deaths were attributed to marasmus and dropsy, which should more accurately be described as hunger oedema (Guinnane [et al.], 2003).

Overcrowding appears to have been closely associated with peaks in mortality and it probably contributed to workhouse deaths. The question arises whether the overcrowding reflects poor administration or external pressure. In Inishowen Union the guardians appear to have worked hard to prevent overcrowding, opening auxiliary workhouses, and closing them when admissions fell; transferring fever cases to temporary fever sheds, and transferring aged and infirm inmates from the workhouse to outdoor relief. According to the records, the number of inmates only exceeded capacity on one occasion, in January 1848, and then only for a brief period and the overcrowding was not significant. By February the board of guardians had opened a house with 50 beds to accommodate the excess. This closed in October 1848. When accommodation was again stretched to capacity in February 1849, they opened an auxiliary workhouse with capacity for 120. It closed in November 1849. But Inishowen escaped relatively lightly during the famine (Cox, 1997a). Rathdrum workhouse (Wicklow) suffered acute overcrowding from November 1847 until mid-January 1848 when the death rate peaked. The number of deaths fell steadily from March 1848, or shortly after overcrowding was relieved by the provision of additional space. A second phase of overcrowding in the winter of 1849/50 was also followed, with a short interval by another mortality peak (Cox, 1997b: Table 164 and ch. 22).

In Inishowen, and in Rathdrum the introduction of outdoor relief played a key role in reducing overcrowding in the workhouses during 1847 and 1848. Parsonstown was the only union in Leinster that did not grant outdoor relief, apparently under pressure from Lord Rosse, who boasted of this. Outdoor relief might have prevented overcrowding in 1848 and in 1849, though by that date outdoor relief was being withdrawn in all unions except those classified as distressed. Enniskillen was very slow to introduce outdoor relief, and when it was conceded the number of successful applicants remained small, with relief almost entirely confined to widows, children and elderly men and women, in line with the instructions issued by the poor law commissioners.(McCabe 1996: 71–74). The position would appear to have been different in the west and south-west. In Ballina and Belmullet, Co. Mayo, up to 30% of the Union population, or half those who had received food rations in the previous year, were on outdoor relief. Of these 53% were children, 19% were men with families, 17% married women and 11% were single men. Able-bodied men and their families also figured prominently on the outdoor relief lists in county Kerry (McCabe, 1997: ch. 20; Foley, 1997: 211–215).

The complex interaction between administrative practices in workhouses and local circumstances makes it extremely difficult to determine whether a specific poor law union's administrative practices were good or bad, given that administrative practices were in turn influenced by the union's finances, which reflected local economic conditions. The high mortality in Rathdrum in January 1847 may have been caused by the tolerant attitude that the board of guardians adopted to overcrowding, their lethargic attitude towards discharging those who could be discharged, or securing additional accommodation. Alternatively it may reflect a serious outbreak of disease in the area, which would have been beyond the guardians' control. A recent paper on workhouse mortality marks the first attempt to apply performance indicators to Irish workhouses, by evaluating their performance while controlling for factors outside the Union's control, such as population, local taxable capacity, and the severity of the famine in the spring/

summer of 1847 (as measured by the proportion being fed at soup kitchens). The findings reveal that while some of the worst performing unions were in the impoverished west, so were some of the best-performing unions. The authors acknowledge that their indicators need to be refined, because their regression fails to highlight some poor law unions other evidence shows to have performed poorly. Enniskillen and Parsonstown fail to make it on the black-list, unlike Ennistymon, although Inishowen, with its energetic programme of white-washing, ranks among the top performers. (Mokyr and Ó Gráda, 2002).

While recent years have seen a major advance in our knowledge of the local aspects of the Irish famine, a lot remains to be done. Yet filling in this story is important, if Irish history is to take on the regional colourings that have served to enrich our understanding of the history of countries such as France or Germany. If we compare the current state of knowledge of the regional and local history of the famine with the local knowledge of the 1798 rebellion – the other historical event commemorated in the past decade – it would appear that the 1798 story is more complete, and the comparative analysis of local aspects is more advanced. Why? The famine generated more source material, it encompasses a longer time-period and a wider geographical area, and most significantly, it demands some quantitative skills – something in scarce supply among Irish historians. The devil is in the detail, and most of that detail is statistical.

V.   Conclusion

The Irish hunger crisis of the 1840s was much more acute than the comparable crises in other European countries. At its peak it was a national, not a local disaster: it claimed the lives of more than 10 per cent of the population, and in the worst-affected areas it lasted for more than ten years. Any comparisons between Ireland and other countries in northern Europe must take the differing incidence into account. Nevertheless the European experiences highlight a number of issues. One is the importance in many continental countries of local relief, provided either by local authorities or by charitable agencies. Although a crisis on the scale of the Irish famine would have challenged any system, we should also recognize that local institutions in Ireland were not geared to provide such relief. The poor law was a new institution, whose creation had been controversial. It imposed a system designed for England on Ireland, taking little if any account of specific Irish circumstances. Charitable agencies were organized on a denominational basis. The Catholic church, the church of the majority of the population and of most of the poor had only recently emerged from the penal laws, and therefore lacked the institutional network found elsewhere in Europe. This shortcoming was most acute in the poorer areas of the west and south-west of Ireland. The contribution of Irish landlords to famine relief has not yet been analysed in a systematic fashion, but in many cases it is evident that self-interest ranked above the needs of the wider community.

The key decisions with regard to Irish famine relief were taken in London, where the policies pursued involved a belief that market forces would offer the most effective mechanism for bringing sufficient food to Ireland. Famine relief policies were designed, not simply to bring about short-term assistance, but to transform Irish rural society. Before the famine appeared British government ministers and senior civil servants were already of the opinion that Irish rural society was seriously flawed. The famine was seen as confirming that view, and as offering an opportunity to bring about a long-term transformation from a subsistence-based agriculture with the potato as the staple diet to a more capitalist type of farming similar to that operating in England. Here again Europe offers counter models. Cases where governments used tariffs and bounties to moderate free market forces during the 1840s crisis, and countries where peasant proprietorship offered a productive and prosperous alternative to English-style capitalist farming. The goal of creating large capitalist farms worked by bread-eating wage-earning labourers was not achieved. Indeed the long-term solution to the Irish land question that emerged towards the end of the nineteenth century was the introduction of continental-style peasant proprietorship.

Bibliography

Archdeacon, T. (2002) 'The Irish Famine in American school curricula', *Eire-Ireland*, 37, 1–2, pp. 130–152.

Bourke, P.M.A. (1967/8) 'The use of the potato crop in pre-famine Ireland', *Journal of the Statistical and Social Inquiry Society of Ireland*, 21, pt. 6, pp. 72–96.

Bourke, P.M.A. (1976) 'The Irish grain trade', *Irish Historical Studies*, 20, pp. 156–169.

Cork Archives Institute (1996) *Great famine facsimile pack*, Cork.

Cowman, D. and Brady, D. (1995) *Teacht na bprátaí dubha: The famine in Waterford, 1845–1850*, Dublin.

Crawford, E.M. (1989) *Famine: the Irish experience*, Edinburgh.

Cullen, L.M. (1972) *An economic history of Ireland from 1660*, London.

Cox, C. (1996) 'Dead Dubliners. The effects of the famine in the North Dublin Union', National Famine Research Project (www.ucd.ie/hii).

Cox, C. (1997a) 'Inishowen Poor Law Union, 1843–52', National Famine Research Project (www.ucd.ie/hii).

Cox, C. (1997b) 'Rathdrum and the Great Famine', National Famine Research Project (www.ucd.ie/hii).

Daly, M.E. (1986) *The famine in Ireland*, Dundalk.

Daly, M.E. (1997) *The buffer state. The historical roots of the Department of the Environment*, Dublin.

Daly, M.E. (forthcoming) 'Irish studies and the Irish past: the challenge of a multidisciplinary approach' in L. Harte, Liam and Y. Whelan (eds), *Beyond Boundaries. Mapping Irish Studies in the Twenty-First Century*.

Devine, T. (1988) *The Great Highland Famine. Hunger, Emigration and the Scottish Highlands in the Nineteenth Century*, Edinburgh.

Donnelly, J.S. (1989) 'Landlords and tenants', in W.J. Vaughan (ed.), *A new history of Ireland Vol. V. Ireland under the Union, I, 1801–70*, Oxford, pp. 332–349.

Donnelly, J.S. (2001) *The Great Irish Potato Famine*, Stroud.

Dyson, T. and Ó Gráda, C. (2002) *Famine Demography. Perspectives from past and present*, Oxford.

Edwards, R.D. and Williams, T.D. (1956) *The Great Famine. Studies in Irish History, 1845–52*, Dublin.

Eirikkson, A. and Ó Gráda, C. (1996) 'Bankrupt Landlords and the Irish Famine', University College Dublin Centre for Economic Research Working Papers 96/10.

Eiriksson, A. (1997) 'Parstonstown Union and Workhouse during the Great Famine', National Famine Research Project (www.ucd.ie/hii).

Fitzpatrick, D. (1997) 'Gender and the famine', in M. Kelleher and J.H. Murphy (eds), *Gender perspectives on nineteenth century Ireland: public and private spheres*, Dublin, pp. 50–69.

Foley, K. (1997) *Kerry during the great famine 1845–52*, Dublin. Ph.D. Thesis University College Dublin.

Grant, J. (1997a) 'The great famine in county Down', in L. Proudfoot (ed.), *Down: history and society*, Dublin, pp. 353–582.

Grant, J. (1997b) 'Local relief committees in Ulster 1945–47', in E.M. Crawford (ed.), *The Hungry Stream, Essays on emigration and famine*, Belfast, pp. 184–198.

Gray, P. (1997) 'Famine relief in comparative perspective: Ireland, Scotland and North-West Europe, 1845–49', *Eire-Ireland*, 32, 1, pp. 86–108.

Gray, P. (1999) *Famine, Land and Politics. British Government and Irish Society, 1843–1850*, Dublin.

Guinnane, T.P., McCabe, D. and Ó Gráda, C. (2003) 'Agency and Famine relief: Enniskillen workhouse during the great famine', Paper delivered at the Fondation des Treilles Workshop.

Hickey, P. (2002) *Famine in West Cork. The Mizen peninsula. Land and people 1800–1852*, Cork.

Kennedy, R.E. (1973) *The Irish. Emigration, marriage and fertility*, Berkeley.

Kildare County Council (1995) *Lest we forget. Kildare and the great famine*, Kildare.

Kinealy, C. (1994) *This great calamity. The Irish famine 1845–52*, Dublin.

Kinealy, C. and Parkhill, T. (1997) *The famine in Ulster*, Belfast.

Kinealy, C. (2002) *The great Irish famine. Impact, ideology and rebellion*, Basingstoke.

Lindsay, D. and Fitzpatrick, D. (1993) *Records of the Irish famine: a guide to local archives, 1840–1855*, Dublin.

Marnane, D.G. (1996) 'The famine in south Tipperary', *Tipperary historical journal*, 9, pp. 1–42.

Marnane, D.G. (1997) 'The famine in south Tipperary', *Tipperary historical journal*, 10, pp. 131–150.

McAtasney, G. (1997) *'This dreadful visitation': the famine in Lurgan/Portadown*, Belfast.

McCabe, D. (1996) 'Enniskillen and the great famine', National Famine Research Project (www.ucd.ie/hii).

McCabe, D. (1997) 'Ballina and the great famine', National Famine Research Project (www.ucd.ie/hii).

McHugh, R. (1956) 'The famine in Irish oral tradition', in R.D. Edwards and T.D. Williams (eds), *The Great Famine. Studies in Irish History, 1845–52*, Dublin, pp. 391–436.

Mokyr, J. (1983) *Why Ireland starved: a quantitative and analytical history of the Irish economy, 1800–50*, London.

Mokyr, J. and Ó Gráda, C. (2002) 'Famine disease and famine mortality', in T. Dyson and C. Ó Gráda (eds), *Famine Demography*, Oxford, pp. 19–43.

Mullin, J.V. (2002) 'The New Jersey Famine Curriculum: A report, *Eire-Ireland,* 37, 1–2, pp. 119–129.

Murphy, M. and Singer, A. (2001) *The Great Irish Famine Curriculum*, Albany.

Murphy, M. and Singer, A. (2002) 'New York State's "Great Irish Famine Curriculum". A Report', *Eire-Ireland*, spring/summer, pp, 109–118.

O'Gorman, M. (1994) 'Great Irish Famine Curriculum, A Report', *Eire-Ireland*, 37, 1–2, pp. 109–118.

O'Gorman, M, (1994) *A Pride of Tigers. A history of the great hunger in the Sctariff Workhouse Union from 1839–1853*, Clare.

Ó Gráda, C. (1997) *Famine 150: Commemorative Lecture Series*, Dublin.

Ó Gráda, C. (1999) *Black '47 and beyond. The Great Irish famine. History, economy, memory,* Princeton.

O'Neill, T.P. (1971) *The state, poverty and distress in Ireland 1815–45*, Dublin. Ph.D. Thesis University College Dublin.

O'Neill, T.P. (1998) 'The famine in Offaly' in W. Noaln and T.P. O'Neill (eds), *Offaly History and Society*, Dublin, pp. 681–733.

O'Neill, T.P. (2000) 'Famine Evictions', in C. King (ed.), *Famine, Land and Culture*, Dublin, pp. 29–70.

Porteir, C. (1995) *Famine echoes*, Cork.

Sen, A. (1981) *Poverty and famines. An essay on entitlements and deprivation*, Oxford.

Solar, P. (1989) 'The Great Famine was no ordinary subsistence crisis', in E.M. Crawford (ed.), *Famine: The Irish Experience*, Edinburgh, pp. 112–133.

Solar, P. (1997) 'The potato famine in Europe', in C. Ó Gráda (ed.), *Famine 150: Commemorative Lecture Series*, Dublin, pp. 113–128.

Solar, P. (2003) 'Irish trade in the nineteenth century' in D. Dickson and C. Ó Gráda (eds), *Refiguring Ireland. Essays in Honour of L.M. Cullen*, Dublin, pp. 277–289.

Stewartstown and District Local History Society (1996) *The famine in East Tyrone*, Stewartstown.

Swinford Historical Society (1995) *An Gorta Mór: Famine in the Swinford Union*, Swinford.

Swords, L. (1999) *In Their own Words. The famine in north Connacht, 1845–1849*, Dublin.

Tóibín. C. and Diarmaid, F. (2001) *The Irish famine. A documentary*, London.

Woodham Smith, C. (1962) *The Great Hunger*, London.

4 The crisis of the late 1840s: what can be learned from prices?

Peter M. Solar, Vesalius College, Vrije Universiteit Brussel

A central element in the crisis of the late 1840s was the rise in the prices of basic food-stuffs, notably grain and potatoes.[1] Prices began to rise in 1845, were acutely high in the spring and early summer of 1847, then fell sharply in late 1847 and early 1848. This paper explores the nature of the crisis using price data at various frequencies from a variety of markets in Europe. First, annual prices for the entire nineteenth century are used to put the 1840s crisis in perspective. This data suggests the importance of comparisons over time, in particular with the period of high prices in the mid-1850s. Second, bimonthly prices for the 1840s and 1850s are used to pursue this comparison and to look at how the crisis transpired in different parts of western Europe. This data shows its early impact in the Low Countries and its more limited impact in parts of southern Europe. Finally, weekly prices for London and Belfast are used to show how the crisis played out in detail in the grain markets of the United Kingdom. This data, along with information from contemporary market reports for London and Belfast, forms the backbone of a narrative showing how the price movements were perceived at the time.

I. The long run: annual prices

Figures 4.1 to 4.4 show the annual movements in wheat and potato prices from 1800 to 1913. In some respects these price series are not strictly comparable. First, some series refer to particular markets – Waterford, Hamburg, Berlin, Breslau, Bruges, Milan and Vienna – whilst others – England, Netherlands – are national averages. Second, in most cases the annual price is the simple average of monthly prices, whereas for England the wheat price is a weighted average of weekly observations (with several changes in the weighting schemes) and for Belfast and Waterford the prices are averages of bimonthly observations (on the English corn averages, see Vamplew, 1980).

The various price series have been expressed in British pounds using series for exchange rates from the London market. They have been put into common measures using a variety of coefficients which are documented in the Appendix. The levels of the series may not be strictly comparable, especially those for potatoes. There may have been differences in the quality of the produce traded in different markets. Price levels could also depend on whether the goods were being sold in small or large quantities.

Price levels could be quite different across markets. The effects of protection for cereals show up quite clearly in Figures 4.1 and 4.2 (Williamson, 1990). Until the late 1840s, when the Corn Laws were repealed, English and, to a lesser extent, Waterford

---

[1] This work on prices would not have been possible with the help and advice of colleagues. I want to thank Rafael Barquin, Jean-Michel Chevet, Giovanni Federico, Liam Kennedy and Gilles Postel-Vinay for sharing price data with me. I would also like to thank Peter Scholliers and Jan Luiten van Zanden for reading and commenting on a draft of the paper.

Figure 4.1   Wheat prices, Northwest Europe, 1800–1913
(£ per 1000 kg)

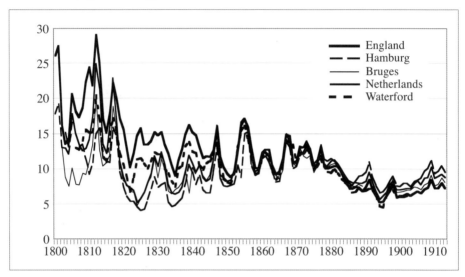

Figure 4.2   Wheat prices, Eastern and Southern Europe, 1800–1913
(£ per 1000 kg)

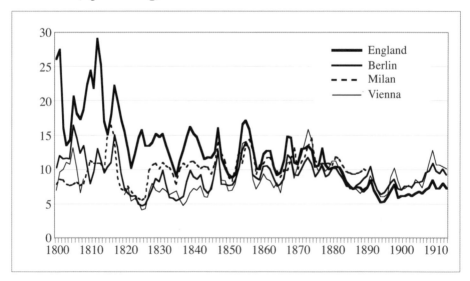

Figure 4.3   Potato prices, Northwest Europe, 1800–1913
(£ per 100 kg)

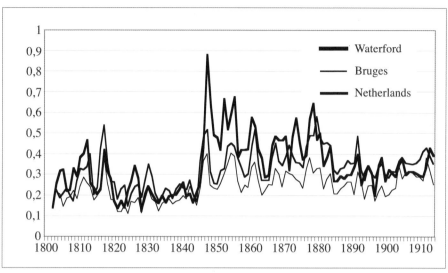

Figure 4.4   Potato prices, Eastern Europe, 1800–1913
(£ per 100 kg)

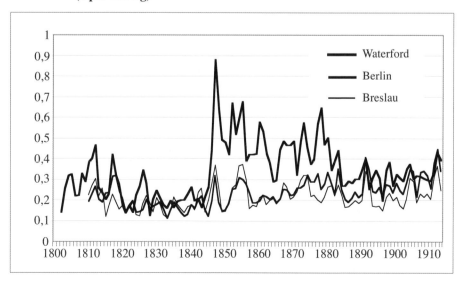

wheat prices were usually well above those on the continent. During the period of relatively free trade in the 1850s, 1860s and early 1870s prices were roughly comparable across northwest European markets, though a bit lower in southern and eastern Europe. Then, from the 1880s, as Germany and other continental countries erected barriers against grain imports, prices in the U.K. were lower. During this last period the Netherlands and Belgium were intermediate cases.

It is less obvious that potato-growing received any effective protection during the Corn Law era (see Solar, 2002). Although more rigorous comparative work is needed, potato prices in Ireland do not seem to have been systematically higher than those on the continent before the late 1840s. After the famine they are distinctly higher, which could have two interpretations. One is that the prices quoted in Ireland were for retail markets and may have been generally higher than prices in the continental markets. But this would suggest that the Irish prices throughout should be adjusted downward to make them comparable to the continental prices and this would only reinforce the point about potato-growing lacking any effective protection. The other interpretation is that the advent of the blight changed supply conditions more drastically in Ireland than it did elsewhere. This could have been due to greater virulence of the blight under Irish weather conditions. Or it could have reflected the much greater reduction in the rural labour supply that took place in Ireland.

Taken together, the wheat and potato price series suggest that before the famine the relative price of potatoes may have been much lower in Ireland than on the continent. This difference in relative prices may help explain why Irish consumption of potatoes was so much higher during the early nineteenth century (Solar, 1997).

The fluctuations in wheat prices, abstracting from the differences in levels, readily confirm that European markets, particularly those in northwest Europe, were quite highly integrated during peacetime in the nineteenth century (Persson, 1999). This was clearly not the case during the wars before 1815 when prices move in all different directions. But from the European, indeed worldwide, crisis of 1816–1818 the year-to-year fluctuations in the series are quite similar, except for certain periods before 1846 when protection decoupled English markets from those on the continent.

As regards the crisis of the late 1840s, in century-long perspective the wheat price peak in the 1847 stands out as severe but not exceptionally so. The peak in 1817 was much more pronounced, which befits the attention that the crisis of 1816–1818 has received from historians (Post, 1977). But what is particularly striking is that the peak in wheat prices in 1855–1856 was not only as pronounced as that in 1847, but it was more prolonged. This raises the question, to which I will return repeatedly: why was there apparently no crisis in the mid-1850s at all comparable to that in the late 1840s?

The fluctuations in potato prices appear to be much less synchronized than do those for wheat prices. Given the costs of transporting potatoes and the much more limited international commerce in this good, this might seem perfectly normal. However, it may be due as much to the difficulties in getting good quotations for potato prices. I shall return to the question of potato market integration when looking at higher frequency observations.

Yet, despite the generally low correlation of potato prices across these markets, the late 1840s and mid-1850s stand out for particularly synchronous movements. The peaks in 1847 and 1854–1855 suggest Europe-wide, rather than local, forces were at work.

The movements of potato prices do mark out the late 1840s as a special period. The peak in 1847 was much more pronounced than that in 1817, and it was also more severe than the peak in the mid-1850s, though again it is worth noting that the high prices in the 1850s were spread over a longer period. The severity of the potato price peak in 1847 may go some way to resurrecting the crisis of the late 1840s, both by comparison with the late 1810s and the mid-1850s. It was, first and foremost, a potato crisis, and where potatoes were the food of the poor, the incidence of high prices was likely to be more devastating in demographic and social terms.

In Ireland the 1840s also marked a persistent upward shift both in the absolute level of potato prices and in the price of potatoes relative to cereals. On the continent potato prices also increased but the change in relative prices was much less. The shift in relative prices was thus in part due to the repeal of agricultural protection in the U.K and in part to the negative productivity shock caused by the introduction of blight. Until effective methods of treating the fungus were developed later in the century, the blight both lowered the average yield of the crop and increased its volatility. This is one regard in which the late 1840s was a structural, rather than merely conjunctural, crisis (Solar, 1989).

II. The medium run: bimonthly prices

Figures 4.5, 4.6 and 4.7 show bimonthly movements in wheat and potato prices in several European markets from 1844 to 1857. Again, there may be problems in comparing the series. Those for the United Kingdom have been collected from market reports and refer to prices as near as possible to the beginning of the month. The continental series are generally based on prices collected by public authorities and in some cases are averages over the month. Again, all of the series have been converted into British pounds using exchange rates and into common measures.

At this higher frequency the wheat prices in northwestern Europe (Figure 4.5) still move together quite closely, which is further testimony to the integration of grain markets, but the southern and eastern European markets (Figure 4.6), at least the ones presented here, are deviant in several respects. Prices at Marseille and Toulouse show much less marked peaks in early 1847 and a much more gradual increase in prices during 1853. At Zaragoza high prices continued into 1848, unlike in northern Europe, and prices continued to rise in late 1856 and 1857 when they were falling everywhere else. Both of these movements are amply confirmed by prices at other Spanish markets, and confirm that the great crisis of the mid-nineteenth century in Spanish agrarian history is 1856–1857, rather than 1847 (Barquin, 2001).

The bimonthly series show quite clearly that the period of high grain prices in the mid-1850s was as severe as that in the late 1840s. Except in the British and Irish markets, the price peak in the mid-1850s was equal to or higher than that in 1847. High prices also lasted for much longer in the mid-1850s. In the 1840s in the United Kingdom the period of very high prices lasted less than a year, from the autumn of 1846 until late summer in 1847. In the mid-1850s, by contrast, the period when prices were high enough to be comparable with those in early 1847 lasted from the autumn of 1853 to the autumn of 1856, fully three years.

The bimonthly data on potato prices (Figure 4.7) is, for the moment, less abundant and refers mainly to British and Irish markets. It is obvious that potato prices had a much stronger seasonal component than did wheat prices, reflecting, no doubt, the fact that this crop could not be stored from one year to the next. Nonetheless, it is surprising

**Figure 4.5 Wheat prices, Northwest Europe, 1844–1857
(£ per 1000 kg)**

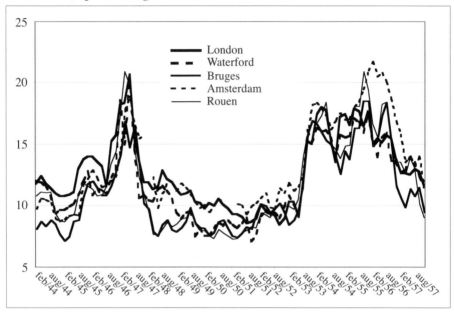

**Figure 4.6 Wheat prices, Southern and Eastern Europe, 1844–1857
(£ per 1000 kg)**

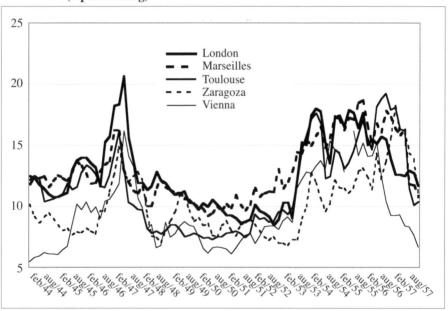

Figure 4.7   Potato prices, Northwest Europe, 1844–1857
(£ per 100 kg)

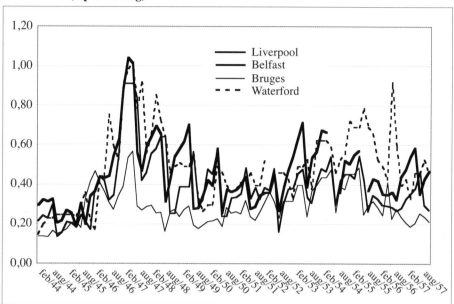

how closely prices at Belfast and Liverpool moved together. Waterford, and even Belgian, prices also showed broadly similar movements.

The continental potato prices did differ from the British and Irish prices in certain respects. Belgian prices rose earlier. Potato prices at Bruges almost doubled in the last three months of 1845 and reached a peak in February 1846 almost comparable to that in the spring of 1847. Prices also rose during this period in Britain and Ireland, but later, in the spring of 1846, and less markedly. As Bourke has shown, Belgium was the epicentre of the blight's diffusion into Europe and the price data correspond to its much more devastating impact there in 1845 (Bourke, 1993: 140–149).

The higher frequency data confirm that the peak in potato prices was more pronounced in the late 1840s than in the mid-1850s. Indeed, in the potato markets at Liverpool and Belfast it is difficult to detect a clearly defined period of high prices in the 1850s. But at Waterford and Bruges a mid-1850s peak is more evident, though it is less distinct than in grain prices.

The more pronounced peak in potato prices may, as suggested above, be a reason why there was a crisis in the late 1840s, but apparently not in the mid-1850s. But it is worth speculating, just for a moment, on why Europe may have been less vulnerable to the prolonged period of high cereal prices in the mid-1850s. The fact that the late 1840s crisis came first may be significant in several respects. First, it eliminated much of the population that was particularly vulnerable, especially in Ireland. In Ireland a large share of the poor died and many others emigrated in the late 1840s and early 1850s. Second, repeal of the Corn Laws in the United Kingdom, and tariff changes elsewhere, may have improved the ability of markets to allocate scarce supplies of grain. Third, public authorities may have learned from the earlier crisis and have been more effective in limiting distress in the mid-1850s. These are merely hypotheses that might be fruitfully examined by comparing these two periods of high prices in greater detail.

III. The short run: weekly prices

Figures 4.8 and 4.9 show the weekly movements in wheat and potato prices at London and Belfast. The price data is shown in all its original detail, in part as a reminder of the problems of working with nineteenth century sources of price data. For wheat and potatoes in Belfast and potatoes in London the newspapers quoted a price range. The difference between low and high prices varies over time, and in some cases one price will increase whilst the other decreases. For wheat in London, for which the quotations were taken from specialist market reports, sometimes three prices were quoted, and the source gives little guidance as to their meaning. It should also be noted that there are quite a number of missing observations, especially for potato prices, and that sometimes prices remain suspiciously constant for long periods.

Nonetheless, the series give a reasonably consistent picture of the movements in grain and potato prices during these years. It is not really surprising that they are consistent, at least for wheat, since the Belfast market reports repeatedly interpreted local price changes in terms of what was happening in English markets. The broad similarity in potato price movements tends to confirm the integration seen in the bimonthly prices for Belfast, Waterford and Liverpool markets.

Figure 4.8   London and Belfast wheat prices, 1845–1847 (sh per cwt)

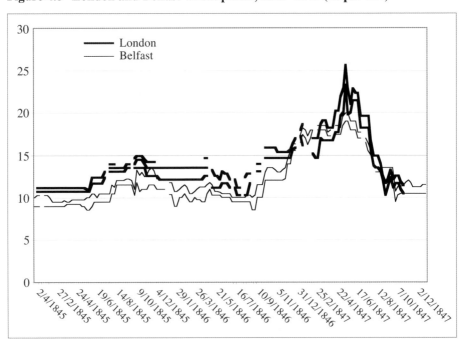

Figure 4.9   London and Belfast potato prices, 1845–1847

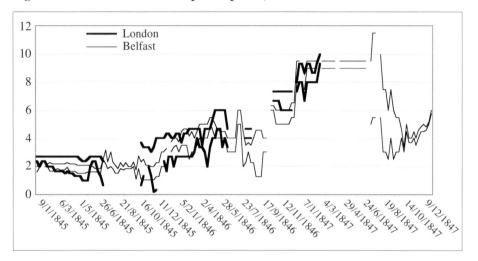

Two features of the weekly price data may be indicators of the disruptions caused by the famine. One is that the range between low and high potato prices becomes quite large in two key periods. In August of 1846 there is a sharp rise in the high price whilst the low price falls, which is probably an indication that both sound and diseased potatoes were present on the market. In July and August of 1847 the gap is also particularly large, though it almost closes by early October. This might again reflect differences in quality, with the high prices representing early potatoes from the crop of 1847 and the low prices older, perhaps diseased, potatoes from the crop of 1846. A second, famine-related feature is the suspicious stability of wheat prices at Belfast from March to June 1846, a period during which prices at London rose sharply, and then fell in stages. Taken together with the fact that the quotations for Belfast potato prices were unchanged throughout the first half of 1846, this suggests that market reporting at Belfast had deteriorated and that the Belfast wheat prices are probably not a reliable indicator during this period. Waterford wheat prices followed the rise and fall of London prices more faithfully, though prices there did remain constant through much of July and August, when there was 'so little business' that the 'quotations are almost nominal' (*WN*, 3 August 1846, 'Waterford markets').

The wheat and potato price series indicate that price movements were often discontinuous. Prices remained relatively stable for extended periods, then rose or fell sharply. In order to understand these movements, or at least how market participants understood them, I shall follow the major movements in wheat prices from the summer of 1845 to the autumn of 1847 using the comments of the *Mark Lane Express* and, to a lesser extent, the *Economist* and the *Belfast Mercantile Register*. The weekly *Mark Lane Express* [*MLE*] was the leading agricultural newspaper in nineteenth-century Britain. It printed market reports from British, Irish and foreign markets, and on its front page summarized them in its "Review of the British Corn Trade" and its "Review of the Foreign Corn Trade".

Wheat prices first started to move upward in the summer of 1845. Even before the result of the British harvest was known, the *MLE* expressed apprehension about rising prices because of low stocks of grain in Britain:

'the abundance of last year's crop, and the favourable manner in which the seed was committed to the ground in autumn, rendered all parties averse to entering into speculations in foreign wheat, more particularly as previous investments, ever since the disastrous year 1842, had proved the reverse of lucrative to those engaged in them. During the winter and spring comparatively little was, therefore, bought abroad, and latterly prices have, in consequence of the unfavourable result of the last crop in many of the principal wheat producing countries in the north of Europe, been so high, in comparison to the value of the article here, as to act as a decided check to business. Meanwhile the stocks of old foreign wheat in the kingdom have been gradually used up; hence we are almost wholly dependent on our own producers for supplies…' (*MLE*, 14 July 1845, "Review of the British Corn Trade"; hereinafter RBCT)

By late September it was judged that 'not only is the crop short in this country, but the harvest has been defective over the greater part of continental Europe' (*MLE*, 22 Sept 1845, RBCT). It had been noted in early September that the partial failure of the potato crop would tend to push up grain prices. Shipments of potatoes from England to Holland were observed, leading the *MLE* to remark that 'the export of agricultural produce from England to the Continent is certainly a new feature' (*MLE*, 1 Sept. 1845, RBCT; 15 Sept. 1845, RBCT). This new feature was also noticed in Belfast, where 'what has caused the alarm to be greater is the quantity of orders already received to purchase and ship potatoes to England and to neighbouring ports of the Continent' (*BMR*, 20 Sept. 1845).

Prices peaked in November and then fell until late January of 1846. Although it was clear that supplies would be short, merchants were starting to hear rumours first that the government would allow free imports of grain, then that the Corn Laws would be repealed altogether (*MLE*, 24 Nov. 1845, RBCT). 'In this state of affairs, the regular course of trade has been interrupted; and so averse are all parties to enter into fresh engagements whilst the important point remains undecided, that business in corn has been completely paralized' (*MLE*, 8 Dec. 1845, RBCT). This uncertainty continued well into 1846 (*MLE*, 5 Jan. 1846, RBCT; 20 Apr. 1846, RBCT). In February the *MLE* advanced a further explanation for slack demand: 'The tightness of money, and the impossibility of obtaining the usual accommodation, have rendered all mercantile men cautious of entering into speculations; and the same reasons have caused parties who purchase for actual consumption to conduct their operations on a more restricted scale than in ordinary times' (*MLE*, 23 Feb. 1846, RBCT).

Prices remained slack through the spring and much of the summer of 1846, leading the *Belfast Mercantile Register* to vaunt its prediction that potato prices would be lower in May 1846 than in November 1845. The peak in early 1846, according to the *BMR*, had been the result of panic and speculation (*BMR*, 2 June 1846).

Between late August and early October prices shot upwards. By then it was clear that the potato crop had failed throughout much of Europe and that wheat crops were not promising (*MLE*, 10 Aug. 1846, RBCT; 24 Aug. 1846, "Review of the Foreign Corn Trade", hereinafter RFCT; 21 Sept. 1846, RFCT; 5 Oct. 1846, RFCT). There had been exports of grain to Britain from France and Belgium and stocks in London were 'trifling' (*MLE*, 5 July 1846, RBCT; 24 Aug. 1846, RBCT). During the last months of 1846 prices were high, but still no higher than the peak that had been reached in November 1845.

Prices, both for wheat and potatoes, jumped again during the last two weeks of 1846 and the first few weeks of 1847. The *MLE* was primarily worried about the low level of stocks:

The enormous importations of 1846…have been almost wholly consumed. The quantity of grain, etc, at present in bond in the United Kingdom is trifling in the extreme; all parties engaged in the corn trade, whether as merchants, factors, milllers, or dealers, are indifferently stocked: that farmers hold less than usual at the commencement of a new year is the prevailing opinion, and for two months we shall probably be without arrivals of importance from abroad (*MLE*, 11 Jan. 1847, RBCT).

The *Economist* (27 Feb. 1847, p. 250) also observed that stocks on the continent, notably in the producing regions of Germany and Poland, were very low. Despite these worries, wheat prices remained relatively stable in late January and February. There were also concerns about the supply of Irish oats drying up, as 'we are now approaching a time when the use of this grain increases: the town is what is technically termed full during the sitting of Parliament, and a greater number of horses have to be fed' (*MLE*, 25 Jan. 1847, RBCT). In fact, oats prices at London and Belfast were extremely high during January, February and March 1847, higher even than in May 1847. Since in many parts of Ireland and Britain oats were an important part of the diet, this meant that the pressures on living standards started well before the spring of 1847.

Wheat prices increased again in early March. One factor in pushing up prices may have been increased demand from France. The French had removed duties on grain and allowed imports in foreign ships. In early 1847 French buyers 'had taken all the wheat and rye they had been able to procure' in the Antwerp market and accounted for 'by far the greater proportion of purchases' on the Hamburg market (*MLE*, 1 Feb. 1847, RFCT; 1 Mar. 1847, RFCT). In late February the French government even ordered six large steamships to the Dardenelles, Gibraltar and the Channel to 'take in tow vessels laden with corn' (*MLE*, 1 Mar. 1847, "Monthly Notes on French Agriculture"). In the London market the *MLE* noted that:

Though there is now no longer anything new in purchases of English wheat being made for shipment to France, small quantities having from time to time been taken in our markets by French buyers for several months past, still a good deal of sensation has been caused this week by the extent of purchases for that country (*MLE*, 8 Mar. 1847, RBCT).

This led the *MLE* to observe that: 'Countries from which we are in the habit, in ordinary years, of receiving supplies, are not only unable to afford us assistance, but actually look to England for aid' (*MLE*, 8 Mar. 1847, RBCT). For example, in May agents of the Baden-Wurttemburg government were puchasing grain in London (*Economist*, 15 May 1847, p. 565). A less market-oriented observer might have said that the English were clearly willing to sell grain to the highest bidder and might have inquired whether the French government, at various levels, was not behind these large purchases, with the result, perhaps, that in late spring and early summer, when shortages were most acute in Britain and Ireland, there were sufficient stocks of grain in France.

There followed a lull in prices during late March and April. The *MLE* attributed this to several factors, including a 'sudden cessation of Irish demand' and 'a material falling off' in shipments to France (*MLE*, 29 Mar. 1847, RBCT). At Liverpool, Cork and Belfast there were large arrivals of maize in late March (*BNL*, 30 Mar. 1847). Yet the *Economist* (3 Apr. 1847, p. 395) was skeptical, thinking in early April that the 'recent reduction of price is, therefore, we fear, rather the effect of a temporary alarm, than of a permanent increased supply'.

The sharpest rise in prices came during the first three weeks of May, reaching a peak with prices almost twice as high as they had been in the spring of 1845 and as they would be by the end of 1847. The *MLE* (10 May 1847, RBCT) put the rise down to the realization that the stocks being held were very low indeed, since up to that point merchants, dealers and millers had been buying only small quantities. These high prices had the effect of sucking into western Europe whatever grain was available. In Romanian ports shipping was so scarce that freight rates almost doubled (MLE, 3 May 1847, 7 June 1847, market reports for Galatz).

A strange inversion of affairs may have occurred in May 1847. In normal times Britain had the highest grain prices in Europe, but shortages on the continent and Britain's central role in the grain trade seems to have turned it into the low-price centre. This even affected Ireland. The *Economist* (18 May 1847, p. 565) noted that large imports into Ireland 'mean that it is cheapest market in Europe…At this moment, an extensive export trade is being carried on from Ireland, and large profits are being realised.'

By the end of May prices were on their way down. The prospects for the grain crop of 1847 appeared good, but it was probably arrivals of grain from the Baltic that eased the pressure somewhat at the end of the month (*MLE*, 31 May 1847, RBCT). The great fall in prices, which took place much faster than the rise, seems to have happened in three, almost discrete, steps, coinciding with the first weeks in July, August and September. In each case 'auspicious reports of grain crops and arrivals from abroad' seem to have led to sharply revised expectations about future prices (*MLE*, 28 June 1847, RBCT; 26 July 1847, RBCT). The falls in prices were devastating for some merchants. In mid-August the *MLE* (17 Aug. 1847, RBCT) noted that: 'The extensive failures in London it is thought will rather assist the market than otherwise, by the withdrawal for a time, of a good deal of stuff which the holders are pressing for sale, in order if possible to meet their engagements'.

To sum up this narrative of wheat price movements, consider the long leading article that the *Economist* in September 1847 devoted to "The Corn Panic—Is it Justified by the Facts?" (11 Sept. 1847, pp. 1045–1048). Harking back to an earlier article in June, when prices were high, the editors focussed on five major factors in judging future supplies: the prospect of the potato crop, the prospects of the grain crops, the stocks existing in farmers' hands, the probable extent of foreign supplies, and the extent of foreign grain held in stock. Potatoes, they thought, would be as scarce as in 1846 because of the reduced acreage sown, something widely known in June. The domestic grain crops would be better than in 1846 but again this was the general opinion held earlier in the summer. Evidence on market sales of domestic produce indicated that stocks of grain were lower in 1847 than they had been in 1846, when they were already 'much below the usual quantity'. Foreign supplies of grain, from America and eastern Europe, had been more forthcoming in the summer of 1847 than during the summer of 1846, but the increase was not judged to be large enough to compensate for the deficiency in domestic supplies and stocks. Nor were imports during the autumn likely to exceed the already very high level reached in the autumn of 1846.

The thrust of the *Economist*'s reasoning was that wheat prices were too low in September 1847. But the article can also be read to suggest that prices had been too high in May and June. That is, the real 'corn panic' was not so much the fall in prices during the summer as the rise in the spring. The article does suggest two reasons why prices might have been driven up. One was a reevaluation by market participants in May and June of the supplies likely to be available from America. Reports from the United States indicated that stocks there were low and that the grain coming from the interior would be used for domestic consumption. The other factor was the 'great excitement produced in our markets by the enormous purchases of the Government...It would not be easy to estimate the whole of the influence which the Irish expenditure has exercised in our grain markets during the past year.' The *Economist* cited the likelihood that no such grants of public money would happen in the fall of 1847, along with the depressed state of manufacturing and railway construction, as demand factors contributing to the fall in prices in the autumn.

IV. Concluding Remarks

What can be learned from prices about the crisis of the late 1840s? A major lesson is, I think, that high prices alone do not make a crisis, a point made elsewhere in this volume by Chevet and Ó Gráda. The more prolonged period of high prices in the mid-1850s did not generate the sort of distress seen in the late 1840s. This comparison, which has only been suggested here, might be usefully developed in further work. The data also show that prices were high throughout Europe in 1846–1847 (and in 1853–1856), yet very high mortality was concentrated in Ireland and high mortality was only observed in pockets elsewhere. Well-functioning grain markets transmitted the price shocks everywhere. Market participants were well aware of developments throughout Europe and in North America and their activities seem to have been quite successful in arbitraging prices. The social effects of high prices depended on local conditions. In this sense the price movements do not help much to localize the crisis. They just provide a context for examining the variations in initial agrarian conditions and in policy responses.

Another lesson that may be drawn from the price data is that the crisis of the late 1840s was, above all, a potato crisis. In the both the short term and the longer term potato prices rose relative to wheat prices. Although the crisis was surely exacerbated by the poor grain crops of 1845 and 1846, even in normal times bread was out of range for many in Ireland and elsewhere who depended on potatoes for subsistence. The devastating failures of the potato crop caused by the blight deprived this class of a major part of its income. High grain prices made relief by government and private charity extremely expensive.

Market participants were keenly sensitive to the government interventions in grain markets during these years. As the crisis took hold, there was a certain balkanisation of grain markets. Many countries prohibited exports of foodstuffs, while at the same time trying to encourage imports by reducing duties. The French and Belgian governments took such measures, and in addition they were notably active in buying grain all over Europe. They bought relatively early, when prices were lower and when supplies were available. By contrast, the British government seems to have piled into the market late, in the spring of 1847, and driven prices sky high for the remaining stocks.

Bibliography

Newspapers

Belfast Mercantile Register [*BMR*]
Belfast Newsletter [*BNL*]
Economist (London)
London Mercantile Price Current [*LMPC*]
Mark Lane Express (London) [*MLE*]
Waterford News [*WN*]

Books and articles

Barquín, R. (2001) *Precios de trigo e índices de consumo en España, 1765–1883*, Burgos.

Bourke, A. (1993) *'The Visitation of God'?: The Potato and the Great Irish Famine*, Dublin.

Jacobs, A. and Richter, H. (1935) *Die Grosshandelspreise in Deutschland von 1792 bis 1934*, Berlin.

Labrousse, E., Romano, R. and Dreyfus, F.-G. (1970) *Le prix du froment en France aux temps de la monnaie stable (1726–1913)*, Paris.

Maddelena, A. de (1974) *Prezzi e mercedi a Milano dal 1701 al 1860*, Milan.

Mitchell, B.R. and Deane, P. (1962) *Abstract of British Historical Statistics*, Cambridge.

Persson, K.G. (1999) *Grain markets in Europe, 1500–1900: integration and deregulation*, Cambridge.

Post, J.D. (1977) *The last great subsistence crisis in the Western world*, Baltimore.

Posthumus, N.W. (1943) *Nederlandsche Prijsgeschiedenis*, Leiden.

Pribram, A.F. (1938) *Materialien zur Geschichte der Preise und Löhne in Österreich, Band I*, Wien.

Riel, A. van (s.d.) 'Constructing the nineteenth-century cost of living deflator (1800–1913)' (Working document project on the reconstruction of the national accounts of the Netherlands: http: //www.iisg.nl/hpw/brannex.html; accessed 2003).

Schneider, J. and Schwarzer, O. (1990) *Historische Statistik von Deutschland, Band XI, Statistik der Geld- und Wechselkurse in Deutschland (1815–1913)*, St. Katherinen.

Schneider, J., Schwarzer, O. and Zellfelder, F. (1991) *Währungen der Welt I, Europäische und nordamerikanische Devisenkurse*, Stuttgart.

Schneider, J., Schwarzer, O., Zellfelder, F. and Denzel, M.A. (1992) *Währungen der Welt VI, Geld und Währungen in Europa im 18. Jahrhundert*, Stuttgart.

Schneider, J., Schwarzer, O. and Schnelzer, P. (1993) *Historische Statistik von Deutschland, Band XII, Statistik der Geld- und Wechselkurse in Deutschland und im Ostseeraum (18. und 19. Jahrhundert)*, St. Katharinen.

Solar, P.M. (1989) 'The Great Famine was No Ordinary Subsistence Crisis', in E.M. Crawford (ed.), *Famine: the Irish Experience*, Edinburgh, pp. 112–133.

Solar, P.M. (1997) 'The Potato Famine in Europe', in C. Ó Gráda (ed.), *Famine 150: Commemorative Lecture Series*, Dublin, pp. 113–128.

Solar, P.M. (2002) 'Ireland and the Corn Laws', [unpublished paper].

Vamplew, W. (1980) 'A Grain of Truth? The Nineteenth Century Corn Averages', *Agricultural History Review*, 28, 1, pp. 1–17.

Verlinden, C. and Scholliers, E. (eds) (1973) *Dokumenten voor de geschiedenis van prijzen en lonen in Vlaanderen en Brabant, Deel IV (XIIIe–XIXe eeuw)*, Bruges.

Williamson, J.G. (1990) "The Impact of the Corn Laws Just Prior to Repeal", *Explorations in Economic History*, 27, pp. 123–156.

Appendix

Sources of the price data shown in Figures 4.1–4.6

The basic price data comes from the following sources. It was converted into British pounds using the exchange rates found in Schneider, Schwarzer and Schnelzer (1993), Schneider and Schwarzer (1990), Schneider, Schwarzer, Zellfelder and Denzel (1992), and Schneider, Scharzer and Zellfelder (1991).

England	Mitchell and Deane (1962), pp. 488–489: average price of British wheat; converted from quarters at 480 lbs per quarter
London	bimonthly: *London Mercantile Price Current*: "wheat, Essex and Kent, white", converted from quarters at 480 lbs per quarter
	weekly: *Mark Lane Express*: "wheat, new red, Essex and Kent" from Coventry & Shepherd's circular; "potatoes, Yorkshire reds", from potato market report
Liverpool	*Gore's General Advertiser* : "potatoes"; converted from measures of 90 lbs
Belfast	*Belfast Newsletter*: "wheat, white", converted from hundredweight at 112 lbs per hundredweight; "potatoes", converted from hundredweight at 112 lbs per hundredweight
Waterford	*Waterford News*: "wheat, white"; barrels converted at 280 lbs per barrel; potatoes, converted from stones at 14 lbs per stone
Netherlands	Riel, A. van (http: //www.iisg.nl/hpw/brannex.html): wheat, converted from hectolitres at 73.5 kg per hectolitre
Amsterdam	Posthumus (1943), p. 7: "Polish Wheat", converted from lasts at 2400 kilogrammes per last
Bruges	Verlinden and Scholliers (1973), pp. 177–182, 203–208: wheat, converted from hectolitres at 79 kilogrammes per hectolitre; potatoes
Rouen	Labrousse (1970), p. 193: Seine Inferieure, converted from hectolitres at 73.5 kilogrammes per hectolitre
Marseille	Labrousse (1970), p. 69: Bouche-de-Rhone, converted from hectolitres at 73.5 kilogrammes per hectolitre
Hamburg	Jacobs and Richter (1935), pp. 52–53, 56–57: wheat
Berlin	Jacobs and Richter (1935), pp. 52–53, 56–57: wheat; potatoes
Breslau	Jacobs and Richter (1935), pp. 52–53, 56–57: potatoes
Milan	Maddelena (1974), p. 379 and Federico (personal communication): wheat, converted from hectolitres at 72 kilogrammes per hectolitre
Vienna	Pribram (1938), p. 594: wheat, converted at 45.2 kg per nord-öesterrei-chischen Land-Metzen
Zaragoza	Barquin, R. (http: //www.iisg.nl/hpw/barquin2.html): wheat, converted from fanegas at 40.79 kilogrammes per fanega

5 The European food crisis and the relief of Irish famine, 1845–1850

Peter GRAY, Queen's University Belfast

For most contemporary and subsequent commentators, the general European subsistence crisis of the 1840s appeared to play at best an 'off-stage' role in the drama of the Great Irish Famine. So extreme and sustained was the Irish experience of famine, and so focused were the political debates concerning relief and reconstruction on the British-Irish relationship, that the European dimensions of the Irish catastrophe have tended, with some exceptions (Solar, 1997; Gray, 1997), to receive relatively little attention. Nevertheless, the Irish crisis did occur within a wider European context, and to understand this dimension it is necessary to investigate rather more closely both the impact continental developments had on Ireland, and the reasons for the ultimate marginalization of the European aspects of the Irish crisis.

This paper will consider four points of focus in which the wider European context impinged most significantly on the debates over Irish relief policy in the later 1840s. Firstly, and perhaps most obviously, was the competition for available food resources, especially between the autumn of 1845 and the early months of 1847. British policy regarding the import and export of foodstuffs to and from Ireland was, and remains, a highly controversial subject, not least because its actions could be contrasted with the public policy of other European governments facing subsistence crises in these seasons. Both British ministers and their nationalist critics were aware of this environment and constructed their arguments accordingly. Next to be considered are the observations of and reactions to the relief policies adopted more generally by European governments in 1845–1847. The British diplomatic service monitored these and made regular reports to London; the British and Irish press also reported on European famine-relief policies, and commented on these as models to be avoided or embraced according to varying political perspectives.

Thirdly, debates about Irish famine relief were rarely restricted to the immediate problem of preventing crisis mortality. For many commentators and political agents, questions of relief were intimately and indissolubly tied to those of reconstruction. The remaking of an Irish society 'dissolved' by the devastations of the potato blight into an entity capable of breaking free from a cycle of vulnerability and famine was, all too often, awarded a higher priority than the 'mere' relief of immediate suffering. Opinions varied very widely on the most desirable modes and blueprints for reconstruction, but European social models, variously conceptualized by their advocates and detractors, were among those most hotly debated.

Finally, the European revolutions of 1848 impacted on Ireland not only through the inspiration they offered to the separatist inclinations of the Young Ireland nationalists, but also through the examples presented (most obviously in France) of radical initiatives in social policy which attracted the attention of commentators on famine policy in Ireland.

I.

The pathways taken by *phytophthora infestans* in 1844–1845 – from North America to Ireland via the Low Countries, France and England – inevitably led Irish observers to draw continental comparisons in the autumn of 1845 (in contrast, the apparent epicentre of the blight in the west of Ireland – and the western Highlands and Islands of Scotland – from summer 1846 tended subsequently to distract attention from the European parallels). Thus, on reporting the first observations of blight in Ireland in September 1845, the *Dublin Evening Post* commented that 'with regard to Holland, Flanders and France, we have already abundant evidence of the wide-spread existence of what we cannot help calling a calamity.' It was in these 'densely packed communities of Europe' (including Ireland) that the risk of disaster was greatest (*Dublin Evening Post,* 9 September 1845).

Alarm over the food supply in the Low Countries had an immediate impact on the European food markets. By late September the Dublin *Pilot* was reporting large Dutch and Belgian purchases of rice and corn in the British and Baltic markets, encouraged by the suspension of duties on foreign grain exports (*Pilot,* 26 September 1845). While the Dutch government limited its activity to the negative step of suspending its corn law, the active interventionism of the Belgian and French administrations in discouraging exports and creating inducements to import were noted abroad (Gray, 1997: 98–99). The developing consciousness that the Irish potato crop had also been severely ravaged by blight led some commentators to demand analogous action. In early November the Dublin Mansion House Committee, behind which the nationalist leader Daniel O'Connell had thrown his still considerable political weight, warned the government explicitly of 'the horrors (…) of the approaching famine', and the rapidly closing window of food availability in the international markets: 'Other foreign countries afflicted by a similar calamity, have already been before us in the market, and are daily enhancing the price of those supplies which our Government might otherwise calculate on'. Specifically, the Mansion House Committee demanded the immediate opening of Irish ports to food imports freed of duty; the prohibition of oats exports from Ireland; a severe diminution of military consumption of oats; prohibition of the distillation from grain; the raising of a loan of £1.5 million to purchase food and subsidize prices; the formation of local granaries; and the initiation of public works of national utility (Mansion House Committee, 1846: 5–6).

The reaction of Sir Robert Peel's Conservative government to the early stages of the Irish crisis, particularly its controversial decision to link it to the abolition of the British corn law, remains a topic of historical controversy. Undoubtedly the prime minister's tactics contained elements of political calculation and expediency – although alongside the apparent concession made to the active free-trade lobby in Britain we need also to remember that the logic of his reformist Irish policy dictated some acknowledgement of the claims of a body like the Mansion House Committee (*Peel Papers*: Graham to Peel, 9 November 1845, Add. MS 40,452, fol. 5). Peel's relatively rapid implementation of elements of the last three of the Committee's demands – through the initiation of public works relief, the establishment of local food depots, and the issuing of grants in aid of local relief subscriptions – demonstrates this awareness of the political expediency of creating relief entitlements, while stopping short of the prohibitionist demands of nationalist opinion.

However, Peel's responsiveness was, as I have argued elsewhere, constrained by an ideological adherence to free trade, and both were underpinned by a specific providentialist interpretation of the meaning of the potato blight (Gray, 1999: 95–141). In 1845–

1846 he attempted to square the circle of combining pragmatic intervention in Ireland with a dogmatic insistence on the adoption of free trade in food. Unlike some other regimes, the Peel government's only initiative to augment food supply for Ireland – the purchase of £100,000 worth of maize from America in November 1845 for distribution by the army commissariat – was undertaken covertly, and was justified as a purely temporary measure to tide Ireland over until the corn bill was fully implemented (unlike wheat, it would admit maize and rice at a nominal duty immediately upon enactment), and as a pump-priming exercise to stimulate private trade and create a demand for the commodity in Ireland (Peel, 1856–1857, II: 173).

It does not follow that the Peel administration, had it survived, would have engaged in any further intervention in food supply. Peel himself ruled out anything other than marginal purchases in April 1846, and the consensus in the administration by early summer was that private trade was indeed meeting Irish requirements (*Hansard*, 3rd ser: LXXXV, 722–726; Gray, 1999: 123–124). Members of the outgoing government subsequently endorsed the policy of the incoming Whig-Liberal government of strict non-interference in the food trade (Gray, 1999: 125). British ministers continued to cast an eye at the vicissitudes of the potato harvest on the continent. In October 1846 the new prime minister Lord John Russell privately expressed comfort at what he believed to be the recovery of the Belgian potato crop, ignoring – as his own government was to do respecting Ireland in 1847 – the fact that acute seed shortages in a season following one of catastrophic failure would render the output of even an untainted crop nugatory (*Russell Papers*: Russell to Bessborough, 22 October 1846, PRO30/22/5D, fols 270–271).

From Summer 1846 Britain was (along with the Netherlands) unmoved in its dogmatic adherence to free-trade orthodoxy in food supply. Aware that the French, Belgian and other government were making large purchases in the American and Mediterranean markets in the wake of the disastrous harvests of 1846, Charles Trevelyan, Assistant Secretary (chief administrator) at the Treasury in London, resisted appeals that the UK follow suit (Parliamentary Papers, 1847: Trevelyan to Routh, 29 September 1846: 98). Issuing his subordinates with reprints of extracts from Adam Smith's *Wealth of Nations*, Trevelyan insisted (with the support of his political superiors) that the market mechanism alone could prevent Irish 'scarcity' developing into 'famine' (Parliamentary Papers, 1847: Trevelyan to Hewetson, 29 September 1846: 98–99; Trevelyan Letterbooks: Trevelyan to Routh, 30 September 1846, vol. 8, fol. 118; Smith, 1846). With mass famine mortality in Ireland undeniable by January 1847 in the wake of extensive press coverage, Trevelyan continued to adhere unwaveringly to the market doctrine; high prices were, he insisted:

'The natural check upon the over rapid consumption of an insufficient stock of food, and that, greatly as we suffer now, we might suffer before long still more intensely if this check were to be removed by any artificial interference. It must also be remembered, that high prices are indispensably necessary to enable us to get our share of the supplies of grain in America, the Black Sea, &c., for the scarcity prevails in France, Belgium, and elsewhere, as much or almost as much as it does in the United Kingdom.' (Parliamentary Papers, 1847: Trevelyan to Douglas, 18 January 1847, p. 501).

This position may have appeared justified in the wake of the massive imports principally of American grain into the UK from late Spring 1847, and the consequent collapse of prices in Ireland, but this was at a cost of an unmediated 'starvation gap' in the winter of 1846–1847.

II.

British observers were generally made aware of continental developments through the reports of the metropolitan press (e.g. *Times*, 24, 29 December 1846, 15 March 1847), but the London government also took a more direct interest in the relief measures adopted by its neighbours. Detailed memoranda on relief policies were requested by the Home Office and supplied by British diplomatic representatives abroad (*Palmerston Letterbooks*: Waller to Palmerston, 12 December 1846, Palmerston to Waller, 22 December 1846, Add. MS 48,553, fols 10–11). Much of this correspondence reflected a close monitoring of the food supply situation. In March 1847 the British ambassador in Paris (coincidently the former Irish viceroy Lord Normanby), reported that in France there was a 'dreadful certainty that it will not be possible to provide sufficient food for all the people between this time and the next harvest. From inquiries made at Odessa and elsewhere the government has become convinced that with every precaution and exertion to secure foreign supplies there will be a deficiency between this and the next crops of one month's duration.' (*Palmerston Letterbooks*: Normanby to Palmerston, 8 March 1847, Add. MS 48,556, fol. 41). The French government's response – to opt for a temporary export prohibition after considering regulating consumption by region – was duly reported to London (*Palmerston Letterbooks*: Normanby to Palmerston, 12 March, 26 April 1847, fols. 43, 50). Other despatches provided detailed analyses of the relief infrastructure in Belgium, expenditure on public works relief (1.5 million francs in 1846–1847) and the parliamentary debates over relief policy; in May 1847, for example, the British minister in Brussels reported the Liberal opposition's attack on the de Theux government for what it claimed was inadequate relief expenditure (*Palmerston Letterbooks*: Waller to Palmerston, 24 November 1846, 13 February 1847, 12 May 1847, Add MS 48,553, fols. 8, 17, 22).

There are a number of reasons why the British administration may have chosen to monitor these developments; France was perceived as a naval and military rival in many spheres (particular whilst Lord Palmerston was Foreign Secretary, as in 1846–1851), its ability to wage war was of particular interest to government. British observers noted with irritation and concern the tendency of the French press and Orleanist politicians to cite the sufferings of Ireland – that 'scandal to the civilized world' according to the *Journal des Débats* – both as proof of British hypocrisy and likely military weakness (*Times,* 3, 6 October 1846, 8 September, 22 November 1847). Belgium, on the other hand, was a state regarded in London as falling under the paternalistic care of Britain (not least because of the dynastic connection between the British and Belgian crowns), whose integrity and internal stability were of direct interest to the UK. Nevertheless, the fact that it was the Home Office – a department with partial responsibility for Irish affairs – that requested the memoranda on European relief initiatives suggests that this information was also required to inform domestic policy making.

Despite the availability of this comparative information, European parallels appear to have been remarkable by their absence in government policy-making processes in 1846–1847 (in marked contrast to the frequent comparisons drawn between the situation in Ireland and the famine in the western Highlands of Scotland). There are perhaps two reasons for this. Firstly, the London metropolitan press, the other main source of information on the continental subsistence crisis, tended towards an overt hostility to what it regarded as the counter-productive interventionism of the Belgian and French governments. Attempted state management of the food supply in Belgium was regarded as anathema by the ascendant free-trade lobby. Its mouthpiece, the *Economist,* condemned the policy as 'absurd' and blamed Flemish famine mortality in 1847 on the Belgian government's vacillation over the renewal of its suspension of agricultural protection in 1846 (*Economist,* 13 February, 3 July 1847). The journal went on to denounce the greater interventionism of Charles Rogier's Liberal government elected in 1847 – not least because of its marked departure from the *laissez-faire* trade and social policies adopted by other liberal regimes facing continuing famine crises, such as Lord John Russell's government in Britain and F.A. van Hall's in the Netherlands (Gray, 1997: 101–103). While acknowledging that extensive expenditure had diminished the political impact of hunger in France, and protesting that an official contrast had been drawn in Paris with the estimated 600,000 Irish starvation deaths by March 1847, the *Times* predicted that heavy French state spending would have negative consequences for the country's economy (*Times,* 11 March 1847). The combination of similarly doctrinaire opinions within the UK government, especially on the part of senior ministers such as Charles Wood and Earl Grey, with the assertiveness of free-trade radicals in parliament – greatly enhanced by their success in attaining a pivotal position in the election of July 1847 – rendered emulation of alternative relief policies difficult.

Secondly, and perhaps more importantly, the dominant paradigm within which Irish relief policy was constructed was one fixated with the British-Irish relationship and which tended to pathologize Irish difference from British social, economic and cultural 'norms' and attribute the underlying causes of Irish famine to that country's 'backwardness'. While there were heterodox thinkers prepared to challenge these assumptions, and divisions over the most suitable modes of 'normalizing' Ireland (and over whether it could or should be obliged to develop without external assistance), the dominant voice in the relief debates in Britain, that associated with the Treasury and its allies in the 'moralist' metropolitan press, had little interest in engaging in any comparative analysis that might detract from the British model. 'Moralist' voices, such as the *Times,* sought to turn continental criticisms of Britain's record on Ireland back on their own social inadequacies. Upbraiding the French government for its silence on French and Belgian suffering whilst it harped upon Ireland's miseries, the *Times* implied that Great Britain alone had escaped the general calamity due to its superior state of social evolution (*Times,* 31 December 1846).

For their part, Irish nationalists, particularly those of radical inclinations, tended to adopt a mirror-image preoccupation with British rule as the ultimate (and indeed the proximate) cause of famine. For nationalist critics of British policy, the policy of some continental states offered a useful contrast to the failure (or to some the malign agency) of British policy. Both the leading writers of the radical *Nation* newspaper in 1846–1848 subsequently appealed to European counter-cases. John Mitchel contrasted the stoppage of export of provisions during the crisis by both the Belgian and Portuguese governments with the free-trade dogmatism of Britain (Mitchel, 1860: 98). Charles Gavan Duffy later took up the same point, adding Hungary, Switzerland and Wurttemberg to the list of export-withholding states, and arguing that famine could have been avoided if Ireland, like Belgium, had been free to manage its own affairs (Duffy, 1883: 45–48). While the radical nationalist case that self-government would have permitted a more effective relief policy could thus be supported by reference to European cases, it was in fact restricted by its preoccupation with only one aspect of policy – the regulation of the export of locally-grown provisions. The Young Ireland writers' dogmatic insistence that, even in the wake of the devastating potato failures of 1845–1848, Ireland produced sufficient foodstuffs to feed its population, made the question of exports paramount and rendered other areas where European parallels might usefully have been drawn – on imports, public works, creating food entitlements and medical relief – marginal to their case (Donnelly, 1996: 26–61).

In contrast, Daniel O'Connell's more moderate and pragmatic style of nationalism was less fixated with exports, and prepared to draw wider connections with continental policy. In a speech made to the Repeal Association on 1 December 1846, O'Connell offered a rather more sophisticated interpretation: in Belgium, 'a free country with its own parliament', the people had been able to apply their own resources to their wants, and the government had got through scarcity with minimal loss through quickly opening the ports and anticipating the wants of the people (the UK government had done the first but failed to do the latter in Ireland – the limitations of the Board of Works in particular were singled out for criticism). If O'Connell somewhat exaggerated for effect the success of Belgian policy, he was more pessimistic about the prospects for Ireland even in the unlikely event of its attaining immediate autonomy – Ireland lacked the reproductive powers of Belgium, and hence the means of immediately supporting itself (*Cork Examiner*, 2 December 1846). If followed that Ireland in the first instance must rely on the surplus resources of Britain, resources it had a moral claim to in reparation for the legacy of British 'misgovernment' of Ireland. O'Connell's tactics in the last year of his life revolved around attempts to cajole and influence the administration into greater expenditure and flexibility, with little discernable effect (O'Connell, 1972–1980: VII, 83, 108, O'Connell to Pigot, 13 August 1846, O'Connell to Labouchere, 4 October 1846; *Hansard,* 3rd ser.: LXXXIX, 942–945). As his health deteriorated in the months preceding his death in May 1847, and as his mass political movement disintegrated under the impact of social dislocation and government patronage of leading Repealers, this voice was lost, and with it the potential to influence official policy.

This 'European' critique of official dogmatism was not restricted to Irish nationalists, but was also adopted, if somewhat fitfully, by some Irish landowners and British opposition politicians. Lord Mornington asked rhetorically in December 1846, 'Is it not singular that in a kingdom miserable in point of extent, under a poor and feeble government, like that of Belgium, immediate steps were taken upon the first suspicion of want of food, and the catastrophe, such as it now afflicts Ireland, was at once averted; as, indeed, it has been stayed in many other parts of Europe?' (*Times,* 25 December 1846). For his part, Lord George Bentinck, leader of the opposition Protectionist Conservatives in the House of Commons and advocate of an extensive scheme of railway construction to provide relief employment in Ireland, was also quick to contrast state interventionism on the continent with British policy:

'I deeply regret to find that whilst the kings of Belgium and Holland, of France and of Prussia, with the Emperor of Austria, and the state of the American Union all combine in the opinion that it is for the advantage of their respective countries to bring the aid of public resources to stimulate private enterprise, and even of themselves to construct works of public utility, the British Government, reined, curbed and ridden by political economists, stands alone in its unnatural, unwise, impolitic and disastrous resolves, rather to grant lavishly for useless and unproductive works, and for Soyer's soup kitchens, than to make loans, on an efficient scale and on ample security, to stimulate private enterprise and great works of well-tried efficacy in opening out the natural resources – in stimulating commerce – in improving and creating ready markets for agriculture, in exiting general prosperity, and last, but not least, in giving honest, honourable and independent employment at high money wages to hundreds of thousands of ablebodied labourers and their families, now pining and dying, and wasting their energies in spoiling the existing roads in Ireland.' (*Times,* 23 March 1847: Lord George Bentinck to William Monsell, 15 March 1847).

To a moralistic bourgeois public opinion in Britain, and its representatives in govern-ment, however, such appeals simply demonstrated the self-serving bankruptcy of the class deemed most responsible for the Irish catastrophe – the landowners. Damning lan-ded obstruction to the extension of the Irish poor law, a measure that would transfer res-ponsibility for the relief of Irish famine to 'Irish property', the *Times* denied that Ireland required external assistance from the British taxpayer or from European or American charity:

'There is not the smallest occasion for these world-wide appeals. Ireland is as well able to help herself as France or any other country. Nay, there are parts of France and Belgium probably still poorer. The only difference arises from the inhumanity of the landowners. The whole earth is doing duty for them. Meanwhile, however, England – that England which is paying 10,000,000*l.* for the relief of Ireland, figures nevertheless before the whole earth, partly as a tyrant, and partly as a beggar ... So long as we weakly suffer the Irish proprietors to be inhuman, we must share the odium of their inhumanity.' (*Times,* 10 May 1847).

For such observers the conclusion was clear: remove the artificial crutch of external aid, allow the 'just measure of pain' of famine to operate naturally, and the inhabitants of Ireland – landlords and peasants alike – would be faced with the moral choice of reforming their behaviour so as to save themselves by productively mobilising the island's resources, or of taking responsibility for their own demise.

III.

In the later 1840s the relief of famine in Ireland was frequently regarded as inseparable from the 'reconstruction' of Irish society. The high priority accorded to reconstruction arose partly from a concern that famine was endemic in Ireland and that relief policies adopted on previous occasions (in 1816–1817, 1822, 1831, and indeed in 1845–1846) had aggravated the underlying susceptibility of the country and discouraged remedial action. As importantly, the emphasis on the primacy of reconstruction also reflected the predominance of providentialist readings of the catastrophe – the assignation of higher meaning to the arrival of the blight and its continuing devastation of Irish society. Although providentialist interpretations varied – with toleration of Irish Catholicism and the existence of the corn laws featuring in early debates as probable causes of divine anger – the prolongation of the Irish crisis (and its echo in the mostly Protestant but 'Celtic' society of the western Scottish Highlands) tended to promote a reading which highlighted the 'unnatural' state of Irish agrarian society as the target of divine intervention, and its rapid transformation as the benign purpose intended (Gray, 2000). If a reconstructivist agenda co-existed with Peel's relief policy in 1845–1846 – in the shape of a concern to replace the discredited potato with imported maize and rice as the subsistence of the Irish poor – this became much more pronounced under the succeeding

Whig-Liberal government. The Russell administration combined a much more acute critique of Irish landlordism as the locus of guilt, and a greater concern with the moral 'backwardness' of all classes in Irish society and their apparent proneness to dependency and inertia. Accompanying this was a generally more 'optimistic' political economy shared with significant sections of the liberal press and public opinion in Britain – a belief (again underpinned by the application of theodicy to the Irish situation) that Ireland was not inherently overpopulated, that there was no real shortage of investment opportunity or capital (or none that could not be easily created through the application of labour power on the underdeveloped soil), and that only the stimulation provided by stern necessity (directed but not unnecessarily relieved by the agency of the state) was required to unleash this. This doctrine, which found its clearest articulation in Charles Trevelyan's *The Irish Crisis*, heavily influenced policy in 1846–1847; from the autumn of 1847 it attained ascendancy (although not universal adherence) within the government (Trevelyan, 1848).

If there was general agreement that the famine had revealed the rottenness of pre-existing Irish social relationships and the need for a 'social revolution' to transform these, there was less consensus on the optimum form that a reconstructed Irish society should take. For the purposes of this contribution I want to give some attention to the advocacy of a 'European' model (in strong and weak forms) in contestation with the more orthodox English (or, more accurately, the Anglo-Caledonian) model for Irish agrarian development.

The 'strong' case for the European model for Irish development was made during the famine years by the heterodox economists W.T. Thornton and J.S. Mill, along with the radical politician Poulett Scrope and social commentators such as Samuel Laing. Thornton and Mill have been credited as the 'rehabilitators' of the idea of peasant proprietary in British economic thought, but both were also active promoters of the application of their theories to Ireland in the later 1840s (Dewey, 1974). Thornton's case, expressed in 1846 and given more explicit application to Ireland in 1848, was that the socio-economic characteristics of most western European peasantries had rendered them relatively prosperous and industrious and encouraged voluntary restraints on the birth rate. Irish misery, in contrast, was due to the social consequences of a system of land tenure which encouraged the opposite (Thornton, 1846: 251–266, 413–439). Thornton was conscious that his advocacy of the superiority of peasant proprietary as model for Ireland had been countered by reference to the European subsistence crisis, and in his 1848 *A Plea for Peasant Proprietors* addressed the subject directly. The distress of 1845–1847, he asserted, had not been confined to small-farm peasant societies – and had led to equal suffering in the estate-based economies of the Baltic and Portugal; the commercial agriculture of Britain had escaped solely due to the accident of its untainted wheat harvests. Heavy reliance on the poor law in England and the sufferings of Ireland pointed to the inadequacies of both social systems in the face of scarcity. In contrast:

'The French peasantry (...) are in general self-dependent; and the interference of the government last year, in order to secure for them additional supplies of food, was a step almost without precedent. What amount of money may have been expended for this purpose, is not very generally known, but it was certainly nothing like ten millions sterling, to which sum it must nevertheless have reached in order to correspond with the amount annually expended on the relief of the poor of the much smaller population of England.'

Besides, it was the urban rather than the rural population which had required food aid in France. In the case of Belgian Flanders, Thornton acknowledged, the very small landowners had and continued to suffer, but these were not husbandmen *per se*, but rural artisans thrown into crisis by manufacturing rather than agricultural distress. Nevertheless, 'their connexion with the land may, and no doubt does, alleviate their misery, but cannot, in any conceivable manner, have helped to produce it … As it is, they are saved from utter destitution by the possession of their plots of land.' (Thornton, 1848: 160–166).

J.S. Mill combined Thornton's theories with his own researches on continental peasant societies to produce a programme for Irish reconstruction published in instalments in the *Morning Chronicle* newspaper in winter 1846–1847. His call was for the creation of a mixed agrarian system in Ireland (the so-called 'Prussian model') incorporating partial peasant proprietary with capitalist farming. This involved the total rejection of what Mill regarded as the orthodox fallacy that Ireland could and should be anglicised:

'We are not sure that it would be doing the Irish a service to make them Englishmen; but we are sure that they are not Englishmen, and cannot, by any device of ours, be made so. To make them work, they must have what makes their Celtic bretheren, the French peasantry, work, and those of Tuscany, of the self-indulgent and luxurious south. They must work, not for employers, but for themselves. Their labour must be for wages only, it must be a labour of love – the love which the peasant feels for the spot of land from which no man's pleasure can expel him, which makes him a free and independent citizen of the world, and which every improvement, which his labour can effect brings to his family as their permanent inheritance.' (Mill, 1846: 913–916).

Mill's rather less idealised mechanism for producing this end (shared by Thornton and Scrope), was the state appropriation of Ireland's waste lands for internal colonization by reclaiming peasant proprietors.

This 'strong' advocacy of the European model was, perhaps surprisingly, echoed by a 'weak' counterpart within the Whig-Liberal administration. Orthodox economists and their government allies were alarmed by signs in 1846–1849 that the prime minister himself was sympathetic towards 'remedial schemes' for Ireland, interfering with Irish land tenures or taking up the initiatives proposed by Mill and Scrope as a means of reviving the 'Justice to Ireland' political strategy of the later 1830s. Russell's personal initiatives (all abortive in the face of strong cabinet and treasury opposition) included an 1847 draft bill for the establishment of peasant proprietors on waste lands, a plan for the universal extension of 'tenant right' in late 1847, and schemes for the promotion of owner-occupation through the agencies of a farmers estate society and 'Prussian land banks' in 1848–1849. All reflected Russell's personal perception that peasant agriculture 'such (…) as exists in Tuscany' had its merits, and his sense that 'the Irish are fashioned more like our continental neighbours than ourselves – that instead of detesting government control they cannot do without it – and we cannot change the nature of the nation in this respect.' (*Hansard,* 3rd ser.: C, 237–254; *Clarendon Deposit Irish*: Russell to Clarendon, 21 May 1848, box 43).

The failure of Russell's remedial schemes owed something to their speculative and potentially expensive nature – but more to the challenge they were seen to pose to the concern for the anglicization of Ireland expressed by the majority of his cabinet colleagues and most of British liberal opinion. Ministerial correspondence and press commentary bears this out, but its most succinct statement can be found in Trevelyan's

Irish Crisis. Extensive state intervention of the sort envisaged by the advocates of internal colonization on reclaimed waste lands, Trevelyan asserted, would not only infringe just property rights but discourage Irish self-exertion; peasant proprietorship was delusional and inapplicable to the Irish situation, while the promotion of English social models should be the aim of all sound policy (Trevelyan, 1848: 172–178). In the place of peasant proprietary, the reconstructive policy most favoured by the treasury moralists in the government, their liberal allies in the press, and by the bulk of British radicals, was 'free trade in land' – a liberalization of the Irish land market which, if supported by continued financial pressure on the existing 'irresponsible' class of Irish landowners, would lead to the replacement of the latter by entrepreneurial British purchasers and large tenant farmers (Gray, 1999: 196–200). If accompanied by the proletarianization of the cottier peasantry through the medium of the extended poor law, this would, in Trevelyan's phrase, serve as 'a master-key to unlock the field of industry in Ireland.' (Trevelyan, 1848: 22–36).

Without an understanding of the preoccupation of key ministers and administrators with this anglicising reconstructive agenda, the Irish relief policy decisions of the government, especially from autumn 1847, make little sense.

Trevelyan received support for his conclusions from orthodox commentary on the Flemish crisis. In a *Times* article entitled 'Flanders and Ireland – a parallel', one author urged the fractious Irish to emulate the Flemings in acknowledging that their analogous problems were mostly beyond the cause or cure of government, but were the general outcome of European economic change which punished adherence to outdated modes of production. Resistance to the advance of capitalized agriculture was the root common to both societies:

'Flanders, like Ireland, suffers from an excess of pauper occupancy; its small farmers are labourers instead of being employers; but the Fleming clings to his plot of ground with the same desperate obstinacy as the cottier tenant in Ireland, and is equally unable or unwilling to perceive that his condition can only be ameliorated by his becoming a paid labourer, and ceasing to be a pauper proprietor.'

The free-traders and economists of Belgium were, the article continued, urging the government to revitalise Flanders by promoting capitalist enterprise, facilitating land consolidation and discontinuing food relief. Ireland's hope lay in the adoption of similar policies rather than regressing into peasant proprietary or 'tenant right' (*Times,* 29 November 1847).

IV.

The 1848 revolutions in Europe posed a series of challenges to British rule in Ireland, not least through the new lease of life they gave to the radical nationalism of Young Ireland and its political offshoot the Irish Confederation (Nowlan, 1965; Kerr, 1994). Alongside the introduction of coercion directed at both political and agrarian activity, the revolutionary moment stimulated further abortive concessionary initiatives on the part of Lord John Russell and led the Lord Lieutenant of Ireland, Lord Clarendon, to urge greater relief expenditure. The miserable failure of the Irish insurrection of summer 1848 tended, however, to convince most British observers of the 'ingratitude' of the

Irish and the necessity of accelerating the process of forced anglicization. To the *Times* the time for conciliation had passed, and all classes in Ireland needed for their own sake to be subjected to strict moral and physical discipline (*Times,* 4 October 1848).

For some observers, the threat posed by continental revolution lay as much in the social example set by revolutionary regimes as in the stimulus provided to nationalism. Lord Clarendon was particularly concerned that news from France had created an expectation of a 'revolutionary millennium' among the masses, and feared that the 'economic fallacies' adopted by the French government would excite false expectations (*Clarendon Deposit Irish*: Clarendon to Oranmore, 4 October 1848, Letterbook III; *Palmerston Papers*: Clarendon to Palmerston, 7 March 1848, GC/CL/483/1). The orthodox liberal economist and political commentator Nassau Senior was equally concerned about the 'socialist' doctrines inherent in the French *ateliers nationaux* (Senior, 1871, I: 1–8).

Advocates of the 'European peasantry' model for Ireland continued to bring their ideas before the British public in the later '40s, and were successful in influencing moderate Irish Catholic opinion (MacMahon, 1848: 331–332). However, despite Samuel Laing's insistence in 1850 that Flanders still offered the best model for Ireland, the negative impression of peasant proprietors created by the European agrarian crises and the 1848 revolutions made this argument difficult to sustain (Laing, 1850: 18–92). To the *Illustrated London News* in September 1849, the densely settled French countryside was as miserable a society as Ireland – proletarianization was the solution for both:

'In both countries a social revolution is needed which shall exalt agriculture as an art, and cause an increase in national wealth and the elevation of the people. We think that Ireland at length is on the right track, and that the stringent operation of the poor law will ultimately turn the small, potato-feeding, near naked farmers, into the meat-eating well-clad labourers of men of capital, skill and industry.' (*Illustrated London News,* 8 September 1849).

Ultimately, an aggressively anglicizing reconstructive agenda took the upper hand in Irish policy-making, and remained dominant in Britain until the historicist turn in economic thought of the 1860s (Gray, 2002).

Although easily defeated and dispersed in 1848, it was the revolutionary Young Ireland cadre, much more than the dispirited and (after 1847) leaderless O'Connellites who were the mould the dominant Irish nationalist memory of the Great Famine. In the formation of this narrative adverse contrasts between the response of the British and European governments to their respective food crises remained useful, but were ultimately marginal to the dominant reading of the Famine as a premeditated assault by a colonial power on the lives of a subject people (Mitchel, 1860: 98). This tradition, if read alongside a mainstream British (and Irish Unionist) recollection of the Famine was an inevitable Malthusian catastrophe falling on a uniquely backward society, may explain the sidelining of the catastrophe's significant European dimensions.

Bibliography

Manuscript sources

Clarendon Deposit Irish, Bodleian Library, Oxford.

Palmerston Letterbooks, British Library, London.

Palmerston Papers, Southampton University Library, Southampton.

Peel Papers, British Library, London.

Russell Papers, National Archives, Kew.

Trevelyan Letterbooks, Bodleian Library, Oxford [microfilm].

Printed and secondary sources

Abel, *Cork Examiner,* Cork.

Dewey, C.J. (1974) 'The rehabilitation of the peasant proprietor in nineteenth-century economic thought', *History of Political Economy,* 6, pp. 17–47.

Donnelly, J.S. (1996) 'The construction of the memory of the Famine in Ireland and the Irish Diaspora, 1850–1900', *Éire-Ireland,* 31, 1–2, pp. 26–61.

Dublin Evening Post, Dublin.

Duffy, C.G. (1883) *Four Years of Irish History, 1845–1849,* London.

Economist, The, London.

Gray, P. (1997) 'Famine relief policy in comparative perspective: Ireland, Scotland, and Northwestern Europe, 1845–1849', *Éire-Ireland,* 32, 1, pp. 86–108.

Gray, P. (1999) *Famine, Land and Politics: British Government and Irish Society, 1843–1850,* Dublin.

Gray, P. (2000) 'National humiliation and the Great Hunger: fast and famine in 1847', *Irish Historical Studies*, 32, 126, pp. 193–216.

Gray, P. (2002) 'The peculiarities of Irish land tenure 1800–1914: from agent of impoverishment to agent of pacification', in D. Winch and P. O'Brien (eds), *The Political Economy of British Historical Experience, 1688–1914*. Oxford, pp. 139–162.

Hansard's Parliamentary Debates, 3rd series, London.

Illustrated London News, London.

Kerr, D.A. (1994) *A Nation of Beggars? Priests, People and Politics in Famine Ireland 1846–52,* Oxford.

Laing, S. (1850) *Observations on the Social and Political State of the European People in 1848 and 1849,* London.

MacMahon, P. (1848) 'Measures for Ireland: tillage – waste lands – fixity of tenure', *Dublin Review,* 25, pp. 331–332.

Mansion House Committee (1846) *Report of the Mansion House Committee on the Potato Disease*, Dublin.

Mill, J.S. (1846) 'The condition of Ireland [11]' (*Morning Chronicle,* 26 October 1846), in A.P. Robson and J.M. Robson (eds), *Collected Works of John Stewart Mill, XXIV: Newspaper Writings, January 1835 to June 1847,* Toronto, 1986, pp. 913–916.

Mitchel, J. (1860) *The Last Conquest of Ireland (Perhaps),* London.

Nowlan, K.B. (1965) *The Politics of Repeal: A Study in the Relations between Great Britain and Ireland, 1841–50,* London.

O'Connell, M.R. (ed.) (1972–1980) *Correspondence of Daniel O'Connell,* 8 vols, Dublin.

Parliamentary Papers (1847) *Correspondence Relating to Measures for the Relief of Distress in Ireland (Commissariat Series), July 1846 to January 1847,* [761], LI, London.

Peel, R. (1856–1857), *Memoirs of Sir Robert Peel,* 2 vols, London.

Pilot, Dublin.

Price, R. (1983) 'Poor relief and social crisis in mid-nineteenth century France', *European Studies Review,* 13, pp. 423–454.

Senior, N.W. (1871) 'Sketch of the revolution of 1848', in M.C.M. Simpson (ed.), *Journals Kept in France and Italy from 1848 to 1852,* 2 vols, London, I, pp. 1–8.

Smith, A. (1846) *Extract from the Fifth Chapter of the Fourth Book of Adam Smith's 'Wealth of Nations',* London.

Solar, P. (1997) 'The potato famine in Europe', in C. Ó Gráda (ed.), *Famine 150: Commemorative Lecture Series,* Dublin, pp. 113–128.

Thornton, W.T. (1846) *Over-population and Its Remedy; or an Inquiry into the Extent and Causes of the Distress among the Labouring Classes of the British Isles, and into the Means of Remedying It,* London.

Thornton, W.T. (1848) *A Plea for Peasant Proprietors, With a Plan for their Establishment in Ireland,* London.

Times, The, London.

Trevelyan, C.E. (1848) *The Irish Crisis,* London.

PART II

A POTATO FAMINE OUTSIDE IRELAND ?

6 Why the Highlands did not starve. Ireland and Highland Scotland during the potato famine[1]

Tom M. DEVINE, University of Aberdeen

In many ways the failure of the potatoes in Ireland and Highland Scotland in the 1840s had remarkably similar effects. The dependency on this single crop was such that blight plunged entire districts into profound crisis. In both the Western Highlands and the west of Ireland, where famine was most acute and its social consequences most serious, the emigration of the poor accelerated beyond all previous levels, landowners promoted mass clearance and set up schemes of assisted passage across the Atlantic. External agencies, whether government or private charities, were forced to establish extensive programmes of relief for distressed districts.[2]

The failure of the potato crop over successive years in the 1840s and early 1850s was, of course, not unique to the Highlands and Ireland. The fungal disease which devastated their subsistence agriculture also wrought havoc throughout western Europe and beyond. But in two senses, the catastrophe in both northern Scotland and Ireland was exceptional. Firstly, the crop deficiency in several years in the two areas was abnormal by standards elsewhere in Europe. Recent estimates suggest that the shortfall in potato yields throughout Europe, even during the period of blight, was usually no more than one third (Solar, 1989: 12–33). The 'largest observed deficiency' in potato yields in France throughout the nineteenth century was 36 per cent, in Germany 31 per cent and in the Netherlands 50 per cent. However, three quarters of the crop was lost in Ireland in 1846 while in the same year, in a sample of distressed Highland districts, 67 per cent experienced complete failure and in another 20 per cent blight destroyed the potatoes 'almost entirely' (Free Church Reports, 1847: 6–13).

In the second place, the crisis was protracted over several seasons. In both Ireland and the Highlands 1846 was a terrible year but it was not unique. Blight also struck in Ireland, especially in the west, in 1845, 1848, 1849 and 1850. Crops continued to be badly affected in the Hebrides and the western coastlands of the Highlands until 1855; only in the following season did clear evidence emerge of sustained recovery from the ravages of the famine years. The moist and moderately warm summers of both regions were ideal for the propagation and perpetuation of *Phytopthora Infestans*.

In one fundamental sense, however, the experience of the two societies diverged dramatically in the 1840s. Between 1,000,000 and 1,200,000 died during the Irish famine through starvation or famine-related disease. In the Scottish Highlands mortality rates did start to climb above 'normal' levels in the latter months of 1846 and early 1847 but the crisis was eventually and successfully contained (Devine, 1988a: 57–67). The potato blight had profound demographic effects in north-west Scotland. A huge emigration was precipitated from the distressed districts. Between 1841 and 1861 Uig in Lewis lost

---

[1] Reprinted with minor bibliographic additions from Devine, 1995.
[2] Key works on the Irish potato famine include Crawford, 1989; Daly, 1986; Edwards and Williams, 1956; Mokyr, 1985; Ó Gráda, 1988; Flinn, 1977; Hunter, 1976; Smout, 1977; Donnelly, 2001.

about half of its population, Jura almost a third, the Small Isles nearly a half and Barra about a third.[3] In addition there was a pronounced fall in both the rate of marriage and the number of births in many affected parishes.[4] These demographic measures illustrate the scale of the social crisis triggered by crop failure. But unlike their counterparts across the Irish Sea the people of the region survived. Misery and suffering increased but contemporary comment, government reports, estate correspondence and surviving burial records all indicate that there was no crisis of mortality.[5]

The purpose of this paper is to outline some of the influences which might help to explain the contrasting fate of the Irish and the Highlanders who were exposed to crop failure on an equally massive scale but with somewhat different results.

I. Scale and potato dependency

Why Ireland starved and the Highlands survived is in part a question of numbers. In much of Ireland and particularly in the poorer districts of the far west the population dependent on potatoes in whole or in part was enormous. Recent estimates suggest that on the eve of the Great Famine, potatoes accounted for about one-third of all tilled ground, three million or so people consumed them as the major element in diet and the crop formed a cornerstone of the agrarian system by which plots of potato-land were let 'on conacre' by farmers to labourers on an annual basis (Bourke, 1968: 72–96). Such was the scale of dependency that some argue effective control of the crisis was beyond the powers of the contemporary state, especially one so thoroughly imbued with such doctrinaire laissez-faire principles as that of early Victorian Britain (Daly, 1986: 84). Others contend that even given the ideological and administrative constraints of the time much more could have been done to save life.[6]

Self-evidently, however, the management of relief was much easier in the Highlands because there the potential victims of crop failure could be numbered in thousands rather than millions. In late 1846, the estimates of those seriously at risk from starvation ranged from 600,000 to 200,000. By 1847 and thereafter it became apparent, however, that the disaster was less extensive. The southern, eastern and central Highlands attracted external relief in 1846 and 1847 but operations were wound down in subsequent years. The blight rapidly diminished in ferocity in these inland districts. In addition, the balance between population and employment opportunities was much better than further west and potatoes were not so much a principal subsistence crop as an important element within a more diverse system of food supply which included grains, fish and vegetables.[7]

---

[3] Calculated from the published census, 1841, 1851, 1861.

[4] Based on calculations form General Record Office, Edinburgh, Parish Registers for Kilfinichen, Tiree, Ardchattan, Glenorchy, Iona, Ardnamurchan, Dornoch, Creich, Clyne, Stornoway, Portree, North Uist, Moidart, Arisaig, Bracadale, Strontian.

[5] The evidence is sifted in detail in Devine, 1988a: ch. 3.

[6] *Scotsman*, 19 December 1846; Parliamentary Papers (further PP) 1847 LIII, *Correspondence relating to the Measures adopted for the Relief of Distress in Ireland and Scotland*, Sir J. Riddell to Sir G. Gray, 24 August 1846; Sir J. McNeill to Sir G. Gray, 27 September 1846.

[7] *Reports of Edinburgh Section of the Central Board* (Edinburgh, 1847–50), Second Report for 1850 of the Committee of Management, p. 11. See too Young, 1996.

Furthermore, as the famine persisted, destitution became concentrated not only in the western maritime districts of croft agriculture but even more emphatically on the islands of the inner and outer Hebrides.[8] The potato blight in the Highlands endured for a long period but gradually became confined to a particular corner of the northern region. As a result, the crisis was much more easily managed than in the west of Ireland. In 1851, the population of the four main Highland counties was almost a quarter of a million. About half of this number lived in areas in receipt of consistent supplies of external aid in the later 1840s while the numbers of inhabitants of parishes 'seriously at risk' (defined as having up to one third of their population on the relief lists between 1847 and 1850) was 66,000 or about 28 per cent of the Highland population (Devine, 1988a: 43–48). By 1848/9, in only Tiree, South Uist, Barra, Skye, Harris and Mull, were conditions similar to the distressed west of Ireland. The administrative problems associated with famine relief in that region were not replicated in the Highlands after 1847. Partly because the crisis could be more easily controlled in Scotland, government in that year was able to delegate responsibility for the entire relief operation to the private and church charities co-ordinated by the Central Board of Management for Highland Destitution.

It may also be that dependency on the potato was not as complete as in the poorest districts of Ireland. One Scottish historian, A.J. Youngson, has described the Highlands as 'almost a potato economy' and R. N. Salaman thought the crop was 'the cornerstone of the social structure' of the region in the nineteenth century (Youngson, 1973: 164; Salaman, 1949: 362). These assertions are probably exaggerated. In 1846 the Free Church investigated the importance of potatoes in the West Highland diet and concluded that they accounted for up to four fifths of popular food consumption in only one third of the districts surveyed (Free Church Report, 1847: 6–12). Both its research and the reports of other contemporary observers describe a Highland diet in which potatoes were very important but which also still included meal, from both oats and barley, milk and, above all, fish.[9] Even in some of the poorest communities along the west coast, the New Statistical Account described how potatoes and herring were consumed twice a day while oatmeal gruel was a common dish for supper (*New Statistical Account of Scotland*, 1845: 110–111). There also seem to have been interesting dietary variations within the social structure of the peasant community. Most crofting (or full tenant) families ate meal and fish regularly whereas semi-landless cottars were more likely to depend on potatoes as their main source of subsistence.[10] The complexity of Highland diet ensured that the potato blight created shortages for some and the threat of starvation for the very poor but did not necessarily threaten the mass catastrophe, which engulfed entire areas of Ireland after 1845.

---

[8] *Report on the Outer Hebrides by a Deputation of the Glasgow Section of the Highland Relief Board* (Glasgow, 1849), p. 9.

[9] P.P. 1851 XXVI, *Report to the Board of Supervision by Sir John McNeill on the Western Highlands and Islands,* Appendix A, *passim*; Macculoch, 1824: 338; Fullarton and Baird, 1838: 15.

[10] P.R.O. TI/420IS R. Grahame to Fox Maule, 3 April 1837; S.R.O. Lord Advocate's Papers, AD58/84, W.H. Sitwell to Countess of Dunmare, 1 October 1846.

II. Economy and society before the Famine

Superficially there were pronounced similarities between the development of the Irish and Highland economies before the 1840s. Both areas suffered from 'deindustrialization' as textile and other manufactures collapsed after 1815: contemporary economists suggested that each also demonstrated the horrors of 'over-population' and confirmed the validity of Malthus's arguments. The west of Ireland like the western Highlands was a region of 'redundant' population and chronic poverty which persistently succumbed to a cycle of subsistence crises which had long disappeared from the rest of Britain. Not surprisingly, therefore, both Scottish and Irish historians, in endeavouring to explain why a biological disaster became a social catastrophe in the later 1840s, tend to argue that the potato blight was but the pretext for a crisis ultimately conditioned by an imbalance between resources and population which became steadily worse after the Napoleonic Wars. Malcolm Gray's Highland Economy 1750–1850, in particular, presents the postwar Highlands in dark colours as a society becoming more vulnerable to crop failure and economic disaster.

Perhaps, however, the pessimistic analysis has been taken too far. The crumbling of the structure of bi-employments which had grown up in the later eighteenth century is undeniable. But not enough attention may have been given to the re-adjustment of west Highland society and economy in the generation after Waterloo, which probably gave it more resilience than the poorest districts of western Ireland by the time of the potato famines.

First, in both Ireland and Highland Scotland, the decades before the 1840s saw a deceleration in population growth due primarily to an increase in out-migration. In Ireland growth fell from 1.6 per cent in 1780–1821 to 0.9 per cent by the 1820s and had dropped to 0.6 per cent in 1830–1845 (Daultry, Dickson and Ó Gráda, 1981; Lee, 1981: 37–56). But there was considerable regional variation within the national trend and in those areas badly hit by the Great Famine growth, though slowing down, was still occurring in the 1820s and 1830s. Emigration was very significant before the 1840s but mainly confined to Ulster, Sligo, Leitrim and some parts of eastern Ireland. Outward movement from the poorest counties of the west, the districts later most ravaged by the potato blight, was still relatively slight (Fitzpatrick, 1984). It was a different story in the western Highlands. In the period 1810 to 1840 Scottish average population increase per annum was 1.48 per cent in 1811–1820, 1.23 per cent between 1821 and 1830 and 1.03 per cent between 1831 and 1840. The West Highlands experienced an even more dramatic fall from 1.46 per cent in 1811–1820 to 0.51 in 1821–1830. Between 1831 and 1840, however, population was actually falling with a decadal rate of –0.03 per cent (Richards, 1982: 99). The safety-valve of emigration operated more effectively in the Highlands than in the poorer parts of Ireland. From the middle decades of the eighteenth century chain migrations linked communities in the Hebrides with specific areas in the U.S.A. and Canada. The dislocation imposed by the creation of the crofting system and later the clearances associated with sheep farming produced a considerable increase in movement (Bumstead, 1982). The sheer scale of recruitment to the British Army between 1756 and 1815, perhaps unparalleled in Europe, cannot but have accustomed men to mobility.[11]

---

[11] This point was suggested to me by Professor Louis Cullen.

The inflation of cattle prices in the later eighteenth century provided the resources for sea migration, while landlords after the Napoleonic Wars were increasingly anxious to promote depopulation through assisted emigration (Cameron, 1970). In more general terms, however, the much greater rate of Highland emigration in the pre-famine decades may also suggest a less impoverished society than the west of Ireland, one where many crofters still had enough stock and goods to sell to raise the necessary capital to start a new life across the Atlantic.

Secondly, the Highland adjustment involved a huge increase in temporary migration in the first half of the nineteenth century. This may be seen as a substitute source of income and employment after the collapse of the kelp manufacture, the decline in army recruitment and the crushing by the state of illicit whisky-making in the 1820s and 1830s.[12] On the eve of the potato famine temporary migration occurred from all parts of the western Highlands with the exception of some areas in the Outer Hebrides. Of course, temporary migrants also came in large numbers from the poorer districts of Ireland and increasingly from the 1820s Irish harvesters became an important source of labour in Scottish agriculture (Johnson, 1970: 224–243; Ó Gráda, 1973: 48–76). But the impression is that Highland temporary migration was more extensive, more diverse and more significant to local economies in the north-west. Both young men and women were involved and they worked in Lowland agriculture, fisheries, domestic service, urban construction and railway building. Equally importantly, before 1840 most temporary migrants seem to have been drawn from the cottar class, the group most dependent on potatoes for subsistence. As will be seen later, the growing connection between this class and seasonal work opportunities in the Lowlands was very relevant to their survival when the potatoes failed in the 1840s.

Thirdly, commercial fishing (especially for cod and ling) and subsistence fishing probably persisted longer in some parts of the Highlands than some commentators have suggested.[13] The New Statistical Account is certainly full of references to stagnation in fishing and the disappearance of the herring from the sea lochs by the 1820s and 1830s. But the evidence of estate papers and the experience of some districts during the potato famine itself arc partly in conflict with the pessimistic view. Many communities still depended on the sea rather than the land and proprietors made determined efforts to consolidate their position while dispossessing crofting townships which had mainly relied on kelp manufacture.[14] Relief officials during the famine pointed out that such areas as western Ross, eastern Lewis and parts of Mull were not seriously distressed because of their fishing traditions.[15] Similar patterns can be detected in the west of Ireland, where both Patrick Hickey and Cormac Ó Gráda suggest that the offshore islands were less affected than mainlanders partly because of the opportunities for fishing (Ó Gráda, 1988: 121; Hickey, 1980: 603). On the other hand, the riches of the sea were more easily

---

[12] This paragraph is a summary of Devine, 1988a: 146–170 and Devine, 1979.

[13] See for example Gray, 1957: 158–169.

[14] MS Diary of J.M. Mackenzie, 1851 (in private hands); Conon House, Conon, Rosshire, Mackenzie of Gairloch MSS Bundle 53, Correspondence re estate affairs, 1847–1853; Macculoch, 1824, IV: 341; Fullarton and Baird, 1838: 16; P.P. 1847 XXVIII, *First Annual Report of the Board of Supervision for the Relief of the Poor*, p. 39.

[15] *Reports of Edinburgh Section of the Central Board* (Edinburgh, 1847–1850), Captain H.B. Rose to Captain Eliot, 1 May 1848.

harvested by the majority of Highlanders. The region most vulnerable to blight was the Hebrides and the western seaboard. Sheep clearances in earlier times had pushed even the people of the inland glens towards the coast. As Sir John McNeill concluded after his survey of the distressed areas in 1851: 'Of fresh fish they can almost always command a supply, for in those districts there are few crofts that are far from the coast'.[16]

Fourthly, the Highlands developed a more effective system of internal communications in the years after the end of the Napoleonic Wars. Irish historians argue that famine relief in the 1840s was constrained by the primitive nature of transport and communications, the isolation of many communities and the under-developed nature of trade in the far west (Daly, 1986: 51; Ó Gráda, 1989: 54–55). Thus the depth of the famine crisis was conditioned not only by a shortage of food in absolute terms but in some localities at least by poor structures of distribution and marketing. Few of these arguments are applicable to the western Highlands. Connections between the region and the Lowlands had expanded on a huge scale since the later eighteenth century as the north west developed as a major source of meat, wool, mutton, fish, kelp, timber, slate and whisky for the southern economy. A tourist trade flourished from the early nineteenth century (Smout, 1983: 5). These trends were both cause and effect of the revolution in communications. From the 1820s steam propulsion began a new era in Highland navigation: 'a bridge of boats now unites the southern mainland with the northern coast and very specially with the Western Isles' (Mulock, 1850: 160). A traveler took five weeks to make the journey from Edinburgh to Tiree in the 1770s; by the 1840s, the round trip from Glasgow to Mull by steamship took less than three days.[17] Partly because of the transport revolution, but more basically because the region had long had an historic dependency on grain imports, the trade in meal from the south was extensive before the 1840s. A structure of retail markets did exist through which the much enhanced supplies of the famine years could flow.[18] Proprietors and many large tenants kept grain stores. Fish merchants provided meal on credit and local traders supplied grain to temporary migrants.[19]

III. The landlord response

To the British government and some later historians Irish landlords were the great villains of the Famine years. More recent judgments suggest that some landowners were very active, a few went bankrupt in the struggle to keep the distressed people of their estates alive and the vast majority did little, either through choice or circumstances (Donnelly, 2001: ch. 6). Considerable emphasis is placed in the literature on the poverty of many proprietors which prevented them playing an energetic role in the Famine: 'By 1843 an estimated one thousand estates, accounting for a rental of over £700,000, one twentieth of the country, were in the hands of the receivers. This figure increased to £1,300,000 by 1847 and £2 million by 1849'(Daly, 1986: 109). Systematic research on the Irish landed class during the Famine has yet to begin but enough is already known to

---

[16] Mc Neill Report, p. IX.
[17] Compare Cregeen, 1964: xx and Bruce, 1847: 5.
[18] *Relief Correspondence,* Sir J. McNeill to Sir G. Gray, 27 September 1846; S.R.O. Treasury Correspondence, Coffin to Trevelyan, 28 September 1847.
[19] *Edinburgh Section Reports*, First Report (1849), pp. 20, 46.

point to significant differences between their response and that of the Highland elite.

The activities of 77 per cent of landowners in the affected areas of the western Highlands in 1846–1847 are known.[20] Almost 30 per cent were singled out for special praise by government officials for their private relief efforts while only 14 per cent were censured for their negligence. Charles Trevelyan was warm in his praise:

'(…) the Treasury have been quite delighted with the whole conduct of the Highland proprietors (…) it was a source of positive pleasure to turn from the Irish to the Scotch case. In the former, everything with regard to the proprietors is sickening and disgusting.'

A key factor in the difference was almost certainly the contrasting financial position of the two groups. Highland landowners also experienced a steep increase in crofter rent arrears in 1846–1849 and many contributed much to famine relief schemes on their estates. On the island of Tiree, the Duke of Argyll's outlay on relief turned a pre-famine surplus of £2,226 into a deficit in 1847 of £3,170. Yet there was no spectacular increase in bankruptcies. Only an estimated 6 per cent of the eighty odd estates in the distressed districts were sold or placed under trust during the famine years as a consequence of landlord insolvency.

The Highland elite may have been in a much stronger position to aid their people than many of their counterparts in the west of Ireland. This relief did not simply take the form of meal distribution and the provision of work. From the middle years of the famine several proprietors also established ambitious schemes of assisted emigration and these, together with private charities in which landlords participated led to the resettlement of over 16,000 people, mostly from the Hebrides, in Canada and Australia (Devine, 1992). Potential emigrants were selected with meticulous care: the poorest, the most destitute and the weakest were given the highest priority. The overwhelming majority belonged to the cottar class.[21] As one landlord put it in 1851: 'I wish to send out those whom we would be obliged to feed if they stayed at home—to get rid of that class is the object'.[22] By removing many of the most vulnerable in the society by coercive means some landlords achieved lasting infamy and opprobrium (Mackenzie, 1883). But they also reduced the chances of a crisis of mortality in the Highlands. Irish proprietors were also active in assisted emigration but the total supported by Highland landowners was a much higher proportion both of the regional population and of the famine emigrations from northern Scotland as a whole (Fitzpatrick, 1984: 19–20).

Two factors probably explain the solvency of the Highland aristocracy. First, a great transfer of estates took place between 1810 and 1840 from the old, indebted hereditary class to new owners who were principally rich tycoons from the Lowlands and England. They were merchants, bankers, lawyers, southern landowners, financiers and industrialists who were attracted to the Highlands for sport and recreation and by its romantic allure. An estimated 74 per cent of estates in the famine zone changed hands in the four decades before 1840 (Devine, 1989: 108–142). Second, there had been a radical restructuring of estate economies in many parts of the western Highlands and islands over the same period. As the labour-intensive economy founded on kelp, fish and cattle

---

[20] This paragraph summarises Devine, 1988b.
[21] See Inveraray Castle, Argyll Estate Papers, Bundles 1335, 1531, 1558, 1804, Correspondence of John Campbell; MS Diary of J.M. Mackenzie, Chamberlain of the Lews, 1851.
[22] Inveraray Castle, Argyll Estate Papers, Bundle 1558, Duke of Argyll to?, 5 May 1851.

stagnated or collapsed, proprietors increasingly laid down more land to more profitable sheep-farming. By the 1840s commercial pastoralism was dominant on the majority of estates.[23] The income of most landlords came to depend on the rental of the big sheep ranchers rather than the petty payments of the crofters.[24] Mutton and wool prices rose during the famine years, sheep rentals were maintained and most proprietors were therefore insulated from the sharp increase in arrears within the crofting sector which occurred in 1846–1849 (Devine, 1988b: 150–152). This resilience allowed many to play an active and energetic role in the provision of relief during the same period.

IV. The crisis of 1846–1847

The potato blight affected Ireland for the first time in 1845, a year earlier than the Highlands, but late 1846 and early 1847 was probably the period of most acute distress in both societies (Ó Gráda, 1989: 46). Close study of these two years provides further insights into the reason for Scottish resilience. Two key differences between the experience of the two societies at this time emerge. First, the role of the state in Ireland was more significant in the relief effort than private charity. A principal agency was the creation of a Board of Works which in return for labour in relief schemes provided work for the needy. The public works carried out in the autumn and winter of 1846–1847 cost the huge sum of £4,848,123. The scale of the Irish crisis was such, however, that even this was not enough to prevent a massive increase in mortality. In addition, scholars have criticized the schemes because money spent on the works did not necessarily have a decisive impact as local organization was often lacking in the areas of most acute distress. Moreover, the system of payment in return for labour penalized the weakest and the unhealthiest who were most in need of support.[25] Government intervention was much more limited in the western Highlands in 1846–1847 and was confined to the establishment of meal depots, maintaining pressure on landowners to provide succour for the poor and sponsoring relief works through the promotion of the Drainage Act.

Ironically, however, the more muted response of the state was probably to the advantage of the stricken Highland population. The Whig government of Lord John Russell would have done everything possible to avoid free or lavish distribution of meal. But the first agency to provide relief in the north west, the Free Church of Scotland, seems to have had a more liberal policy.[26] The government's initiatives in Scotland, especially those in the far west, have been criticised for poor organisation. But the Free Church in the Highlands was in an excellent position both to guide funds to the worst hit areas and at the same time to attract subscriptions from its mainly middle class adherents in the Scottish cities. It was in essence an embryonic relief organisation which

---

[23] This generalization is based on a survey of the relevant entries in the *New Statistical Account*, 1845.
[24] See, for example, Conon House, Conon, Mackenzie of Gairloch MSS, Report by Thomas Scott on accounts of Dr. Mackenzie as factor, 1843–1846; National Library of Scotland, Sutherland Estate Papers, Dept. 313/2159–2160; *McNeil Report*, Appendix A, *passim*.
[25] Ó Gráda, 1989: 54–55; Daly, 1986: 84. For a further comparative perspective see Young, 1994: 325–340.
[26] The Free Church's activities are chronicled in Free Church Reports, 1847 and its newspaper *The Witness* for 1846 and early 1847.

through its local parishes, synods and ministers could be activated to provide ready assistance. All contemporary observers agreed that its response was immediate, generous and vigorous and showed no sign of denominational prejudice. In fact, the Catholic islands of Barra and South Uist were among the first to receive succour. A further telling illustration of the church's imaginative effort was its scheme for transporting 3,000 Highlanders to the labour markets of the Lowlands for seasonal employment in 1847.

A second important distinction between the two societies in this phase of crisis was the general economic context in Scotland and Ireland. Cormac Ó Gráda states that:

'Unfortunately for Ireland, the height of the Famine period – late 1846 and early 1847 – was one of financial crisis in Britain. The 'railway mania' which began in 1845 had run its course, and bad harvests in both Ireland and Britain in 1846 led to a huge trade deficit and consequent drain of bullion. The ensuing sharp rise in the cost of credit embarrassed many companies. The value of cotton output fell by a quarter.' (Ó Gráda, 1989: 46)

The economic depression therefore massively intensified the problems caused by crop failure. The Highland population was again more fortunate. Only in the latter months of 1847 and early 1848 was Scotland plunged into industrial recession. At the end of 1846 the Board of Supervision of the Scottish Poor Law confirmed that 'there was an unusual demand for labour at rates of wages probably unprecedented'.[27] The greatest railway construction boom of the nineteenth century was under way and did not abate until the late autumn of 1847.[28] Wages in the east coast herring fishery in the season of 1846 were 'at least one third higher than was customary' and in the same year the agricultural labour market in the Lowlands 'was never better able to bear the influx of Highlanders'.[29] Prices for Highland black cattle were also buoyant in 1846 and the first few months of 1847.[30]

Throughout the worst period of the potato failure, the vigour of the Lowland economy was therefore able to absorb increasing numbers of Highland temporary migrants who on their return released a great stream of income throughout the north west. It was the boom in 1846 and 1847 in temporary migration which provides one answer to the question which puzzled relief officials in the destitute districts, namely why so many of the poor were able to pay cash for meal.[31] Amartya Sen's familiar argument suggests that some famines are caused less by an absolute shortage of food than by the absence of 'entitlements' to food through the inability of the population to buy that which is available (Sen, 1981). One probable reason therefore why the Highland population survived was that a higher proportion than in the west of Ireland in 1846–1847 had the purchasing power to make good some of the deficiencies in subsistence brought about by the failure of the potatoes.

---

[27] P.P. 1847–1848 XXXII, *Second Annual Report of the Board of Supervision*, p. XV.

[28] *Scotsman*, 3 February 1847; *North British Daily Mail*, 1 May 1847.

[29] S.R.O. HD16/101, Minutes of Committee appointed to watch the progress of events connected with the potato failure (1847); *Inverness Journal*, 20 August 1847.

[30] West Highland cattle prices are recorded in the *Inverness Courier, Scotsman and Witness*, 1846–1848.

[31] *Edinburgh Section Reports*, Fourth Report (1848), R. Eliot to W. Skene, 3 February 1848; S.R.O. HD6/2, Treasure Correspondence, Sir E. Coffin to Mr. Trevelyan, 28 September 1847 and Captain E. Rose to Sir E. Coffin, 28 March 1847.

V.   Conclusion

The stark contrast in the fate of the Irish and the Highlanders during the potato famines is partly explained by the enormous difference in scale and the numbers affected in the two societies. However, this paper has argued that west Highland society was also more resilient than the poorer districts of Ireland. Potato dependency was not as great and population pressure not as acute; the landlord class was more active in relief and the peasant economy more diverse. The proximity of an industrialized society to the south and east was also of singular importance. The advanced economy of the Lowlands provided a host of seasonal work opportunities for Highland temporary migrants. It produced the surplus wealth which allowed the very rich to acquire insolvent Highland estates before the 1840s and also enabled the philanthropic organizations to raise the necessary funds to alleviate the threat of starvation in the north west.

Bibliography

Bourke, P.M.A. (1968) 'The Use of the Potato Crop in Pre-Famine Ireland', *Journal of the Statistical and Social Inquiry Society of Ireland*, 12, pp. 72–96.

Bruce, J. (1847) *Letters on the Present Condition of the Highlands and Islands of Scotland*, Edinburgh.

Bumstead, J.M. (1982) *The People's Clearance: Highland Emigration to British North America, 1770–1815*, Edinburgh.

Cameron, J.M. (1970) *A Study of the Factors that Assisted and Directed Scottish Emigration to Upper Canada, 1815–55*, Glasgow. Unpublished Ph.D. Thesis, University of Glasgow.

Crawford, E.M. (ed.) (1989) *Famine: The Irish Experience 900–1900: Subsistence Crises and Famine in Ireland*, Edinburgh.

Cregeen, E.R. (1964) *Argyll Estate Instructions, 1771–1805*, Edinburgh.

Daly, M. (1986) *The Famine in Ireland*, Dundalk.

Daultrey, S.G., Dickson, D. and Ó Gráda, C. (1981) 'Eighteenth-Century Irish Population: New Perspectives from Old Sources', *Journal of Economic History*, 42, pp. 601–628.

Devine, T.M. (1979) 'Temporary Migration and the Scottish Highlands in the Nineteenth Century', *Economic History Review*, 2nd series, 32, pp. 344–359.

Devine, T.M. (1988a) *The Great Highland Famine: Hunger, Emigration and the Scottish Highlands in the nineteenth century*, Edinburgh.

Devine, T.M. (1988b) 'Highland Landowners and the Highland Potato Famine', in L. Leneman (ed.), *Perspectives in Scottish Social History: Essays in Honour of Rosalind Michison*, Aberdeen, pp. 141–162.

Devine, T.M. (1989) 'The Emergence of the New Elite in the Western Highlands and Islands, 1800–60', in T.M. Devine (ed.), *Improvement and Enlightenment*, Edinburgh, pp. 108–142.

Devine, T.M. (1992) 'The Flight of the Poor: Assisted Emigration from the Scottish Highlands in the Nineteenth Century', in C.J. Byrne, M. Harry and P. Ó Siadhail (eds), *Celtic Languages and Celtic Peoples*, Halifax, pp. 645–660.

Devine, T.M. (1995) 'Why the Highlands did not starve: Ireland and Highland Scotland during the Potato Famine', in S.J. Connolly, R. Houston and R. Morris (eds) *Conflict, Identity and Economic Development: Ireland and Scotland 1600–1939*, Edinburgh, pp. 77–88.

Donnelly, J.S. (2001) *The Great Irish Potato Famine,* London.

Edwards, R.D. and Williams, T.D. (eds) (1956) *The Great Famine: Studies in Irish History,* Dublin.

Fitzpatrick, D. (1984) *Irish Emigration 1801–1921*, Dublin.

Flinn, M.W. (ed.) (1977) *Scottish Population History from the Seventeenth Century to the 1930s,* Cambridge.

Free Church Reports (1847) *Report of the General Assembly of the Free Church of Scotland Regarding Highland Destination*, Edinburgh.

Fullarton, A. and Baird, C.R. (1838) *Remarks on the Evils at Present Affecting the Highlands and Islands of Scotland*, Glasgow.

Gray, M. (1957) *The Highland Economy, 1750–1850*, Edinburgh.

Hickey, P. (1980) *A Study of Four Peninsular Parishes in Cork, 1796–1855*, Dublin. Unpublished M.A. Thesis, National University of Ireland.

Hunter, J. (1976) *The Making of the Crofting Community,* Edinburgh.

Johnson, J.H. (1970) 'The Two "Irelands" at the Beginning of the Nineteenth Century', in N. Stephens and R.W. Glasscock (eds), *Irish Geographical Studies in Honour of E. Estyn Evans*, Belfast, pp. 224–243.

Lee, J. (1981) 'On the Accuracy of the Pre-Famine Irish Censuses', in J.M. Goldstrom and L.A. Clarkson (eds) *Irish Population, Economy and Society*, Oxford, pp. 37–56.

Macculoch, J. (1824) *The Highlands and Western Islands of Scotland*, London.

Mackenzie, A. (1883) *The History of the Highland Clearance*, Inverness.

Mokyr, J. (1985) *Why Ireland Starved: A Quantitative and Analytical History of the Irish Economy, 1800–45*, London, revised edition.

Mulock, T. (1850) *The Western Highlands and Islands Socially Considered*, Edinburgh.

New Statistical Account of Scotland (1845), 15 vols, Edinburgh.

Ó Gráda, C. (1973) 'Seasonal Migration and Post-Famine Adjustment in the West of Ireland', *Studia Hibernica*, 13, pp. 48–76.

Ó Gráda, C. (1988) *Ireland Before and After the Famine. Explorations in Economic History, 1800–1925*, Manchester–New York.

Ó Gráda, C. (1989) *The Great Irish Famine*, Basingstoke.

Richards, E. (1982) *A History of the Highland Clearances*, London.

Salaman, R.N. (1949) *The History and Social Influence of the Potato*, Cambridge.

Sen, A. (1981) *Poverty and Famines*, Oxford.

Smout, T.C. (1977) 'Famines and Famine Relief in Scotland', in L.M. Cullen and T.C. Smout (eds), *Comparative Aspects of Scottish and Irish Social History 1600–1900*, Edinburgh, pp. 21–31.

Smout, T.C. (1983) 'Tours in the Scottish Highlands from the Eighteenth to the Twentieth Centuries', *Northern Scotland*, 5, pp. 99–121.

Solar, P.M. (1989) 'The Great Famine was No Ordinary Subsistence Crisis', in E.M. Crawford (ed.), *Famine: the Irish experience 900–1900: subsistence crises and famines in Ireland*, Edinburgh, pp. 112–133.

Young, L. (1994) 'Paupers, property and place: Poor law policy and practice in England, Scotland and Ireland in the mid-nineteenth century', *Environment and Planning D: Society and Space*, vol. 12, pp. 325–340.

Young, L. (1996) 'Spaces for Famine: A Comparative Geographical Analysis of Famine in Ireland and the Highlands in the 1840s', *Transactions of the Institute of British Geographers*, 21, no. 4, pp. 666–680.

Youngson, A.J. (1973) *After the '45*, Edinburgh.

7 "So worthy an example to Ireland". The subsistence and industrial crisis of 1845–1850 in Flanders

Eric VANHAUTE, Ghent University

I. A dynamic peasant economy

Up until the nineteenth century, the agriculture of Flanders was that of a peasant economy.[1] After the disappearance of serfdom in the High Middle Ages, most holdings in the Flemish countryside were small household farms characterised by peasant survival strategies (Verhulst, 1990; Thoen, 2001, 2004). In addition, an extensive rural flax industry developed in the heart of this region, reaching its zenith at the beginning of the nineteenth century (see Figure 7.2).

This type of agriculture, called 'Flemish husbandry', was based on equilibrium within the holding, within the village economy and in the regional context. To begin with, all holdings, large and small, were mixed farms. The combination of arable farming and the breeding of small stock and, when possible, cattle, was the key to success in peasant agriculture. Above all, the arable land had to produce grain (wheat, rye, maslin, spelt, also buckwheat) and, from the eighteenth century on, more and more potatoes, these together being the main ingredients of the human diet. In addition, some land was cultivated for grass and hay, industrial crops (such as flax, hop and coleseed), fodder crops (turnips, peas, spurrey, clover, etc.) and certain fruit and vegetables. The cattle supplied meat, dairy products and provided traction power and manure. Because of extremely high labour input, rotation systems were elaborated and agricultural productivity was high. Typically, in the middle of the nineteenth century, Flemish smallholdings were often less than 0.5 hectare, often tilled by spade. Almost all of these smallholdings cultivated rye and potatoes. About 60% also grew vegetables, 40% fruit and 30% coleseed. Five out of every ten of these tiny holdings grew a second crop such as turnips. In holdings between 0.5 and 2 hectares (still too small to be self-sufficient), 50% of the land was used for grain, 15% for potatoes, 10 to 15% for clover and 10 to 15% for flax. These holdings often kept one or two cows (but not horses) (Thoen and Vanhaute, 1999).

These small family holdings were deeply embedded in the local village economies but also participated in regional and national economies, through local markets and larger farms, and even in the international economy, via linen export. Large farms and smallholdings were linked to each other via complex dependence relationships and credit systems in the form of labour, goods, services and sometimes money. Smallholders exchanged their labour surplus for the capital and goods surplus (such as horsepower)

---

[1] Vanhaute and Van Molle, 2004. This overview focuses on the sand and sand-loam region of Inner-Flanders, situated in the Belgian provinces of East- and West-Flanders, excluding the coastal region and the river polders (Figure 7.1).
I am grateful to Cormac Ó Gráda for his suggestions and corrections.

When the potato failed

Figure 7.1 Map of agricultural regions in Flanders

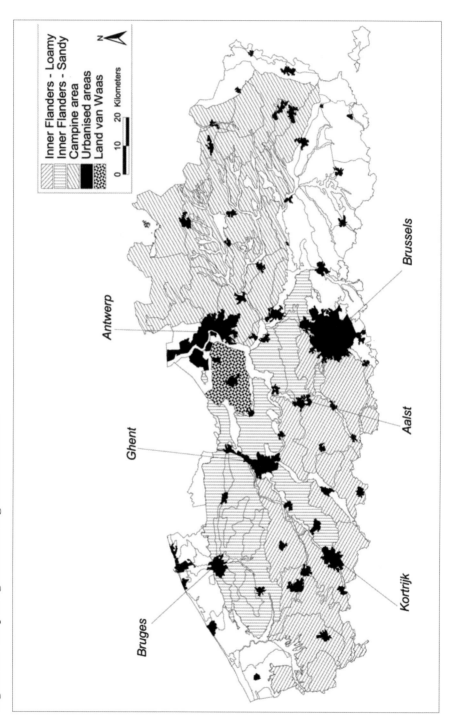

124

of the larger farmers. These local credit networks linked subsistence farming to the external markets.

Moreover, the mixed holding had to maintain a balance between producing enough to live on and still have sufficient left to exchange on the local and regional market circuits. The small family farm, with its typical intensive mixed agriculture, could only survive thanks to self-sufficiency supplemented with income from the sale of some arable farming produce (e.g. industrial crops and fruit), and meat and diary produce (e.g. butter and eggs), and, especially, from (proto-)industrial flax processing. Regions such as the (coastal and Scheldt) polders and the surrounding clay soil areas that supported larger holdings, generated additional exchange relationships through demand for agrarian labour and the sale of agricultural produce.

All these factors determined the particular character of the Flemish commercial peasant economy (Vanhaute and Van Molle, 2004; Lambrecht, 2002; Thoen, 2001, 2004). For centuries, mixed agriculture guaranteed the survival of the large majority of families in Flanders. In addition, until the nineteenth century, this system of household farming was the most important driving force behind regional and national economic growth and the biggest source of regional wealth. The last period of accelerated growth started in the middle of the eighteenth century, resulting in levels of agricultural yield in the middle of the nineteenth century that were the highest until then. The increased productivity of land and livestock was the result of further refinements of the mixed holding type of agriculture and an increasingly higher labour input in small to very small holdings.

II. High profits and high costs

Between 1750 and 1850, the population of the whole of Belgium almost doubled. In the already densely populated Flemish area, population grew by 75%. After 1800, the population increased with annual growth rates of 0.7 to 1%. In 1846, the two Flemish provinces had 400,000 more inhabitants than in 1801, a growth of 40% (from 1.02 million to 1.43 million inhabitants). This increase was an entirely rural phenomenon, related to the success of the 'traditional' agrarian society. Permanent long-distance emigration hardly occurred. In 1850, population density in Flanders had increased to 233 inhabitants per km², one of the highest at that time. The region only had one centre of urban growth: the industrial city of Ghent.

The demographic and financial pressures (see below) on husbandry had a favourable effect on yields. In the eighteenth century, the agriculture of the Southern Netherlands was strikingly productive (Vandenbroeke, 1975: 621–626). It was able to feed a rapidly increasing population. In addition, approximately 5% of the grain harvest could be exported as surplus. Only through a permanent pursuit of improving physical yields in arable farming could a structural food shortage be avoided.

The increase in total agricultural output was due in large part to diversification and further improvement of the existing production methods. Rising food production was the combined result of the increase in yields as a consequence of a more intensive soil cultivation in arable farming, the spread and differentiation of crop rotation (without fallow), the introduction and spread of new crops (potato), and longer, often permanent stabling of livestock.

Table 7.1   Population and agricultural output in Belgium, 1760-1850 (growth per annum)

	Population growth	Output agriculture	Output arable farming	Output livestock farming
1760–1810	+0.53%	+0.35%	+0.62%	–0.11%
1810–1850	+0.97%	+0.93%	+0.93%	+0.94%

Source: Dejongh, 1999.

Table 7.2   Agricultural land in Belgium, 1760–1850

	c. 1760	c. 1810	c. 1850
Agricultural land (mio hectare)			
Arable land (plus fallow)	1.37		1.46
Pasture land	0.33		0.35
Woodland	0.59		0.55
Heath land	0.43		0.35

	c. 1760	c. 1810	c. 1850
Subdivision arable land (%)			
Total hectares (mio)	1.13	1.21	1.32
Grains	83.1%	71.7%	67.4%
Potatoes	1.7%	6.1%	9.1%
Industrial crops	4.2%	6.8%	5.1%
Fodder crops	11.0%	15.4%	18.4%

* exclusive fallow, horticulture and after crops

Source: based on Dejongh, 1999.

Nevertheless, by the beginning of the nineteenth century, tension was building between population increase, farm structure and production volume. In spite of yield increases, the agricultural sector in the Southern Netherlands could not keep pace with population growth. Whereas agricultural production grew at average annual rate of 0.58% between 1760 and 1850, population grew at a rate of 0.69% in the same period. However, in spite of occasional supply crises, this imminent problem did not result in a structural hunger crisis. This is related to the fact that the Southern Netherlands shifted from being a bread grain exporter to a grain importer (10 to 15% of needs in the mid-nineteenth century). Moreover, as a consequence of the enormous success of the potato, arable farming was able to keep pace with population growth (with an annual output increase of 0.74% between 1760 and 1850, against 0.30% for the livestock sector).

In the first half of the nineteenth century, soil yields rose to levels never seen before. In the middle of the nineteenth century, average bread-grain yields (also oats and barley) per hectare were 40 to 50% higher than a century before and potatoes, although a young

Table 7.3   Average arable yields in Flanders and Belgium, 1760–1850

	kg/hectare c. 1760	index c. 1760	c. 1810	c. 1850
East- and West-Flanders				
Wheat	1100	100	121	143
Rye	1050	100	123	146
Potatoes	8700	100	119	161

	kg/hectare c. 1760	index c. 1760	c. 1810	c. 1850
Belgium				
Wheat	940	100	115	144
Rye	930	100	123	141
Potatoes	7300	100	132	177

* Yields in a 'normal' year. Conversion of 1 hectolitre in kilograms: wheat 78 kg, rye 71 kg, potatoes 66 kg.

Source: based on Dejongh and Vanhaute, 1999.

crop increased even more. Thanks to this and the expansion of cultivated acreage – an additional 17% between 1760 and 1850 as a result of land reclamations and further reduction of fallow – a structural food shortage could be avoided.

Animal husbandry played a considerably smaller role in maintaining food supply. The equilibrium between animal husbandry and arable farming, the central axis in mixed farming, came under severe pressure. Because total livestock hardly increased between 1750 and 1850 (+ 3%), occupation of heads of livestock per hectare of farmland dropped from 2.4 to 2.1. Demographic growth strengthened the role of agriculture as producer of the staples: bread grains and potatoes.

However, the physical yield increase had its limits. Expressed in yield ratios (the ratio sowing seed/harvest), productivity growth in grain and potato cultivation was rather modest. A greater output was achieved by denser sowing and planting. The key to physical yield increase was a higher labour input. Labour intensification on the field – digging, manuring, weeding, etc. – explains the survival of the rural way of life up until the third quarter of the nineteenth century. Average labour input per hectare in Belgium increased by almost 50% between 1760 and 1850 (Dejongh, 1999: 256). Most likely, the physical growth of Flemish agriculture went hand in hand with a stagnating or even decreasing labour productivity. For good reason, foreign observers, surprised by the intensive cultivation of small plots of land spoke of the Flemish 'horticulture'.

It can be seen that the success of arable farming averted a structural supply crisis in Belgium in the first half of the nineteenth century. This can be related to the success of the potato crop from the middle of the eighteenth century. Because of this tuberous plant's high yields, in comparison to bread grains, the same plot of land could support twice the number of people. It is true that growing potatoes was more labour-intensive and required more fertilizer but because of the easy access to labour this was no problem.

Cultivation of the potato expanded, particularly in areas with many smallholdings and low incomes, as was the case in Flanders. The growth of potato cultivation had both a positive and negative effect: it increased the calorie yield of the land and could thus feed more people but at the same time, food became more monotonous and the fragmentation of smallholdings further increased.

Table 7.4   Potato culture in Belgium and Flanders, first half 19th century

		c. 1810	c. 1840
potato cultivation (% arable land)	Belgium	6%	14%
	Flanders	9%	16%
yields potatoes (kg /ha)	Belgium	10000	14000
	Flanders	11200	15000
production breadgrains per capita		195 kg	175 kg
production potatoes per capita		110 kg	300 kg

Notes: 1) 'normal' (pre-crisis) years (decrease of potato land 1840–1850 –17%);
2) production without import and export
Source: based on Goossens, 1993 and Gadisseur, 1990.

Around 1760, potatoes represented hardly 3% of total arable output (in production value), whereas by 1840, this had increased to almost 20%. This also meant that in terms of daily calorie consumption, from 1760 up until the potato crisis the bread grain to potato ratio shifted from 9: 1 to 6: 4 respectively. Average potato consumption of a Belgian adult round 1840 was 1 to 1.5 kg per day. In many Flemish villages, it was more.[2]

In Belgium, the number of people employed in agriculture reached an all-time high in the mid-nineteenth century. Between 1750 and 1850, the agricultural population (those who worked in agriculture on a full-time or part-time basis) increased by two thirds, to over 1.2 million (Segers, 2003: 14–17). This was the consequence of a further recourse to small-scale subsistence agriculture related to the lack of alternative means to make a living. Nevertheless, this increase was smaller than general population growth, so that the proportion of the population employed in agriculture (full-time or mainly) fell from approximately 65% to 55% in this period. Taking into account part-time labour, this still meant that in the middle of the nineteenth century, two thirds of all Belgian families (urban families included) depended to a greater or lesser extent on an agricultural income. However, hardly one in three families (20 to 25% of total population) could live on agriculture. The other households were forced to supplement their agricultural income with other earnings.

---

[2] According to Gadisseur's calculations (1990: 670–682), in the 1840s only half of the total potato production was meant for human consumption, which would mean average daily human consumption was about 0.4–0.5 kg per person (total Belgian population). In these calculations a large part of the harvest (up to 50%) was used as pig feed (about 4 kg per day per adult pig). We estimate per capita consumption at 0.6-0.7 kg per person per day. Consumption figures in Flanders were 50% higher than average for humans and 100% higher for pigs. See also *Exposé de la Situation du Royaume. Titre IV*: 56–58.

These developments meant that Belgian rural society became characterised by increasing differentiation and polarization. In the most densely populated regions of the country, Flanders and the western part of Brabant, 40 to 50% of the farms were less than one hectare, and 80 to 85% less than five hectares. Typical holding size fluctuated between one and two hectares (Vanhaute, 2001). During the eighteenth and nineteenth centuries, land fragmentation increased, due to the combination of partible inheritance, increasing debt among peasants, severe population pressure and the introduction of the potato. As a consequence, the need for income from other sources increased further.

In addition, land and farms increasingly had to be rented. In Inner Flanders in the second half of the eighteenth century, two out of three farms were cultivated on lease. Increasing land competition increased the rents. Whereas in the mid-eighteenth century the annual rent of a hectare of arable land was the equivalent of thirty times the daily wage, by the turn of the century this price had doubled and by 1850 it had tripled.

Higher rents became the major cause of mounting debts within the peasant population. Increases in productivity were skimmed off by landowners. It is no accident that the prices increased the most in regions where farm-fragmentation was greatest, leasing was dominant, and cottage industry was widespread. These areas also saw accelerated commercialization of rural life (many small and regional markets) and the revival of small and medium-sized cities. However, these changes were not just the consequence of rural society's internal dynamics. Another reason was that there was a growing (sub)urban bourgeoisie that profited from rising flows of money from the productive countryside. Landowners, the bourgeoisie of big and medium-sized cities, but also traders and artisans in villages, saw their fortunes grow. This was also thanks to the increasing demand for credit, so part of the rents was ploughed back into agriculture in the form of loans. Farmers contracted huge debts in their struggle for a piece of arable or pastureland of

Figure 7.2   Areas of flax cultivation and linen weaving in eighteenth century Flanders

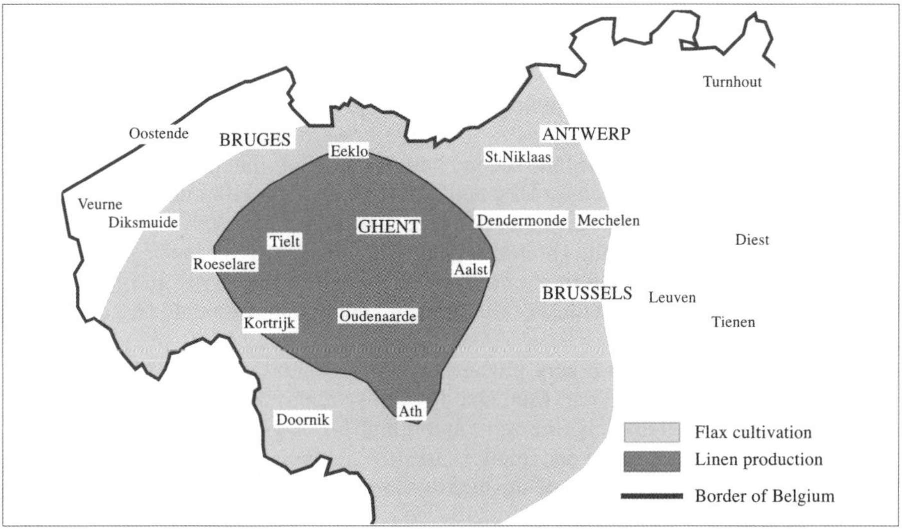

Source: Thoen, 2001: 120.

129

their own. Proto-industrial expansion probably increased the demand for credit in the villages. Creditors used their position to appropriate properties under debt.

The Flemish peasants responded to this increased financial pressure by working even harder on the land, and augmenting their income at the spinning wheel and the loom. In the first half of the nineteenth century, a quarter to half of the population of Inner Flanders worked in the rural flax and linen industry. Until the 1840s, 300,000 to 400,000 villagers earned extra income in this proto-industrial labour. Decreasing yarn and cloth prices from the 1820s, however, increased pressure on the Flemish peasants' income. By the 1830s, one out of every five Flemish families was registered as indigent.

Because of the (unequal) labour, credit and lease relationships, the greatest part of the surpluses produced by household farming were drained away. The Flemish peasant economy was thus responsible for a large part of the 'national' economic growth. However, a high social price was paid for this growth and by the middle of the nineteenth century, the impoverishment of the countryside was clearly apparent. The village economies were unable to support the population growth that occurred from 1750 on, and eventually the agricultural system reached its limits in the middle of the nineteenth century.

III. The subsistence crisis of 1845–1850

III.1. An agricultural crisis

The direct cause of the mid-19th century subsistence crisis in Europe was the failure of potato harvests in the years 1845–1850. Compared to other countries, the Belgian potato fields were affected much earlier (from mid-July 1845) by the potato blight, phytophthora infestans (Bourke, 1964; Solar, 1997). The potato blight meant that 87% of harvests were lost and in Flanders, the epicentre of the potato disease, losses mounted up to 95% of the crop. To make matters worse, more potatoes than normal had been planted to make up for the disappointing yield of winter crops such as wheat and coleseed that had been affected by the severe winter of 1844–1845. Over the following years, harvests were also poor because fewer potato seedlings were planted. In the years from 1846 until 1850 (with the exception of 1849), the harvests were only 40 to 60% of what they 'normally' were. It was not until the second half of the 1850s that pre-crisis yields were achieved again. In the provinces of East and West Flanders, the situation was even more distressing. In 1846, the acreage under potatoes was reduced by 30% and this was still 23% in 1850. It was not until the 1860s that pre-crisis acreage was reached again. Physical yields remained well below normal until the second half of the 1850s. In Flanders between 1846 and 1850 barely a third of the 'normal' potato harvest could be gathered in.

The food situation became very precarious late 1846 and in the first half of 1847, because of poor bread-grain harvests. Due to bad weather conditions in 1846, the rye harvest fell by more than half (the most important bread grain by far), although the losses for wheat and maslin were smaller (10%). Calculated in grain equivalents, the combined loss of bread-grain and potato harvests in 1846 was 66% (calculation according to contemporaries: Jacquemyns, 1929: 258–259). This meant that there were only 125 litres of grain equivalents (bread grains and potatoes) available per head, compared to

Table 7.5   Average yields and acreage of potatoes in Belgium and Flanders, 1840–1854

| | Yields – kg/hectare | | Acreage – hectare | |
	Belgium	Flanders	Belgium	Flanders
'normal year' (1840–1844)	14,000	15,000	164,000	56,200
1845	600–1,300	600–1,200		
1846	10,700	6,000–8,000	123,000	38,800
1847	10,700	6,500	126,000	39,900
1848	7,600	5,000–6,500	130,000	41,100
1849	13,800	9,500	134,000	42,200
1850	6,800	5,500–7,000	137,000	43,400
1851–1854	7,000–10,000	7,000–12,000		

Source: based on Gadisseur, 1990: 292, 406, 536; Jacquemyns: 1929: 255.

375 litres in previous years. Because all harvests in that year were affected (half the bean and pea harvests were lost too), the threat of famine loomed. Luckily, the bumper grain harvests of 1847 and the reasonable harvests in subsequent years reduced the threat of famine.

Soon after the potato disease broke out, the national government stopped food exports. In addition bread grains, and to a limited extent, potatoes were imported. Bread grain imports increased from 25.8 kg per capita in 1845 to 38.4 kg in 1846 and 32.4 kg in 1847 (Degrève, 1982).[3] Imports of (seed) potato and other vegetables (8 kg per person per year in 1846–1847), rice (3 kg per person per year) and various types of flour (1.5 kg per person per year) were much more limited. These imports made up for approximately one third of the grain deficit.

The insidious impoverishment process meant that the average Belgian's diet fell from about 2850 Kcal per day around 1800 to about 2450 Kcal in the 1840s.[4] The differences between rich and poor also increased markedly. About the middle of the century, labourers in the cities and the countryside had hardly 2000 Kcal a day to live on. Their diet was based mainly on potatoes (average 0.8 to 1 kg per day), bread grains (0.5 to 0.7 kg per day) and buttermilk (0.75 litres per day).

This diet was impoverished even further by the poor harvests in the years 1845–1847, although people tried to supplement this with turnips and carrots. Scarcity inflated market prices as can be seen in Figure 7.4 which shows average annual market prices in

---

[3] Total amount of food imports in Belgium increased from 90.46 million Belgian Francs in 1841–1845 to 104.89 million Belgian Francs in 1846–1850. Imports from France grew fastest in these crisis years. Imports from the Netherlands, Prussia and the United States grew also considerably (*Exposé de la Situation du Royaume, Titre IV*: 157–158).

[4] Segers, 2003: 255–273. National consumption data, derived from estimates of production, import, export etc. (figures for 1800 based on Vandenbroeke, 1975: 593). The diet includes bread, potatoes, buckwheat, meat, butter, fish, vegetables, sugar, buttermilk, beer etc.

131

Figure 7.3 Import and export of breadgrains, Belgium 1840–1855 (metric tons)

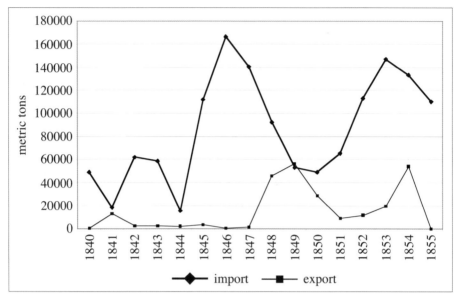

Figure 7.4 Market prices of wheat, rye and potatoes, Belgium 1831–1860 (Belgian francs/100 kg)

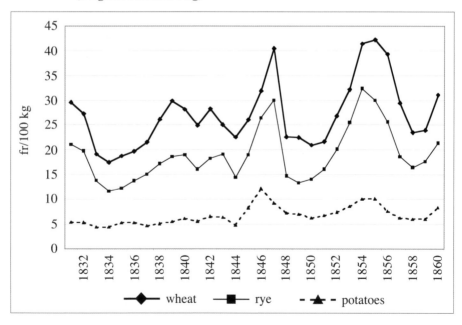

Belgium in 1831–1860 (Gadisseur, 1990: 756–760). Prices reached a peak in the spring of 1847, after the partial failure of grain harvests. In the spring of 1847, potatoes were sold at 3.5 times the 1844 level. Rye cost 2.4 times as much as in 1844 and wheat cost twice as much. Rice was 3 times as expensive while peas and beans were 1.8 times as expensive as in 1844. Prices for meat and diary produce increased far less over the same period: butter by 1.5, pork by 1.3 and beef by 1.1 times (Sabbe, 1975: 493).

The increase in livestock numbers slowed down after the crisis years, and sometimes halted completely. Between 1846 and 1856, in Belgium cattle rose by 4%, but the number of horses (–6%) and pigs (–8%) dropped. In 1856, in Flanders there were 13% fewer pigs. This was probably directly related to the lack of fodder caused by the potato blight. A striking feature is the increase in the number of goats (30% in the same period). Goats have been considered as the 'poor people's cows'.

III.2. A proto-industrial crisis

A crisis in the rural flax industry coincided with the subsistence crisis of 1845–1847. Up until then, this industry had provided tens of thousands Flemish families with crucial additional income. Labour participation in the Flemish linen industry was still rising during the first decades of the nineteenth century, and reached more than 300,000 women and men. In the Inner Flanders' textile regions, at least half of the labour force worked part-time (Gubin, 1983). Flemish flax processing lost the commercial battle against mechanized cotton and linen production. The most important destination of Flemish linen was the foreign market but export levels fell from 4.5 million kg in 1835 to less than 2 million kg in 1848 and later, even though the price of linen cloth was halved (Jacquemyns, 1929: 14, 163).

The only way merchant-entrepreneurs could reduce their losses was to cut wages and reduce the quality of their goods. In consequence, the real income of spinners and weavers went into free fall. By 1850, a weaver's daily wage would buy him less than 3.5 kilograms of rye, whereas in 1750 the daily wage was worth four times this amount.

The national government tried to help the ailing flax industry by an active customs policy, promoting trade treaties, giving subsidies to *comités industriels* and by organizing model ateliers. In the 1840s, about 2.5 million Belgian Francs were spent on subsidizing and promoting the rural flax industry. These initiatives could not prevent prices (and wages) and the demand for handmade cloth going down even further. Provincial and local governments supported the same initiatives. Eventually, by about 1850, people began to acknowledge that the traditional cottage industry based on flax processing no longer had a future and entrepreneurs and governments gave up their efforts.

III.3. Disease and death

Figure 7.5 clearly highlights the crisis years of 1845–1847. It shows increased mortality and declining birth rates that resulted in negative population growth in 1847 (Devos, 2003, vol. 2: 10–11, 125). Compared to the reference years of 1841–1845, 1847 had a surplus mortality of 23,000 (+30%), and the period of three years from 1846 to 1848 had a surplus mortality of 44,000 (+15%). The number of births decreased by 47,000 during the same years (–12%). There were 17% fewer marriages.

Figure 7.5   Birth and mortality rates, Belgium 1830–1860 (promille)

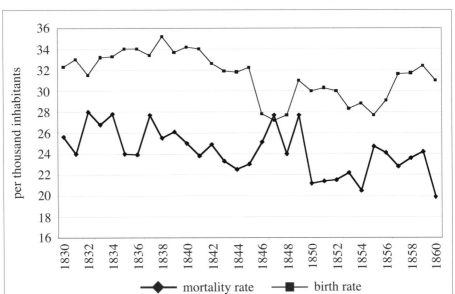

Figure 7.6   Mortality rates, East- and West-Flanders 1835–1860 (promille)

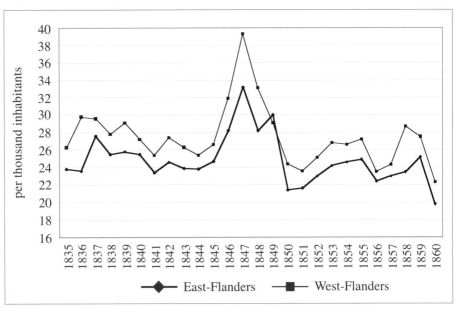

As indicated in the charts and maps of Figures 7.6 and 7.7, high mortality in 1846–1847 was limited to the geographical area of Inner-Flanders. The highest rates were found in West-Flanders in the districts of Roeselare and Tielt (47 to 53 per thousand in 1847) and the cities of Bruges (40 per thousand) and Tielt (52 per thousand). In 1847, some villages in these regions had mortality rates of higher than 80 per thousand. Total excess mortality in the two Flemish provinces was 15,000 (+40%) in 1847 and 29,500 in 1846–1848 (+27%). In the Tielt region, mortality rates of more than 100% increase were seen (Jacquemyns, 1929: 352–362). Life expectancy at birth in the Flemish regions decreased: a 32 to 35 years average in 1841–1850, against 37 years in Brabant and more than 39–40 years in the other Belgian provinces (Devos, 2003, vol. 1: 154). In the crisis years in Flanders, 18% fewer births than normal and 30% fewer marriages were registered. In the linen district, the declines were 30% and 40%, respectively.

Most deaths were a consequence of nutrition-related diseases, such as dysentery and typhus. In 1846–1848, typhus was registered in half of the Flemish municipalities (46,000

Figure 7.7   Mortality rates in Belgian communities, 1846–1847 (promille)

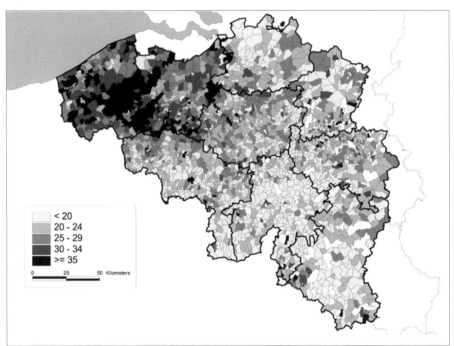

Source: *Population. Mouvement de l'état civil 1841–1850* (Mortality figures 1846 and 1847); *Recensement général de la population de 15 octobre 1846* (Population figures 1846).

registered sick persons and 10,000 registered deaths). From 1848 through to 1849, a cholera epidemic took hold resulting in 5,900 registered deaths in Flanders (in Belgium 22,400 deaths). Striking differences in local mortality rates were seen, reflecting the impact of local outbreaks of dysentery or typhus. Mortality increases in the years 1846–1847 were mainly seen in the adult population. The share of the 16–65 year age-group in rural mortality in East- and West-Flanders increased from 33% to 37% in 1845–1846 to 42% to 46% in 1847–1848. In the autumn of 1847, half of all deaths were in this age-group (whereas it would have been normal if this was a third: Devos, 2002, vol. 1: 84 and vol. 2: 198-203). Moreover, excess mortality affected more men than women (proportion of 54 to 46 respectively in the spring of 1847).

The general health of the population can be assessed by looking at how tall people are. In the crisis years 1845–1847, more than a quarter of male army recruits were shorter than 1.57 metres whereas after 1850 this was less than a fifth. At the beginning of the nineteenth century, the average height of men was 1.66 metres but after the crisis years, in 1850, this had dropped to 1.62 metres. In Southwest-Flanders, men were on average another 3 to 4 cm shorter (Devos, 2003: 160–164, 171).

A huge surge of emigration failed to materialize. According to official statistics at the time, nearly 14,000 Flemish citizens left to go to foreign countries in the period between 1845–1850. Internal migration was also minimal and there was no massive flight from the rural areas to the city. Villages in East- and West-Flanders lost on balance approximately 20,000 inhabitants during these years. The only industrial city, Ghent, grew by just under 9,000 inhabitants. In total, the provinces of West- and East-Flanders lost, respectively, 1.3% and 4.5% of their population in the years 1844–1848. In the linen producing districts, this was 4% to 9%.

III.4.   Criminality and unrest

Criminal statistics for the 1845–1850 crisis years show some remarkable tendencies.[5] First of all, the number of cases and charges appearing before the criminal court (*Tribunaux correctionnels*) strongly increased. In the period from 1840 to 1844, approximately 17,000 to 19,000 cases involving an average of 26,500 suspects were handled per year. By 1847, this had increased to 32,894 cases involving 38,235 suspects, i.e. an increase of almost 50%. The biggest increase in charges concerned mendicancy (9 times higher in 1847, compared to 1840–1841) and vagrancy (3 times higher), petty theft (3 times higher), trespassing on public woods and land (2.5 times higher) and pillage (*et autres délits ruraux*) (3.5 times higher). On the other hand, the number of cases of physical violence decreased. The profile of suspects also changed. At the beginning of the 1840s, 19% of suspects were female, and 11% were under sixteen. In the years from 1846 to 1848, a quarter of the suspects were female and 20% at least were under sixteen. Women and children were mainly charged for mendicancy (31% of suspects were women, 22% were children under sixteen), entering public woods and lands (28% women), insulting behaviour (33% women), petty theft (25% to 30% women, 13% children) and stealing crops at night (50% women, 20% children).[6] The total number of children in Belgian confined in prisons and *dépôts de mendicité* rose from 4,400 in 1845, through 8,800 in

---

[5]   All statistics are taken from *Exposé de la situation du Royaume, Titre 3*.
[6]   Averages for 1841–1849; no yearly figures are available.

1846 to 13,000 in 1847. In Belgium, over the years from 1845 to 1847, some 26,000 children were temporarily interned.

In addition, the number of convictions increased. At the beginning of the 1840s, an average of 78% of suspects was actually sentenced (of which 48% were imprisoned), but by the period from 1846 to 1849 this had risen to 85% (two thirds actually went to prison). Mendicancy (91% sentences, compared to 77% in 1840), theft (82% against 71%) and pillage (69% against 41%) were more severely dealt with. The number of people sentenced to prison remained around 10,000 before the crisis years. This increased to 20,787 in 1846 and 28,348 in 1847, and then fell again.

The number of cases and charges before police courts (*Tribunaux de simple police*) also rose, from 14,400 in 1840–1841 until almost 23,500 in 1847. Remarkable was the rise in cases against common prostitutes or '*filles publiques*' (7 times higher than in 1840), and against those who grazed their livestock on other people's land and blocked public roads (2 times higher).

All this information seems to indicate that governments and possibly ordinary citizens were less tolerant in this period. This view is supported by an increase in the number of police by-laws, rising from approximately 200 per year before 1844 up to 1,116 in 1846 and 1,374 in 1847. Police statistics also show a striking increase in the number of fires and deaths by drowning during the 1846–1847s.

Finally, the number of Crown Court cases (*Cours d'assises*) increased from approximately 375 per year in 1840–1845 to 616 in 1846 and 579 in 1847. This was a consequence of twice as many cases of nocturnal theft (with aggravating circumstances) and damage to property.

In East- and West-Flanders, the number of arrested and convicted persons rose by 160% and 250%, respectively, between 1841 and 1847 (Jacquemyns, 1929: 331). Most of them were arrested for minor offences, and detained only for a short period. The population of the prisons (*les maisons centrales*) rose by 25% between the early 1840s and 1847 while in the local arrest houses (*maisons de sureté et d'arrêt*) the number of prisoners doubled.

There was also a sharp increase in the numbers of beggars who often 'worked' in groups. In the winter of 1846–1847, the Bruges police arrested 6,000 beggars. They were mostly sent back to their own villages but some were confined in the *dépôts de mendicité*.[7] In the five years from 1845 to 1850, all rural villages set up their own safety measures such as night patrols and field watches. We could only find scattered evidence of collective food riots in the spring of 1847, mostly in cities (Bruges, Kortrijk, Ronse, Ghent). There is one record of a grain ship being looted near Ghent. Plans for a hunger march in April 1846 were aborted prematurely.

III.5. National and local authorities

In 1834, Belgian Parliament approved a system of sliding import duties on grains. The lower the internal prices, the higher import duty would be and the higher the internal prices, the lower the import duty. Emphasis was on protection of the own markets and

---

[7] In the 1840s, Belgium had *dépôts* which had the capacity to provide 4,000 to 5,000 people with relief from poverty. In the 1830s, these institutions helped a little under 2,000 people. This increased to 3,000–4,000 at the beginning of the 1840s and to 10,000 in 1847. By 1850, the number went down again to 4,500.

on controlling the price level of basic foodstuffs. The reaction of the central government to the harvest failures of 1845 and 1846 completely fits in with this 'traditional' policy.

The government reacted quickly. In September of 1845, the Belgian government already proclaimed the import of grains, potatoes and other foodstuffs would be duty free and at the same time prohibited the export of, for example, bread or biscuits. These laws were extended until the beginning of 1850. Moreover, the government bought food from foreign countries. For example, in the spring of 1846, a 100,000 Belgian Francs credit was used to buy 5.5 million kg of seed potatoes. As stated earlier, these measures had a favourable effect on imports. Another policy was to support local governments financially, e.g. to support the rural flax industry. In the years 1845–1847, national government allotted 4.8 million Belgian Francs to this. Most of it went to the two Flemish provinces (approximately 3 million Belgian Francs). In addition, the creation of industrial aid committees and working schools was supported.

In the third place, funds were allotted to subsidize public works (in co-operation with the town councils on a 50/50 basis). In the 1840s, various government bodies (including town councils) spent 14.7 million Belgian Francs on public works in the two Flemish provinces, compared to 3.9 million Belgian Francs during the previous decade. According to their own calculations, central government spent 8 million Belgian Francs to alleviate problems during the crisis of the 1845–1850s.[8] Finally, projects for land reclamation and drainage were stimulated. The reclamation law of March 1847 forced all the municipalities to sell their uncultivated land and reintroduced tax exemption for newly cultivated land. However, this did not have any effect in the short term. Other initiatives such as colonization came to nothing and the same went for plans to stimulate overseas emigration.

The shocks of the complex societal crisis were mostly absorbed within the village communities themselves. As soon as it became clear that the harvest was going to fail, these village communities responded immediately. They increased poor relief and financed initiatives to create additional jobs (public works, purchase and sales offices for flax, linen yarn and cloth, work-houses, lace-ateliers) and the local elites organised food handouts. Order became an issue and local patrols and night watches maintained the 'social' peace and tried to stop the itinerant poor from entering the village.

The main policy instruments were the local institutions of poor relief. In Belgium, relief policy was locally co-ordinated. The logic of the relief system was to provide assistance as much and as long as possible within the (official) municipality of domicile. Each municipality had, as made compulsory by Communal Law, its own local relief institution (*bureaux de bienfaisance*, in bigger cities also *hôpitaux*). The poor relief institutions were administered by a council, which was made up of the local elite.

These poor relief institutions were financed by their own resources (movable and immovable possessions) and, increasingly by municipal authorities. Municipalities had

---

[8] That is about 1.8 Belgian Francs per inhabitant. Total expenses of the central government in the 1840s ran up to 120–130 million Belgian Francs per year. In the period from 1845 to 1847 central accounting registered a deficit of 27 million Belgian Francs, resulting especially from decrease in income (*Exposé de la situation du Royaume, Titre III*: 679. *'Dépenses resultant des mesures prises à l'égard de la crise alimentaire de 1846–1848 et de la crise industrielle des Flandres'*).

the right to (and did) collect separate taxes intended for poor relief administration (cities: *octrois*). The institutions rarely received (as in the 1846–1847s) financial support from the national government. There was only one central workhouse for the two provinces of Flanders (located in Bruges). The maximum capacity was about 500 to 600 persons. In the period between 1845 and 1849, some 10,800 men, women and children were given assistance.

The city of Bruges is a good example of the central role of the local *bureau de bienfaisance*. In the winter of 1846–1847, 247,000 litres of soup, 250,000 kg of coal, 64,000 Belgian Francs worth of bread coupons (for cheap bread) and 40,000 Belgian Francs of direct financial support were distributed among the registered poor. In 1847, 142,500 Belgian Francs were spent to support 21,532 inhabitants, which constituted nearly half of the population. The city of Ghent spent about the same amount on bread coupons and subsidizing grain prices.

Table 7.6   Number of registered poor, supported by local poor institutions, 1844–1850 (% of total population)

	East-Flanders	West-Flanders
1844	14.5%	26.7%
1845	21.6%	32.5%
1846	28.2%	35.4%
1847	29.5%	36.8%
1848	26.9%	34.1%
1849	25.5%	31.2%
1850	23.4%	27.3%

Source: Vermeersch, 2003: 126-127.

The number of registered poor in Flanders, already high, rose sharply in the crisis years. In 1847, some linen-producing regions and some cities (Bruges, Kortrijk), 40% of the population was registered poor. The assistance given to the poor was not consistent. Only 14% received support all year round, 22% were supported for more than half of the year, but the rest only for less than half a year. In West-Flanders, total expenditure by municipal relief institutions in 1846–1849 ran up to 9.15 million Belgian Francs, more than the total relief sum of the central government. Only a minor part of these huge costs could be paid for from the institutions' own resources. The remainder came from additional support from the local community and, to a much lesser extent, central government, from the sale of properties and from fund raising actions. In the crisis years the poor institutions were virtually bankrupt and were only able to keep running because of massive subsidies and private initiatives organised by the local elites and the Church. A local private committee in support of the poor relief of Bruges managed to raise 130,000 Belgian Francs in 1847, of which 50,000 outside Flanders. A begging trip from the curate of Tielt to the industrial city of Liège brought in 15,498 Francs for the local poor fund. Nonetheless, it seems that local traditions of raising funds for the poor came under pressure in the crisis years. The shortfall was compensated for through more forceful fund raising by local authorities (e.g. higher local taxes) and the Catholic Church.

III.6. After the crisis

Towards the middle of the nineteenth century, 'traditional' Belgian agriculture reached the limit of its capacity. The combination of population growth, land fragmentation and high rent debts demanded higher physical yields and greater income differentiation. This entailed increase in labour input, the refinement of crop rotation schemes, the introduction of new crops like potatoes, and sufficient spreading of economic risks. To this we should add the combination of production for private consumption and for the market, of agricultural income and income from non-agrarian activities, of independent labour in the own holding and labour exchange with bigger farms in and outside the village.

The double crisis of the 1840s (subsistence and industrial) demonstrates that the balance within the rural survival model was lost. Already precarious family incomes were threatened even further and community relations in Flemish villages came under pressure. A massive social crisis was averted in the 1845–1847 hunger years because of a combination of four elements:

– the partial alleviation of food shortages and the speedy restoration of grain supply after the summer of 1847;

– the use of land even if small and under lease at a gradually increasing price;

– the resilient village society, with local elites who were able to relieve the most urgent distress of the poor;

– support from central, provincial and especially local governments, which not only provided concrete help but in doing so acknowledged the seriousness of the crisis.

Although the crisis was averted, Flemish agriculture ended up in a dead-end situation by the middle of the nineteenth century. This was the result of an unfortunate combination of a further parcelling out of agricultural land and farms, a further fragmentation of landownership, an increasing amount of (small to very small) leasehold farms and ever-increasing rents. This negative spiral had agriculture in its hold for several more decades. The double land competition between tenants and between landowners further increased purchase and lease prices of rural property. It became clear that this rural survival model was doomed. Age-old processes of land fragmentation and loss of property on the countryside were brought to a climax after 1850. The rapid growth of registered agricultural holdings mainly made up of the category of micro-holdings: i.e. smaller than one hectare. Micro-holdings more than doubled between 1846 and 1880. By 1880, 51% of all holdings were even less than half a hectare, compared to 43% in 1850.

IV. Why Flanders did not starve: a comparison with Ireland [9]

'No country on the face of the earth presents so worthy an example to Ireland as Belgium.(…)
Like Belgium we have the small farming system to a great extent, with an abundance of hands to
cultivate minutely; but we are ignorant, indolent, and careless, idle and poor.' (Thomas Skilling,
The Science and Practice of Agriculture, Dublin, 1846: 39).

1.   Both regions were characterized by a dominant rural/agrarian peasant economy,
based on small to very small holdings (both in Flanders and Ireland the big majority –
two thirds to three quarters – of the holdings were smaller than two hectares). In both
societies, agriculture was based on a high labour input on small plots of land, together
with a low, and even decreasing labour productivity.

The significant growth acceleration within these economies after 1750 went hand in
hand with a rapid population increase. Between 1800 and 1845, the population increased
by 60% in Ireland and by 40% in Flanders, almost exclusively in the countryside. Both
regions were marked by a high population density (certainly per hectare of arable land)
and by an extreme fragmentation of the holdings. In spite of the impressive economic
and demographic growth rates, both regions were very much impoverished at the
beginning of the 1840s, mainly because of the deteriorating income position of both
tenant farmers and wage labourers. This generated a rapid polarisation in both societies,
and a growing group that was very vulnerable to (periodical) food shortages.

So, both regions were in a structural decline since the end of the eighteenth and early
nineteenth centuries. In both regions, more families than ever depended on different and
uncertain forms of wage labour (Flanders: cottage industry, Ireland: farm labour, migrant
labour; proto-industrial activities in Ireland disappeared already in the early nineteenth
century). Already in the 1830s, about one third of the Irish population was evaluated as
poor (Poor Inquiry 1835). In Flanders, about one-fifth received some kind of poor relief.
From the 1830s, the downward trend of both nominal and real wages intensified.

It seems that the vulnerability of rural society was lower in Flanders. Here, economic
growth after 1750 was based on the increasing intensification of the 'Flemish husbandry',
in combination with the vast expansion of rural flax and linen industry. Growth within
the Irish rural economy was much more export-dependent, less embedded in a village
economy (Ireland provided 80% of the total British grain imports in the 1830s). This is
illustrated by the massive Irish emigration movement, which started already decades
before the Famine (about 1.5 million people in 1801–1845). In the words of Donnelly:
'Altogether, then, it seems reasonable to conclude that though Ireland was certainly not
careering towards economic and social disaster in the decades before 1845, about half
of the population were victims of some degree of immiseration and stood dangerously
exposed to a foreign and devastating plant disease' (Donnelly, 2001: 11).

2.   Both regions can be considered as 'peripheral' within the context of the own nation-
state. The big difference is that Flanders was, also literally, closer to the centre of political
(state) power. Flemish (elite-conservative) interests were defended more successfully
in Brussels. These interests aimed at the survival of the Flemish village economy, and its

---

[9]   Information on Ireland is based on Ó Gráda (1999), Donnelly (2001), Vermeersch (2003), the
articles of Ó Gráda and Daly in this volume, and the literature mentioned in these publications.

built-in power relations. Examples are the support of the rural linen industries until 1850 and the respect for local autonomy. Within the Belgian quasi-democracy, regional and even local elites were able to find their way to defend their interests (representation on munici-pality, province or state level). All tendencies in favour of centralisation could be resisted.

In London, Irish interests were severely underrepresented (in 1805, after The Act of Union, Ireland was appointed 105 seats of a total of 658 in the British House of Commons, although it had about 40% of the total population of the Union). The Irish representatives mainly came from the class of Anglo-Irish landlords, largely disconnected from the former Irish village economy. Although some efforts were made to restructure the Irish society before 1845, in the eyes of the authorities in London, the Irish famine was predominantly a local problem. This was 'undeniably the source of the problem: the refusal of the British government to treat Ireland as part of the United Kingdom and its famine as an imperial responsibility' (Donnelly, 2001: 25).

3.   In contrast with Ireland, the Belgian administrative structure was based on small municipalities (communes). They had a high degree of local autonomy, and their own elected or appointed councils (municipality, poor relief, Church). This guaranteed a strong power position of the local elites, protected by an elitarian ballot system. Three levels of intermediary administrative structures (cantons, arrondissements, provinces) streamlined the links between the municipality and the national state. Around 1850, the two provinces of Flanders counted 515 municipalities, with an average of 2785 inhabitants (cities included).

Nineteenth-century Ireland under British rule was marked by a further tendency towards centralisation (e.g. police force, poor relief, education). The administrative structure was based on counties (with an average population number of 265,000) and, from 1838 in the case of poor relief, poor law unions. These institutions controlled administration, police, public works, poor relief, etc.

4.   In the first half of the nineteenth century, both Irish and Flemish rural societies strongly depended on the potato. The success of the potato in both regions was related to population increase, further fragmentation of smallholdings, and increasing poverty and social polarisation. But, there were also big differences between the social agro-systems. As explained earlier, the Flemish farming system was successful in two ways: a high agricultural productivity and high rents. This yielded the paradox of a rich agri-culture and poor farmers. This was an extremely resilient farming system, with a high degree of crop variation, even on the smallest plots of land, and with high (physical) yields. Nevertheless, the population increase entailed the increasing cultivation and consumption of potatoes. Still, the dependence on the potato was significantly lower than in Ireland. Grain consumption was still high, and alternatives as vegetables, carrots, and turnips were available. Moreover, in the nineteenth century, a tradition of importing grain was built up. Grain imports rose almost tenfold in the 1840s. In general, Flemish agriculture was considered as more efficient and more productive than Irish farming. In the 1850s, the Belgian agronomist De Laveleye claimed that 1,000 farmers in East Flanders could feed more than 4,000 people, whereas the Irish figure was only 1,000 to 1,500. This probably exaggerates the gap between the two agricultures. On the eve of the famine, Irish agriculture was rather successful. It could feed about 10 million people, of which 8 to 8.5 in Ireland and the remainder via exports in Britain.

Above all, potato cultivation was extremely successful in Ireland. Only 50% of the harvest was destined for human consumption, 30% for animal consumption. Nevertheless, about one-third of the population relied predominantly (and more than half heavily) on the potato. Consumption figures were extremely high: up to 5 to 6 kg a day per adult worker in the lowest classes and 3 kg per capita a day in the lower middle classes. Market (grain) agriculture was oriented towards export to Britain. Commercial farmers were dependent on external markets and prices.

5. Obviously, the crisis of 1845–1850 hit the Irish society much harder than the Flemish. In Ireland, the first attack of phytophthora infestans in 1845 was much weaker than in Flanders. Then potato production fell back from 68% (of a normal, pre-crisis harvest) in 1845 to 20% in 1846 and 14% in 1847. After 1845, the Irish potato harvests met only one-third of the minimum standard for human consumption. Prices went up as from the winter of 1845–1846. Substitute foods (grain, maize) were insufficient to prevent a large part of the population from starvation. In Ireland, mortality rates rose by 330% between 1844 and 1847, whereas in Flanders the rise was only 40% on average. The extreme excess mortality continued from 1847 to 1850. The total excess death rate is estimated at 1 million, the number of averted births at about 0.5 million.

According to Peter Solar's calculations, domestic food supply fell back by 38% during the crisis years. Thanks to rising imports, total consumption in Ireland in the years 1846–1850 was only 12% less than in 1840–1845 (Solar, 1989). Mass starvation was mainly triggered by the unequal availability of food, the lack of purchasing power and the devastating effects of epidemic diseases (typhus, relapsing fever, dysentery and, also, smallpox and cholera).

The Famine prompted mass emigration to Great Britain, United States, Canada and Australia. Between 1845 and 1855, about 2.1 million Irish men, women and children left the island (of which 1.5 million to the United States). Only a small portion (5%) of this mass movement consisted of assisted migration (paid by government or private funds). In 1851, 6.5 million Irish lived in Ireland, about 2 million Irish abroad.

Harvest failures in Flanders were severe in 1845 (potatoes) and 1846 (potatoes and bread grains). In 1846, the shortage of bread grains and potatoes is calculated to be 50% (harvest failures minus imports). From the summer of 1847 onwards, the situation improved, but potato harvests remained uncertain until well into the 1850s. Some abundant grain harvests after 1846 and a (temporary) increased import of grain secured the markets for bread cereals. Hunger or food uncertainty was no longer an issue in Belgium after the summer of 1847. Mass migration was never a realistic option in Belgium/Flanders (although the Belgian government supported some experiments).

6. The Belgian and the British state had a different response to the food crisis, partly explained by the different impact of the famine (see also Gray, 1997 and Gray, this volume). As told, the Belgian government had a rather quick and differentiated reaction to the outbreak of the potato blight. She regulated import and export and adjusted customs policy, subsidised local authorities, poor administrations, industrial committees and public works, and organised or stimulated repression when local networks failed (workhouses, prisons).

The British response to the Irish crisis was very diverse and very incoherent. At the outset, it relied on the initiatives of local relief committees, the promotion of food imports (maize) and the distribution of food through specially created depots. Later on in late 1846 and early 1847, the main emphasis switched to massive public works (with a maximum of 700,000 people involved) and, after this experiment was aborted, on soup kitchens. In June and July 1847, a maximum of more than three million persons per day were provided with relief. The soup kitchen scheme was terminated in September 1847. After that, the government relied mainly on the poor law system based on centralised workhouses. Besides, an adaptation of the poor law drastically reduced the relief entitlements of rural smallholders.

The total sum of British relief expenditure in the years 1845–1850 was £8.1 million (204 million Belgian Francs), of which £4.5 million were loans, to be paid back by Irish taxpayers. So, aid was designed to place the heaviest burden on the local, i.e. Irish, taxpayers. Due to deferred and cancelled payments, the total effort of British treasury can be evaluated at £7 million (177 million Belgian Francs; about 6.4 Belgian Francs per inhabitant). British authorities put the responsibility of the famine on Irish land-lords, who should bear the consequences. At the same time, they saw the crisis as an opportunity to restructure rural Ireland in the image of the English countryside.

The overall opinion is that British policy was characterized by a complete misjudge-ment of the nature and the extension of the crisis. An active food provision policy (imports, distribution, soup kitchens) was not maintained in the worst years. Public works were organised in extreme bad working and weather conditions. The workhouses were heavily overcrowded. Perforce, outside relief (soup kitchens) was re-introduced in 1848, serving meagre meals to more than 800,000 people. All by all, the impact of the disaster was too overwhelming, the ideology of the free market too deeply rooted in the London elite and the financial basis too weak (workhouses went even bankrupt), to have a public initiative that could do more than work in the margins. Peter Gray evaluated this policy as a 'culpable neglect of the consequences of policies leading to mass starva-tion' (Gray, 1999).

7. As stated before, the main shocks of the Flemish food and industrial crisis were absorbed by existing local economic and social networks. We pointed to the active policy of the different local and regional administrations, to the wide discretion left to local administrators (adjusting poor relief policy and control systems to local needs), to the local controls on petty criminality (e.g. local night patrols, locally organised police forces), migration and mobility, beggars and strangers, and the effects of epidemic diseases.

This local autonomy was actively supported and controlled by an energetic provincial administration (run by representatives of the local communities). The main lever in this decentralised policy were the institutions of poor relief, dominated by the local elites and Church representatives, and key element in the control system within village society.

Since the reform of 1838, the Irish Poor Law was based on the British system of workhouses. The New Poor Law of 1847 further centralised the relief system. Ireland with its more than eight million inhabitants was subdivided in 130 Poor Law Unions, containing an average of over 60,000 persons. The logic of the relief system was institutionalised indoor relief. Aid distribution outside the workhouses for non-structural poor (able to work) was abolished. The initial capacity of the workhouses (places for 100,000 people or 1.25% of the population) was increased during the crisis, but the sys-tem was never adequate to sustain 3 to 4 million poor.

8.   Local and regional elites in Flanders still had large interests in the functioning (and profits) of the rural society (property, trade, subcontracting). In the middle of the nineteenth century, they were still powerful enough (although only for a short time to come) to redirect national policies towards their interests. In general, political disputes (catholic/liberal) were not fought on the back of the rural society. The Catholic Church was still hegemonic in Belgian society and as such more a binding, than a dividing factor.

In Ireland, the gap between the (mainly Anglo-Irish) landlords, some of whom owned vast estates, and the villagers was much wider. Nor did these local/regional landlords have much influence on the London government and administration. Much of the land was owned by often passive or 'absentee' landlords, who did not resist an increasing land fragmentation that brought them rising rents. When the crisis struck, they sought to undo the damage through mass evictions (about 100,000 families in the crisis years).

The survival of the village economy was not a motive in the strategies of the Irish elites. They were first of all concerned about their own survival, being also beset by the British government. Catholic and Anglican clergymen were much more active. Catholic priests acted also as 'bell-ringers', or communicators about the situation in the provinces. The Catholic Church organised international relief actions. Also, some private initiatives, such as the soup kitchens organised by The Society of Friends (Quakers), were – in relative terms – impressive. However, this did not trigger co-ordinated protest against British politics.

V.   Conclusion

In a pioneering article, Peter Solar states that the impact of the blight in Ireland and in the rest of Europe 'needs to be seen through the prism of local economic and social structures' (Solar, 1997: 123). The two factors he stressed are the structures of land ownership, income and occupation, and the impact of (the crisis in) domestic manufacturing (mainly linen industry). He added two other elements: public and private relief policies and the impact of the cereal crop failures of 1846. Although several authors have stressed the differences in national public welfare and relief measures (e.g. Ó Gráda, 1999; Gray, 1997 and Gray, this volume), a more integrated analytical model as suggested by Solar is still lacking. This comparative research has to start from the regional and even local level, stressing the differences in impact of the crisis (see also Daly, this volume).

The 1840s crisis in Flanders is characterised by at least three dimensions:
1.   Flanders faced a very severe subsistence crisis in the years 1845–1847. After an almost complete loss of the potato harvest in 1845 and a very poor grain harvest in 1846, the situation at the beginning of 1847 turned out to be very uncertain. Bread grain yields returned to their normal level in 1847 and potato yields stabilized to around 50% of the level of the pre-crisis years for some time to come. This, together with higher grain imports, relieved the immediate pressure on the food supply.
2.   The 1840s witnessed the final collapse of the proto-industrial linen industry. Around 1840, about 150,000 Flemish rural families earned some (minimal) income from flax processing, spinning, and weaving. Ten years later, almost 90% of this industry

had disappeared.

3.   The tensions within the age-old agro-rural society based on a 'commercial peasant economy' brought the system at the edge during these crisis years. The system cracked, burst, was pushed to and, eventually, over its limits. In the next decades, the system further disintegrated. It became crystal-clear that it lacked the remaining power to sustain a majority of the rural population (stabilisation of the physical productivity, smaller holdings, ever higher land rents, diminishing possibilities to combine incomes etc.).

The crisis of the 1840s was and is a decisive turning point in the history of the Flemish agro-rural society. Nevertheless, even then, the social effects of the crisis were endured mostly by the disintegrating village economy.

1.   The existing peasant economy (high crop yields on extremely small holdings, as much variation in crops as possible, exchange relations within the villages and on local and regional markets) was able to guarantee a minimal and basic food supply and income for the majority of the rural population (except for one or two years).

2.   The strong position of local institutions, combined with an active interest of the local elites, guaranteed the survival of the basic social safety nets (not without severe difficulties). Their active role did avert a total breakdown of the rural society during the crisis years, but could not prevent the dissolution of the Flemish peasant society in the next decades.

'Famine is both event and structure' (Murton, 2000; Arnold 1988). Both event and structure explain the different effects of the famine of the 1840s in Flanders and Ireland. The potato disease struck Ireland later, but much harder than Flanders. On the other hand, the combined crisis in Belgium (agricultural and industrial) struck at the heart of Flemish rural society. The political response differed in both countries, but it is unlikely the nineteenth century state apparatus could do more than take care of the wounds. Most emphasis must be laid on differences in the local and regional structure of society. It is clear that the Flemish commercialised village economy, even though severely weakened after a century of increasing stress, was much more capable of absorbing the shocks of the crisis of the 1840s than the uprooted Irish society.

Bibliography

Arnold, D. (1988) *Famine. Social crisis and historical change*, Oxford.

Bourke, A. (1964) 'Emergence of potato blight, 1843–1846', *Nature*, pp. 805–808.

Degrève, D. (1982) *Le commerce extérieur de la Belgique, 1830–1913–1939. Présentation critique des données statistiques*, Brussels.

Dejongh, G. (1999) *Tussen immobiliteit en revolutie. De economische ontwikkeling van de Belgische landbouw in een eeuw van transitie, 1750–1850*, Louvain. Unpublished PhD Thesis University of Louvain.

Dejongh, G. and Vanhaute, E. (1999) 'Arable productivity in Belgian agriculture, c.1800–c.1950', in B. Van Bavel and E. Thoen (eds), *Land productivity and agro-systems in the North sea area (Middle Ages–20the century). Elements for comparison*, Turnhout, pp. 65–83. (CORN Publication Series; 2).

Dejongh, G. and Segers, Y. (2001) 'Een kleine natie in mutatie. De economische ontwikkeling van de Zuidelijke Nederlanden/België in de eeuw 1750–1850', *Tijdschrift voor Geschiedenis*, 2, pp. 171–194.

De Laveleye, E. (1863) *Essai sur l'économie rurale de la Belgique*, Paris.

Devos, I. (2003) *Allemaal beestjes. Mortaliteit en morbiditeit in Vlaanderen, 18de–20ste eeuw*, Ghent. Unpublished PhD Thesis Ghent University.

Donnelly, J.S. (2001) *The great Irish potato famine*, Phoenix Mill.

Exposé de la situation du Royaume. Période décennale de 1841–1850 (1852), Brussels.

Gadisseur, J. (1990) *Histoire quantitative et développement de la Belgique au XIXe siècle. Vol. IV, 1a: Le produit physique de la Belgique 1830–1913. Présentation critique des données statistiques. Introduction générale. Agriculture*, Brussels.

Goossens, M. (1993) *The economic development of Belgian agriculture. A regional perspective, 1812–1846*, Louvain.

Gray, P. (1997) 'Famine relief policy in comparative perspective: Ireland, Scotland, and NorthWestern Europe, 1845–1849', *Eire – Ireland*, 32, 1, pp. 86–108.

Gray, P. (1999) *Famine, land, and politics. British government and Irish society, 1843–1850*, Dublin.

Gubin, E. (1983) 'L'industrie linière à domicile dans les Flandres en 1840–1850. Problèmes de méthode', *Belgisch Tijdschrift voor Nieuwste Geschiedenis, Revue belge d'histoire belge contemporaine*, 14, pp. 369–401.

Jacquemyns, G. (1929) *Histoire de la crise économique des Flandres (1845–1850)*, Brussels.

Lambrecht, Th. (2002) *Een grote hoeve in een klein dorp. Relaties van arbeid en pacht op het Vlaamse platteland tijdens de 18de eeuw*, Ghent.

Lindemans, P. (1952) *Geschiedenis van de landbouw in België,* 2 vols, Antwerp.

Murton, B. (2000) 'Famine', in K.F. Kiple and K.C. Ornelas (eds), *The Cambridge World History of Food. Volume II*, Cambridge, pp. 1411–1427.

Ó Gráda, C. (1999) *Black '47 and beyond. The great Irish famine in history, economy, and memory*, Princeton.

Sabbe, E. (1975) *De Belgische vlasnijverheid. Deel 2. Van het Verdrag van Utrecht (1713) tot het midden van de 19de eeuw*, Kortrijk.

Segers, Y. (2003) *Economische groei en levensstandaard. Particuliere consumptie en voedselverbruik in België, 1800–1913*, Louvain.

Solar, P. (1989) 'The great famine was no ordinary subsistence crisis', in E.M. Crawford (ed.), *Famine. The Irish experience. 900–1900: subsistence crises and famines in Ireland*, Edinburgh, pp. 112–131.

Solar, P. (1997) 'The potato famine in Europe', in C. Ó Gráda (ed.), *Famine 150. Commemorative Lecture Series*, Dublin, pp. 112–127.

Thoen, E. (2001) 'A 'commercial survival economy' in evolution. The Flemish countryside and the transition to capitalism (Middle Ages–nineteenth century)', in P. Hoppenbrouwers and J.L. Van Zanden (eds), *Peasants into farmers? The transformation of rural economy and society in the Low Countries (Middle Ages – nineteenth century) in light of the*

Brenner debate, Turnhout, pp. 102–157 (CORN Publication Series; 4).

Thoen, E. (2004) ''Social agro-systems' as an economic concept to explain regional differences. An essay taking the former county of Flanders as an example (Middle-Ages–nineteenth century)', in B. Van Bavel and P. Hoppenbrouwers (eds), *Landholding and land transfer in the North Sea area (late Middle Ages – 19th century)*, Turnhout, pp. 47–66 (CORN Publication Series; 5).

Thoen, E. and Vanhaute, E. (1999) 'The "Flemish Husbandry" at the edge. The farming system on small holdings in the middle of the nineteenth century', in B. Van Bavel and E. Thoen (eds), *Land productivity and agro-systems in the North sea area (Middle Ages – 20the century). Elements for comparison*, Turnhout, pp. 271–294 (CORN Publication Series; 2).

Vandenbroeke, C. (1975) *Agriculture et alimentation*, Ghent–Louvain.

Vanhaute, E. (2001) 'Rich agriculture and poor farmers. Land, landlords and farmers in Flanders in the eighteenth and nineteenth centuries', *Rural History. Economy, Society, Culture,* 1, pp. 19–40.

Vanhaute, E. and Molle, L. Van (2004) 'Het einde van de overlevingslandbouw, 1750–1880', in Y. Segers and L. Van Molle (eds), *Leven van het land. Boeren in België 1750–2000*, Louvain, pp. 13–47.

Verhulst, A. (1990) *Précis d'histoire rural de la Belgique*, Brussels.

Vermeersch, N. (2003) *Een vergelijkende studie van de aardappelcrisis in Ierland en Vlaanderen in de periode 1845–1850*, Ghent. Unpublished MA Thesis, Ghent University.

8 The consequences of the potato disease in the Netherlands 1845–1860: a regional approach

Richard PAPING and Vincent TASSENAAR, University of Groningen

I. Introduction[1]

Being the wealthiest country of the world in the 17th and 18th century in per capita terms, the Netherlands lost this position around the mid-19th century (Maddison, 2003: 58–59). Economic growth per capita had been limited or even absent for more than a century (Van Zanden and Van Riel, 2000; Smits e.a., 2000; Wintle, 2000; Paping, 1995: 14–16; De Vries and Van der Woude, 1997). Dutch industry was relatively less technologically advanced and also trade and transport lost ground, so the highly productive agricultural sector had become the prime mover. This stagnant economy did not remain untouched by the failure of the potato harvest in 1845–1846. However, recently estimated national figures do not offer a very consistent view of these crisis years (Table 8.1).

Table 8.1 Measures of Dutch Real Gross National and Domestic Production, Income and Expenditures per capita, 1840–1860 (1840-1844 = 100)

	1840/ 1844	1845	1846	1847	1848/ 1852	1853/ 1857	1858 1860
Gross National Product	100	97	96	97	104	108	106
Gross National Income	100	106	102	100	106	96	110
Gross National Expenditures	100	90	88	88	103	102	106
Gross Domestic Product	100	98	98	99	105	108	105
Gross Domestic Income	100	107	105	102	108	96	110
Gross Domestic Expenditures	100	90	88	88	103	102	106

Source: Smits e.a., 2000: 228-229, 231-232, 234-235.

Per capita expenditures fell considerably; national production remained nearly stable, while real income developed very well in 1845 to decline somewhat in the next two years. Real income per capita did not fall below its 1840/1844 level. Interestingly, according to these figures real income did decline during the next period of exorbitant prices (1853–1857: Crimean War), while expenditures remained relatively untouched, and production was on a fairly high level. In sum, these macro figures suggest that the period of the potato blight experienced mainly a consumption crisis accompanied by

---

[1] An earlier version was presented at the workshop: *Welfare Effects of Economic Growth, and Standard of Living*, 14 May 2004, University of Groningen, The Netherlands. Among others, especially Ben Gales and Geurt Collenteur are thanked for their comments.

increasing savings of certain groups in society, while the period of the Crimean War formed more or less a real income crisis with falling savings. It has to be stressed, however, that the national figures in Table 8.1 are estimates which can be quite unreliable in the short run.

In the century before 1845 the potato conquered an important position within the Dutch diet. Some writers even characterise the Netherlands as 'the most potato-dependent country after Ireland' (Wintle, 2000: 53). In a lot of poor households the potato was even delivering the most calories, mainly carbohydrates, and vitamins. It is important to stress that the Dutch lower social classes – urban and rural labourers, cottagers, artisans and small tradesmen – were particularly dependent on the potato (Van Otterloo, 1990: 24–42). Because of this, the tremendous fall in the production of consumable potatoes, as a result of the potato disease after 1845, created a lot of misery (Terlouw, 1971; Bergman, 1967). The consequences, however, differed between regions, mainly because of the differing social-economic systems existing in the Netherlands, although the vulnerability of the soil for the potato disease was also important. We will study the differences in the short-term and mid-term consequences of the potato disease for the standard of living between the Dutch provinces using the periods 1840/1844, 1845, 1846 and 1847, 1848/1852, and 1853/1860. The period 1840/1844 (sometimes 1842/1844) describes the situation before the potato blight. Figures for 1845, 1846 and 1847 show short run effects, while the periods 1848/1852 and 1853/1860 (sometimes 1853/1856) give some insight into the long term effects, although the Crimean War is a complicating factor.

After describing in brief the social and economic characteristics of the Dutch provinces, we focus on the appearance of the potato blight and what this meant for the agricultural production. We then treat the consequences of the potato blight in five sections respectively on consumption and trade, on prices, on the biological standard of living measured by human height, on poor relief and on fertility and mortality.

II. Characteristics of the Dutch provinces

In the Netherlands, fairly huge differences between social-economic systems existed within a small territory. A very straightforward division is that between coastal and inland provinces (Van Zanden, 1985: 8–9, though Utrecht does not fit completely into this scheme). The provinces of North and South Holland formed a modern heavy urbanised region. The other coastal provinces (Groningen, Friesland, Zeeland) were less urbanised, being characterised by an extremely market-oriented capitalistic agriculture with farmers and proletarised labourers within a specialised economic system (Paping, 1995; Priester, 1991; Blauw, 1995; Priester, 1998). Agriculture was mostly directed to livestock and diary production (North Holland, most parts of Friesland, and South Holland) or to arable production (mainly in Groningen and Zeeland) for the national and international market.

The economic system of the inland provinces (Drenthe, Overijssel, Gelderland, North Brabant, Limburg, and to a lesser extent Utrecht) was in general less 'modern' and more self-contained (Bieleman, 1987; Slicher van Bath, 1957; Bieleman, 1995; Van den Eerenbeemt, 1996; Philips e.a., 1965; Knippenberg, 1995). The agriculture was by Dutch standards less capitalistic with lots of small farms, cottagers and labourers with small plots of land. It was directed partly towards self-provision, which resulted in a relatively non-

Figure 8.1   The Dutch provinces around 1850

specialised production of both grain and livestock, the (still considerable) surpluses being sold on the market. Apart from proto-industry in some inland regions, specialised non-agricultural rural activities were relatively unimportant. Cities filled in this last gap, making urbanisation, although differing enormously between the inland provinces, quite high (Table 8.2).

Table 8.2   Characteristics of the Dutch provinces around 1850

	Population November 1849	Percentage urbanisa- tion 1840	Percentage agriculture 1849	Male agric. lab. force per farm 1859	Potato produc- tion hl/cap 1842/44	Main geographical characteristics
North Holland	477,079	64%	16%	3.7	0.9	Coast, clay
South Holland	563,425	48%	22%	4.2	2.7	Coast, clay
Groningen	188,442	23%	40%	5.4	7.3	Coast, clay & peat
Friesland	247,360	19%	45%	4.5	7.7	Coast, clay & peat
Zeeland	160,295	24%	48%	5.9	4.7	Coast, clay
Utrecht	149,380	42%	31%	3.8	2.6	Inland, sand, etc.
Drenthe	82,378	26%	54%	3.9	7.3	Inland, sand & peat
Overijssel	215,763	32%	44%	2.4	5.9	Inland, sand etc.
Gelderland	370,716	23%	47%	3.5	7.1	Inland, sand etc.
North Brabant	396,420	23%	44%	2.9	5.2	Inland, sand
Limburg	205,261	16%	47%	2.3	3.8	Inland, sand
The Netherlands	3,056,519	35%	36%	3.5	4.5	–

Source: Population: *Bijdragen*, 1878; Urbanisation (percentage of population in agglo-merations above 5.000 inhabitants): De Meere, 1982: 34–35, 130; Agricultural male labour force: Oomens and Den Bakker, 1994: 30–31. Number of farms and other agricultural firms estimated from figures of 1889 in *Uitkomsten*, 1894: 170–173, corrected for the development using the change in the number of 1 horse-farmsteads 1850–1883: Van Zanden, 1985: 377 (revised for Groningen). Potato production per capita: see Table 8.5 combined with Hofstee, 1978: 191 (population 1843).

However, it has to be pointed out that it is very difficult to generalise inasmuch as enormous differences also existed within each province. For example, the province of Groningen is characterised as specialised, but comprised not only a quite modern coastal part on sea clay soil, but also modern industrialising peat colonies such as the Veen-kolonien, older peat colonies in South Westerkwartier, new peat digging areas and some relatively backward sand villages in Westerwolde. Inland Gelderland (sand and river clay parts) is described by Bieleman (1995) as characterised by the existence of a great amount of agricultural systems, and an agriculture which was far more dynamic than was formerly thought. North Brabant consisted for the most part of sandy regions with a small scale extensive agriculture. However, the northwestern part of this province with clay soil agriculture resembled South Holland with its large market-oriented farms.

The transport system within most of the inland provinces was far worse than that in the coastal provinces. Waterways played an important role, connecting nearly all places of some size in Holland, Zeeland, Friesland and Groningen. For example, a regular sys-tem of barges for the transport of passengers connected most cities in these provinces (De Vries, 1981). Although large parts of the inland provinces seem economically more backward, exactly in parts of these provinces (Overijssel, Gelderland and North Brabant) an important proto-industry in textiles existed, which developed into a modern factory industry during the 19th century.

III. The potato blight and the agricultural production

In the Netherlands, potatoes were partly grown by large and medium-sized farmers as part of an advanced cultivation system. Presumably of even more importance was the small scale culture by peasants, cottagers, farm labourers and non-agricultural households. In the non-clay parts of Friesland a rising group of so-called gardeners grew mainly potatoes and vegetables (Bieleman, 1992: 132, 150–152). In the river clay area of Gelderland, especially in the Tielerwaard (37%), the county of Culemborg (39%) and the Bommelerwaard (59%), the production of potatoes dominated, comprising 26% of the sown area in 1845 (Bieleman, 1995: 38–39, 48–50, 59–60). In this area the labour intensive potato was mainly produced by very small farmers and labourers who hired plots of land from the larger farmers. A usual condition was to deliver half the yield (or a third) to the owner (who sometimes also ploughed and delivered manure), as in for example Gelderland and Groningen. By the 19th century the potato had become the most important crop in the small gardens of labourers and the lower middle classes.

As in most other parts of Europe, the potato disease first appeared in Dutch fields in the summer of 1845. Already in early July the first symptoms were noted in North Holland, and possibly also elsewhere, though only in the course of August and especially in September did the size of the disaster become completely clear. Provincial reports showed that already by mid-September 65,516 of 79,477 hectares sown with potatoes in nine of the eleven provinces were touched by the disease (Terlouw, 1971: 269). For the Netherlands as a whole the potato yields fell by three-quarters, and mostly only the cheaper factory potatoes could be lifted, inasmuch as the harvest of edible (winter) potatoes in a lot of cases completely failed. That the potato disease struck so hard was due to the hot wet weather of the summer of 1845 (Bergman, 1967: 393–394).

Fortunately, there are lots of provincial data on Dutch potato production in the 1840s, while for the 1850s the figures are more or less complete. These official statistics have some weak points. Firstly, they were mainly assembled by civil servants as mayors, who did not always have a completely reliable picture of the agricultural yields. Secondly, it is likely that a part of the small-scale cultivation of potatoes by households for their own use was neglected. In several Friesian municipalities no potato production was reported, because they were grown 'only in small gardens' (*Algemeen Verslag*, 1849–1850). Even in municipalities with an agriculture mainly directed at dairy farming, a lot of rural households grew potatoes for their own use.

The consequences of the potato blight on the yields per hectare are shown in Table 8.3.[2] Really disastrous were the harvests in South Holland (15 hl) and Zeeland (8 hl); yields in 1845 were hardly enough to get seed-potatoes for the next year. Surprisingly, the hectare yields in nearby North Holland were – although still very unsatisfactory – some ten times higher with 107 hl. The scanty data on yields in 1846 show that in this year the returns were still poor, though far better than in the first year. The potato disease

---

[2] On Friesland 1845: Bergman, 1967, reports 20 hl/ha (p. 393) and 58 hl/ha. (p. 430). On Limburg 1846: Philips e.a., 1965: 118, mentions 38 hl/ha. On the total Dutch productivity: Saltet, 1917: 459, mentions 179 hl/ha for 1842/44, 45 hl/ha for 1845 and 62 hl/ha for 1846, which he derived from Doorman, 1847: 42. These figures are, however, not in accordance with the production statistics.

Table 8.3 **Average production of potatoes per hectare in the Dutch provinces, 1842-1860 in hectolitres**

	1842/44	1845	1846	1847	1848/52	1853/60
North Holland		107			(108)	118
South Holland		15			(99)	125
Groningen	179	45	61	139	107	153
Friesland	(178)	66	(66)	106	112	119
Zeeland	158	8	82	95	96	115
Utrecht	(134)	34		134	117	122
Drenthe	(169)	67	(70)	137	(97)	132
Overijssel		61			121	103
Gelderland		50	107		(143)	132
North Brabant		31	90	120	94	116
Limburg	(116)	36		107	87	106
The Netherlands	(162)	43	(84)	(124)	(112)	122

Source: *Algemeen verslag*, 1845–1860; *Statistisch Jaarboek*, 1851; Van Hall, 1846; Bernhardi, 1846; *Verslag van de Gedeputeerde Staten*, 1842–1860; Priester, 1998: 606-609; Bergman, 1967: 430; *Algemeene Landhuishoudelijke Courant*, 1847–1851. Between parentheses: Drenthe: data partly delivered by Jan Bieleman comprising 22 of the 34 municipalities in 1842–44, 1846, 1849–50; Friesland 1846: hectares estimated from graph in: Spahr van der Hoek, 1952: 643; Friesland 1842/44, Utrecht 1842/44, Limburg 1842/44, North Holland 1848/52, South Holland 1848/52, Gelderland 1848/52: amount of hectares unknown for some years. The Netherlands: estimates based on total production and the development in hectares for some provinces.

was checked by drought in August and September, which stopped *phytophthora* penetrating the potato tubers (Bergman, 1967: 394–395). In 1847 yields returned to almost pre-disease levels. However, in some provinces potato yields did not structurally reach those pre-disease levels in the long run. The potato disease remained harassing the harvests in every province one year more and the next year less until after 1860 (see also Figure 8.2). An important way of coping with the disease was to grow early brands of potatoes, which were less vulnerable for the disease.

Average yields remained some 30% lower because of the potato disease. From 1845 onwards, considerable shifts in the cultivation of potatoes took place. In the decades before 1845 the number of hectares cultivated with potatoes showed a steady growth, which was halted to some extent after that date. Because especially potatoes sown in clay soil were extremely vulnerable for the potato disease, the cultivation of potatoes decreased structurally in Groningen, Friesland, South Holland and Zeeland, while in sandier regions like Drenthe, Overijssel, Gelderland and North Brabant the amount of potatoes grew. Within these provinces also changes took place. Factory potatoes (for example to make potato flour) sown on former peat areas, became more important, while the cultivation of edible potatoes in the clay parts diminished. A clear example is the province of Groningen, where in the clay parts large-scale potato farming disappeared, whereas in the peat districts the cultivation of potatoes recovered quickly, and in the long run even showed an increase.

In the peat districts of Groningen and Drenthe farmers concentrated on growing factory potatoes, which appeared in the long term to be less vulnerable than potatoes destined for human consumption mostly grown in the clay parts. Uncomfortably, the statistical figures do not make a division between these two different branches of potatoes. However, from different sources on the production of potato flour and potato gin (compare Figure 8.2) the amount of potatoes used can be estimated to be less than 500,000 hl till 1857 or no more than 2–3% of the total production of potatoes, with 1845 as an exception: a lot of potatoes which could be gathered that year were suitable only for factory processing.

Table 8.4   Hectares sown with potatoes in the Dutch provinces, 1842-1860

	% pot. 1845	1842/ 1844	1845	1846	1847	1848/ 1852	1853/ 1860
North Holland	13%		2,287			(2,634)	3,578
South Holland	18%		12,310			(7,942)	9,554
Groningen	8%	7,404	8,469	5,771	5,361	4,980	6,103
Friesland	22%	(10,500)	10,816	(8,250)	7,006	7,654	9,543
Zeeland	5%	4,655	4,732	2,942	3,601	3,888	4,369
Utrecht	13%	(2,872)	3,264		3,059	3,230	3,872
Drenthe	10%		2,682		3,143	(3,227)	4,121
Overijssel	13%		7,326			8,968	9,655
Gelderland	15%		17,712	13,082		(20,054)	20,980
North Brabant	10%		14,131	12,600	14,329	15,885	18,562
Limburg	9%	(6,537)	7,527		7,600	7,877	7,658
The Netherlands	11%	(82,000)	91,256	(69,000)	(79,000)	(86,339)	97,994

Source: See table 8.3. Between parentheses figures concern only part of the years mentioned; for the Netherlands rough estimates only.

NB: % pot. 1845 is the percentage of potatoes cultivated in 1845 as the total amount of arable land around 1850 given by Van Zanden, 1985: 88.

Farmers responded to the disastrous potato harvest of 1845 by reducing the area cultivated in 1846. An important factor seems to be the shortage of seed-potatoes in the spring of 1846, although the enormous fall in money yields of a hectare of potatoes also played a large role. Prices of potatoes indeed did rise, but the price increase in 1845–1846 was far less than the fall in hectare yields. In Groningen the average prices of a hl consumption potatoes in 1844 was 1,33 guilders, in 1845 2,17, in 1846 2,68 and in 1847 2,03 guilders. While in the Netherlands bad harvests normally caused higher prices – as in 1816–1817 –, which more than compensated the fall in yields, making those farmers capable of producing enough market surplus to be better off, this wasn't at all the case for potato growers during the potato blight.

In 1847 and following years the area under potatoes was restored quickly in the Netherlands, although it was only in the middle of the fifties that the level of 1845 had again been reached. However, in important potato regions as Friesland and South Holland the cultivation of potatoes significantly decreased, as was the case in the other provinces with clay soils, with the exception of North Holland. The urbanised province of North Holland is in many ways an exceptional case, it was the only province were the majority of the potatoes consumed had to be imported, the agriculture being nearly completely directed towards livestock production.[3] In provinces with mainly sandy soils the area under potatoes had already returned to its old level around 1847, to rise quickly afterwards, especially in North Brabant and in Drenthe. In the last province this is due to the booming production of factory potatoes in newly reclaimed peat districts.

Table 8.5   Total production of potatoes in the Dutch provinces, 1842–1860 (in 1,000 hectolitres)

	1842/44	1845	1846	1847	1848/52	1853/60
North Holland	412	245	155	201	284	425
South Holland	1,452	186	348	802	788	1,201
Groningen	1,325	377	353	747	525	951
Friesland	1,819	713	521	745	843	1,154
Zeeland	735	37	242	341	370	508
Utrecht	386	110	216	409	379	468
Drenthe	565	178	227	432	319	549
Overijssel	1,215	446	541	1,061	1,083	998
Gelderland	2,565	885	1,398	2,566	2,869	2,770
North Brabant	2,041	433	1,137	1,715	1,492	2,161
Limburg	757	271	679	817	682	885
The Netherlands	13,271	3,880	5,818	9,836	9,633	11,991

Source: See Table 8.3.

It has already become clear that '*phytophthora infestans*' did not disappear after the 1840s, becoming endemic in the Netherlands and being already in 1853 accepted as a 'normal disease' for potatoes (Bieleman, 1992: 133–140). Because of the disease the potato yields per hectare remained considerably lower in the fifties than before 1845 (Table 8.3). In 1861 the disease even returned heavily, spoiling large parts of the potato harvest for example in Friesland. In the period 1845–1860, total potato production did not structurally return to pre-1845 levels (Table 8.5), despite the growth of hectares in the fifties of the 19th century. The pre-blight position of the inland provinces of Gelderland and North Brabant as the most important potato suppliers was reinforced by the potato blight. In two other inland provinces of Utrecht and Limburg the average production in the period 1853–1860 was also somewhat higher than before the blight.

The decrease in potato production was largest in Friesland, followed by Groningen. One could say that by 1850 Friesland lost its position as an important surplus producer of potatoes for the Netherlands, as was the case for the clay parts of Groningen where potato production was marginalized (Groningen potato production became concentrated in the peat districts).

The changes in potato production between 1848/1852 and 1853/1860 are also of interest for the long term consequences of the potato blight. The rise in total production

---

[3] Van Zanden, 1985: 88: percentage of agricultural land used for arable production around 1850: North Holland 12%, South Holland 31%, Groningen 59%, Friesland 21%, Zeeland 72%, Drenthe 32%, Overijssel 33%, Gelderland 45%, Utrecht 27%, North Brabant 55%, Limburg 80%.

in the 1850s was centred mainly in the clay regions where the drop in production was heaviest in the previous years, a sign that the potato disease lost its strength and that the relatively modern clay farmers were capable to find adequate countermeasures against '*phytophthora infestans*', by using more suitable races and tracks of land. In the sandy inland provinces of Overijssel and Gelderland the peasants failed to increase the production considerably in this period, due especially to falling yields per hectare. However, in sandy inland North Brabant and Limburg potato production showed a completely reversed picture.

It can be concluded that the Netherlands was most heavily hit by the potato disease in the year 1845/1846, and to a lesser extent in 1846/1847, and that afterwards potato yields remained considerably below the pre-disease years. In the short term the cultivation of potatoes fell significantly, while in the long run a shift in production from clay soil to sandy regions took place.

IV. Consequences: consumption and trade

From the mid-18th century to 1845 the potato made a rampant push into the daily diet of the Netherlands. Of course, Dutchmen were familiar with the potato before 1750 but after that date rising prices and demographic stress made the highly productive and the high-caloric potato an increasingly more attractive alternative for corn. The first half of the 19th century saw a particularly fast rise in daily potato consumption. In this period the Netherlands were confronted with a rapidly rising population, which could not have been fed on the same level were it not for a rise in potato consumption. In 1845 the Minister of the Interior wrote that the potato was 'the most general and the most important foodstuff for the lower and even for a part of the middle class in the Netherlands' (quoted by Bieleman, 1992: 132). In the Utrecht countryside labourers' families were heavily dependent on potatoes, eating them three times a day and consuming at least 30 hl annually (Frieling, 1853: 409, 413).

It is possible to make estimates of the actual human consumption of potatoes in the Netherlands (Figure 8.2). Table 8.2 shows that the production of potatoes per capita in the period 1842–1844 can be estimated at 4.5 hl using government statistics. Presumably total potato production was higher in reality, since part of the small scale production of potatoes by households was probably omitted. This underestimation is difficult to take into account in our calculations. We estimate fodder – mainly for pigs but also for cows – as 10% of total gross production of potatoes in official statistics, which is possibly a bit low. Also a part of the potatoes were used in potato flour factories[4] and potato gin distilleries[5], and some were needed as seed-potatoes for the next year (the figure of 14 hl per hectare from Priester, 1991: 355 for the province of Groningen 1851–1852 is

---

[4] Data on expenditure on potatoes by the large Scholten potato flour factory in Groningen was kindly supplied by Dorien Knaap. The expenditure of the few smaller firms is roughly estimated taking some scattered remarks into account: Knaap, 2000.
[5] *Bescheiden*, 1861: 212–213, gives yearly production figures till 1859 in hl.. Some 9 hl potatoes are needed to produce 1 hl of potato gin according to the Groningen production statistics of 1855–1857: *Verslag Gedeputeerde Staten*, 1858. De Meere, 1982: 95, however, calculates using 7.5 hl potatoes for 1 hl gin.

used for the Netherlands as a whole). Some potatoes were exported, but they constituted a negligible proportion of total production, for example only some 1–2% in 1843–1844 (see also Table 8.9).[6]

Figure 8.2 Estimated yearly human consumption of potatoes in the Netherlands, 1840–1860 (hl per capita)

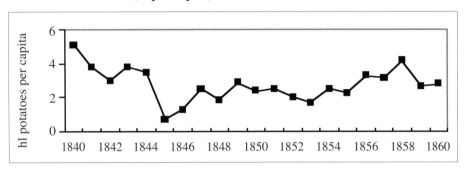

Around 1845 the government estimated the annual consumption of potatoes to be 2.5 hl per capita, while at the same time Vissering (1845: 11–15) used in his calculations a normal consumption of 4 hl per capita. Our estimates suggesting a normal yearly consumption of 3–4 hl per capita is somewhere in-between. The potato disease caused the number of potatoes per capita available for human consumption in the Netherlands as a whole to fall from an estimated average of 3.8 hl in the period 1840–1844 to a dramatic low of 0.7 hl for the year following the harvest of 1845, and 1.3 hl for 1846. In the following years this figure fluctuated between 1.7 and 2.9 hl. Only after 1856 was the average Dutchman again able to eat ca. 3 hl potatoes or more per annum.

Estimates for the province of Groningen using the same method as in Figure 8.2 result in a per capita consumption of 4 to 6 hl in the decade before 1845 (Paping, 1995: 249–250, 258, 382–383).[7] Until the mid-1850s, Groningen potato consumption remained about 2 hl per capita. In the 1830s, potatoes in Groningen supplied some 23% of the calories, followed by rye bread with 17%, groats and other meal (mainly from barley and buckwheat) with 15%, and meat with 10%. In the fifties potatoes' share fell to only 14% of the calories, with rye bread (20%) and groats and buckwheat meal (17%) becoming again the most important and the share of beans increasing from 5% to 8%. As Table 8.2 shows the potato production per capita in the province of Groningen was comparatively high by Dutch standards, which presumably was going together with a relatively high human consumption, even if one, as we did, takes into account that the bulk of the Dutch factory potatoes were grown in the peat districts of Groningen.

---

[6] Export and import figures: Terlouw, 1967, 286 (1839–1845); *Statistiek van den handel,* 1847–1861 (1846–1860). See also: Pilat, 1989: 84–85; Bergman, 1967: 394.

[7] Consumption data on rye and wheaten bread, groats and other meal, beans, peas, potatoes, butter and meat, other products estimated at delivering 20% of the calories. Estimated total calories per day per head developed in the following way: 1830/1839: 2,692; 1840/1849: 2,620; 1850/1859 2,631.

The figures on the total production of potatoes per capita in Table 8.6 can not be transformed easily into consumption figures also due to the important shipments between provinces (see later). Counted in hl the fall in per capita production in 1845 was largest in Groningen (5.3 hl), followed by Drenthe (5.1 hl), Friesland (4.8 hl) and Gelderland (4.7 hl). In relative terms in 1845 the fall was largest in South Holland and Zeeland, where taking into account the need for seed-potatoes the net potato harvest was about zero. In most provinces per capita production of potatoes improved somewhat in 1846, though in Groningen and Friesland the situation worsened. Only Limburg stands out by having a nearly normal potato production. Utrecht, North Brabant and Gelderland lifted more than half the ordinary production; nevertheless, the fall in absolute terms in Gelderland was with 3.3 hl per capita enormous in 1846. In that respect the province of Drenthe also has to be mentioned with 4.5 hl below pre-blight level.

In the post-blight years per capita consumption recovered in all provinces. This recovery was complete in the inland provinces of Utrecht, Gelderland and Limburg, and later also in North Brabant and Drenthe. In Friesland, Groningen and Zeeland per capita production remained around half the usual amount till the mid fifties, limiting the possibilities to sell potatoes to other provinces severely.

Table 8.6   Production of potatoes per capita in the Dutch provinces, 1842–1860

	1842/44	1845	1846	1847	1848/52	1853/57	1858/60
North Holland	0.9	0.5	0.3	0.4	0.6	0.8	0.9
South Holland	2.7	0.3	0.6	1.4	1.4	1.9	2.1
Groningen	7.3	2.0	1.9	3.9	2.8	3.7	6.3
Friesland	7.7	2.9	2.1	3.0	3.4	3.9	5.0
Zeeland	4.7	0.2	1.5	2.1	2.3	2.9	3.5
Utrecht	2.6	0.7	1.4	2.6	2.5	2.8	3.3
Drenthe	7.3	2.2	2.8	5.2	3.8	5.4	7.0
Overijssel	5.9	2.1	2.5	5.0	5.0	4.2	4.6
Gelderland	7.1	2.4	3.8	6.9	7.7	6.7	7.7
North Brabant	5.2	1.1	2.8	4.2	3.7	4.8	6.2
Limburg	3.8	1.3	3.3	4.0	3.4	3.8	3.8
The Netherlands	4.5	1.3	1.9	3.2	3.1	3.4	4.2

Source: See Table 8.3.

Due to its bulk, the potato was not a particularly attractive agricultural product to transport to the cities. In pre-blight years consumption levels in towns were therefore lower than on the Dutch countryside. The province of Groningen had a rather high potato consumption, partly while it was less urbanised; in the municipality of Ten Boer (clay soil), for example, labourer households produced and consumed more than 50 hl of potatoes each year (Paping, 1995: 250). Market figures for the city of Leiden (South Holland) suggest a minimum consumption of 2.5 hl per capita around 1840 (Calculated using a rate of 70 kg per hl from Pot, 1994: 310, 313), taking into account the potatoes from city gardens and bought directly from the countryside, annual human consumption of potatoes must have been somewhere around 3 hl in Leiden.

Around 1810 consumption per capita in Amsterdam (North Holland) can be estimated on 2.0 hl (Van der Maas and Noordegraaf, 1983: 208–209), three decades later it was possibly around the same level, given an average market supply of 408,000 hl or 1.9 hl per capita in 1838–1840 (Knotter and Muskee, 178). Given the lack of potatoes produced in North Holland, most potatoes consumed in Amsterdam were imported from other provinces. Zeeland, Friesland and Gelderland are mentioned in this respect (Knotter and Muskee, 1983: 157, 160, 178; Posthumus, 1943, 49; Van der Maas and Noordegraaf, 1983: 194–195). Amsterdam data clearly show that massive inland shipments of potatoes were taking place already before 1845. In the period 1851–1855 annual consumption per capita in Amsterdam can be estimated at 1.8 hl. So it can be concluded that in the largest city of the Netherlands the per capita potato consumption fell far less than the overall Dutch production.

Interestingly, supply on the market of Leiden during the potato blight years also fell only to a limited amount: in 1842/1844 2.4 hl per capita, in 1845 2.7 hl (presumably mostly supplied in the months before the disease), in 1846 1.9 hl, in 1847 1.5 hl, in 1848/1852 2.0 hl. Leiden's urban population was capable of bidding high prices for the potatoes it needed in 1845–1850, enough to raise its share of total potato supply. This is clearly the case if we look at the gross production figures per capita for South Holland (Table 8.6). Although more evidence is needed on this point, the data on Leiden and Amsterdam strongly suggest that the Dutch urban population, who in first instance ate fewer potatoes than the rural population, did not experience such a dramatic fall in potato consumption as production figures suggest. The consequence was that the fall in consumption in the countryside was considerably higher than implied by the average figures for the Netherlands presented in Figure 8.2. However, this need not imply that the urban population was better off during the potato blight. Far more than the rural population, they were dependent on purchases for their food supply. Even during the blight potatoes remained a relatively cheap kind of food, especially compared with wheaten and rye bread which was an important alternative in the Holland cities.

Excises offer us detailed information on the consumption of meal destined to bake wheaten or rye bread (Table 8.7 and 8.8). Wheaten bread was considerably more expensive than rye bread, even if we take into account the amount of money paid per calorie. Remarkably, in the different provinces existed widely diverging eating habits concerning bread and other food (Van Otterloo, 1990: 23–24). The consumption of bread (from rye or wheat) wasn't in every province of equal importance. The inland provinces Limburg (122 kg in 1847) and North Brabant (119 kg) had the highest average yearly total consumption of bread meal in the period 1840/1844, followed by Zeeland (113 kg), Gelderland (112 kg), Drenthe (99 kg), South Holland (96 kg), North Holland (93 kg), Overijssel (90 kg), Utrecht (89 kg). The northern provinces of Friesland (79 kg) and Groningen (76 kg) stand out with a very low bread meal consumption, which has to do with the high consumption of groats made from barley and possibly also with the great popularity of potatoes in these provinces.

In response to the failure of the potato harvest in 1845 and 1846 the consumption of rye bread increased in nearly all Dutch provinces. This increase, however, was by no means large enough to compensate completely for the loss of calories due to the fewer potatoes available. Interesting is what happened in 1846 and 1847. As elsewhere in Europe the rye harvest also failed in 1847, being only half its ordinary magnitude.[8] This

---

[8] The gross production of rye in the Netherlands was in millions of hl in 1837/1841 2.4; in 1842

Table 8.7   Average consumption of human rye meal per capita in the Dutch provinces, 1840–1855

	1840/44 kg	1840/44	1845	1846	1847	1848/52	1853/55
North Holland	44	100	98	101	96	102	101
South Holland	31	100	105	100	121	107	119
Groningen	68	100	107	104	93	112	103
Friesland	66	100	106	109	99	116	105
Zeeland	14	100	105	94	167	170	184
Utrecht	44	100	108	110	108	115	119
Drenthe	93	100	107	107	90	93	87
Overijssel	80	100	113	113	101	115	112
Gelderland	90	100	103	102	93	110	110
North Brabant	102	100	103	115	104	111	115
Limburg	(70)			97	100	104	106
The Netherlands	62	100	105	105	101	111	111

Source: *Statistisch Jaarboek*, 1853–1857. Limburg (1847=100, consumption in 1847 is 70).

NB: the taxation of the milling of rye (and wheat) was abolished in 1856.

resulted in very high prices of all kinds of grain. In the wheat province of Zeeland people in first instance reacted with eating less rye bread and more wheaten bread, however, when prices in 1846–1847 began to rise the amount of wheat was cut back, while rye bread became increasingly popular. It is clear that the limited availability of rye was not a problem for the inhabitants of Zeeland, they were capable and prepared to pay a high price. In a way this can be said of the Dutch people in general in the years of the potato crisis. Although the consumption of rye bread fell somewhat in 1847 as a result of the failure of the rye harvest, its extent was limited compared to the fall in production. In 1846 and 1847 combined, net import of rye grew by 1.9 million hl, enough to compensate for the harvest losses of 1846/1847 (Table 8.9).

In the wheat provinces of South Holland and Utrecht rye bread was also eaten a lot more in 1847, which was again due to a shift from expensive wheaten bread to cheap rye bread (see also Table 8.8). In the rye provinces of North Brabant, Overijssel, Drenthe and Friesland the consumption of rye bread partly compensated for the loss of potatoes, but only in 1846, inasmuch as this consumption fell considerably in 1847. Clearly, 1847 was the worst year, especially, in the potato producing provinces of Groningen and Gelderland, and also in Drenthe. The inhabitants were unable to find compensation for potatoes in rye bread, also taking into account that in the second half of 1847 the situation concerning the bread prices again returned to normal (see also Figure 8.3). In these provinces the majority of the inhabitants did not seem to have been able to buy itself a way through the potato and rye crisis of 1846/1847.

2.6; in 1843 3.4; in 1844 3.0; in 1845 2.9; in 1846 1.6; in 1847 3.8; in 1848 3.4; in 1849 3.7; in 1850 3.4: *Statistisch Jaarboek*, 1851; *Staatkundig*, 1850.

In the long-term in most provinces rye bread offered some compensation for the lack of potatoes. Nearly everywhere the consumption of rye bread was significantly higher from 1848 onwards than before 1845. Only Drenthe was an exception, pointing to grave long-term consequences of the potato blight in this province, worsening the everyday diet to a considerable extent.

North Holland also attracts our attention. The consumption of rye bread there was stable in 1846, but declined in 1847. In 1845 and 1846, some compensation for potatoes was found in a rising consumption of wheat in this rich province dominated by Amsterdam, which accounted for nearly half of its inhabitants; but this rise could not be sustained in 1847, an indication of the strongly negative consequences of the potato blight. In the long term the population of North Holland was also unable to find compensation in a growing consumption of rye bread, while the consumption of wheaten bread declined heavily during the Crimean War years. Interestingly, the situation in Amsterdam itself differed somewhat.[9] Its consumption of rye bread rose during the potato blight years, suggesting that its rural hinterland experienced an important fall. Directly after 1848 a strong shift towards rye took place in Amsterdam, which does not show up in the provincial figures, suggesting that the countryside was experiencing a shift in the other direction towards wheat. This development is difficult to explain, but more or less in line with what was happening in Zeeland and South Holland. It must be kept in mind, however, that because potato production and also probably consumption was very low in the North Holland countryside, the rural population there was less heavily hit by the blight.

Table 8.8   Average human consumption of wheat meal per capita in the Dutch provinces, 1840–1855

	1840/44 kg	1840/44	1845	1846	1847	1848/52	1853/55
North Holland	49	100	106	113	102	99	89
South Holland	65	100	113	117	94	107	103
Groningen	8	100	107	113	95	115	103
Friesland	13	100	96	104	100	106	103
Zeeland	99	100	112	120	96	109	107
Utrecht	45	100	102	106	85	99	97
Drenthe	6	100	107	107	90	93	87
Overijssel	10	100	103	108	93	94	86
Gelderland	22	100	101	99	70	98	73
North Brabant	17	100	106	124	91	108	98
Limburg	(53)			122	100	115	95
The Netherlands	35	100	109	115	95	105	100

Source: See Table 8.7.

---

[9] Calculated from Knotter and Muskee, 1983: 157, 176. Rye meal: in 1840/44 36 kg = 100; 1845 = 105; 1846 = 106; 1847 = 103; 1848/1852 = 114, while meal of wheat: 1840/1844 68 kg = 100; 1845 = 108; 1846 = 111; 1847 = 100; 1848/1852 = 91.

The data on wheat consumption show that nearly everywhere wheaten bread was to some extent a substitution for the potato in 1845–1846. However, the high prices of wheat in 1847 caused the Dutch to give up part of their expensive wheat-consuming habits. In the long term three systems show up. In rich provinces like South Holland, Groningen and Friesland the consumption of wheaten bread increased, although some of the gain was lost during the Crimean War. In the inland provinces of Drenthe, Overijssel, Gelderland and to a lesser extent Utrecht, wheat lost ground after 1848 and even further during the Crimean War. Strange is the favourable development of the consumption of wheat in North Brabant and Limburg, suggesting a fast recovery (their rye bread consumption also rose). After 1853, however, in these southern provinces a fast shift from wheat to rye bread took place.

Table 8.9 Net import figures (a trade deficit is positive) of agricultural products for the Netherlands, 1840–1850 (in 1000 hl and in numbers)

	1840/44	1845	1846	1847	1848/50
Wheat	281	239	287	132	53
Rye	851	803	1,703	1,840	1,156
Barley	158	445	295	68	207
Buckwheat	60	172	217	155	181
Oats	−169	−341	−328	−485	−671
Potatoes	−92	247	102	−90	−13
Cattle above 2 year	−20,320	−31,797	−46,685	−59,687	−49,238
Calf	−8,286	−14,136	−13,373	−24,219	−27,536
Sheep	−36,297	−53,671	−108,769	−145,157	−144,825

Source: *Statistisch Jaarboekje*, 1851, 1853; Terlouw, 1971: 286; *Statistiek van den handel*, 1847–1851. The net import of potatoes for 1845 is an estimate based only on figures for part of the year. Livestock: export figures only.

To stabilise food consumption levels during the potato blight and the failure of the 1846 rye harvest, heavy imports were necessary in the Netherlands. As already mentioned the Netherlands were a (small) net exporter of potatoes in pre-disease years, which contrasts sharply with the other important arable products. On average in the 1836–1845 period 0.11 hl wheat, 0.29 hl rye, 0.05 hl barley and 0.02 hl buckwheat per capita were imported into the Netherlands (Terlouw, 1971: 291). The Dutch indeed were capable to attract a growing amount of arable food products on the international market during these difficult years (Table 8.9). Several official trade measures were taken by the Dutch government to stimulate imports and to counter exports, a topic dealt with extensively in previous publications (Terlouw, 1971; Bergman, 1967). Imports of rye were massive in 1846 and 1847, but also remained on a higher level in the three following years, making a higher rye bread consumption attainable. The same was true to a lesser extent for buckwheat which was milled to grits. In 1846 and 1847 the Netherlands again resumed some of its old position of grain store of Western Europe. Not only did imports of rye, wheat and buckwheat increase enormously, but exports speeded up in 1846 and 1847.[10] This

---

[10] The export of rye rose from 868 hl in 1840/44 to 38,520 hl in 1846/47. to fall again to 576 hl

position could, however, only be retained for wheat in 1848–1850, while the important large international rye trade again disappeared from the Dutch market.

Another sign that the Dutch were prepared and able to buy themselves a way through the potato crisis is the development of the net trade of potatoes. Already in 1845 and again in 1846 the Dutch were able to secure large amounts of foreign potatoes for their own country. Although in the light of the size of the disaster the shift in trade figures from 1840/1844 to 1845 seems modest, the change of 340,000 from 1840/1844 to 1845 supplied an extra 10% of available potatoes at the end of 1845. In 1846 net imports were already lower, and in 1847 the Netherlands started to export potatoes again. Trade figures for grain suggest that the trade balance of the Netherlands deteriorated significantly in 1845–1847, however, this was not the case for oats. Table 8.9 shows that the oats export rose during the potato blight, while exports of livestock products also increased – mainly destined for Great Britain. These rises were partly to compensate for imports of other products, but also partly a sign of a flourishing Dutch agriculture.

Table 8.10 Total consumption of livestock, 1840–1852

	1840/44	1845	1846	1847	1848/52
Cattle above 2 years	135,613	146,286	137,335	131,502	132,353
Calf	123,713	112,114	109,666	100,961	96,459
Sheep	140,867	135,126	114,735	88,457	101,343
Pigs	331,965	420,395	318,463	265,171	354,262
Meat per capita (kg)	23.9	23.2	20.1	17.1	22.9

Source: Estimated from *Staatkundig*, 1853. The weight of a calf is estimated to be 30 kg (65% meat); weight of pigs (80% meat) changing according to Groningen figures; weight of sheep 35 kg (55% meat); weight of cattle 250 kg (63% meat): Paping, 1995: 373, 387–388 .

As a result, meat consumption deteriorated significantly in 1846 and 1847, to regain nearly its former level in the 1848–1852 period. The fast increase in the export of sheep meant a considerable fall in consumption of mutton. Although the figures of the number of pigs slaughtered in 1845 are impressive, the resulting amount of bacon presumably is not. Because of the failure of the potato harvest there wasn't enough fodder available for the pigs, which made it impossible to fatten them in the ordinary way. The average weight of pigs slaughtered by institutions in the city of Groningen fell from a norm of 140–150 kg to 112 kg in 1845, 123 kg in 1846 and 115 kg in 1847, only to rise again to 142 kg in the 1848/1850 period (Paping, 1995: 252–253, 373).

in 1848/50. The export of wheat rose from 6,443 hl in 1840/44 to 19,398 hl in 1846/47, to increase further to 31,782 hl in 1848/50.

V.   Consequences: prices and food riots

In the Netherlands the crisis was at its gravest in the first half of 1847, when the prices of rye and of most other unprocessed food products rose in some months to nearly three times their usual level (Figure 8.3).[11] Because Dutch nominal wages were nearly constant, these high prices caused huge problems for the wage-owning class in the cities, who had to buy every piece of food. The urban middle and upper classes, however, do not seem to have felt much impact of the potato blight, because their earnings were more flexible, they had more reserves, and food formed a smaller part of their budget. In the countryside it was a similar story, but for the rural lower classes the situation was even worse, because they also missed income in kind by losing most of the potatoes in their gardens. For the market-oriented farmers and a part of the middle classes in the countryside the potato blight years were not bad. The high agricultural prices made large profits possible. Only when potatoes were the main crop, as for instance for many peasants and cottagers in Friesland and Gelderland (de Bommclcrwaard), were the effects extremely negative.

Figure 8.3   Monthly market prices of rye in Amsterdam and Nijmegen (Gelderland), 1844–1848 (in guilders per hl)

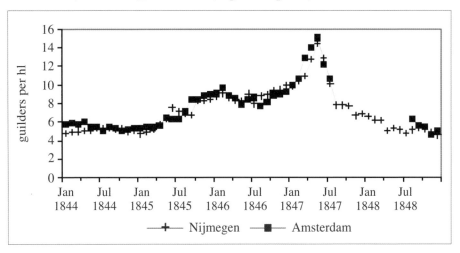

Price increases in September 1845 caused social unrest in several cities in South Holland (Leiden, the Hague and Delft) and North Holland (Haarlem) (Bergman, 1967: 404–413). Mobs smashcd windows of shopkccpcrs to forcc thcm to cancel recent price rises. The riots had, however, more to do with fear for the future than that the food supply in the Dutch cities was really in danger at that moment. Rumours of the complete failure of the potato harvest in newspapers made lower class people unjustly afraid for starvation in the coming winter. As shown in Figure 8.3 prices not even doubled, and although many Dutch people must have been hungry in the winter of 1845–1846, the

---

[11] Source: Amsterdam, Prussian rye: Posthumus (1953: 22–23). Nijmegen: Tijms (1983: 179–180).

situation still was quite bearable and disorder vanished in the coming months. In the Netherlands the worst was still to come.

As argued the Dutch countered the potato and rye crisis by buying food elsewhere. In the spring of 1847 this strategy became increasingly difficult to maintain because food supplies everywhere in Europe ran short of demand. Speculation caused exorbitant prices especially in the months May and June 1847. On 24 June in the harbour city of Harlingen in Friesland the shipping of new potatoes to England combined with the high price of bread instigated riots. Social unrest spread quickly to several other Frisian towns and also to some parts of the countryside. As Bergman (1967: 410) states it 'Houses and shops were looted, shopkeepers and farmers were forced to hand over their foodstuffs'.

Things really got out of hand in the city of Groningen, where a mob of unemployed labourers and poor women begged the mayor for bread and work, and it proved impossible for the government to calm them down with lower bread prices. The so-called 'Bread Revolt' of 28 June 1847 ended in a shooting-party in which four civilians were killed and at least thirteen wounded by soldiers (Gout, 1976/77). The mob wounded a total of 49 soldiers by throwing stones. Rigorous governmental reaction prevented further disorders in the Groningen countryside, and possibly elsewhere in the Netherlands. In the large cities in the provinces of Gelderland (Arnhem, Nijmegen, Zutphen) and Overijssel (Deventer, Zwolle) riots also took place at this time.

Real hunger was probably the cause of all this – mostly urban – disorder in June 1847. Social unrest broke out mainly in cities of provinces with a previously relatively high production of potatoes. Also it has to be remarked that apart from North Holland (where

Table 8.11 Price developments of several products in Groningen, 1840–1860

	1840/44	1845	1846	1847	1848/52	1853/60
Potatoes	100	151	186	141	145	162
Barley	100	118	124	173	87	130
Wheat	100	85	103	144	85	111
Rye	100	106	141	157	93	139
Rye bread	100	108	133	153	93	113
Buckwheat	100	121	128	157	89	126
Peas	100	99	147	162	93	125
Beans	100	144	159	119	100	147
Butter	100	97	114	114	97	124
Meat (beef and bacon)	100	98	120	142	103	152
Several (gin, beer, eggs)	100	101	104	119	97	118
Cloth/textile	100	82	74	79	81	88
Peat	100	118	97	105	108	134
Building material	100	96	94	97	96	105
Price-index cons. all	100	103	109	114	95	118
Price-index cons. poor	100	106	117	121	97	121

Source: Paping, 1995: 363–377, 406–407. Price-index cons. all relates to total household consumption. Price-index cons. poor relates to the consumption of pauper households.

potato production was of only small importance), Groningen and Friesland were the only provinces where the potato harvest in 1846 was worse than in 1845. The situation definitely became difficult in these clay soil provinces. Potato consumption had probably been relatively high among the urban working classes in these potato provinces. The potato blight made potatoes nearly inaccessible for these groups, and the more expensive alternatives had become also very costly.

A Groningen database of prices of 36 products shows that the aggregate price level did not change dramatically in 1846 and 1847, mainly due to falling prices of textiles and building material. However, if one focuses on basic foodstuffs the outcome is negative. The price of potatoes was 86% higher than usual in 1846, and that of barley 73% higher in 1847. In 1845 only potatoes and beans were considerably more expensive. In 1846 this was already the case for potatoes, rye, peas and beans, although more luxury food products like wheat, butter and meat were still quite cheap. In 1847 the prices of wheat and meat also had also risen. It has to be considered that prices in May and June 1847 were much higher than indicated in Table 8.11 (compare Figure 8.3). In the period 1848–1852 food prices returned to normal levels again. Only potatoes remained relatively expensive, as a result of the structurally lower supply due to the potato disease. Remarkably, during the Crimean War prices rose more than during the potato crisis, pointing at the enormous impact disturbed trade relations have in an open market economy.

VI. Consequences: the biological standard of living

Changing human stature can be seen as an outcome of developments in nutrition, morbidity and labour input, the so-called biological standard of living (Tassenaar, 2000: 24–36). The effects of the potato blight on average height seem indeed very obvious (Figure 8.4). One could be surprised that there was no visible effect in 1845 or 1846, however, height data are less than totally revealing for several reasons. Firstly conscriptions and ensuing height measurements usually took place in February or March, so if we analyse the 1845 conscription data we have to keep in mind that those data were gathered before the potato blight. Secondly, it takes some time before changes in nutrition or the disease environment affect height data. Since the potato blight came to the Netherlands only in the autumn of 1845 it seems logical that the effects only could become visible in the data of cohorts starting from 1847. Effects of changing conditions in nutrition, hygiene or medical care work out some years later in height data. Crises are especially important for adult height when they take place during the adolescent growth spurt. Boys who in 1845 were on a peak of their velocity curve, i.e. their adolescent growth spurt, which was around the age of 16–17, were measured only one, two of three years thereafter as conscripts aged 19 years. The average heights of Dutch conscripts from those cohorts were 1.5–2.0 centimetres below that of cohorts that were measured in the early forties.

Data for the percentage of undersized conscripts (<1.57 metres at the moment of measurement) are available for only seven of the eleven provinces for the period of 1842–1860: the urbanised province of North Holland, the modern coastal clay soil provinces of Groningen and Zeeland, and the more traditional inland sand provinces of North Brabant, Limburg, Drenthe and Utrecht, the last province, however, being more

Figure 8.4 The development of the percentage of undersized conscripts in the Netherlands, 1842–1860

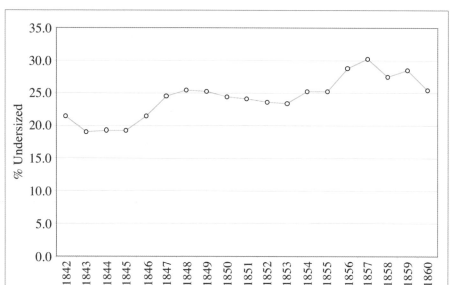

urbanised. Figure 8.4 demonstrates that the percentage of undersized conscripts in 1847 and following years were substantially higher than during the period of 1842–1846. A recovery took place in the early 1850s as a result of improving consumption, but this was followed by a second increase in the mid-1850s as a result of the high food prices during the Crimean War.

Table 8.12 The percentage of undersized conscripts in several Dutch provinces, 1842–1860

	1842/46	1847	1848	1849	1850/54	1855/60
North Holland	26.5	29.9	31.4	30.0	29.1	36.9
Groningen	19.4	22.8	24.9	24.9	24.6	28.3
Zeeland	15.4	18.0	23.3	25.8	20.4	22.1
Utrecht	20.5	26.5	30.4	28.8	29.3	–
Drenthe	18.8	26.1	23.0	22.3	23.7	26.4
North Brabant	14.5	20.6	19.9	22.3	21.8	20.5
Limburg	19.9		19.7*		18.0	21.8

*1847–1849.

Source: Tassenaar, 2000: 286–289. Data of Limburg are based on a small annual sample: Rutten, 1995. The numbers are too low for a yearly comparison.

Comparing these data with those on potato production per capita in 1845–1846 (Table 8.6) – and excluding the provinces in which potato-production was limited, i.e. North Holland – one would expect the most clear effects to be found in Groningen, Zeeland and Drenthe, while developments should be most favourable in Limburg and possibly Utrecht. Table 8.12 shows that this picture is not completely reflected in the height data. By comparison with normal years (cohorts 1842–1846) it seems clear that especially Utrecht, Zeeland and to a lesser extent North Brabant were hit heavily by the potato blight. Conscripts from North Holland were not much shorter after the potato blight, which is not surprising inasmuch as the potato was an unimportant crop in this province. Furthermore the standard of living situation in this province was already very bad before the blight.

The developments in Drenthe and Groningen are remarkable. In Groningen effects were especially visible in municipalities which can be characterised as fully market-oriented and agricultural (Zeeman, 1861). In the potato-exporting province of Groningen the regions with industry or a less market-oriented agriculture were less strongly affected by the disappointing yields. The potato blight had a positive effect on the potato flour industry in some parts of the province, especially after 1850. Drenthe had only one 'bad year' (the 1847 cohort), which was mainly a result of decreasing heights in so-called buckwheat areas, while in 1845 and the foregoing years there was almost no production of buckwheat. Regression analysis shows that there was a negative relation at a municipal level between the production of potatoes per capita before 1845 and the height of conscripts from 1847 onwards in Drenthe (Tassenaar, 2000: 252–253). Considering our findings on production and consumption it is not surprising that in Limburg the percentage of undersized conscripts remained quite stable during the whole 1840s.

The biological standard of living did not really recover significantly immediately after the end of the potato blight. This suggests that the potato disease also caused a long term deterioration of the standard of living. The period of high prices in the mid-1850s aggravated the situation even more. Looking at the cohorts of 1855–1860 it seems that in the most urbanised province (North Holland), and in Groningen with its numerous labourers, the percentage of undersized conscripts increased most. The lower classes in these provinces were hit heavily by the high prices during the Crimean War. North Brabant, Limburg and Zeeland on the other hand, remained nearly untouched, while Drenthe took a middle position. From these provinces the relatively favourable development in Zeeland in the fifties is again difficult to explain, per capita potato consumption did not completely recover and wage dependable farm workers were dominating the population of this province.

It is to be expected that the potato blight, like any other subsistence crisis before the transport revolution, hit the inhabitants of urban areas harder than rural people. We have data for four cities in the Netherlands: Leiden and Rotterdam (South Holland), Groningen city and Goes (Zeeland). The situation in Leiden became particularly bad, although potato consumption in Leiden fell far less than in the Netherlands as a whole. The percentage of undersized conscripts in this industrial town in decay nevertheless increased with a quarter, from almost 36% of the conscripts in 1842–1846 to 45% in 1847–1849. In 1848 conscripts were on average three centimetres shorter than eight years before, even though the percentage of undersized conscripts in Leiden was already twice as high in the years before the potato blight (cohorts 1842–1846).

Table 8.13 The percentage of undersized conscripts in four Dutch cities, 1842–1860

	1842/46	1847	1848	1849	1850/54	1855/60
Rotterdam (South Holland)	22.8	26.3	27.6	28.0	28.8	35.4
Leiden (South Holland)	35.7	43.3	46.0	45.9	41.0	49.2
Groningen (Groningen)	20.5	23.1	24.8	23.9	25.6	32.0
Goes (Zeeland)	25.6		34.9*		34.7	43.9

*1847–1849.

Source: Figures are reconstructed with the reversed method: Tassenaar, 2000: 288–289 using figures in Oppers, 1963.

In Goes there was also a strong increase of the percentage of undersized conscripts just after the potato blight. This rise was stronger than the rise in the province as a whole, which, as mentioned above, was already high for national standards. The city of Groningen experienced a decrease in biological living standards in line with the general picture of the province. In the case of Rotterdam there was only a modest decline in the biological standard of living compared to Leiden. As both a harbour and industrial town Rotterdam was booming in this period, which could explain this apparently contradictory outcome. This is in line with the relatively modest decline in industrial regions in Groningen.

In the four cities studied the biological standard of living also did not recover immediately after the potato blight years, apart from the partial exception of the very poor town of Leiden. Clearly, the main impact of high prices during the Crimean War period was on the urban population throughout the Netherlands, speeding up the share of undersized conscripts till enormous proportions. At the end of the 1850s, a third (Groningen, Rotterdam) or even a half (Leiden) of the conscripts had not been fed well enough to reach a stature of 1.57 at the age of 19.

For Drenthe a database on individual level is available which means that the figures of Drenthe can be both subdivided on a regional and occupational level (Tassenaar, 2000). In the first half of the 19th century this province experienced spectacular population growth, due to a combination of migration (expansion of peat-digging activities) and a very low mortality rate. At the beginning of the 19th century the biological standard of living, i.e. the average height, was relatively favourable in comparison with other provinces in the Netherlands. But this advantage was diminishing between the early 1830s and the early 1840s.

After 1845 this process accelerated. The potato fields, which had sustained the biological living standard of the labourers and small peasants for so long, did not yield enough any more. The regions that experienced the biggest declines in the biological standard of living were not those with the highest demographic growth, but those with the highest potato production. It were the small peasants and the farm labourers workers from the north of Drenthe, where arable farming was dominated by the potato, who suffered enormously from the bad harvests.

Figure 8.5   Average heights of sons of farmers and sons of labourers in Drenthe, 1840–1861

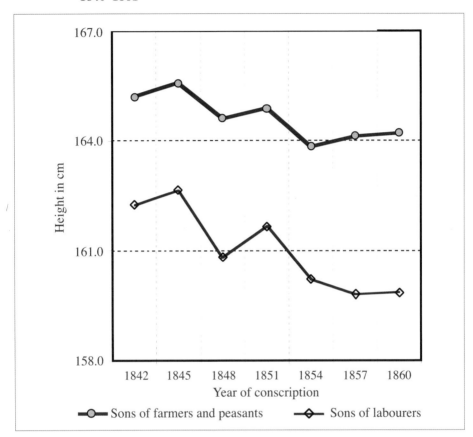

In general the biological standard of living of the sons of labourers was more affected by the potato crisis than that of the sons of farmers. Before 1846, many labourer families rented a plot of land to cultivate potatoes. After 1846, some of them gave up this survival strategy. This meant that a working-class family consumed fewer carbohydrates than before. The nutrition intake of labourers worsened and consequently influenced the growth of boys as Figure 8.5 demonstrates.

Within the variety of farmers taken together in Figure 8.5 there was a large difference between peasants directed partly towards self-provision and 'large' well tot do farmers. The sons of these well-to-do farmers could keep their daily nutrition intake on the same level in contrast with the sons of peasants. However, the decrease in average height for this last group was less severe than for the labourers. Lower social strata were hit more severely than their counterparts from higher social strata. As a consequence of the potato blight the average height of the conscripts from different social strata diverged.

Concluding, if we take the biological standard of living into account it can be stated that during the potato blight years the situation worsened mostly in the province of

Utrecht, which is not completely in line with other indicators. A possible explanation is that the figures to a considerable extent show a rise in urban poverty, this province being dominated by the large city of Utrecht. The height indicator clearly suggests that the urban population was hit mostly – both in the short and in the long term – by the potato disease, which presumably was caused by its complete dependence on purchases for foodstuffs. In the countryside the poor were hit more than the well to do. In the short run the inland sandy provinces, with the notable exception of Limburg, were as vulnerable as the coastal clay soil provinces. In the long run the picture is confusing with coastal Zeeland and inland North Brabant and Limburg doing quite well, while coastal Groningen and North Holland, but also to some extent Drenthe doing comparatively badly. At least it is clear that pre-potato-disease biological standard-of-living levels were beyond the reach of most Dutchmen (and Dutchwomen) in the fifteen years following the blight.

VII. Consequences: paupers and poverty

After the French period (1795–1813) a system of civil poor relief boards was established in the Netherlands. However, in reality most of the burden of relieving the paupers fell on numerous religious poor relief boards, mainly Roman Catholic and Dutch Reformed, though the other less important denominations also had so-called '*diaconieën*'. Part of these poor relief boards were subsidised by the local government. Since the 1820s the national government had been trying to persuade poor relief boards to send their healthy paupers to large working institutions for paupers in the countryside in Drenthe and Overijssel to reclaim land, the so-called 'Societies of Benevolence'. Condemned beggars and tramps were also imprisoned there. Poor relief boards, however, were often very unwilling to send their own villagers to these institutions, for financial (it was an expensive solution), practical and social reasons. For this reason, these pauper institutions only played a minor role during the potato-crisis and its aftermath.

Most religious poor relief boards received quite a stable income from properties, alms and several other sources. This stability made them completely unsuitable for solving cyclical poverty problems during economic crises. They could organise extra collections, or they could sell some of their properties or borrow funds, unattractively decreasing their income stream in the long run. The municipal council could also put larger subsidies at the disposal of the poor relief boards. Actually all these kinds of measures were taken during the potato-crisis.

Fortunately, we have quite reliable provincial statistics on the number of paupers, although they are not flawless (De Meere, 1982, 43–45; Griffiths, 1979: 10–13). Table 8.14 shows that official poverty highly diverged between provinces. These differences are only partly reflections of relative poverty; they also reflect different relief systems (Van Zanden, 1991: 37–38). In some provinces it was nearly impossible for an able-bodied unemployed or partly employed labourer to get support from the poor relief boards, while in others places this was quite common. Especially in North Holland, and to be more precise in Amsterdam, the majority of the labourer families supplemented their income with donations from poor relief boards, which resulted in very high rates of pauperism. In the other Dutch coastal provinces and also in Utrecht poor relief boards were less generous, though still many ordinary labourers families were relieved in this area. The Groningen countryside stands out, with pauper percentages of less than 6%

before 1845 (Paping, 1995: 285, 410–411), figures which are more in line with nearby Drenthe and Overijssel. Only widows, the elderly, the disabled, and orphans were accepted by the poor relief boards, being in this way some kind of a social insurance for bad times for a majority of the population. The average amount of money given to paupers in these provinces was relatively high, because a large part of the paupers endowed were nearly completely dependent on poor relief, in contrast with the situation in North Holland were deficient earnings were supplemented. In the other inland provinces Gelderland, North Brabant and Limburg the percentages of paupers were also low, but in these regions it seems to have been somewhat easier to obtain support. It has to be remarked that in larger Dutch cities the percentages of supported people were nearly always considerably higher than in their rural hinterland, a tendency probably explaining the high percentage of paupers in urbanised inland Utrecht. In Maastricht, the capital of Limburg, the share of paupers around 1840 (15–20%) was considerably higher than the provincial figures, and this share rose to ca. 35% during the potato blight years (Gales et al., 1997: 199).

Table 8.14 Paupers as a percentage of the population in the Dutch provinces, 1840–1860

	1840/44	1845	1846	1847	1848/52	1853/60
North Holland	23.2	26.7	29.0	27.8	26.6	21.0
South Holland	13.0	16.7	18.2	19.1	18.5	14.5
Groningen	7.8	10.1	11.3	11.5	10.5	10.1
Friesland	14.7	18.3	20.2	21.4	19.2	18.5
Zeeland	(12.0)	12.7	16.2	15.9	15.4	13.1
Utrecht	12.7	14.6	15.0	17.5	17.1	17.6
Drenthe	4.5	5.9	7.0	7.8	6.2	4.4
Overijssel	6.8	8.2	9.8	10.0	8.7	8.3
Gelderland	8.8	11.1	12.4	12.6	11.7	17.3
North Brabant	8.8	12.4	15.6	17.0	15.6	13.9
Limburg	(10.7)	14.6	15.7	16.2	15.8	14.8
The Netherlands	12.5	15.4	17.2	17.7	16.7	14.8

Source: 'Verslag omtrent het armwezen', 1841/2–1852/3, Bijlagen. *Statistisch Jaarboek*, 1853–1863. Limburg only figures on 1842–1844, Zeeland only on 1844, because of different counting procedures. Figures relate to both home-sitting poor and inhabitants of charitable institutions and poorhouses. Population 1840–1850: Hofstee, 1978: 190–191; 1860: Oomens, 1978: 46–47 (official figures), interpolation for the period 1851–1859.

Already in 1845 the number of paupers began to rise in all Dutch provinces, signifying that more and more households did not feel able anymore to earn enough for themselves as a result of rising prices (wage earners) or falling incomes (potato growers). Surprisingly, in absolute terms the share of paupers rose mostly in North Brabant. In this province the nature of poor relief seems to have changed fundamentally during the potato blight, shifting from relieving persons really incapable of earning any income, to also relieving the unemployed and underemployed, as in South Holland and Friesland. With the notable exception of Drenthe and possibly Overijssel, in quite a few other provinces such structural changes took place to some extent.

Why the number of paupers in North Brabant increased more rapidly is still unexplained. However, we already saw a quite heavy deterioration of the biological standard-of-living in this province. A likely explanation is that potatoes in North Brabant were grown mainly for household use by poor peasants and textile workers. This subsistence agriculture had no financial reserves to counter the potato blight with purchases of alternative foodstuffs. On the other hand the high intake of bread in North Brabant and its favourable development at least in 1845 and 1846 seems to contradict this suggestion (see Table 8.7 and 8.8).

Equally interesting is the question why the share of paupers in Limburg rose so rapidly in the period 1845–1847 while other indicators suggest that this province remained relatively untouched by the potato failure after 1845. Of course poor households in Limburg also felt the burden of the higher prices, although consumption and height figures suggest that they were able to cope. The developments in Limburg point to the fact that in all Dutch provinces the increase in pauperism was similar in the period 1845–1847. In Groningen, the rise in the number of paupers was relatively limited, however; in this province suddenly 69 temporary large-scale weekly winter distributions of foodstuffs (groats, beans etc.) and money for non-pauper poor households were organised in 1846 and 1847. From 10% to a maximum of 30% of the rural households could be reached in this way (Paping, 1995: 290–292). The provincial government supported this strategy, afraid as it was that if the mass of able-bodied farm labourers received poor relief once, some would be reduced to long-term paupers. In none of the other provinces does this kind of temporary initiatives seem to have been taken, indicating the severity of the crisis for the Groningen rural poor.

In some 90 Dutch locations (mainly cities) regular winter distributions were organised all through the forties. In the winters 1845/6 and 1846/7 the amount of money needed for this nearly doubled, but considering the high price level the amount of food distributed did rise only marginally. The same was true of the expenditures by the poor relief boards on paupers living at home or in local institutions, which rose from about 6.5 million to about 8.5 million Dutch guilders; hardly enough to compensate for the high price level.

After 1847 the share of paupers did not quickly return to pre-famine levels, although there was some decline in all provinces. The share of paupers fell most in North and South Holland, though only in North Holland and Drenthe did the share of paupers again fall to its pre-1845 level. Although the share of paupers in North Holland remained higher than anywhere else in the Netherlands, the differences became smaller. In Utrecht and surprisingly in Gelderland, the share of paupers showed even an increase in the 1850s. However, in Gelderland this unexplained rise might have something to do with changing counting procedures.

VIII. Demographic consequences

The potato blight years 1846–1847 marked the last period, before the end of the Second World War, when people were really talking of famine in the Netherlands, especially in the river clay area of Gelderland. As mentioned in the Bommelerwaard a large part of the population depended for its income on potatoes, comprising according to some reports four-fifths of the sown area, and the region was deemed to be near to starvation (Beekman, 1990: 9). The loss of the harvest had catastrophic results in this region. The local vicar Hooyer (1847) wrote a pamphlet to raise funds to help the inhabitants of the Bommelerwaard (Bergman, 1967: 400). He stated that a national campaign to supplement the funds of the local poor relief boards had come too late to save a lot of people from starvation. If we put the number of deaths in 1841/1844 at 100, 1845 is 110, 1846 is 126, 1847 is 162, 1848 is 125, 1849 is 141, and 1850/1854 is 97. A comparison of these figures with the national and provincial ones (Table 8.15) shows that only in 1847 mortality was relatively high, and even in that year the differences were not striking. So, it seems an exaggeration to speak of wide-spread starvation in the Bommelerwaard, though the effect of the potato disease on the mortality rates in this region was higher than elsewhere.

The death rate of farmers (ca 35% of the population) and labourers (ca 40% of the population) rose some 20% more than that of other occupational groups in the period 1846/1850 (Beekman, 1990: 14–22). Interestingly, mortality in labouring families was relatively high in 1846 and 1847, while within farmer families there seems to have been a delayed effect in 1848 and 1849. Mortality was especially higher in the 3-to-9 and 40-to-69 year age categories in the period 1846–1850 (Beekman, 1990: 15–19). The important 40-to-69 year age group was hit mostly in 1846 and 1847, resulting in a lot of fatherless and motherless children. Young children aged 3 to 9 showed a higher mortality in 1848 and 1849 suggesting that the bad food situation in previous years had weakened their general health, making them more vulnerable for all kind of diseases.

According to Van Zanden (1991: 25) the excess mortality in the Netherlands as a result of the food crisis in the period 1846–1849 was nearly 0.5% of the population, being lowest in North Brabant, Limburg and, surprisingly, Gelderland (0.1–0.2%) and highest in North Holland and Drenthe (0.6–0.7%). However, whether his calculations can be completely trusted is open to doubt, especially since he includes in his calculations the relatively good years of 1848 and 1849. The relatively high excess deaths in the Dutch coastal area can be attributed to a maleria epidemic in exactly the same years. On the other hand it can be suggested that malaria took so many lives because a lot of people were weakened by an insufficient food-intake in the preceding years. Hofstee (1978: 24, 145–146, 175; idem, 1981: 72–73) also considers the potato crisis and the resulting food shortages as the cause of the high mortality in 1846 and 1847, while the high mortality of 1848 and 1849 he relates partly to cholera. According to him, the high mortality was concentrated in provinces with mostly clay (diluvial) soil, while it was less in sandy (alluvial) regions. Table 8.15 clearly shows that it is indeed dangerous to mix figures of the potato crisis years 1846 and 1847 and the post-crisis years 1848 and 1849. Mortality was higher in the relatively prosperous post-crisis years

The mortality figures for 1845 for every province are very normal, and in this way sharply contrast with the following four years. In 1846 when the consequences of the failure of the potato crisis began to be felt, mortality in every province began to rise. However, there were large differences between provinces. The figures suggest that the thinly populated inland province of Drenthe was already heavily hit in 1846, and this was also to a lesser extent the case in the coastal potato growing provinces of Zeeland and Friesland. In the following year mortality rose significantly in all the coastal provinces, and also in Utrecht. Only in urbanised North Holland did mortality rates rise above 50% of the normal figures. Mortality increases were on the other hand com-

Table 8.15 The development of mortality in the Dutch provinces, 1840–1849

	1840/44 %	1840/44	1845	1846	1847	1848	1849
North Holland	30.1	100	98	131	151	124	135
South Holland	30.1	100	102	122	130	128	165
Groningen	22.1	100	100	123	143	140	133
Friesland	21.5	100	95	133	141	138	130
Zeeland	31.7	100	90	135	129	106	102
Utrecht	26.7	100	100	115	133	132	171
Drenthe*	20.4	100	104	137	118	125	125
Norg	44.9	100	51	163	303	180	263
Overijssel	24.1	100	100	119	122	119	127
Gelderland	22.7	100	104	111	116	124	114
North Brabant	21.9	100	103	111	118	120	111
Limburg	22.9	100	99	106	119	107	105
The Netherlands	25.8	100	100	122	132	124	134

Source: *Jaarboekje*, 1842–1849; *Statistisch jaarboek*, 1851; Hofstee, 1978: 191: population figures 1842.
* The mortality numbers of Norg (comprising the pauper colony of Veenhuizen, whose inhabitants mainly came from the western part of the Netherlands) are excluded from the figures of Drenthe.

paratively very moderate in the sandy inland provinces of Limburg, North Brabant, Gelderland and Overijssel; mortality in Drenthe also fell to this level in 1847. The effects of the potato blight do not seem to have been enough to result in 'famine-like' circumstances in these provinces. The higher mortality rates in the Bommelerwaard in the river clay district of the Betuwe were offset by lower rates in the more sandy regions of Gelderland (Veluwe and Achterhoek).

The provincial figures show that the potato crisis had its largest effects on mortality in the coastal clay parts of the Netherlands, while the sandy inland parts were hit far less. Only the case of Drenthe does not fit completely into this scheme for 1846. This deviation cannot be blamed on the large beggar colony lying within its frontiers, because we have corrected for that. Death rates in colonies like Veenhuizen were indeed dramatically high, especially in 1847 and in 1849, however, the mortality registers show that most deaths concern people who were brought their recently from North and South Holland and other provinces.

In 1848 mortality rates did not return to old levels, but remained high, especially in the coastal areas, with Zeeland as an outstanding exception. In 1849 mortality reached again a peak in the Netherlands, being on average 34% higher than normal. Responsible for this high level were especially Utrecht and South Holland, where an epidemic of cholera asiatica raged through the region, being responsible for some one third of deaths in 1849. According to contemporary statistics 22,460 persons died of cholera in 1848–1849 in the Netherlands ('T Hart, 1990: 85, 180–182, 211–213, 248, 303). Coming from Russia and Germany, the epidemic had already struck Amsterdam and the cities of Groningen and Utrecht by October 1848, although most casualties fell in July and August

1849. Comparatively untouched by the cholera were the south-eastern provinces of Gelderland, Limburg, North Brabant and also Zeeland, while in most of the coastal provinces mortality was high in 1849.[12]

Figure 8.6 Monthly development of the number of births and deaths in the Netherlands, 1840–1849

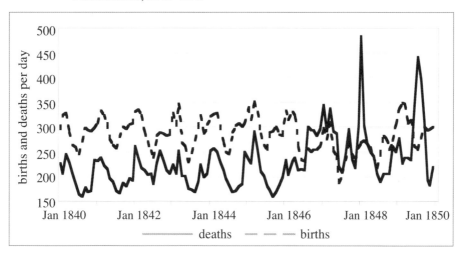

Monthly death rates make it easier to relate mortality to specific causes (Figure 8.6). Mortality showed a clear pattern with high death rates in the first months of each year. The loss of nearly all potatoes during the harvest of 1845 did not raise the number of deaths in any way the first 8–9 months. Maybe the mortality rate remained a little bit higher during the early summer of 1846. However, in August 1846 death rates began to rise extraordinarily to remain high till April 1847. This mortality was partly the product of malaria in the coastal provinces, where malaria epidemics were a 10–15 yearly recurring disaster (De Meere, 1982: 84–92).[13] It is of course also tempting to relate these excess deaths to the weakening of the population as a result of the potato blight, but then the fall-off in mortality in the disastrous months of 1847 May, June and July to near-normal levels is not easily explained. Clearly, this is a sign that starvation was not the prime factor moving the death rate in this period.

In the autumn of 1847 the death rate remained relatively high and in January 1848 it speeded up to reach by far the highest level in the period under observation. In every Dutch province mortality doubled. A micro investigation of death registers of the city of Groningen showed that from about 28 December 1847 to 19 January 1848 mortality

---

[12] Cholera deaths in 1848–1849 as a percentage of the total number of deaths in 1849 were: North Holland 23%; South Holland 37%; Groningen 23%; Friesland 14%; Zeeland 4%; Utrecht 43%; Drenthe 19%; Overijssel 17%; Gelderland 12%; North Brabant 0% (no figures); Limburg 8%.

[13] Malaria was also in some parts endemic, which partly explains the structurally higher death rates in Zeeland, North Holland and South Holland in pre-disease years (Table 8.16). Until the second half of the 19th century these provinces were extremely unhealthy to live in.

was indeed enormous. Especially from 4 January to 12 January it was more than three times above normal. It wasn't malaria, because then mortality would not have risen so much in the inland provinces, nor are there signs of a small-pox epidemic, and the cholera epidemic was yet to come. It was an icy spell, but by no means exceptional; possibly we are dealing with a widespread influenza epidemic. That this short-term national rise in mortality had something to do indirectly with a long-term deterioration of health caused by the potato blight cannot be completely ruled out.

After this unexplained mortality crisis, death rates fell again to a little above normal for a year and a half, to rise again significantly in the months from June 1849 to August 1849 due to the cholera epidemic already mentioned. Two statements have to be made about the high mortality rates in 1848 and 1849. Firstly, of course it is possible to relate the strength of the cholera epidemic in these years to the weakening of the population caused by the bad food situation in 1846–1847 (Van Zanden and Van Riel, 2000: 251; De Meere, 1982: 112). The cholera epidemic began in August 1848, just a year after the fall in food prices, giving people little time to restore their health situation. However, by far the most casualties fell in 1849, as Figure 8.6 clearly shows. Secondly, the cholera epidemic wasn't the only explanation of the high mortality rates in 1848–1849. Only a little more than half of the excess mortality in 1848–1849 can be attributed to the epidemic, leaving still an unexplained 40%–45% of excess deaths, due in major part to the national death crisis in January 1848.

More signs of what Van Zanden and Van Riel (2000: 251) call a classical 'subsistence-crisis' can be found if we consider the Dutch monthly birth rates. Famine will in general result in the postponement of conceptions, in lower female fertility, and in more inter-rupted pregnancies or very premature births. The consequences will be seen between three and nine months afterwards. Monthly births – taking into account a correction for the distinct seasonal fluctuations – were very stable till October 1845. In November and December a slight and temporary downturn occurred, after which the birth rate recovered completely. From May 1846 onwards the number of births decreased, reaching a low of 15% below ordinary level in September and October 1846. This fall in the birth rate began too early to relate it completely to the malaria epidemic of autumn 1846. On the other hand, it began about nine months after August 1845, suggesting that the problems caused by the potato blight indeed resulted in a significant decrease in female fertility.

The birth rate remained rather low for several months and starting in March 1847 it fell even more to 23% below the non-crisis norm in June 1847. There are several possible explanations for this birth crisis in the spring of 1847. Possibly, the fall in fertility was a combined effect of the malaria epidemic of August 1846–April 1847 and the high food prices of the winter of 1846/1847. The number of births stayed 10% to 20% below ordinary level till June 1848. In July 1848 the birth rate was back to normal. By October 1848 the number of births again was 15% below normal as a short-term effect on con-ceptions of the very high death rate in January 1848. It has to be remarked that the cholera epidemics of 1848–1849 left no trace in the birth rate, because compared to malaria epidemics only a relatively small part of the population was infected by this very deadly decease. In conclusion, although the consequences of the potato blight are difficult to separate completely from the effects of malaria epidemics which struck the Netherlands simultaneously, it is clear that the blight resulted in a fall in the number of births. Comparing the birth rate between August 1846 and June 1848 with the figures for 1840–1844 suggests approximately 30,000 averted births in this period.

IX. Conclusion

We tried to show the consequences of the potato blight in the Netherlands mainly by presenting provincial figures on all kind of variables. In 1845 about three-quarters and in 1846 about half of the potato harvest was lost, resulting in a short-term fall in the cultivation of potatoes, which recovered already quickly after 1846. A shift in potato cultivation from (coastal) clay soil regions to (inland) sandy soil regions took place. The potato crisis in the Netherlands was seriously aggravated by the loss of half the rye harvest in 1846. The consequences of these harvest failures for the food consumption were mainly checked in this rich country by purchasing alternatives, partly on international markets. Imports of food were paid for by rising exports of livestock and oats.

However, the part of the population which wasn't able to buy it's way through the potato crisis came in a vulnerable position. Because nominal earnings did not rise significantly, urban lower class suffered a lot especially in 1847, which resulted in food riots in some places. Potato consumption in the cities, however, fell relatively little, aggravating the situation in the countryside. The rural lower class which grew potatoes themselves came into serious difficulties, their real earnings declined while they had to buy more food to compensate for the lost potatoes. Although the situation of the lower class deteriorated enormously during 1846 and especially the first half year of 1847, there are little signs of starvation. Mortality did indeed rise, but the rise is difficult to connect directly to the potato blight, considering the quite low death rates during the most difficult months of May–July 1847, when prices rose to about three times their normal level. On the other hand, an indirect effect by way of a deteriorated state of health caused by reduced food intake is possible. Also a considerable part of the fall in birth rate in 1846–1847 can definitely be attributed to the economic distress accompanying the blight.

The results of the analysis of several indicators of standard of living for the several provinces appears to be a little confusing, with different indicators suggesting different provinces suffering the most (Table 8.16). If we limit ourselves to the short term consequences, the consumption situation seems to have been worst in the potato growing provinces of Gelderland, Friesland, Groningen and Drenthe, while Limburg and to a lesser extent North Brabant were relatively well off. This contrasts sharply with the development in the number of paupers, where North Brabant shows the greatest absolute and relative increase. In Gelderland and Groningen the number of paupers developed more in line with the Netherlands as a whole. However, Groningen was also the only province were large-scale winter distributions of non-paupers were organised, suggesting that in reality poverty during 1846–1847 rose much more than official poverty figures suggest. If we turn ourselves to the biological standard of living measured by height (we miss data for some provinces) the provinces of Utrecht, North Brabant (!) and Zeeland stand out as experiencing the largest downturn, while in Limburg there was no effect to be seen at all. Groningen and Drenthe only showed a relatively moderate fall in the biological standard of living. An analysis of mortality rates in 1846–1847 showed that in coastal provinces the number of deaths rose more than in the inland provinces.

In Table 8.16 a rough measure for the general development of the standard of living in the Dutch provinces during the potato blight is presented, taking into account all five indicators used and giving them the same weight. Clearly the situation in the two coastal clay provinces Friesland and Groningen situated somewhat in the periphery was worst. This result contrasts with Van Zanden (1991: 8) who mentions only Friesland and Zee-

Table 8.16 Ranking of the development of welfare measures in the Dutch provinces during the potato blight

	Potato production	Bread consumption	Height	Paupers	Mortality	Average	Riots in 1847
North Holland	10	5	3	5	0	4.6	
South Holland	6	7	–	4	5	5.8	
Groningen	0	2	3	8	3	3.3	*
Friesland	0	5	–	3	1	2.5	*
Zeeland	3	10	1	7	3	4.9	
Utrecht	8	4	0	9	6	5.3	
Drenthe	1	3	3	10	5	4.3	
Overijssel	4	7	–	9	7	6.8	*
Gelderland	3	0	–	8	10	5.1	*
North Brabant	4	9	2	0	9	4.8	
Limburg	8	–	10	5	10	8.2	

NB: 0 is most negative, 10 is most positive.

Potato: the absolute fall in potato production per capita of 1845 and 1846 compared with the period 1842/1844; Bread: the absolute fall in consumption of wheaten and rye bread per capita in 1846/1847 compared with 1840/1844 (Limburg is missing); Height: the percentage rise in the undersized conscripts in 1847/1849 compared with 1842/1846 (several provinces are missing); Paupers: the percentage rise in the percentage paupers from 1846-1847, compared with 1840/1844; Mortality: The relative rise in the number of deaths in 1846-1847, compared with 1840/1844.

land, while according to him the crisis was less in Groningen, which he attributes to a larger share of freeholders. The inland sandy provinces of Limburg and Overijssel remained comparatively the most untouched by the failure of the potato blight. Rural market-oriented regions seem to have suffered the most. In less market-oriented parts, it was easier to get hold of alternatives for the lost potatoes, because of the large amount of self provision. In urban areas there were more possibilities (because of the greater liquidity) to buy alternatives. However, for the urban lower class which run completely short of money as a result of the high price level, this expensive strategy was unattainable.

In the long term the potato blight had two other effects. First, for the next fifteen years food consumption of the Dutch population was lower than before 1845. Although potato yields recovered – however, remaining about 30% per hectare lower than before 1845 – it was only after 1860 that the average height of Dutchmen again began to rise structurally. Secondly, a much higher proportion of the population had become dependent on poor-relief in the Netherlands, and in most of the provinces it took a very long time to return again to the old situation. In several provinces the potato blight had made it normal to support households of unemployed or underemployed able bodied poor.

Bibliography

Algemeen verslag wegens den staat van den landbouw in het Koningrijk der Nederlanden (1845–1860).

Beekman, V. (1990) 'De invloed van de mislukte aardappeloogsten van 1845/46 op de sterfte in de Bommelerwaard', Unpublished student essay rural history, Wageningen University.

Bergman, M. (1967) 'The potato blight in the Netherlands and its social consequences', *International review on social history*, 12, pp. 390–431.

Algemeene Landhuishoudelijke Courant (1847–1848); Continued as *Landhuishoudelijke Courant* (1849–1850), and as *Landbouw Courant* (1851).

Bernhardi (1846), 'Over de aardappelziekte in het jaar 1845', *De Vriend van den Landman*, 10, pp. 278–298.

Bescheiden betreffende de geldmiddelen, eerste stuk (1961), 's-Gravenhage.

Bieleman, J. (1987) *Boeren op het Drentse zand 1600–1910. Een nieuwe visie op de 'oude' landbouw*, Wageningen.

Bieleman, J. (1992) *Geschiedenis van de landbouw in Nederland 1500–1950*, Meppel/ Amsterdam.

Bieleman, J. (1995) 'De Gelderse landbouw voor 1850', in J. Bieleman et al. (eds), *Anderhalve eeuw Gelderse landbouw, De geschiedenis van de Geldersche maatschappij van landbouw en het Gelderse platteland*, Groningen, pp. 34–64.

Bijdragen tot de Algemeene Statistiek van Nederland (1878) part 1.

Blaauw, M.J.E. (1995) *Van Friese grond. Agrarische eigendoms- en gebruiksverhoudingen en de ontwikkeling in de Friese landbouw in de negentiende eeuw*, Leeuwarden.

Doorman, J. (1847) *Neerlands financiewezen van den vroegen en tegenwoordigen tijd*, Utrecht.

Eerenbeemt, H.F.J.M van den (ed.) (1996) *Geschiedenis van Noord-Brabant, deel 1: Traditie en modernisering 1796–1890*, Amsterdam/Meppel.

Frieling, F.H.C. (1853) 'Verslag van den toestand der arbeidende klasse, vooral ten platten lande, in de provincie Utrecht', *Tijdschrift voor Staathuishoudkunde en Statistiek*, 8, pp. 405–452.

Gales, B.P.A. et al. (1997) *Het Burgerlijk Armbestuur. Twee eeuwen zorg voor armen, zieken en ouderen te Maastricht, band 1*, Maastricht.

Gout, D. (1976/77) 'Het broodoproer in Groningen in 1847', *Groningse Volksalmanak*, pp. 63–84.

Hall, H.C. van (1846) 'Bijdragen tot de statistiek van den Nederlandschen landbouw', *Tijdschrift ter bevordering van Nijverheid*, 11, pp. 172–233.

Hofstee, E.W. (1978) *De demografische ontwikkeling van Nederland in de eerste helft van de negentiende eeuw; Een historisch-demografische en sociologische studie*, Wageningen.

Hofstee, E.W. (1981) *Korte demografische geschiedenis van Nederland van 1800 tot heden*, Haarlem.

Hooyer, C. (1847) *De groote nood des hongers in en bij den Boemelerwaard. Een waar verslag voor alle menschenvrienden in ons vaderland*, Zaltbommel.

Jaarboekje over (....) uitgegeven op last van Z.M. den Koning (1842–1849), 's Gravenhage.

Knaap, D.A. (2000) 'Het W.A. Scholtenconcern (1840–1900): first mover in de Nederlandse aardappelmeelindustrie', *NEHA-Jaarboek voor economische, bedrijfs- en techniekgeschiedenis*, 63, pp. 8–42.

Knippenberg, H. (1995) 'Het hart van Nederland. De provincie Utrecht in de periode 1800–1940', in K. Mandemakers and O. Boonstra (eds), *De levensloop van de Utrechtse bevolking in de 19ᵉ eeuw*, Assen, pp. 7–36.

Knotter A. and Muskee, H. (1986) 'Conjunctuur en levensstandaard in Amsterdam 1815–1855. Een onderzoek op basis van plaatselijke accijnzen', *Tijdschrift voor Sociale Geschiedenis*, 11, pp. 153–181.

Maas, J. van der and Noordegraaf, L. (1983) 'Smakelijk eten. Aardappelconsumptie in Holland in de achttiende eeuw en het begin van de negentiende eeuw', *Tijdschrift voor Sociale Geschiedenis*, 9, pp. 188–220.

Maddison, A. (2003) *The World Economy: Historical Statistics*, Paris.

Meere, J.M.M. de (1982) *Economische ontwikkeling en levensstandaard in Nederland gedurende de eerste helft van de negentiende eeuw; Aspecten en trends*, 's-Gravenhage.

Oomens, C.A. (1989) *De loop der bevolking van Nederland in de negentiende eeuw*, CBS Statistische Onderzoekingen M35, 's-Gravenhage.

Oomens, C.A. and Den Bakker, G.P. (1994) 'De beroepsbevolking in Nederland 1849–1990', *Supplement bij de sociaal economische maandstatistiek*, part 2.

Oppers, V.M. (1963) *Analyse van de acceleratie van de menselijke lengtegroei door de bepaling van het tijdstip van de groeifasen*, Amsterdam.

Otterloo, A.H. van (1990) *Eten en eetlust in Nederland 1840–1990. Een historisch-sociologische studie*, Amsterdam.

Paping, R.F.J. (1995) *Voor een handvol stuivers. Werken, verdienen en besteden: de levensstandaard van boeren, arbeiders en middenstanders op de Groninger klei, 1770–1860*, Groningen.

Philips, J.F.R., Jansen, J.C.G.M. and Claessens, Th.J.A.H. (1965) *Geschiedenis van de landbouw in Limburg 1750–1914*, Assen.

Pilat, D. (1989) *Dutch agricultural export performance (1846–1926)*. Groningen.

Posthumus, N.W. (1943) *Nederlandsche prijsgeschiedenis, deel 1*, Leiden.

Pot, G.P.M. (1994) *Arm Leiden. Levensstandaard, bedeling en bedeelden, 1750–1854*, Hilversum.

Priester, P.R. (1991) *De economische ontwikkeling van de landbouw in Groningen 1800–1910. Een kwalitatieve en kwantitatieve benadering*, Groningen.

Priester, P.R. (1998) *Geschiedenis van de Zeeuwse landbouw circa 1600–1910*, Wageningen.

W.J.M.J. Rutten, W.J.M.J. (1995) 'De levensstandaard in Limburg van de Franse tijd tot aan de Eerste wereldoorlog. Een analyse van de lichaamslengte van Limburgse lotelingen', *Studies over de sociaal-economische geschiedenis van Limburg*, 40, Leeuwarden/Maastricht, pp 123–160.

Saltet, R.H. (1917) 'Aardappeloogsten en hun invloed op het volksleven', *Vragen van den dag*, 32, pp. 454–466.

Slicher van Bath, B.H. (1957) *Een samenleving onder spanning. Geschiedenis van het platteland van Overijssel*, Assen.

Smits, J.P., Horlings E. and Van Zanden, J.L. (2000) *Dutch GNP and its components, 1800–1913*, Groningen.

Spahr van der Hoek, J.J. (1952) *Geschiedenis van de Friese landbouw*, part 1, Leeuwarden.

Staatkundig en staathuishoudkundig Jaarboekje, 1850.

Statistiek van den handel en de Scheepvaart van het Koninkrijk der Nederlanden, 1846–1850 (1847–1851), 's-Gravenhage.

Statistisch Jaarboek voor het koningrijk der Nederlanden (1851–1863).

Tassenaar, P.G. (2000) *Het verloren Arcadia. De biologische levensstandaard in Drenthe, 1800–1860*, Capelle a.d. IJssel.

Terlouw, F. (1971) 'De aardappelziekte in Nederland in 1845 en volgende jaren', *Economisch- en Sociaal-Historisch Jaarboek*, 34, pp. 263–308.

'T Hart, P.D. (1990) *Utrecht en de cholera 1832–1910*, Zutphen.

Tijms, W. (1983) *Prijzen van granen en peulvruchten te Arnhem, Breda, Deventer, 's-Hertogenbosch, Kampen, Koevorden, Maastricht en Nijmegen: Historia Agriculturae XI-2*, Groningen.

Uitkomsten der beroepstelling in het koningrijk der Nederlanden op den 31-12-1889, 's Gravenhage (1894).

Verslag van de Gedeputeerde Staten aan de Staten der provincie Groningen gedaan in derzelver vergadering (1842–1860).

'Verslag omtrent het armwezen' (1841/2–1852/3), *Verslag der Handelingen van de Staten-Generaal*.

V(issering), S. (1845) *Eenige opmerkingen ter zake de aardappelteelt*, Amsterdam.

Vries, J. de (1981) *Barges and capitalism; Passenger transportation in the Dutch Economy 1632–1839*, Utrecht.

Vries, J. de and Woude, A.M. van der (1997) *The first modern economy: success, failure, and perseverance of the Dutch economy, 1500–1815*, Cambridge.

Wintle, M. (2000) *An economic and social history of the Netherlands, 1800–1920*, Cambridge.

Zanden, J.L. van (1985) *De economische ontwikkeling van de Nederlandse landbouw, 1800–1914*, Wageningen.

Zanden, J.L. van (1991) *'Den zedelijken materiëlen toestand der arbeidende bevolking ten platten lande'. Een reeks raporten uit 1851*, Groningen.

Zanden, J.L. van and Riel, A. van (2000) *Nederland 1780–1914. Staat, instituties en economische ontwikkeling*, Amsterdam.

Zeeman, J. (1861) 'Rapport van de commissie voor statistiek over de lotelingen in de provincie Groningen van 1835–1861', *Nederlandsch tijdschrift voor geneeskunde*, 5, pp. 691–723.

9   The crisis in Prussia[1]

Hans H. Bass, Bremen University of Applied Science

I.   Introduction

Causes, consequences and coping strategies in the subsistence crisis of 1847 were different in the various parts of Prussia. This is not surprising, given the size and the economic diversity of the country. Mid-19th century Prussia, home to 16 million inhabitants, stretched approximately 1,200 km East to West (Aachen–Memel) and up to 400 km North to South. The state, administratively organized into 26 counties (*Regierungsbezirke*) in eight provinces, consisted of two major parts, which were geographically not directly connected with each other. In economic respect, Prussia included regions[2] as diverse as the manor house-dominated East-Elbia, proto-industrial Upper Silesia and East Westphalia, the factory area of the Wupper Valley, smallholding and viniculture areas along the Rhine river, and areas characterized by market-oriented medium-scale agriculture and farming in Lower Rhineland, Saxony, and Lower Silesia.

Agricultural production in Prussia as a whole increased considerably during the first half of the 19th century. Not only did this sustain a growing population with on average enhanced diet, but also expanded the century-old grain export trade from the Baltic area. However, this does not mean that Prussia had already escaped the danger of subsistence crises. Especially in 1847, hunger was widespread. On the one hand, the margin between food production and the amount of consumption necessary to satisfy the basic needs of the population on average was still small. Yet in the course of the argumentation of this paper it will become clear that more factors have to be taken into consideration to explain this subsistence crisis in Prussia than a harvest related food availability decline. Thus, the following section (II) discusses conditions underlying the 1847-crisis, especially production, consumption, and trade of food, and the population dynamics. The next section (III) analyses the subsistence crisis of 1847 in Prussia, particularly in the framework of the 'food availability decline' approach and Sen's 'loss of entitlements' approach, and, finally (IV), some conclusions and comparative thoughts are presented.

---

[1] The author wishes to thank the participants of the 2003 Dublin Workshop, especially Mary Daly and Pat McGregor, for their very useful comments on a first draft of this contribution, as well as Michael Hecht, who provided detailed price data, and Andreas Kunz, who provided the map. As always, any remaining mistakes are the sole responsibility of the author.
[2] An economic region is defined here with respect to similarity judged by one or more features. A region in this sense ('homogeneous region') is not necessarily congruent with a region defined by intra-regional interdependence of functions ('functional region') or by political borders ('administrative or planning region') – see Schätzl 1998: 94–95 for the different concepts. It is obvious that in this view some of the counties consisted of two or three distinct economic regions (like Minden County which comprised the proto-industrial Minden-Ravensberg area and the agrarian surplus Paderborn area), while on the other hand various counties can be grouped together as the long-distance grain export region of Prussian East-Elbia.

II. The pre-famine situation

II.1. Food production

The increase in food production[3] in Prussia between the beginning and the middle of the 19th century was due to higher factor inputs (arable land, labour, capital) as well as progress in the partial productivity of factors (Wehler, 1987: 27–53, esp. 40 ff.). The latter resulted *inter alia* from changes in property rights, i.e. the general establishment of sole proprietorship of land, the formal abolishment of serfdom in 1810 (Schönthaler, 2002), and the restructuring of the agricultural production system. Where soil conditions allowed, a system dominated by rye as a universal crop was being replaced by a crop system based on wheat and potatoes. Wheat, traded over long distances, served as a cash crop for the larger farms and manors, while the higher calorie-per-acre potato served as a subsistence food crop for the rural poor, was marketed over short distances as food for the urban poor, and was used as fodder. In addition, potato distilling instead of rye distilling had become common practice, particularly in the East of the country. By-products of distillery served as fodder in stable keeping. Thus, meat production increased, and the manure promoted in turn the cultivation of wheat.

Between 1800 and 1850 there had been an increase of average area yields of wheat by 50 per cent to 1,300 kg (= 4.6 mill. kcal) per hectare, compared to an increase of rye yields of 28 per cent to 1,160 kg (= 4.1 mill. kcal) per hectare (computed with data from Von Finckenstein, 1934: 53, 58). The average area productivity for potatoes does not seem to have increased much during this period, as potato cultivation significantly relied on claiming marginal (i.e. less fertile) lands. For the territory of the latter German Reich, estimates are 8,600 kg (= 7.3 mill. kcal) per hectare potato yield in 1850 (computed with data from Bittermann, 1956: 34–35)[4] – only about 60 per cent of what could be produced in Flanders (see Vanhaute, this volume).

----

[3] Production and consumption data in mid-19th century sources are given in 'Scheffel', a dry measure. A Berlin *Scheffel*, according to *Preußische Maß- und Gewichtsordnung vom 16. Mai 1816,* is equivalent to 0.549615 hl; the minimum weight of a scheffel for various types of food as calculated by the Royal Magazines is given as 90.5 *Pfund* of pulses, 85.5 *Pfund* of wheat, 80.5 *Pfund* of rye, 55.5 *Pfund* of barley, and 45.5 *Pfund* of oats; a *Pfund* is equivalent to 0.46771 kg (Von Reden, 1853/54: 2302–2304). This leads to the following *minimum* weights per Scheffel: pulses 42.3 kg, wheat 40.0 kg, rye 37.7 kg, barley 26.0 kg, and oats 21.3 kg. Data used in modern agro-business refer, for instance, to 77 to 79 kg/hl (www.agrigate.ch/preise/de/richtpreise/ pr_brotgetreide_00-10_d.htm) for marketable wheat, i.e. that estimates for a *Scheffel* of wheat could be between 42.3 kg and 43.4 kg or about 6 to 9 per cent more than the minimum weights given in the contemporary source. In this paper we added 3 per cent to the minimum weights as given above and converted scheffel into kilogram by the following rates: pulses 43.6 kg, wheat 41.2 kg, rye 38.8 kg, barley 26.8 kg, and oats 21.9 kg. For potatoes, a wide range of estimations exists. Here, 47.0 kg per scheffel is used as a conversion figure.
[4] Estimations of the 1840s/50s' average potato yield using Von Lengerke's estimation of area usage and the production estimations provided in Table 9.1, arrive at 6,500 kg (= 5.5 mill. kcal) per hectare (Schubert's data) and 10,000 kg (8.5 mill. kcal) per hectare (Von Lengerke's data), respectively. Both figures seem misleading. See also Harnisch, 1984: 210 for a positive assessment of Bittermann's data quality.

While in the beginning of the 19th century five times more rye than wheat was produced in Prussia, it was only three times as much in the mid of the century. Rye production had increased 1.4-fold, while wheat production increased 2.2-fold, yet potato production increased 13.3-fold (computed from data of Krug, 1805 and Von Lengerke, 1851; both quoted in Von Reden, 1853: 88–91). In mid-19th century, 55% of arable land was used for all sorts of grain, 11% for potatoes, 11% to grow fodder and 22% as fallow (estimation by Schubert, 1846; quoted in Von Reden, 1853: 90). On average, the share of potato production was no *quantité négligeable* – although by Irish standard it was not particularly high, as Solar (1997) rightly pointed out.

Estimations on the total amount of food production in Prussia and its various uses are provided in Table 9.1. It should be kept in mind, however, that harvest failures happened every few years. For instance, failures of more than 20 per cent less than average were recorded in the Rhineland between 1816 and 1850 six times in the 24 years for which quantitative estimations exist (see Bass 1991: 57).

Table 9.1 "Average" food production, Prussia c. 1850

in thousand tons	(L)	(S)	in thousand tons	(L)	(S)
1. Wheat	**808**	**653**	**4. Oats**	**1,661**	**1,523**
o/w Consumption	61%		o/w Horse fodder	84%	
Distillery	1%		Human consumption	1%	
Brewery	1%		Export	1%	
Export	26%		Seed	14%	
Seed	11%				
2. Rye	**2,487**	**2,765**	**5. Pulses etc.**	**327**	**299**
o/w Consumption	81%		o/w Consumption/Seed	89%	
Distillery	0%		Export	11%	
Export	3%				
Seed	14%				
3. Barley	**514**	**690**	**6. Potatoes**	**13,184**	**8,472**
o/w Consumption	57%		o/w Consumption	57%	
Distillery	10%		Distillery	7%	
Brewery	16%		Fodder	21%	
Export	4%		Seed	14%	
Seed	13%				

Sources: L – Von Lengerke (1851), S – Schubert (1846); both quoted in Von Reden (1853: 88-89).

II.2. Food consumption

According to semi-official estimations (Von Reden, 1853: 91) the average food intake per capita and year in the late-1840/early-1850s was 126 kg rye, 31 kg wheat, 0.5 kg oats, 17 kg pulses, and 470 kg potatoes. From these figures average calorie intake per day can be estimated to have been between 2,650 and 2,800 kcal – for the 'average' Prussian little more than half a kilogram of potatoes per day difference from what modern studies consider the nutritional minimum (2,200 kcal per day).[5] Estimates that include the consumption of meat, alcoholic beverages, rice, and sugar arrive at figures around 3,000 kcal (computed from contemporary estimations in 'Versuch ...' 1851 by Bass, 1991: 52); a calculation based on indirect evidence (Helling, 1977) estimates an average intake of 2,610 kcal per capita per day. Both figures, floor and ceiling, demonstrate a moderate increase in caloric intake per capita between the beginning and the middle of the 19th century.

Average figures, however, do not mean that much in a notably stratified society. It is equally important to realize that the intensification and diversification of agricultural production had compositional effects on diets:

Enough to eat had men in 1805 in the coarsest food as in 1831; already in 1805 the population of the Prussian State could not precisely be termed poor. However, there is even in the most common food progress in that respect that besides grain there is so much potato food added. The main progress, however, is in the more sophisticated consumption [...]. (Dieterici 1846: 153)

In plain language, this meant more meat for the rich, and more potatoes (and spirits) for the poor (see also Teuteberg, 1979: 364).

Several contemporary observers describe the low quantity, quality, and the monotony of food, which the lower strata of society actually could afford in 'normal' years (with malnourishment as a potential consequence of an insufficient intake of proteins, minerals, and vitamins). A medical account on one of the state's poorest regions, the East Elbia Bromberg County, states:

The majority of the inhabitants of the county live in utmost poverty and misery [...]. In rural areas, many individuals lack any kind of housing; in the open fields, they dig themselves in like moles and only cover their holes with a light roof. The usual food of the common man are sauerkraut and potatoes, at the most bread, bacon, pork, solid and coarse dumplings, milk, butter, cheese, herrings, other fish, onions, garlic [...] Before consumption these foodstuffs usually develop unhealthy properties by much too long storage at ill-suited places [...] Water, bad beer, corn and potato spirits are the usual beverages available [...]. (Ollenroth, 1833)

There is (anecdotal) evidence on similar conditions also from other parts of Prussia. On Upper Silesia, the social revolutionary Wolff wrote: 'The day wage for agricultural labourers is mean in the extreme. [...] Their diet consists almost solely of potatoes and schnapps' (Wolff in *Neue Rheinische Zeitung* of 25.04.1849, quoted by Engels, 1876).

---

[5] It should be pointed out, however, that the caloric value of food is only a very rough measurement of its nutritional value, as other components (such as proteins, fat, and vitamins) are neglected. The caloric value was calculated with figures from Schall and Schall (1967) and with figures from FAO (1949). Schall and Schall give 358 kcal per 100 g of wheat (peeled), 354 kcal per 100 g of rye (partially peeled), 359 kcal for peas, and 85 kcal for potatoes with skin. The use of different varieties of grain and different estimation methods arrive at different caloric values (for details of the estimation process see Merrill and Watts, 1973). Using the earliest available FAO data (FAO/Chatfield 1949) – to exclude the effects of modern bioengineering – the figures are 334 kcal per 100g of wheat (whole meal; 364 kcal for white flour), 319 kcal for rye (whole meal; 349 kcal for flour), 385 kcal for oatmeal. Using the Schall and Schall data would result in a slight upward bias, as these data refer to the further processed grain (I am grateful to Richard Paping for this hint). This also, however, seems to be justified to even out the lack of consideration of vegetables in the sources.

In the Province of East Prussia, according to the statistician Von Reden (1852: 365), one third of the rural population 'abstained' from bread as common daily food and depended only on potatoes. On Rheinbach, in the hilly Rhineland, an official yearbook states: 'Food for humans consists mainly of potatoes and black bread' (Statistik des Kreises Rheinbach für die Jahre 1859 bis 1861, quoted in Böhm, 1998). Early-19th century potato varieties were reported to 'make the throat feel rough and burning', probably due to higher solanin contents (Körber-Grohne, 1994: 144 quoting an unspecified 1818-source from H. Brücher, 1975). Buckwheat, another 'poverty culture' (Lis and Soly, 1982: 136) despite its considerable nutritional value, was the 'main food' of the agrarian proletariat in sandy East Westphalia (Der Regierungsbezirk Minden, 1832: 21). It was also cultivated in newly claimed moor soils, for instance in East Prussia, and in low mountain ranges, such as the Eifel in the Rhineland province (see also Körber-Grohne, 1994: 339–349).

Based on this information one can agree to Wehler (1987: 41) that throughout Prussia potatoes (and buckwheat) played a much more important role for the poor than indicated by the production figures, and that for poor people only narrow margins separated a modest livelihood from hunger.

II.3. Economic regions and grain markets

In mid-19th century Prussia, four types of regions can be distinguished according to the usual ratio of food production to food consumption, or their economic 'openness' for extra-regional grain trade (for a similar concept see Gailus, 1990: 230). Table 9.2 and Figure 9.1 provide a cluster analysis, i.e. counties are combined, which had a similar demographic and economic profile in relevant variables, namely:

– Grain-export regions serving international markets (the provinces East-Prussia, parts of Pommerania and parts of Posen province). This region was sparsely populated, had a high concentration in landholding and a low share of industrial income opportunities. Wheat exports mainly took place via Dantzig and Stettin and served Berlin, Hamburg, Amsterdam, Cologne, and England. Some areas in these counties, however, can be termed peripheral, especially in Gumbinnen County and parts of Königsberg and Köslin Counties;

– Agricultural surplus regions, especially in the fertile *Börde* area, which exported grain and animals for slaughter to neighbouring regions (parts of Düsseldorf, Münster, Minden, Liegnitz, and Magdeburg Counties). The risks and costs of overland trade in the pre-railway era, however, prevented the farmers of the region from engaging in long-distance trade (Kopsidis, 2002: 99);

– Smallholder areas, partly vine producing (in Trier and Koblenz Counties), and subsistence production (hilly areas like Eifel mountains in Aachen County), with a low share of industrial employment;

– Food importing regions with a comparatively high level of industrial employment;

– Proto-industrial areas (parts of Minden and Oppeln Counties), factory areas (in Düsseldorf and Arnsberg Counties), and a few urban agglomerations (Cologne, Breslau, Berlin).

A prerequisite for economic openness are transport possibilities. In Prussia, transport capacities had grown considerably during the first half of the 19th century, while at the same time they had become more evenly spread throughout the country (Bass, 1991: 71–72). State-built roads, for instance, increased from 3,200 km in 1816 to 10,400 km

Figure 9.1 Food import and export regions, Prussia 1850

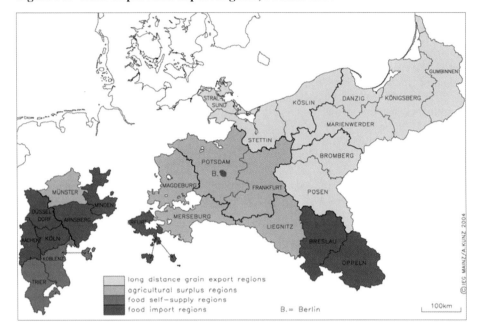

in 1842, while the coefficient of variation among the Prussian provinces decreased from 1.15 to 0.54. Freight capacity of inland ships similarly increased by more than 90 per cent between 1831 and 1842, while transport costs sank by 40 per cent in sea-ship transportation (1816 to 1846) and 20 per cent in inland-ship transportation (Weser River, 1818 to 1846). Consequently, in 1806 sea transport added 2.1 per cent to a long-term average wheat price per 100 km, but only 1.4 per cent in 1846. Land transport added 35.9 per cent per 100 km in 1838, but only 19.4 per cent in 1860 on highroads (and 3.7 per cent in the same year if the railways could be used).

Transport possibilities are also the physical foundation for market integration.[6] Although the level of food prices showed a considerable and permanent West-East slope, grain market integration – measured by the similarity of price time series of different market places – was already quite strong in Prussia in the first half of the 19th century (Fremdling and Hohorst, 1979; for a detailed study on intra-regional market integration [Westphalia] see Kopsidis, 1996; Kopsidis, 2002). Additionally, year-to-year movements of prices for rye and for potatoes show a strong correlation (r = 0.84 on average for prices in Prussian provinces 1816–1850, de-trended by using multiples of a moving average; see Bass, 1991: 62–63). Thus, markets seem to have been flexible enough to

---

[6] A market is integrated if the 'law of one price' (Jevons) holds. The process of integration can be described, for instance, by increasing price movement synchronisation on different markets. On the other hand, however, for agricultural markets price synchronisation does not necessarily indicate market integration, as climatic variables may be highly correlated and influence prices on various markets in the same direction independent of actual economic integration.

Table 9.2   Grain importing/exporting regions, Prussia 1846/49

Type of economic region	(1) Population density per km², 1849	(2) Concentration index, landholding, 1849	(3) Industrial employment per 100 inhabitants 1846	(4) Wheat and rye consumption (in TT), c. 1850 (est.)	(5) extraregional grain exports (+)/ imports (−) (in TT), (est.)
Long distance grain export region	41	0.3070	0.9	800	+ 250
Agricultural surplus region	60	0.2220	2.6	700	+ 180
Food self-supply region	76	0.0854	1.6	160	0
Food import region	102	0.1652	6.1	900	− 150
(1)-(3) unweighted average; (4) sum; (5) net cross boundary only	68	0.2234	3.1	2,560	+ 285

Long distance grain export regions include the Counties of Marienwerder, Gumbinnen, Köslin, Königsberg, Bromberg, Stralsund, Dantzig, Stettin, and Posen. Agricultural surplus regions include the Counties of Merseburg, Potsdam excluding Berlin, Frankfurt, Liegnitz, Magdeburg, and Münster. Food self-supply regions are the Counties of Trier and Koblenz. Food import regions include the Counties of Oppeln#, Minden#, Cologne, Breslau, the city of Berlin, Erfurt, Aachen, Düsseldorf, and Arnsberg. Sources: (1) computed with data from Von Reden, 1853; average excludes Berlin; (2) computed in analogy to the Gini-Index. Differences due to the peculiarity of data source ('Übersicht …', 1852) are explained in Bass, 1991: 296–297; (3) without sideline weaving; computed with data from Von Reden, 1853. Note that the denominator is the figure of all inhabitants and not only the gainfully employed persons; (4) estimated consumption plus exports plus seed (app. 13 % of production) adds up to the 'average production' in Table 9.1; (5) the estimate is based on the following specific data: Cologne – Schwann, 1915, III, 210, 420, data for 1847 only: +30 TT; Dantzig – Von Lengerke, 1852: 566 ff., wheat only, average 1840/50: +93 TT; Aachen: HStA Düsseldorf, Reg. Aachen Nr. 1701 – wheat and rye, average 1840/50: +9 TT; scattered information on the 1840s/50s in Von Reden, 1853 on Liegnitz (+24 TT), Berlin (−52 TT), and Magdeburg (rye and wheat exports +59 TT). However, Magdeburg County needed grain imports in years of bad harvests because of the great amount of special culture crops, i.e. sugar turnips, chicories, and potatoes. The total cross boundary wheat export in the 1840s/50s was 179 TT on average according to Onishi, 1973: 184; the export of wheat and rye here is estimated from figures in Table 9.1.
Notes:
*. unweighted average
#: predominant proto-industrial cottage industry
TT: thousand metric tons

———————

[7] As can be derived from Figure 9.2, however, the volatility of potato prices was much less than the volatility of grain prices. An explanation may be that speculation with potatoes, involving the storage and the possibility to physically transport them to a different market, was limited.

191

balance supply and demand of different types of basic foods between different localities, although in the first half of the 19th century potatoes definitely were a 'Thünen commodity' (a low price per weight inhibited long-distance trade).[7] Prussia also had long played a mayor role as a supplier of the European grain market. It provided the early-industrialising European regions (see Borchardt, 1965 on 16th and 17th-century Dantzig–Amsterdam trade), while during the first half of the 19th century England was the main export des-tination, absorbing about two third of Prussian wheat exports. The price-elasticity of wheat exports from Dantzig to England was considerable, indicating a responsive commercial agriculture: an increase in English wheat prices by one per cent caused the Dantzig expor-ters to increase wheat exports on average by 1.86 per cent in the same year and 1.67 per cent in the following year (Bass, 1991: 227–229). Finally, sophisticated economic mecha-nisms existed to make international and interregional grain trade efficient – specifically to be mentioned are deals on the forward market, which were legalized in 1842.

In food price history, the crisis of 1845/47 plays the role of a watershed, dividing a period of 25+ years of low prices following the 1816/18-famine and a similarly long high-price period up to a new political and economic history watershed in the 1870s. The observation of a rising price level validates the argument of Solar (1997) that the subsistence crisis of 1847 was a 'large, negative, and persistent productivity shock'. The average price of rye 1820 to 1844 was 96 Mark / ton, for potatoes it was 28 Mark / ton. From 1845 to 1869 the prices were 153 Mark / ton and 47 Mark / ton, respectively (sources see Figure 9.2). It is interesting to note that the relative price of potatoes to rye remained stable, which probably sets Prussia apart from other regions in Europe.

Food prices obviously reacted to supply changes. As argued in section II.1, harvest failures did happen rather frequently, and are indicated by rising prices. Price reactions were much stronger, however, than deviations of yields from the average (as already shown by Gregory King; see Wrigley, 1987: 92–98), because demand for staple food was price-inelastic[8], supply was only moderately price-elastic.[9] Thus the amount of food availability decline associated with price heights should not be overestimated. On average, a 100 per cent increase in prices indicates a 23 per cent decrease in supplies.

Considering the enhancements in transport capacity and the indications of market integration one may assume that regional differences between food supply and demand in Prussia were under usual circumstances evened out by extra-regional grain-trade. Physical potential and economic mechanisms for increasing or decreasing the ratio between

---

[8] Under several assumptions (including the price-inelasticity of supply, i.e. closed markets, and constant consumption behaviour over time), an iso-elastic demand-curve can be described as $D=ap^b$ with b representing the price-elasticity of demand. Linearization by logarithmical transformation leads to $\log D = \log a + b \log p$, for which the parameters can be estimated by linear regression. Data are derived from a consumption tax on grain, which was levied in urban areas. Urban demand-elasticity for rye was estimated to be –0.23, which means that a 1 per cent increase in prices resulted in a 0.23 per cent decrease of consumption. The values derived from this estimation for seven Prussian provinces 1838–1850 are significant on a 95% level (average $r = -0.68$). The highest elasticity was estimated for Potsdam County (–0.37), the lowest for East Prussia (–0.15); see Bass, 1991: 294–295.

[9] As is estimated in Table 9.2, food-import regions normally imported about 15% of the grain consumption. Adding 25 % more imports, which would have put a lot of strain on transport cap-acities, would have resulted only in an increase of supply of about 4%.

regional food production and regional food consumption existed (although probably not enough for extraordinary shortages). Thus it may be concluded that by the mid-19th century, regional food scarcities in Prussia had ceased to be purely natural phenomena: enhanced transport possibilities reduced the occurrence and the severity of under-supply crisis – and increased the risk of insufficient food intake due to losses of income opportunities, as will be shown below in more details.

II.4. Food, health, and population dynamics

Health, mortality, and natality within the Prussian population during the first decades of the 19th century were recurrently influenced by food intake shortages. A food-intake to health nexus is shown in a cross regional study by Baten, 1996. It can also be shown in a longitudinal approach by correlating food prices as indicators of relative scarcity of food with anthropometric data. Health conditions, indicated by the share of those permanently unable for military service among all medically examined potential recruits, and rye prices in the respective birth year in the 1820s and 1830s are moderately strong correlated (up to r = 0.69 Frankfurt/Oder County, n = 20; see Bass 1991: 83).

Visual inspection also shows that years of high prices of basic food (1831, 1847, 1855) coincided with mortality peaks and natality lows in the same year or the following

Figure 9.2   Mortality, natality and food prices, Prussia 1816–1870

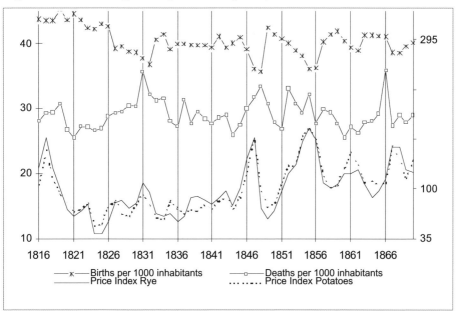

* Prices (right scale) were calculated as index figures: the average 1816–1870 = 100.
Sources: Preußische Statistische Jahrbücher; Zeitschrift des Königlich Preußischen Statistischen Landesamts, no. 47 (1907), Besondere Beilage, 84–85, both in: www.learn-line.nrw.de/angebote/eda/medio/preussen.

year (see Figure 9.2; generally on these crises see Abel, 1974; Abel, 1986; Bass, 1991; Bass, 1994a). Over the long run (1816/1870), however, prices and raw mortality figures are statistically not strongly linked to each other (r = 0.16 for rye prices and mortality, 1816–1870; r = 0.37 for the period 1820–1850). The same holds true if price data are lagged for one period. With respect to natality, correlation is slightly stronger (r = –0.40 for rye prices and natality, 1816–1870). The picture is blurred, *inter alia*, by cholera mortality, which is independent of food intake, in 1831/32, 1837, and 1848/50 as well as by war-related mortality (1866).

Deconstructing population movements on a regional basis shows that the incidents of demographic crises, defined as a significant negative deviation from a region's 'normal' population growth rate[10], differed: from the 1830s to the 1850s, the manor based long-distance grain exporting regions in East Elbia were particularly prone to demographic crises (Bass, 1991: 42–46).

The various economic regions also show different demographic reactions to food price increases (see Bass, 1991: 78–89). Both shock reactions and recovery reactions are much stronger in the East than in the West. Adjusted for cholera mortality, for instance in Königsberg County (East, long-distance grain exports) a 1% increase in rye prices led to a 1.0% (B_0) decrease of the relative population growth rate in the same year, a

Table 9.3   Demographic vulnerability by rye price shocks, Prussian counties 1821–1850

Type of Region	County	B_0	B_1	B_2
East	Protoindustrial	Oppeln	+0.08	**–1.86 (a)**	+0.40
East	LD Export	Königsberg	–1.04 (a)	**–1.70 (b)**	+0.87 (c)
West	Protoindustrial	Minden	–0.47 (a)	**–0.54 (a)**	+0.25
West	Surplus	Münster	–0.84 (a)	**–0.54 (c)**	+0.25
Middle	Import	Erfurt	–0.31 (b)	**–0.47 (a)**	+0.20
Middle	Surplus	Frankfurt/O	–0.41 (a)	**–0.32 (b)**	–0.12
West	Industrial	Düsseldorf	–0.60 (a)	**–0.14**	–0.12

Note: Relative population growth rate figures are adjusted for cholera mortality. The equation for a multiple regression analysis is

RELATIVE POPGROWTH$_{t0}$=C+B$_0$RYEPRICE$_{t0}$+B$_1$RYEPRICE$_{t1}$+B$_2$RYEPRICE$_{t2}$

Significance of t-values of regression coefficients is (a) 99%, (b) 95%, (c) 90%, otherwise below 90%. As year-to-year prices reflect two successive harvest years, B_0 may not have a satisfying selectivity. Autoregression can be excluded in all cases (Durbin-Watson test).

Source: Bass, 1991: 89f. (includes all test statistics as well as data for all other counties).

---

[10] Regional population growth rates provide a comprehensive picture of natality, mortality, and net-migration. To neutralize differences in the population growth level between the counties, we calculated the relative population increase in each county as a multiple of the county's 10-yrs moving average population increase. Baten (2003: 393) is right, however, that this procedure is not completely satisfactory as it 'overestimates the number of crisis years in counties with rapidly growing populations (such as Berlin), since a higher total growth might imply higher variance'.

1.7% (B_1) decrease in the following year, and a 0.9% (B_2) increase (demographic rebound) in the second year.

The explanation can partly be seen in the dominant economic system. A higher weight of a commercially oriented agricultural sector implies stronger demographic shock reactions to harvest deficits, caused by a reduction of both income opportunities and the amount of food which could be purchased by a given income. Below-average harvests are both a necessary and a sufficient condition for subsistence crises only in grain-export regions and in self-sufficient regions, while in the two other types of regions additional factors have to come in (see Figure 9.3). Furthermore, it could also be shown that the vulnerability of a county's demographic system to price shocks (measured by the sum of the regression coefficients) depended on wealth (as measured by tax indicators, the population share of the poor, and medical supply indicators) and the equality in land distribution (Bass, 1991: 86–89).

Figure 9.3 Potential relations: Harvest results and subsistence crises

Harvest result		Structural characteristic of region		
	I. Long-distance exports, manors	*II. Short-distance exports, medium-sized farms with some surplus*	*III. Self-supplying (no extra-regional food trade)*	*IV. Food import region*
below average	Subsistence crisis: cash crop price effect relevant for owners, while volume effect affected incomes of labourers; food crop failures aggravated crisis	Subsistence crisis only if harvest was very low, because price effect and turnover effect of traded grain worked in different directions, given a low price elasticity of demand for grain[1]	Subsistence crisis	Subsistence crisis if industrial incomes lost
average	Subsistence crisis if terms of trade deteriorated so much that labourers lost income	–	–	Subsistence crisis if industrial incomes considerably lost
above average	–	–	–	Subsistence crisis if industrial incomes strongly lost

[1] This is what Abel called the "anomaly of grain markets", i.e. that lower harvest can represent higher incomes for farmers. However, as shown in Bass, 1991: 35-39, it is important to consider market quotas to qualify this argument.

III. The subsistence crisis of 1847

III.1. Immediate causes and the course of the crisis

Peter Solar (1997) identified three factors having caused the European subsistence crisis of 1847: potato blight, drought, and structural changes in industry. In Prussia, all three factors contributed to the crisis, although in different degrees. Moreover, in some parts of Prussia other factors ensued, which transformed the subsistence crisis of 1847 into a series of demographic crises: the Polish uprising (as far as Posen province is concerned), and the outbreak of cholera.

III.1.a.   The crisis in the agricultural sector

The subsistence crisis of 1847 developed from harvest failures: Already in 1845, crops were below average. In all parts of the state, potatoes were affected by occurrences of *phytophthora* disease (in the East: for instance County Administration of Bromberg, Report of 09.03.1846, quoted in Bass, 1991: 221; in the West: Nolte, 1984).

The following year, spring and early summer weather was abnormal. The meteorological station in Erfurt recorded a very wet April, but precipitation in May, June, and July 1846 was far below average. While the long-term average was 189 mm in these three months, in 1846 it was only 94 mm – the second-driest late-spring/early-summer period in 43 years (it was only lower in 1842: 67 mm; one value is missing). The figures for Gütersloh (Minden County) are similar: the long-term average of May to July was 203 mm, in 1846 there was only 104 mm precipitation – the driest conditions in 34 years (see Figure 9.4). On the background of the changes in the agricultural production structure, as outlined above, the social consequences of these weather conditions set the 1846 harvest apart from earlier harvest failures:

Figure 9.4   Precipitation, long-term average and 1846

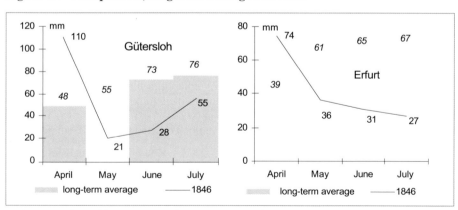

Source: adopted from www.ncdc.noaa.gov/oa/climate/-ghcn/ghcn.SELECT.html. The reference period for Erfurt is 1827-1870, for Gütersloh it is 1837-1870 (measurements here started later).

For the actual proletariat class [...] nowadays a wet harvest failure is less disadvantageous because the flourishing of potatoes provides some substitute particularly for him. This was the case in most places in 1816, while the dry year of 1846 also significantly damaged the potato crop. (Roscher, 1852: 52)

On the other hand, the drought seems to have checked the blight in 1846 (although it is still reported in some sources; see Nolte, 1984; Petter, 2000: 196).

Contemporary estimates indicate – although not unchallenged (Engel 1861: 272) – that in autumn of 1846 both potato and cereal crops dropped to between one half and three quarters of a 'good average' yield; the Eastern Provinces generally had better rye and worse potato crops than the Middle and the West. The potato crop was reported to have been most affected in Pommerania and East Prussia and least affected in the Rhineland; the rye crop was most affected in Westphalia and the Rhineland, and least affected in East Prussia (see Table 9.4). In 1847, there was another potato crop failure in the Eastern parts of the country. In this year, precipitation in May and June was also considerably below average: Erfurt reported precipitations in these two months to have been even lower than in 1846. Rye yields in 1847 were, however, above average.

Table 9.4   Estimates of yields, selected Prussian provinces 1846–1847

Province	Crop	Shares of a "good average"	
		1846	1847
East Prussia (E)	Rye	**0.66**	1.20
	Potatoes	**0.34**	**0.33**
Pomerania (E)	Rye	**0.63**	1.22
	Potatoes	**0.31**	**0.52**
Westphalia (W)	Rye	**0.43**	1.37
	Potatoes	**0.60**	**0.87**
Rhineland (W)	Rye	**0.48**	1.23
	Potatoes	**0.72**	**0.91**
Unweighted average	*Rye*	*0.57*	*1.22*
of eight provinces	*Potatoes*	*0.53*	*0.67*

Source: Von Reden, 1853: 94–95. No data provided for 1845. E = Eastern State, W = Western State.

As a reflex to the harvest failure, prices of rye and potatoes in spring 1847 climbed to more than double the previous years' average. A detailed representation of prices in the province of Saxony (De Boor, 2000: 48; Hecht, 2000: 107) shows that food prices steadily climbed from summer to November 1846, stayed more or less stable on a high level during winter and early spring 1847, before they climbed strongly in mid-April 1847. They reached their peak in mid-May 1847 and declined sharply (with the new harvest) in mid-July 1847. While rye prices finally dropped to 19% below the ten years' average in 1848, potato prices remained high even in 1848 with 18% above this average.

The general picture seems to be very much the same in the western (importing) and the in the eastern (exporting) provinces (see Figure 9.5). The eastern provinces, however, show a somewhat more coherent course in the various market places, while there are more differences between the individual market places in the West. In absolute terms, prices in the less wealthy eastern parts of the state did not reach the peak price in the West.

Figure 9.5   October and May prices of rye, West/East of Prussia 1840–1850

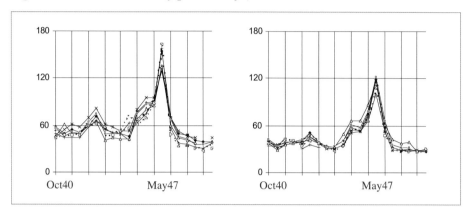

Prices in silvergroschen / scheffel. Left diagram: Western Provinces Rhineland and Westfalia (Aachen, Cologne, Kleve, Elberfeld, Münster, Minden, Paderborn). Right diagram: Eastern Provinces Silesia, Posen, East Prussia (Glogau, Breslau, Neisse, Posen, Fraustadt, Bromberg, Thorn).
Sources: Amtsblätter der preußischen Regierungen, various issues.

III.1.b.   The industrial crisis and exogenous factors

In addition to the food price increase, there was a cyclical industrial crisis in the second part of the 1840s. The timing of the crisis, however, was different in various industrial sub-sectors (and exactly the reverse of what was the sequence in France: see Vivier in this volume). Textile industry in Prussia had been in a cyclical crisis already in 1846. Yet metal industry, particularly iron production, and railway construction were at their heights in 1846: In this year, new railway lines amounted to 1,100 km – a result that was achieved again not earlier than 1870. Iron rod production since 1844 followed a new output growth path. Seen from this basis year, the production in 1847 had doubled. Only towards the end of 1847, when food prices had already decreased, a cyclical downswing in the monetary sector appeared, followed by a downswing in heavy industry. Most modern studies on the mid-1840 crises (Bergmann, 1979; Spree and Tybus, 1979; Metz, 1980) therefore see a clear separation between the agricultural harvest-related crisis and the industrial, cyclical crisis, thus rejecting the Abel-Labrousse thesis of crisis transmission by the shift of effective demand to food. Recently, however, Berger and Spoerer (1998) argued again that high food prices reduced demand for industrial products and thus employment opportunities in the industrial sector.

In 1848, in the Eastern provinces of Prussia cholera broke out. It caused, for instance, 11% of deaths in Dantzig County and 13% of deaths in the city of Berlin. In 1849, even one out of four deaths in Berlin was caused by cholera ('Übersicht …', 1857). Eventually, in 1850 the disease reached the central provinces of Prussia. In Posen Province, the

Polish uprisings of 1846 and 1848 added to economic tensions and demographic reactions. For some parts of the country, thus there was not a single subsistence crisis, but instead a bundle of economic and demographic crises in the late 1840s, only partly tied together by causal chains.

III.2. Effects on income and food consumption

In the East-Elbia *long-distance export region,* the de-feudalisation at the beginning of the 19th century had created large manor house estates and a landless agrarian proletariat. Estimates are that around 1850 three in four households in Posen did not own any land (Borowski 1963). As legal marriage barriers no longer existed, as industrial employment was not created, and as the Poor Law checked migration, *supply* of labour was fairly 'unlimited' (W.A. Lewis) – in great contrast to labour *demand*, as incomes of farm labourers had increasingly become dependent on production volumes. Manor house files (quoted in Bass 1991: 229) indicate that around the mid of the 19th century threshing was remunerated by some 8 per cent of the threshed corn and that two third of the labour used for potato digging was done by external piece workers. In the harbour of Dantzig, for instance,

the turn-over of the huge quantities of stored grain provides income opportunities in winter to the non-steadily employed workers. In years when the grain stocks are small, there is great poverty, as there is a lack of other employment in winter. (Von Reden, 1853: 355)

The joint grain and potato crop failure in autumn 1846 caused two-sided pressure on the labourers (scissor effect). First, there was an increase in expenses, as food supply from markets could be secured only at higher prices or generally had to be bought as an alternative to otherwise home-grown potatoes. Secondly, there was a reduction in income opportunities for reapers or from other types of agriculture-related labour or transport.

Thus, it is not surprising that in 1847 grain exports from the starving region increased. While in 1846 wheat exports from Dantzig were 69% of the de-trended average volume, this figure in 1847 – when the English Corn Laws were repealed – was 106% (Bass 1991: 234).

The loss of 'entitlements to food', triggered off by the scissor effect, translated into sheer hunger. E. von Saucken, a liberal politician and lord of the manor, wrote about his visiting labourer lodgings in East Prussia:

In the lodging there was [a man called] Dauksch, 45 years of age, able and willing to work, but idle in spite of his many attempts to find work and thus completely without any means of subsistence; the wife with the child as a result of the disaster confined to bed, pale and emaciated. Since some days she had had only water for food [...] the last food had been small, unripe potatoes with herring brine or once a day some watery porridge. (Königsberger Zeitung, 12.12.1846)

In February 1848, the crisis had extended to the artisans' sector. An administrative report relating to a town with some 8,000 inhabitants in Posen province said that day labourers and artisans were so weakened that they were unable to work:

During the heavy cold they sit in their homes and starve. As soon as weather allows they spread to the neighbouring villages and beg. (County administration of Posen, letter from 21.02.1848, quoted in Bass, 1991: 225)

In *agricultural surplus regions*, usually the situation of rural class division was not that extreme, and more food sources existed for the rural poor. This is shown by an albeit 30 years older government report on the Northern Rhineland:

The only business in this area is agriculture [...] The inhabitants are [...] either peasants or day labourers. [...] The peasants grow rye, buckwheat, vegetables (esp. potatoes), and hay for fodder, and for sale wheat, barley, oats, and tobacco. They also fatten some animals for slaughter and sell young cattle and pigs. [...] Among the peasants, there is considerable wealth, particularly in fertile years [...]. The day labourers are there only to help the peasants; they do not seek external income, and do not engage in sideline production; they spin rarely – at the most for domestic demands – and support themselves only by their hands. In their cabbage gardens, they plant vegetables, especially potatoes, and sometimes a few dozens of tobacco plants for sale. Their main food, potatoes, is planted jointly with the peasants; the labourers provide seed and manure, the peasant provides the land, he provides horse work, they provide manual labour; the yield is shared according to the different sources. The milk from their cows and the meat of their pigs is consumed in their homes; bread and all other necessities have to be bought by their daily wage which is secured all the year round [by various agricultural activities; hay making and threshing was paid in kind.] (Von Coeverden, 1816)

However, in 1846 some regions, notably Münster County (Province of Westphalia), seem to have experienced such low harvests (compare Table 9.4) that the joint decline of home-grown food and agricultural income opportunities for the day labourers' families resulted in hunger. From the perspective of the market-oriented peasants, the (negative) volume effect had overcome the (positive) price effect of the dearth.

In *subsistence regions*, the crop failure directly led to a deficit in food consumption. This can be understood by another government official's report on a district in the Eifel hills in Rhineland:

The mass of the population consists of small landowners, who partly – and this also only in favourable years – can grow their basic supply of vegetables themselves, and partly, in addition to this, for more or less months grow their own grain. However, to secure the remaining needs of the year, they have to try to sell the few additional products of their land or to have earnings as day labourers. The latter, given the large number of this class, is of low importance. The wealthier landowners need day labourers only at certain times of the year. (District Commissioner of Daun district, report of 29.09.1843; quoted in Mergen, 1973)

In *food-import dependent industrial and proto-industrial counties* (Rhineland, Saxony, East Westphalia), the harvest failure of 1846 resulted in price increases as it did in the other parts of Prussia. However, food consumption here was, to a considerable degree, dependent on three non-agricultural income sources: textile industry, metal industry, and railway construction. Due to imports triggered off by increasing price differentials between surplus and import regions, food shortage was less severe in the import regions until iron and railway industries entered the bust period in autumn 1847.

III.3. Demographic effects

Hunger affected mortality and natality throughout Prussia. By comparing the mortality in 1847 with the average mortality in the years 1816–1850, the excess mortality amounted to 2.6 per mille points, or 42,000 deaths. As shown by Figure 9.6 the demographic toll was strongest in the long-distance grain export regions, also in 1848. In addition, the proto-industrial area in Upper Silesia was hard hit. There was nearly no demographic impact of the harvest failure according to this data in the agricultural surplus regions, with the remarkable exception of the County of Münster. Only moderate occurrences of a subsistence crisis can be seen in the industrialised area.

Figure 9.6   Subsistence crises, Prussian counties 1845–1850

	Long-distance grain export									Agricultural surplus						Subst.		Proto-industrial and industrial								
	Mw	Gb	Ks	Kb	Bb	Sd	Dz	St	Pn	Me	Pd	Ff	Lg	Md	Ms	Tr	Kz	Op	Mi	Kl	Bl	Bn	Ef	Ac	Dd	Ab
1845	2																									
1846	1			1																		1				
1847		3	2	3	1								1		3	1		3	1			1	1			1
1848	3	3		3	3	2	3		3									3								
1849																										
1850																										

Source: Bass 1991: 45. Note: All data given here are corrected for cholera mortality.
1 – less than 50 per cent of 10yrs moving average population growth rate
2 – less than 75 per cent of 10yrs moving average population growth rate
3 – less than 100 per cent of 10yrs moving average population growth rate (i.e. population decrease)

Already contemporaries commented on the differences in the demographic impacts of the food price increase. The economist and statistician Schubert (1847; quoted in Von Reden 1853) was of the opinion that structural factors had contributed to the heavy and frequent subsistence crisis in East Elbia in the late 1840s. In particular, he named the rural population growth which led to a relative de-urbanisation; the increase of landless rural labourers; an insufficient progress in agriculture, but nevertheless strong exports; a lack of alternative employment; the generally low standard of living; and lack of traffic communications, i.e. the lack of a sufficiently developed internal market. Friedrich Engels focussed the Eastern proto-industrial area:

Upper Silesia [...] in autumn 1847 was struck by a famine as severe as that which was simultaneously depopulating Ireland. As in Ireland, famine typhus also broke out in Upper Silesia and spread like the plague. The following winter it broke out once again, yet without any failure of the harvest, flooding or other calamity having occurred. What is the explanation? (Engels, 1876a)

Engels, following Wolff, stressed the particularly heavy burden exerted by the (German) ruling class on a (predominantly Polish) working class. Wilhelm Wolff had written on the landless labourers:

Their diet consists almost solely of potatoes and schnapps. If only the laborer had even had these two items in sufficient quantity, then at least starvation and typhus would have spared Upper Silesia. When, however, the staple food became steadily dearer and scarcer as a result of potato blight, and the day wage not only failed to rise but actually fell – people had resort to plants which they picked in the fields and woods, couch grass and roots, making soup with stolen hay and eating the flesh of dead animals. Their strength evaporated. Schnapps became more expensive – and even worse than before. [...] The stomach of the peasant, weakened by hay and couch-grass soups, could no longer take such medicine. Considering the poor clothing, the filthy, unsanitary housing, the cold in winter, and the lack either of work or of strength to work, one realizes how, no more and no less than in Ireland, these famine conditions very soon gave rise to typhus. [...] They were continually exploited and drained dry by the state and the robber-knights to such an extent that at the slightest increase in their misery they were bound to perish... (Neue Rheinische Zeitung 25.04.1849, quoted in Engels, 1876b)

A multiple regression analysis (Bass, 1991: 265–269) widely supports these ideas: It could be shown that neither the absolute level of prices in 1846/47 nor the difference between these prices and the average prices 'explain' the demographic data. The most significant variables turned out to be prosperity indicators such as trade taxes and medical provision:[11] The fewer inhabitants a physician had to care for, and the larger the non-agricultural sector was, the higher was the population growth of 1847, i.e. the less severe was the subsistence crisis. There was no simple link between high food prices and low population growth and no support of the hypotheses of a high demographic impact of the regional crop shortfall – the overall level of development of a region was of importance for the demographic consequences of the subsistence crisis.

III.4. Political coping strategies

It seems to be a ubiquitous phenomenon that assistance given by a society to its weakest members is less a function of their objective needs but of their claim making power. The readiness and possibilities of the needy to communicate, the knowledge of a society about the extent of their deprivation, the sympathetic identification with the victims (more likely in sudden and incidental catastrophes than in structural and chronic problems) – all this positively contributes to the extent of social assistance (Barton, 1969: 216 ff.). Pressure groups such as powerful industrial bourgeoisie, active local administrations or urban masses creating unrest have been more probable to channel help than a dispersed, quietly suffering rural population (L. Tilly, 1983). An articulation of the claims can thus be understood as an intervening measure, which helped to avert potential subsistence crises. Were protests in 1847 suitable to bring about social or administrative emergency aid? And what were the costs for the rioters? Or, to put it into a different perspective: was emergency aid a worthwhile investment in security? – as argued by Ludolf Camphausen, a grain trader in Cologne, who became Prussia's prime minister in 1848/49: 'The increase of grain prices is horrible; sometimes we are worried, although the impression of what we did for town and country is still strong' (letter from 10.03.1847 to his brother Otto,

---

[11] The dependent variable was a county's relative population growth (POP47), defined as a multiple of a moving 10-yrs-average. Independent variables were short-term economic factors, such as de-trended grain and potato prices (POTATOPRICE) and harvest estimates, as well as structural variables, such as indicators for social polarization, industrial income opportunities, overall prosperity (such as inhabitants per physician: INHAB/PHYSICIAN), and technical advances in agriculture and infrastructure. The most appropriate equation turned out to be POP47 $= -2.85 - 0.79$ INHAB/PHYSICIAN $+ 0.37$ POTATOPRICE ($t_1 = -4.49$ sign. 99 %, $t_2 = 2.11$ sign. 95 %, F$=10.07$, $R_{sq}=0.43$, $d_w=1.57$). It is interesting to note that the regression coefficient for potato prices has a positive sign. The reason is that there is also a poverty indicator hidden here, as in West-Prussian industrialised regions potato prices were higher than in the impoverished East.

in Hansen, 1942: 172). Riots and their results will be discussed in the first part of this subsection, while the second part addresses government policies.

III.4.a.   Riots

To date, 138 food protests are known to have happened in Prussia between late 1846 and summer 1847 (see Gailus, 1990; Bass, 1991; 241 ff.; Gailus, 1994; Hecht, 2004 for a comprehensive history of food riots in Prussia in 1846/47). Riots started as early as December 1846 in Hagen in the industrial Ruhr area (Westphalia) among the ironworkers and in January 1847 among railway workers near Münster (Westphalia). On a massive scale, food riots in the form of export blockades, market disturbances, and looting took place in late-April/early-May. Compared to the prices, which – at least in the centrally located city of Magdeburg – had their climax in the week around April 17th, 1847, riots seem to have been a lagged re-action, as their occurrence culminated in the two weeks between April 24 and May 7, 1847 – or in a different interpretation: contributed to bringing prices down (see Figure 9.7), although it is also important to note that the Prussian King officially declared a state of emergency April 23rd, 1847, which possibly triggered off expextations of government intervention and thus contributed to the price decrease.

Figure 9.7   Weekly prices of rye and potatoes and temporal distribution of food riots in Prussia, 1846–1847

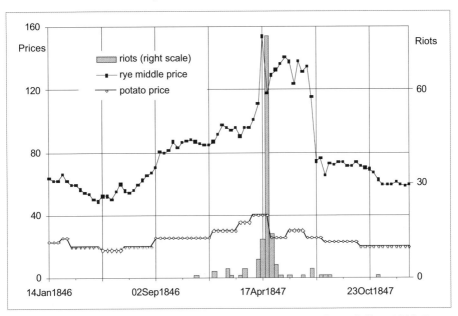

Source: Temporal distribution of riots computed with data from Gailus, 1990; Bass, 1991. Price data (local price in Saxony province) provided by Dr M. Hecht. Prices are given in silvergroschen per scheffel.

Due to the general character of the food price increase, one would expect the riots to be Poisson-distributed (i.e. a truncated normal distribution) over the different regions. The empirical distribution, however, is different (see Table 9.5): there were regions of intense protest as well as regions where no protest occurred at all. Regions particularly prone to protest were in the long-distance grain export zone the counties of Bromberg and Posen (foreshadowing the ethnic and political conflicts of 1848 in this non-German part of Prussia; for a detailed regional study see Bass, 1994b), Stettin and Marienwerder Counties, as well as Breslau County, a net import region for grain. There were nearly no riots in the self-supplying counties and in the industrial areas of Rhineland and Westphalia provinces, or in most of the short-distance grain export regions. There were also no riots in the peripheral and particularly backward County of Gumbinnen. A middle position is taken by Saxony (in normal times predominantly an agricultural surplus region; for detailed regional studies see Benninghaus, 2000), as well as by proto-industrial Upper Silesia.

Table 9.5   Regional distribution of food riots, Prussia 1847

Number of riots per county	0-2	3-5	6-8	9+
Hypothetical distribution (Poisson)	3	14	9	2
Empirical distribution	14	2	4	6

Source: Computed with data from Bass, 1991; Gailus, 1990. χ^2 statistics for comparison of the two distributions is 61.39 (critical value for a distribution with 3 degrees of freedom, 95 per cent probability: 7.82).

There is no mono-causal explanation for this geographical distribution of protests (see Hecht, 2000: 94 f. for a critical review of previous approaches). At least three different elements have to be distinguished, the combination of which may have caused people to press the administration to create survival opportunities (similar: R.Tilly, 1990: 26f.).

Firstly, people revolted when *endangered* by food deprivation, particularly where seeing the *venas abiertas* (Galeano) making this fate probable (a fact which is particularly stressed by Gailus, 1990; 1994), such as in the important grain trade centre Stettin. On the other hand, people probably did not 'riot' when starvation was already too extreme, but looked for less visible methods of individually securing food resources (such as stealing or begging).

The *second* ('Thompsonian') dimension of an explanation of social protest in subsistence crises comprises horizontal possibilities for communication and immediate causes, although not necessarily with a neat concept of 'moral economy' in mind – there are symbolic actions, such as setting a 'fair price' as well as incidents of trivial appropriation. An account of the first form is given by the Municipal authority of Gostyń (County of Posen):

At today's weekly market four or five wagons loaded with grain were surrounded by an uncountable mass of people of the poorer class. Some of them climbed up and asked the owner of the grain whether he wanted to sell the grain for a considerable price. As the farmer refused, they pulled out the grain sacks from the wagon and sold it for the set price, the sack for 6 Talers. (letter from 07.05.1847 quoted in Bass, 1991: 255)

On the other hand, the District Commissioner of Wongrowiec (County of Bromberg) reported:

Recently several important manor houses in this district were reduced to ashes obviously mainly to seize hold of the meat of the burnt sheep, as crowds of people including many women came flocking to these barns, with bags and knives. Some ate the still steaming cadavers on the spot, others carried them away in their bags. (letter from 02.06.1847, quoted in Bass, 1991: 256)

Over the course of time the form of riots changed from the first to the second type, reflecting both increasing misery and the experience of repression.

Thirdly, vertical communication between those in authority and their subjects was important – paternalistic approaches as well as a sort of negotiation reduced the inclination to violent action and often secured aid by preventive policies (Benninghaus, 2000: 141 f.).

Did rioters succeed? On the local level, there are several examples indicating that the danger of riots or the actual protest did have, albeit limited, positive results – not only what was actually looted, or what had been blockaded from export, but also mobilisation of communal or societal aid. Examples include the introduction of a local tax for the rich to subsidise bread for the poor, rent credits, and soup kitchens. However, the stick normally came along with the carrot. There were military action, trials, and corporal punishments on the 'cost' side. And sometimes, there was simply a lack of food availability, which limited the success of riots:

Being afraid of a repetition of the incidents which had happened, the traders and the owners of grain stocks reduce their prices [which in this district in May 1847 had been in fact the highest in the whole county; H.B.] – unfortunately, however, the supply is low. (District Commissioner of Gnesen, County of Bromberg, letter from 04.05.1847, quoted in Bass 1991: 249)

III.4.b.   Government policy

In case of food emergency the mid-19th-century Prussian government could have used a wide range of policies. Supply-side instruments could have included direct food aid (used in the famine of 1816, although rather unsuccessfully; see Bass 1991: 128 ff.) or a tariff reduction, as in Prussia between 1824 and 1856 considerable tariffs were levied on grain imports in order to protect the East-Elbia producers. Demand-side policies could include job creation, in the construction of roads and fortresses, as well as a reduction of the urban indirect taxes on grain. However, centrally administered emergency aid was under the double pressure of ideology, which pleaded, at least since the 1820s, against interference in markets, as well as from a real constraint by the state's budget. The effects of the Napoleonic Wars and the reorganization of the Prussian state had caused a heavy debt burden. By law originating from the post-Napoleonic reform period, new debts would have to be approved by a national diet. As the ruling class tried to avoid this, apart from a secret 'second' budget, austerity was imperative. Debt service was officially reported to come to 22 per cent of a 52-million-Taler budget in 1821, but was reduced by strict austerity to 11 per cent of the 64-million-budget (o/w 44% were for civil expenses) of 1847 (Borchardt, 1968: 158).

Nevertheless, the central authorities did react in 1846. December 4th, 1846 a sum of up to 1 million Taler was designated from a shadow budget to buy rye as an intervention stock (Petter, 2000: 205, 221–222) – in terms of the civil budget the mobilised amount was considerable, yet it was not a transfer but a price regulation effort and could be reclaimed by the sales. Only the Provinces Rhineland and Westphalia, as well as Upper Silesia, South Posen, and parts of East Prussia were designated for this type of aid, more or less a reflex of the harvest estimates in the various parts of the country as perceived by the authorities. Driven by the increasing tensions, from winter 1846 to September 1847 central authorities had even invested a total of 5.1 mill. Taler – but as these supplies came late to market, no sales credits should be granted, and most stocks should be sold at market prices, one might doubt the price regulating effect of this action. At the end, there was a burden of 2.5 mill. Taler on the budget.

With regard to public works, it is paradoxical that employment in the Eastern parts of the country was reduced in 1846/47 rather than expanded. In the Province of East Prussia, high road building run by the state in 1845, involving 130,000 Taler just for one East Prussian county (Marienwerder), had provided employment for tens of thousands of workers. In summer 1846, however, work stopped due to a rather chaotic management, but also due to a lack of funds. Out of the 150,000 Taler designated for employment creation in the whole country in January 1847, 60,000 Taler were promised to factory owners in Rhineland, and the whole province of East Prussia received with 50,000 Taler only about a quarter of what had been provided the year before. Thus it seems that apart from general reservations against state intervention, the national dimension of the subsistence crisis was asking too much of the central government. Only April 17th, 1847 another 500,000 Taler were designated for employment creation. This aid came too late for a real effect, especially as wages were so low that labourers could not sustain themselves on these wages and thus were too weak to work (see Bass, 1990: 254). In addition, public work schemes became also a victim of 'high' politics: Due to a constitutional conflict (the rejection of an Eastern-Railway loan by Parliament), in June 1847 the King immediately stopped all railway work along the Eastern line. Out of a total of 770,000 Taler for employment generation and seed potatoes, East Prussia received 28%, the Rhine Province 22%, Silesia 14%, and Westphalia 12%.

Different approaches of government with regard to the eastern and the western parts of the country can be shown by the tariff policies: In the Rhineland province, a 25 percent export tariff on grain was introduced as early as January 8th, 1847. This might have helped to stop grain exports in time. The same tariff, however, was introduced in the Eastern provinces as late as May 1st, 1847 when most shipping of grain had already been completed. In Dantzig and Königsberg the *import* tariff for grain was suspended – with the paradox result that traders re-exported Russian grain to Western Europe. Interestingly enough, one instrument, which could have helped to reduce the decline in food availability in the Eastern provinces, was also not used (although often demanded) before May 1847: the prohibition of spirit distillation.

In view of very limited resources, the obvious inequality of treatment of the various parts of the country may have been a result of different negotiation skills and commitment of the administrative authorities to lobbying (as argued by Petter, 2000: 208 f.). It may also be argued that the early incident of riots in Rhineland and Westphalia supported the lobbying of factory owners for additional funds from the central government for employment creation (Petter, 2000: 217). With regard to the tariffs and the industrial use of potatoes, however, the opposing interest of industrialists and manor-house lords has to be taken into consideration.

The unbalanced relief aid also had a structural reason. The Prussian poor law of 1842/43 had designated the local authorities as responsible for relief (although, as argued by some local authorities in 1847, quoted in Petter, 2000: 208, local authorities were by law not responsible to take care of the able-bodied unemployed!). The consequence was that poor relief in Prussia was not particularly abundant in areas where distress was greatest, but where the rich were willing to afford charity, i.e. in urban areas and in the western parts of Prussia (for an excellent overview of Prussian poor law see Schulz, 1995).[12]

To sum up: In terms of financial funds, the involvement of the central authorities in Prussia was not minor, but there was a significant bias in favour of industrial regions, aid arrived late (sometimes later than the army, which was sent in to crack down on hunger riots), and government assistance strikingly lacked efficiency. Generally, civil society on the local level was a more effective agent of redistribution than the state.

IV. Conclusion and comparative thoughts

Already for the contemporaries of the subsistence crisis of 1847 in Prussia, the famine in Ireland was the yardstick for assessment (for instance Wolff, 1849 – see above). Compared to Ireland, where one million famine-related deaths from a population of eight million are the generally accepted estimation (see Daly in this volume), the over-all demographic consequences of the famine in Prussia are very moderate (some 40,000 famine-related deaths of a two times larger population; see above). Compared to other parts of the continent, however, such as Flanders, Denmark, and Sweden (see the con-tributions of Vanhaute, Henriksen and Gadd in this volume) the amount of human suffe-ring particularly in the eastern parts of Prussia was larger.

Contemporaries also discussed supply-side ('food-availability decline'-type, FAD) and demand-side ('entitlement'-type) factors to explain the frequent subsistence crises in the Eastern parts of Prussia in the mid-19th century. Believing in the progress of agriculture, opinion leaders denied the idea of a famine of the FAD-type in Prussia on general grounds:

First, there is a large difference between what food man needs to survive and what he usually consumes with a feeling of well-being. The gap between these two limits of consumption probably is larger than the gap between good and bad harvests in countries where man already subjugated the soil to an extent that a general and total failure has not to be feared. Secondly, the lack of sufficient food under the most populous class of inhabitants is by no means always the result of bad harvests. It is very probable that even with very moderate grain prices he lacks means to buy his keep when customary businesses slacken or the hand of the landlord or capital owner weighs too heavily on him. Alms were collected in London to save the poor Irishmen from real famine while at the same time the London market was nearly overcrowded by Irish wheat. Even if such glaring contrasts cannot happen here, it might not be very rare at the same time and in the same province to have complaints about difficulties to purchase a basic living and it not being worthwhile to grow corn because prices are too low. (Hoffmann, letter to the Minister Von Brenn of January 21, 1837, quoted in Bass, 1991: 15–16)

---

[12] An urban and pro-western bias is even visible in the 'international aid', as Germans in Cincinnati/ Ohio in April 1847 formed a 'Committee for the Poor in Germany', which provided 3,000 Dollars for five German cities, including in Prussia Berlin and Düsseldorf (see Holtmann, 1996).

Our analysis lends support to this view. Interestingly enough, the results are very similar to Mokyr's (1983) finding that the extent of famine even in Ireland, especially in 1846, was a result of structural poverty. Independent of the share of land which was used for growing potatoes, excess mortality during the Great Famine depended on the average wage incomes and the standard of living of a region, measured by such indicators as literacy rate and quality of housing. Moreover, the Prussian case largely validates Vanhaute's complex-causes hypothesis (in this volume) developed from the Flanders case. According to his proposition, the risk to starve depended on the diversification of income sources, namely proto-industrial rural sideline activities; the diversification of crops as a more or less unconscious insurance against the risk of harvest failures; the actual decline of the potato crop; and extra-regional trade relations, depending on income differences between the various regions. Considering the different regional food supply-systems (short-distance exporters, long-distance-exporters, and net importers), our study proposes an interpretation of the 1847-subsistence crisis in Prussia against the background of structural poverty with dominant demand-side causes, regionally already communicable but socially restricted in its effects. In our view, distribution was a more important element than production in causing the 1847 subsistence crisis in Prussia.

Bibliography

'Lebensmittelpreise in Preußen 1816–1870' (1907) *Zeitschrift des Königlich Preußischen Statistischen Landesamts*, 47, Besondere Beilage, http://www.learn-line.nrw.de/angebote/eda/medio/preussen/preuspr.htm.

'Übersicht der durch die Cholera im Preußischen Staate herbeigeführten Todesfälle seit ihrem Erscheinen1831 bis jetzt' (1857) *Mitteilungen des Statistischen Bureaus zu Berlin*, 10, pp. 231–250.

'Übersicht der ländlichen Erwerbsverhältnisse in den verschiedenen Regierungsbezirken des preußischen Staates am Ende des Jahres 1849' (1852) *Mitteilungen des Statistischen Bureaus zu Berlin*, 5, pp. 65–84.

'Versuch, statistisch zu ermitteln, wie hoch die Verzehrungs- und Verbrauchs-Gegenstände an Quantität und Wert im preußischen Staate gegenwärtig durchschnittlich auf den Kopf der Bevölkerung zu berechnen sind' (1851) *Mitteilungen des Statistischen Bureaus zu Berlin*, 4, pp. 209–227.

Abel, W. (1974) *Massenarmut und Hungerkrisen im vorindustriellen Europa. Versuch einer Synopsis*, Hamburg and Berlin.

Abel, W. (1986) *Massenarmut und Hungerkrisen im vorindustriellen Deutschland*, 3rd ed., Göttingen.

Barton, A.H. (1969) *Communities in Disaster. A Sociological Analysis of Collective Stress Situations*, New York.

Bass, H. (1991) *Hungerkrisen in Preußen während der ersten Hälfte des 19. Jahrhunderts*, St. Katharinen.

Bass, H. (1994a) 'Famines in early nineteenth-century Prussia', in *Proceedings Eleventh International Economic History Congress*, Milano, pp. 103–112.

Bass, H. (1994b) 'Hungerkrisen im Rheinland und in Posen, 1816–1848', in M. Gailus und H. Volkmann (eds) *Der Kampf um das tägliche Brot*, Opladen, pp.151–175.

Baten, J. (1996) 'Der Einfluß von Einkommensverteilung und Milchproduktion auf die regionalen Unterschiede des Ernährungsstandards in Preußen um die Mitte des 19. Jahrhunderts: Ein anthropometrischer Diskussionsbeitrag', *Archiv für Sozialgeschichte*, 36, pp. 69–83.

Baten, J. (2003) 'Anthropometrics, consumption, and leisure: the standard of living', in S. Ogilvie and R. Overy (eds), *Germany. A New Social and Economic History*, Vol. III, London, pp. 383–422.

Benninghaus, C. (2000) *Region in Aufruhr. Hungerkrise und Teuerungsprotest in der preußischen Provinz Sachsen und in Anhalt 1846/47*, Halle.

Berger, H. and Spoerer, M. (1998) *Nicht Ideen, sondern Hunger? Wirtschaftliche Entwicklung im Vormärz und Revolution 1848 in Deutschland und Europa*, Hohenheim. (Diskussionsbeiträge aus dem Institut für Volkswirtschaftslehre; 162).

Berger, H. and Spoerer, M. (2001) 'Economic Crises and the European Revolutions of 1848', *Journal of Economic History*, 61, pp. 293–326.

Bergmann, J. (1979) Ökonomische Voraussetzungen der Revolution von 1848, in J. Bergmann, K. Megerle and P. Steinbach (eds), *Geschichte als politische Wissenschaft*, Stuttgart, pp. 24–54.

Bittermann, E. (1956) *Die landwirtschaftliche Produktion in Deutschland, 1800–1950*, Kühn-Archiv, vol. 70, Berlin.

Böhm, R. (1998) 'Ein verkümmerter Menschenschlag', in *700 Jahre Rheinbach*, Teil VI, www.general-anzeiger-bonn.de/region/kommunen/rheinbach/rheinbach_700_6.html.

Boor, A. De (2000) "Wir gehen einer schauerlichen Catastrophe entgegen'. Die Teuerungsproteste in Halle am 22. April 1847', in C. Benninghaus (ed.) *Region in Aufruhr. Hungerkrise und Teuerungsprotest in der preußischen Provinz Sachsen und in Anhalt 1846/47*, Halle, pp. 39–54.

Borchardt, Karl (1968) *Staatsverbrauch und öffentliche Investitionen in Deutschland, 1780–1850*, Diss. Göttingen.

Borchardt, Knut (1965) 'Integration in wirtschaftshistorischer Perspektive', in E. Schneider (ed.) *Weltwirtschaftliche Probleme der Gegenwart*, Berlin, pp. 388–410.

Borowski, S. (1963) *Kształtowanie się rolniczego rynku pracy w Wielkopolsce w okresie wielkich reform agrarnych, 1807–1860*, Poznań.

Engel, E. (1861) 'Die Getreidepreise, die Ernteerträge und der Getreidehandel im preußischen Staate', *Zeitschrift des Statistischen Bureaus zu Berlin*, 1, pp. 249–289.

Engels, F. (1876a) 'Preußischer Schnaps im Deutschen Reichstag' (first published in: *Der Volksstaat*; translated in *Marx and Engels, Collected Works*, vol. 24, pp. 109–128).

Engels, F. (1876b) 'Wilhelm Wolff' (first published in: *Die Neue Welt*; translated in *Marx and Engels, Collected Works*, vol. 24, pp. 129–171) www.marxists.org/archive/marx/works/1876/wolff.

FAO / Chatfield, C. (1949) 'Food Composition Tables for international use', *Nutritional Studies*, No. 3, Washington DC, http://www.fao.org/documents/show_cdr.asp?url_file=/docrep/x5557e/x5557e00.htm.

Fertig, G. (1997) 'Demographischer Wandel, Marktentwicklung und Regionenbildung in Westfalen, 1750–1870: Skizze eines Forschungsprojektes', *Westfälische Forschungen* 47, pp. 725–738.

Fremdling R. and Hohorst, G. (1979) 'Marktintegration der preußischen Wirtschaft des 19. Jahrhunderts. Skizze eines Forschungsansatzes zur Fluktuation der Roggenpreise zwischen 1821 und 1865', in R. Fremdling and R.H. Tilly (eds), *Industrialisierung und Raum: Studien zur regionalen Differenzierung im Deutschland des 19. Jahrhunderts*, Stuttgart, pp. 56–101.

Gailus, M. (1990) *Straße und Brot. Protest in den deutschen Staaten unter besonderer Berücksichtigung Preußens, 1847–1849*, Göttingen.

Gailus, M. (1994) 'Food Riots in Germany in the Late 1840s', *Past and Present*, 145, pp. 57–103.

Hansen, J. (1942) *Rheinische Briefe und Akten zur Geschichte der politischen Bewegung 1830–1850*, vol. 2, part 1 (Januar 1846 – April 1848), Bonn.

Hecht, M. (2000) 'Mitteldeutschland als Protestregion: Geographie, Chronologie und Typologie der Subsistenzunruhen 1847', in C. Benninghaus (ed.) *Region in Aufruhr. Hungerkrise und Teuerungsprotest in der preußischen Provinz Sachsen und in Anhalt 1846/47*, Halle, pp. 93–116.

Hecht, M. (2004) *Nahrungsmangel und Protest. Teuerungsunruhen in Frankreich und Preußen in den Jahren 1846/47*, Halle.

Hoffmann, J.G. (1837) Letter to the Minister Von Brenn, 21. 1. 1837, *Zentrales Staatsarchiv Merseburg*, Rep. 87 B, Nr. 12706, fol. 137 RS f.

Holtmann, A. (1996) *'Ferner thue ich euch zu wissen ...'. Die Briefe des Johann Heinrich zur Oeveste aus Amerika 1834–76*, 2nd ed., http://www.uni-oldenburg.de/nausa/zuroev/000.htm.

Kopsidis, M. (1996) *Market Integration and Westphalian Agriculture, 1780–1880. Market-oriented Economic Development of a Smallholder Agricultural Sector*, Venice.

Kopsidis, M. (2002) 'The Creation of a Westphalian Rye Market 1820–1870: Leading and Following Regions, a Co-Integration Analysis', *Jahrbuch für Wirtschaftsgeschichte*, 2, pp. 85–112.

Körber-Grohne, U. (1994) *Nutzpflanzen in Deutschland. Kulturgeschichte und Biologie*, Stuttgart. (1st ed. 1987, 3rd ed. 1994).

Lis, C. and Soly, H. (1982) *Poverty and Capitalism in Pre-Industrial Europe*, 2nd ed., Brighton.

Mergen, J. (1973) Von der Eifel nach Nord-Amerika, in *Heimatjahrbuch 1973*, www.jahrbuch-daun.de/VT/hjb1973/hjb1973.21.htm

Merrill, A.L. and Watt, B.K. (1973) *Energy values of food. Basis and derivation*, Washington DC, http://www.nal.usda.gov/fnic/foodcomp/Data/Classics/ah74.pdf.

Metz, R. (1980) Agrarpreiszyklen und Wirtschaftskonjunktur. Spektralanalytische Untersuchungen zu Kölner Agrarpreisreihen des 19. Jahrhunderts, in W.H. Schröder and R. Spree (eds), *Historische Konjunkturforschung*, Stuttgart, pp. 255–288.

Mokyr, J. (1983) *Why Ireland starved. A Quantitative and Analytical History of the Irish Economy, 1800–1850*, London.

Nolte, B. (1984) *Chronik der Commune Fürstenberg: 1800–1919*, herausgegeben im Auftrag des Förderkreises für Kultur, Geschichte und Natur im Sintfeld, Paderborn.

Ollenroth (1833) Zur medizinischen Topographie und Statistik des Regierungs-Departements Bromberg im Großherzogtum Posen, MS of 05 June 1833, *Wojewódzkie Archivum Państwowe w Bydgoszczy*, Reg. Bromberg I 1918.

Onishi, T. (1973) *Zolltarifpolitik Preußens bis zur Gründung des Deutschen Zollvereins. Ein Beitrag zur Finanz- und Außenhandelspolitik Preußens*, Göttingen.

Petter, A. (2000) 'Armut, Finanzhaushalt und Herrschaftssicherung: Staatliches Verwaltungshandeln in Preußen in der Nahrungskrise von 1846/47', in C. Benninghaus (ed.) *Region im Aufruhr. Hungerkrise und Teuerungsprotest in der preußischen Provinz Sachsen und in Anhalt 1846/47*, Halle, pp. 187–243.

Der Regierungsbezirk Minden. Geographisch-statistisch-topographisches Handbuch (1832) Minden.

Roscher, W. (1852) *Über Kornhandel und Theuerungspolitik*, Stuttgart and Tübingen, http://www.digitalis.uni-koeln.de.

Schall, H. sr. and Schall, H. jr. (1967) *Nahrungsmitteltabelle zur Aufstellung und Berechnung von Diätverordnungen für Krankenhaus, Sanatorium und Praxis*, 19th ed., Leipzig.

Schätzl, L. (1998) *Wirtschaftsgeographie 1. Theorie*, 7th ed., Paderborn.

Schönthaler, M. (2002) *'Nach dem Martini-Tage 1810 gibt es nur freie Leute'. Der Verlauf der Bauernbefreiung in Preußen und ihre ökonomischen Folgen,* http://www.uni-marburg.de/archivschule.

Schulz, G. (1995) 'Armut und Armenpolitik in Deutschland im frühen 19. Jahrhundert', *Historisches Jahrbuch*, 115, pp. 388–410.

Sen, A. (1981) *Poverty and Famines: An Essay on Entitlements and Deprivation*, Oxford.

Solar, P.M. (1997) 'The Potato Famine in Europe', in C. Ó Gráda (ed.), *Famine 150: Commemorative Lecture Series*, Dublin, pp. 113–124.

Spree, R. and Tybus, M. (1979) *Wachstumstrends und Konjunkturzyklen in der deutschen Wirtschaft von 1820 bis 1913. Quantitativer Rahmen für eine Konjunkturgeschichte des 19. Jahrhunderts*, Göttingen.

Teuteberg, J. (1979) 'Der Verzehr von Nahrungsmitteln in Deutschland pro Kopf und Jahr seit Beginn der Industrialisierung', *Archiv für Sozialgeschichte*, 19, pp. 331–388.

Tilly, L. (1983) 'Food entitlement, famine, and conflict', *Journal of Interdisciplinary History*, 14, pp. 333–349.

Tilly, R.H. (1990) *Vom Zollverein zum Industriestaat*, Munich.

Von Coeverden, A.J.N. (1816) Gehorsamster Bericht die Hungers Noth in der Düffelt betreffend, MS of 09 September 1816, *Hauptstaatsarchiv Düsseldorf*, Regierung Kleve 91, fol. 5 passim.

Von Finckenstein, H. W. Graf Finck (1934) Die Getreidewirtschaft Preußens von 1800 bis 1930, *Vierteljahreshefte zur Konjunkturforschung*, Sonderheft 35, Berlin.

Von Reden, F. W. (1853/54) *Erwerbs- und Verkehrs-Statistik des Königstaats Preussen. In vergleichender Darstellung*, 3 Teile, Darmstadt, http://www.digitalis.uni-koeln.de.

Wehler, H.U. (1987) *Deutsche Gesellschaftsgeschichte 1815–1845/49*, Munich.

Wrigley, E.A. (1987) 'Some reflections on corn yields and prices in pre-industrial economies', in E.A. Wrigley (ed.), *People, cities, and wealth. The transformation of traditional society*, Oxford.

10 The consequences of the potato blight in South Germany

Gunter MAHLERWEIN, Gimbsheim

I. Introduction

In his 1979 essay on 'The economic pre-conditions of the 1848 Revolution' in Germany Jürgen Bergmann pointed to the paradox that although, by contrast with Prussia, statistical data on cereal and potato production in southern Germany show no fall in 1845/46 – on the contrary their crops were better than average – several sources speak of increases in the prices of crops in those same south German regions (Bergmann, 1979: 29–30).[1] Bergmann cannot resolve this paradox, and the same may be said of the present contribution, because research on this subject is only rudimentary. Bergmann hints at a possible answer, however, that agrarian economic growth was characterized by significant regional differences in the first half of the 19th century, so that crop failure and crop damage varied considerably by region. Perhaps interregional differences in harvests are at least part of the solution. Particularly in the socially, politically, and economically

Figure 10.1 Map of South Germany and Switserland

---

[1] Thanks to Christine Hach for helping with the translation.

fragmented regions of southern Germany, it is possible that growing conditions and crop yields varied from village considerably to village. The question of the consequences of potato blight cannot therefore be answered on the large scale. The only clues will be found in regional studies, microstudies and village chronicles that refer to the situation in Rheinhessen, Baden, Württemberg, Bavaria and – by way of comparison – to the Swiss canton of Bern.

II. The extent of potato growing in South Germany

First, there is the issue of how much of the land was under potatoes, about which it is impossible to make generalisations at the state level. The proportion of agricultural land under potatoes in the four districts of Württemberg (Swabia) varied between 2.7 per cent and 7.5 per cent after 1846, when the acreage under potatoes had decreased by 30 per cent as a consequence of the blight (Hippel, 1984: 163). In the eastern parts of Württemberg the potato never rivalled cereals in importance. In Bavaria it is reckoned that on average about 10 per cent of the land was under potatoes in the middle of the 19th century, an average made up by intensive potato cultivation in the Bavarian Palatinate, less intensive cultivation in Franken, where wheaten bread and pork were the staple foods, and little potato cultivation in the rest of Bavaria where large scale grain cultivation dominated the landscape (Sandberger, 1975: 733; Loos, 1999: 531–532; Lindner, 1999: 79). The example of Rheinhessen shows that in addition to such interregional differences, there was even more intra-regional variation (Mahlerwein, 2001: 202–210). In Rheinhessen potatoes had been grown since the 1730s, though at first as fodder only. In 1770 the potato was widely diffused; in that year 84 out of 105 families of the Rheinhessen village of Alsheim stored potatoes. The supply crisis of 1770/71 prompted an increase in potato cultivation. In 1771 only 2 per cent of the fields in the village of Hamm on the banks of the Rhine were planted with potatoes, but in 1804 this had already risen to 8.4 per cent. In Offstein 22 per cent of the fields were already planted with potatoes by 1789. The average percentage for fifty-eight Rhein-hessen villages in the early 1820s was only 6 per cent, but this percentage varied from 2 to 30 per cent depending on the village.

This exceptional inter- and intra-regional variation in potato cultivation is obviously linked to social development. The importance of the potato varied with population density and the percentage of landless people. The proportion of poor smallholders, a feature linked to the system of partible inheritance common in southwest Germany at the time, was also tied to growing potato cultivation. It is striking that in the four districts of Württemberg the most potatoes were grown in the most densely populated areas, whereas in the less densely populated 'Donaukreis' in the eastern parts of Bavaria corn was the staple food of all social classes (compare data in Pfister, 1994: 21 with Hippel, 1984: 163).

All authorities agree that the potato was an immensely important feature of the diet of the lower classes. Utz Jeggle describes his research area, the Swabian Kiebingen, as one where the potato achieved monocultural status with its small farmers (Jeggle, 1977: 265). Wolfgang von Hippel confirms that in Württemberg small farmers were the main cultivators of potatoes, as does Waltraud Loos for Oberfranken (Hippel, 1984: 163; Loos, 1999: 531). That small farmers with little land turned to potato growing is quite consistent with the opinion of an 18th-century Alsacian agrarian reformer that a 4 to 5 person household could be fed with a goat and a quarter of a 'Morgen' (about 700–800 m²) planted with potatoes (Boehler, 1994: 760). Growing potatoes on a part of the village green, or in a little field or garden, might suffice for the subsistence of day labourers, small artisans, and small farmers. The potato spread quickly because it made few demands on soil quality, because it had three to five times the nutritional value of corn, and also because it required neither plough, horses, oxen nor mills – just a spade and lots of manual labour.

The example of Rheinhessen may be used to illustrate the differentiation in cultivation across social class (Mahlerwein, 2001: 207–209). The database of 58 villages contains some whose area under potatoes strikingly exceeds the average. A high degree of potato cultivation indicated either a numerous lower class, or else commercial opportunities. If the production in average years yielded more than the equivalent of a kilogram per day per person, then a market-oriented potato culture is indicated. Potatoes were then planted in the crop rotation system on fields which were reserved to corn culture before. There were three outlets for the commercial growth of potatoes: directly by delivery to the nearest town market, indirectly by feeding as cattle fodder, and distilling.

Feeding potatoes to cattle meant more meat for the market and also – because the cattle were no longer out on grass – more manure which improved the amount of crops immensely. This is especially relevant for potato distilling. It is the main reason for the Rheinhessen-Palatine agrarian revolution of the late 18th and early 19th century. Cattle were fed with the massive amount of distillery residues, and year-round stable fattening produced more manure for use as fertilizer, with the result that within a relative brief time cereal production doubled or even trebled (Mahlerwein, 2002: 46–53). Mennonite farmers were the pioneers of this development, as illustrated by the striking thirty per cent of land under potatoes in the all-Mennonite village of Ibersheim. In other villages with above-average potato cultivation, it is striking that the inhabitants didn't have sufficient space for growing cereals and root crops for subsistence. This indicates a high percentage of almost landless producers.

III. The potato blight in South Germany

Because of the regional and local differences in potato cultivation, the impact of the potato blight on the rural society of south and southwest Germany differed considerably by district. Like everywhere else, the long lasting rainfalls of the summer of 1845 favoured a quick spread of the blight. In Rheinhessen there were big crop failures (Schmahl, 1999: 14). A chronicler from Riedlingen in Swabia noted in 1846 that because the year had been extraordinarily wet the potatoes had been blighted in the autumn 1845, so that many had to be fed to cattle or else thrown away entirely (Steim, 1998: 36). In Württemberg only 45 per cent of the normal yield was harvested (Hippel, 1984: 184). The bulk of the crop rotted in the ground. The Swiss poet Jeremias Gotthelf dramatically described the virulent disease and the reaction of the farmers in his country:

Now there is a disease, nobody knows where it comes from. The fields were black like shrouds, it was a cruel pestilence. The potatoes had plague spots and whoever ate those potatoes, man or animal, would have to die. (Hardegger, 1996: 219)

A major part of the harvested potatoes rotted in the cellars, so that the damage was much higher than 55 per cent. For the year 1845 there are more data from Württemberg (Hippel, 1984: 184) that show the loss in soil and cellar. This also shows that 1845 marked only the beginning of years of potato blight. Although the potato never failed completely, the cumulative effect over the years 1846–1853 – allowing for the relatively 'good' years of 1848 and 1849 – was very serious.

Table 10.1   Yield of the potato harvest in Württemberg, 1846–1853 as a percentage of the yield in a normal year

Year	Yield (as percentage of an average harvest)	Percentage of potato crop affected by blight
1846	45	25
1847	49	33
1848	84	16
1849	90	16
1850	35	32
1851	20	43
1852	51	11
1853	44	0

Source: Hippel, 1984: 184.

The impact of the potato blight on rural society depended on the importance of the potato and the social context of its cultivation. Moreover, the agrarian crisis of 1846/47 in South Germany can only be seen in conjunction with other crop failures.

The wet summer of 1845 not only brought potato blight, but it also prevented grain crops from ripening sufficiently. In Rheinhessen the farmers were told in August to cut the ears from the halms and dry them at home (Schmahl, 1999: 14), while in Upper Swabia thunderstorms ruined the harvest (Steim, 1998: 36). This was the beginning of a decade of crisis where crop failures were the consequence of wet summers and cool springs (Pfister, 1995: 135). In the following year, 1846, potato and grain yields were also poor. In Württemberg the loss of potatoes was 55 per cent, of peas, lentils and broad beans 35 – 40 per cent, and of grain 15 – 24 per cent, relative to average harvest levels (Müller-Harter, 1993: 180). In Rheinhessen, where 76 per cent of an average potato crop was harvested, the rye harvest was only 34 per cent its average level (Schmahl, 1995: 63). In Rheinhessen, unlike Württemberg, the potato crop of 1847 matched the pre-blight average, and in 1848 it was above average (Mahlerwein, 2004: 33). But then in the early 1850s the grain harvests failed again and again, so that in Rheinhessen there was a decade of crisis between 1845 and 1855 (Schmahl, 1999: 54–55).

IV. The economic crisis of the 1840s

The crisis that began in 1845 hit the rural lower classes especially hard, and that in the midst of a long drawn out economic crisis. Low corn prices during the depressed 1820s worsened not only the agricultural situation, but also meant lower wages and less work for day labourers, with the result that day labourers and small craftsmen faced financial problems as consumers in the 1830s when cereal prices were rising. As a consequence of this development the number of people who had to be taken care of by communal poor relief increased immensely (Mahlerwein, 2004: 30–31). In Württemberg from 1842 on, very dry years brought along a decrease in cattle numbers, a rise in corn prices and medium to bad vintages (Hippel, 1984: 180). So the price increase of 1845 caused by crop failures started off at an already high price level. In 1845 the cost of bread for a four-person Rheinhessen family increased by 17.6 per cent relative to 1844, and in 1846 by 60.3 per cent, whereas in the first half of 1847 they had to spend as much as they did in the whole of 1844 (Schmahl, 1999: 55). In Württemberg corn prices increased by 81 per cent between January 1846 and May 1847 (Müller-Harter, 1993: 182), and the price of potatoes increased by 112 per cent between 1845 and 1847 (Kaschuba, 1982: 65). The enormous increase in corn prices cannot be explained by the crop shortfall of 15 per cent in the case of spelt and 24 per cent in the case of rye. A much more important factor must have been the increased demand in consequence of the potato's failure.

The lower classes, who relied particularly on home-grown potatoes, now had to resort to more expensive grains (Kaschuba, 1982: 65). Few potatoes were bought because of the blight, and because storage problems were immense. The increased prices left many families in dire need. If as in Sinsheim (Baden) in February 1847 a four pound (2 kilo) loaf of bread cost 28 Kreuzer, and a day labourer only earned 28 Kreuzer a day, it becomes clear that the landless part of the rural society hardly had a chance of making a living (Rhein-Neckar-Raum, 1998: 360). Drastic reports of impoverished families became common. The Mainz correspondent of the emigration newspaper *Wisconsin-Banner* carried a report in July 1847 about the situation in Rheinhessen:

the poorer classes suffer from black hunger – a poor mother with a baby on her arms crying bitterly for one or two potatoes for her hungry children. There are families who haven't had a bite of bread for one or two weeks. (Schmahl, 1999: 15)

Georg Fettermann from Ober-Flörsheim in Rheinhessen wrote to his brother who emigrated to Pennsylvania in May 1847:

the misery of the lower classes was immense, the poor came from the forests and other regions (the nearby located Palatine and Odenwald) and begged for a handful of potatoes. (Schmahl, 1995: 62–63; Schmahl, 1999: 19)

Reports from the Black Forest speak of skinny horses and of thin bran gruel as the only food reserves, of famished children fainting from weakness at school, and of impoverished people who didn't leave their bed any more because of hunger (Steim, 1998: 38). More than one-third of the households in Alsheim/Rheinhessen depended on communal support in the winter of 1847 (Mahlerwein, 2004: 33); in regions where cereals, bread, and potatoes were much more expensive – as Georg Fettermann wrote to his brother – the proportion of people no longer able to make a living was much higher. There was a marked contrast in fortunes between the lower classes, on the one hand, and the farmers, who could sell their crops at a price that more than made up for the decline in yield, on the other. This may be seen in the increased building activities of farmers during the expensive crop years, as mentioned by Fettermann, a stone mason, to his brother in America (Schmahl, 1995: 61).

V. The reaction towards the potato blight

Measures taken by the state and the municipalities against the crisis caused by the potato blight followed old patterns. The orders issued by the state seemed almost futile: recommendations regarding harvest and storage methods, prohibitions against grain buying for distillation, and attempts of market regulation (Schmahl, 1999: 15). Coping with the misery was mainly the task of the municipalities. The activities of the municipal council in the Rheinhessen town of Alsheim are an example for similar attempts in countless villages and towns. Already in November 1845 the village council decided to buy and store potatoes to sell as seed potatoes to the poor in the spring, in order to guarantee the supply of the year 1846. In 1846/47 many families were directly supported with bread and money by the municipality, or else sold bread at subsidized prices. To supplement the income of the poor, communal work was given but only a few profited from the increased number of communal jobs (Mahlerwein, 2004: 33). In the cities of Heidelberg and Sinsheim (Baden) soup-kitchens were set up for the poor (Rhein-Neckar-Raum, 1998: 360; Nolte, 1994: 291). In many regions the support commissions founded by the municipality or the state were responsible for the coordination of the relief campaigns. In addition to administrative relief actions, non-governmental clubs were established to mobilize relief. Not only in the big cities such as Mannheim or Heidelberg – as Paul Nolte supposes – but also in the countryside, as in Riedlingen or Altheim in Swabia, poor relief clubs were founded with the aim of collecting donations and organizing soup kitchens (Nolte, 1994: 291; Steim, 1998: 37, 45). The new clubs were founded in response to official pressure. In addition, previously existing clubs attempted to raise money through charity events (Steim, 1998: 43).

Fear of social unrest was the main motivation behind public and civil actions. The usual suspicion that the hunger crisis was not a consequence of insufficient storage but a division problem that could be solved by fighting speculation, was verified. This is shown by the crop stocktaking (*Fruchtaufnahme*) of 1847 which listed all private storage in the country. In Württemberg (Müller-Harter, 1993: 230–233) as well as in the Swiss canton of Bern (Frey, 1991: 308–313), the amounts stored would have been sufficient for all, had they been distributed fairly across the population. A count taken in Switzerland revealed that the lower the amount of food stored, the greater the proportion of potatoes in the total (up to 90 per cent), whereas in households with large stocks stored and thus in a position to sell off surplus, the share of grain was more than 75 per cent (Frey, 1991: 313). The amount of storage makes clear that in Switzerland, Württemberg and in other regions grain was held back in order to be sold at a higher price in the months before the new harvest. Not only farmers and corn merchants but also millers and bakers were suspected of hoarding. The protests were usually aimed against those groups. Already in July 1846 there was a 'bread revolution' where people were aggressive against bakers in Mainz/Rheinhessen (Schmahl, 1999: 15). In the spring of 1847 riots were reported of numerous cities in Baden, Württemberg, Franken and Bavaria: Mannheim, Nürnberg, Munich, Bamberg, Schweinfurt, Augsburg (Rhein-Neckar-Raum, 1998: 360; Lindner, 1999: 80).

The anti-speculation riot in Swabian city of Ulm on May 1st 1847 is especially well documented (Müller-Harter, 1993). The riots started at the potato market in Ulm. Because prices were high, many potatoes were brought to the market, which clearly showed that, although difficult to store, great stocks of potatoes were being hoarded for sale in the months before the harvest when prices are highest. When farmers and customers could not agree on a price and the sellers threatened to take their potatoes home again, pillage started and people tried to fix a price. The riots extended to the grain market. Then a mill and a public house were raided, and it took the military several hours to restore order.

Whereas in Ulm and many other towns craftsmen, day labourers, and factory workers were the main participants of the riots, which were sparked off by acute supply shortages, in the Badish Odenwald small farmers also took part in the riots because the conflicts there were motivated by general political problems as well. In contrast with other rural regions, the agrarian reforms had not yet fully taken place and the rural population was doubly burdened of having to pay feudal rents and state taxes. The poor relief was too much of a burden for impoverished villages. The rioters called for the 'day of revolution' on the April 12th 1847 and their threats were directed not only against the nobility, civil servants, and Jews, but also against the mayors and the members of the village councils (Nolte, 1994: 291–292). More than at other places, those riots were the basis of the 1848 Revolution, which had its starting point in the Odenwald area of Baden (Ries, 1998: 264).

Though the numbers of emigrants cannot be compared to those leaving Ireland, an increase in emigration from southern Germany and Switzerland was certainly a consequence of the agrarian crisis of 1845–1847 (Hippel, 1984: 206; Schmahl, 1999: 16; Pfister, 1995: 135). Yet despite the increasing municipal burden imposed by the rapid increase in the numbers of the poor seeking relief, radical solutions like that adopted in the Rheinhessen village of Gimbsheim remained an exception. Here the municipality got rid of 200 people by paying their passage to America, so that the municipality would no longer be obliged to pay their poor relief (Schmahl, 1999: 16).

The demographic consequences of the agrarian crisis varied from region to region. Whereas Christian Pfister reports an increased mortality and a reduced birth rate in the Swiss canton of Bern (Pfister, 1995: 135), research in Rheinhessen found no striking deviations (Rommel, 1996: 160; Rettinger, 2002: 203–207).

No doubt South Germany and Switzerland were hit by the agrarian crisis of 1845–1847 with a harshness that varied according to region. The role of the potato blight within this crisis cannot be completely identified, given the present state of research.

The potato may be seen as triggering the crisis in regions where it was produced and consumed on a considerable scale, which cannot be said for some eastern regions of South Germany. But the consequences of the potato blight for the development of the crisis in other regions can be clearly stated. First, it led to the loss of the ability to survive on home-grown potatoes for many of the poor, who had become dependent on the potato as basic food. Second, the failure of the potato crop increased the price of corn, leading merchants and producers to hold back their supplies and exacerbating the crisis.

Bibliography

'Arbeitskreis der Archive im Rhein-Neckar-Dreieck' (1998), *Der Rhein-Neckar-Raum und die Revolution von 1848/49,* Ubstadt-Weiher.

Bergmann, J. (1979) 'Ökonomische Voraussetzungen der Revolution von 1848. Zur Krise von 1845 bis 1848 in Deutschland', in J. Bergmann, K. Megerle and P. Steinbach (eds), *Geschichte als politische Wissenschaft. Sozialökonomische Ansätze, Analyse politik-historischer Phänomene, politologische Fragestellungen in der Geschichte,* Stuttgart, pp. 24–54.

Boehler, J.M. (1994) *Une société rurale en milieu rhénan: La paysannerie de la Plaine d'Alsace (1648–1789),* Strasbourg.

Frey, W. (1991) *Das Janusgesicht der Agrarmodernisierung: Der Verlust der sozialen Tragfähigkeit. Der demographische, ökonomische und soziale Transformationsprozess des bernischen Amtsbezirkes Konolfingen zwischen 1760 und 1880,* Bern.

Hardegger, J. (1996) *Das Werden der modernen Schweiz, Quellen, Illustrationen und andere Materialien zur Schweizergeschichte, Bd.1: Vom Ancien Régime zum Ersten Weltkrieg,* Basel.

Hippel, W.v. (1984) *Auswanderung aus Südwestdeutschland. Studien zur württembergischen Auswanderung und Auswanderungspolitik im 18. und 19. Jahrhundert,* Stuttgart.

Jeggle, U. (1977) *Kiebingen – eine Heimatgeschichte. Zum Prozeß der Zivilisation in einem schwäbischen Dorf,* Tübingen.

Kaschuba, W. and Lipp, C. (1982) *Dörfliches Überleben. Zur Geschichte materieller und sozialer Reproduktion ländlicher Gesellschaft im 19. und frühen 20. Jahrhundert,* Tübingen.

Lindner, W. (1999) 'Eine Revolution fällt nicht vom Himmel. Ökonomische und soziale Indikatoren der Revolution 1848/49', in G. Schweinfurt, U. Dippold, U. Wirz (eds), *Die Revolution von 1848/49 in Franken,* Bayreuth, pp. 77–96.

Loos, E. (1999) *"Behufs der Bestimmung des im Bezirk herrschenden Kulturgrads" – die Physikatsberichte in der Mitte des 19. Jahrhunderts als Beitrag zur Sozial- und Kulturgeschichte Mittelfrankens,* Ansbach.

Mahlerwein, G. (2001) *Die Herren im Dorf. Bäuerliche Oberschicht und ländliche Eliten-bildung in Rheinhessen zwischen 1700 und 1850,* Mainz.

Mahlerwein, G. (2002) 'Le rôle du travail dans la révolution agricole. L'exemple de la Hesse-Rhénanie aux XVIIIe et XIXe siècles', *Histoire et Sociétés Rurales,* 18, pp. 41–63.

Mahlerwein, G. (2004) *Alsheim-HALASEMIA. Geschichte eines rheinhessischen Dorfes. Band 2: Von der französischen Revolution bis heute,* Alsheim.

Müller-Harter, M. (1993) *Ulm 1847. 1. Mai. 7.00 bis 13.00 Uhr. Auf der Suche nach den Hintergründen eines Teuerungstumultes,* Tübingen.

Nolte, P. (1994) *Gemeindebürgertum und Liberalismus in Baden 1800–1850,* Göttingen.

Ries, K. (1998) 'Bauern und ländliche Unterschichten', in C. Dipper, U. Speck (eds.), *1848-Revolution und Deutschland,* Frankfurt/Main,Leipzig, pp. 262–271.

Pfister, C. (1994) *Bevölkerungsgeschichte und historische Demographie 1500–1800,* München.

Pfister, C. (1995) *Im Strom der Modernisierung. Bevölkerung, Wirtschaft und Umwelt im Kanton Bern 1700–1914*, Bern.

Rettinger, E. (2002) *Die Umgebung der Stadt Mainz und ihre Bevölkerung vom 17.–19. Jahrhundert. Ein historisch-demographischer Beitrag zur Sozialgeschichte ländlicher Regionen*, Stuttgart.

Rommel, M. (1997) *Die Wormser und ihre Stadt 1750–1875. Demographische, soziale und konfessionelle Aspekte des Wandels von der Ackerbürger- zur Fabrikarbeiterstadt*, Darmstadt.

Schmahl, H. (1995) '"…Man hörte schon vieles und verschiedenes…". Briefe einer rheinhessischen Familie nach Amerika 1839–1858', *Alzeyer Geschichtsblätter*, 29, pp. 52–74.

Schmahl, H. (1999) '"Deutschland liefert uns gegenwärtig eine schlimme Zeit…". Lebensbedingungen in Rheinhessen in den Jahren vor 1848', *Mainzer Geschichtsblätter*, 11, pp. 7–19.

Schmahl, H. (2000) *Verpflanzt, aber nicht entwurzelt. Die Auswanderung aus Hessen-Darmstadt (Provinz Rheinhessen) nach Wisconsin im 19. Jahrhundert*, Frankfurt/Main.

Steim, K.W. (1998) *Revolution von 1848/49 im Oberamt Riedlingen*, Bad Buchau.

11 The crisis in France. A memorable crisis but not a potato crisis

Nadine VIVIER, Université du Maine

If we wish to compare the different European countries as they faced the mid-19th century crisis, we need to stress some common features, among them the potato blight, and some differences, particularly those related to their political contexts.[1] The French crisis was distinctive in two ways: it was especially long-lasting and has had an important historiography. The subsistence crisis of 1846–1847 was hardly over when the revolution of February 1848 created a new crisis. Although the topic of this book relates to the crisis of 1845–1847, the difficulties that followed for the next few years (1848–51) need to be described, mainly because French historiography has often considered the two-fold crisis as a single critical event.

The first research to be carried out in economic history on the mid-nineteenth crisis was instigated in 1948 by Ernest Labrousse. In 1953 he edited a collection of work done by his students on several regions of France, focused on economic analysis, particularly price levels. Labrousse sought to explain the outbreak of the revolution in 1848, by giving the economic crises as a major reason (Labrousse, 1949). According to his view, a process similar to the Revolution of 1789 occurred again for two reasons. On the one hand, economic and social conditions did not fundamentally change: the price of bread seemed to rule people's behaviour. On the other hand, the revolution's moral objectives were not attained either. The economic crisis of 1848 was particular, according to Labrousse's interpretation, because it took the form of a 'transitional crisis': it combined the features of a traditional subsistence crisis with those of a new type, the capitalist crisis. It was also a struggle among three parties: aristocracy, middle class and proletariat.

The rise of quantitative research led to a shift in focus from national to regional studies. Several theses devoted to mid-century life in particular regions of France were presented between the 1960s and the 1980s. Although they studied the economic situation, the focus was now on social life and its consequences for politics. This research presented a much more complex outlook on the causes of the revolution and on various aspects of the crisis: instead of a single crisis, several could now be outlined, and these crises affected different parts of the country in different ways, with local variations for example in the Alps as shown by Philippe Vigier (1963) or in Burgundy studied by Pierre Lévêque (1983) (see also Agulhon, 1970; Désert, 1975).

Labrousse's approach influenced research throughout the years 1950–1980; it also inspired English-speaking historians who enriched social history (Price, 1975). In the 1980s, when belief in a future revolution that would severely change society had faded, historians were no longer so eager to depict a past revolution but preferred to make long-term studies of the economy.

---

[1] The author wishes to thank the participants of the 2003 Dublin Workshop, among them especially Carl-Johan Gadd, for their useful comments on a first draft of this contribution.

Recent economic history has proposed a new interpretation of the mid-nineteenth century crisis. Scholars have paid less attention to the study of economic health than to the structural difficulties of capitalism. The gap between large companies on the one side, and shops and the production of artisans on the other, is now seen as a fundamental struggle between a financial aristocracy and the mass of producers. The recent works dwell on interpretations of several aspects: the reality of the crisis (what was the part played by the shortage, and of speculation in the price increases?), the popular responses to the subsistence crisis, the social and political crisis (Démier, 1997).

I. The pre-crisis situation

I.1. The economic context in France

The French economy had been changing quickly before the crisis of the 1840's. Ancient industrial structures coexisted with modern ones, modern agricultural regions with traditional ones; this mosaic explains the debates of historians and their opposed estimations, according to which aspect they focus on. The French economy grew rapidly during the July Monarchy, principally in the twelve years 1833–1845: important efforts to modernise credit, industry and transport (roads, waterways, beginning of railways). In 1837, Jacques Laffitte founded the Caisse générale du commerce et de l'industrie and he was followed by a few others who all favoured a credit system based on a larger number of customers that could provide companies with the funds they needed. Industrial production increased, divided between a traditional part (handicrafts), which was by far the most important, and a modern part, which developed mainly in large and mechanised companies (essentially in textiles, metallurgy and mines). The number of steam-engines in use grew from 615 in 1830 to 5000 in 1847 (Figure 11.1).

However, agricultural activity was still the predominant industry. The July Monarchy's government had been very active from 1836 onwards, introducing various measures to encourage modern agricultural methods.[2] Historians debate the estimated depth of changes in agricultural productivity. Some of them see a French agriculture still like that of the ancien régime (Clout, 1977; Price, 1983b), others challenge this view, showing in some areas considerable changes in production: specialisation of agricultural production (wine, silk, cattle breeding...), increases in wheat yields thanks to an improvement of the soil through the addition of lime. The cottage industry was very active (wool and wood, small-level metallurgy...). Economic historians have measured agricultural output and argued that around 1835 it grew at twice the rate of the population growth.

---

[2] It is often said that the government sought to encourage capitalist farming by large landowners. I can assume encouraging smallholdings was not at all neglected, as can be seen by the pressure upon local councils to have them lease out small plots of land, and by *comices* (agricultural shows) to which many small tenants participated in some regions. The secretary in charge of agriculture in 1835, Passy, supported small farms in his publications.

Figure 11.1   Agricultural and industrial production in France, 1830–1870

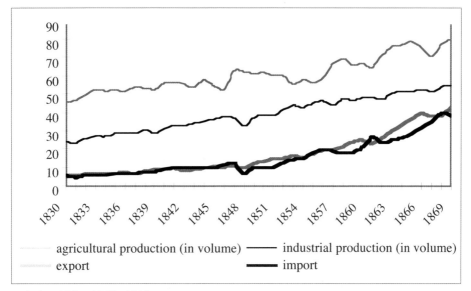

index 100 = 1908–1912
Source: Lévy-Leboyer and Bourguigon, 1985, 333–335.

I.2.   Food production and trade

The desire of the State to have statistical data at its disposal led Napoléon to create a special department of statistics. More or less abandoned in the 1820s, the Statistique department became very active with improved methods in the 1830s. In 1836, the ministry asked for an agricultural enquiry, including acreage devoted to the various crops, their output and a census of animals. All the data were collected in each village and reviewed by the prefect and a commission. Mayors were required to indicate the amounts of various cereals, beverages and meat that were consumed in the village, each year. This information was collated at the department level and related to the population to provide figures on average per capita consumption. Yet even this reliable enquiry presented some failings. In so far as many rural families were self-sufficient, most of the food eaten was not marketed. So the data were actually only estimates. Some elements of diet were not recorded: fish, game, dairy products, fruits and garden products. And of course, the statistics gave the arithmetic mean of food consumption by inhabitant, peasant or bourgeois, baby or adult. Similar failings have been mentioned for the Prussian data (Bass, this volume).

From the last decades of the 18th century output increased. The total output of cereals rose from 132 million hl in 1815 to 204 million hl in 1836 in a country of 33,500,000 inhabitants. The major production was wheat: the area devoted to wheat climbed up to 5,58 million ha in 1836 and the yield rose from 8,59 hl/ha in 1815 to 12,45 in 1836 – which is the average for the whole territory, including mountains – or to 14,98 in north-west France.

Table 11.1 Production and consumption of cereals and potatoes in 1836

France total	Area Ha	Production 1000 hl	Yield Hl/ha	Estimated consumption (%)			
				Seed	Human food	Live-stock feed	Industry
Wheat	5,586,786	69,558	12.45	17.7	81.8	0.1	0.4
Oats	3,000,634	48,899	16.29	16.3	4.6	78.9	0.3
Rye	2,577,253	27,811	10.79	18.2	79.7	1.6	0.4
Barley	1,188,189	16,661	14.02	16.1	50.6	20.3	13.0
Maslin	911,325	11,829	12.98	16.7	82.2	0.9	0.2
Buckwheat	651,461	8,469	13.00	10.4	74.1	15.4	0.0
Maize	631,731	7,620	12.06	3.7	75.3	21.0	0.0
Potatoes	922,075	96,233	104.37	10.6	81.4	8.0	0.0
Pulses	296,995	3,460	11.65	11.8	71.3	11.8	0.4

Source: Statistique de la France.

As proudly notified in the *Statistique de la France* (1836) (p. XXV), 'To the cereals that were formerly the whole diet of people, have now been added potatoes, légumes secs (dried vegetables (pulses)) and garden products (....) They give now each year a prodigious mass of supplies.' The potato was recorded as being grown in Vivarais and in Dauphiné as early as the 16th century. Then, in the 1760s, agricultural societies, working for greater output, tried to popularise the tuber. Parmentier's prize-winning essay for the Académie de Besançon in 1771 praised potatoes because they might reduce the calamities resulting from grain shortages (Suchet, 1870). The catastrophic harvest of 1816 convinced many people to eat potatoes. The land area sown with potatoes rose from 560,000 ha in 1817 to 922,075 in 1836. Potatoes were grown for human diet and for pigs, but unlike the situation in Denmark or Prussia (see Henriksen and Bass, this volume), they were not distilled. Like pulses, they were the food of the poor.

The geography of cultivation, yields and consumption was very similar. I give here the map of consumption only (figure 11.2a). Potatoes were not important in the south which was too hot and dry, in the South-West where maize was the staple crop, and in regions where popular opposition to this tuber continued: the Paris Basin and Normandy, which also had more lucrative specialisations (Désert, 1955). Five areas had an important production level of potatoes: in the north-east, Alsace and Lorraine, where small peasants cultivated cereals and potatoes without fallow; in the west, Maine and Brittany, especially Léon on the north coast of Brittany; the Massif central and the central Pyrénées. Average yield in France was 104 hl/ha. Since the weight of an hl was estimated at 68.3 kg (data given in 1852), the average for the whole country, including southern areas, was 7,130 kg/ha. But in the main areas of production, yields rose to 211hl/ha or 14,411 kg/ha in Finistère and 231 hl/ha or 15,777 kg/ha in Alsace. Those figures may be compared to 8,600 kg/ha in German Reich (Bass, this volume), to 134 to 179 hl/ha in the Netherlands (Paping-Tassenaar, this volume) and 14,000 to 15,000 kg in Flanders (Vanhaute, this volume).

**Figure 11.2a
Consumption of potatoes, 1836
(hectolitres/habitants/year)**

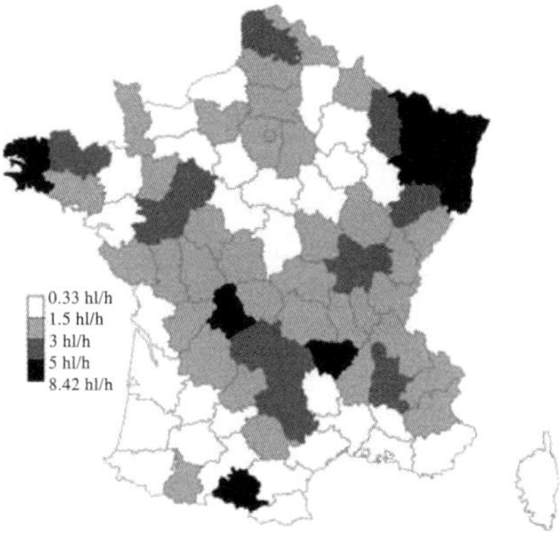

**Figure 11.2b
Average price of a hectolitre
of potatoes, 1836**

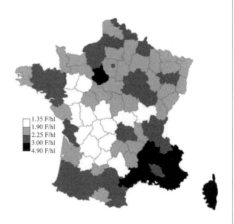

Source: Statistique de la France, 1836

Source: Statistique de la France, 1836

**Figure 11.3
Consumption of wheat and rye,
1836 (hectolitres/habitants/year)**

**Figure 11.4
Main areas of surplus and shortage
for wheat and potatoes in 1835–1840**

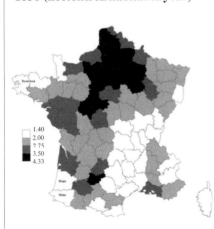

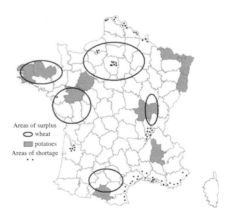

Source: Statistique de la France, 1840

Source: Statistique de la France, 1840

227

Wheat was the leading bread grain, even the exclusive grain in towns, and could be used as a cash crop by peasants who consumed secondary cereals themselves. The wheat trade varied according to shortages, but the usual trade routes can be described. Some granaries sent grain to the most densely populated areas: the Paris Basin fed Paris; Dauphiné and Bresse, Lyon; Brittany, Bordeaux. Rivers (Seine, Loire and Saône), waterways (canal du Midi) and ports along the western littoral played a major role in this trade. Long distance movements by sea took surpluses from Brittany to Mediterranean Europe.

By contrast, other cereals and potatoes were predominantly used to meet local needs, to feed the peasants. The potato trade was small, more especially as they could not be stored and were heavy and of low value. Most areas produced largely what they themselves could consume. Exchanges usually occurred between neighbouring areas. Globally, the north east and Massif Central were self sufficient. The north needed surpluses. Brittany sent 1,13 million hl through the ports of Brest and Morlaix to French Flanders. As transports were still insufficient, in spite of progress, striking differences in food prices could be seen. The less output in a region, the higher the price. The exceptions are Paris, well stocked and with moderate prices, and regions with high exportation such as Brittany where prices were higher. Figure 11.4 summarises roughly the import and export regions.

I.3. Calorific intake of the population

The maps (Figures 11.2a and 11.3) of consumption of potatoes and cereals (wheat and rye) show the diet. Potatoes are eaten in the areas of production. Cereals are the main part of the diet in towns. Using the *Statistique de la France* published in 1840, Hugh Clout (1980: 189–212) developed a study of calorific intake. He explained his methods and the failings of the source (fish, poultry and game were missing) and counted only carbohydrates, meat and beverages. 'The average French citizen consumed 857,000 calories per annum, whilst his counterpart in Limousin, the Pays de l'Adour and the middle Garonne was consuming more than 1,170,000 calories each year (…) In harsh contrast were the 'hungry' pays, with annual calorie intakes of less than 720,000 in Champagne, Franche-Comté and Massif central. Diets in the central provinces were unquestionably the most deficient and unhealthy (…) Parisians, on average, ate well during the July Monarchy (…) probably better than the citizens of any other European city'. By contrast, 'the diet of most peasants is inferior to those in most other nations. No meat, white bread or wine; only black bread, potatoes and water; this is how a third of the French people eats'. Such was the observation of Léonce de Lavergne twenty years after the *Statistique*' (1857: 391).

The map of the height of young men, either made from the number of conscription-free undersized men (Broca in 1867 quoted by Van Meerten, 1990, 760) or made from the height of conscripts in the military registers from 1803 to 1826 (Le Roy Ladurie, 1973) show two parts in France: north of a line Normandy-Geneva, young men are taller. The average size was 1,65 m, but men from the north, the north-east and Paris had a slightly higher stature (1,66m in Paris, 1,68m in North department), thanks to their higher and better average calorific intake which included more meat. In the west and the south-west, where the average income per inhabitant was lower, young men were smaller: 1,641m in Aquitaine where intake was high but essentially made up of carbohydrates, 1,637m in Brittany where people ate very poorly in spite of a high production level, but there was a high density of population and a large part of the production was sold.

Also Van Meerten developed a mathematical model in which variations in median height of French conscripts are predicted with great accuracy by a lagged series of per capita income. His results (Van Meerten, 1990: 769) show that 1847–48 were years of a slight decline of median height (from 163,85 cm in 1835–1845 to 163,99 cm in 1846, 163,68 cm in 1847, 163,77 cm in 1848, 163,93 cm in 1849 and 164,01 cm in 1850). The stature fluctuated between 163,7 cm and 164,0 cm during the following years 1850–66, and raised over 164,6 cm after 1867. In a recent study, Laurent Heyberger shows that the prices of cereals did not matter any more for the generations born after 1835 (Heyberger, 2003). The crisis of 1847 had only a small impact and was the last one. Structural improvement in economic welfare explains the growth of young men's size.

II. The mid-century crisis

II.1. The agricultural crisis of 1846: shortage and high prices

In the context of buoyant economic growth, a slowdown in industrial activities occurred around 1845: textile factories complained about difficulties in selling their products. 'Low prices of manufactured wares are prejudicial to the mill-owner and to the worker. Several workers have been dismissed and are unemployed', wrote the préfet of Sarthe during the first semester of 1846 (A.D.S., 9M21).[3] Everywhere in the industrial regions of western France, similar complaints were sent to the government. The crisis affected also tanneries, and the building industry. The traffic on the river Sarthe reveals the difficulties (traffic of building stones: 1840 = 4,000t.; 1845= 791t. and 1846= 248t.; hemp 1840 = 300t.; 1845= 164t. and 1846= 16t.) (A.D.S., 3S).

Agriculture suffered from long periods of rain and flooding. The 1845 harvest was only 'passable' (A.D.S., 1N4, Rapport du préfet au conseil général, 1845): no major price increases but no reserve either (see Solar, this volume). According to some testimonies, a new and morbid disease of the potato was observed in 1843 in the east of France. 'In the year 1843, people first observed a potato disease and worried [in Franche-Comté]. They tried to regenerate potatoes with seedling. But soon the disease escalated to a considerable extent' (Suchet, 1870, 18). Was this *phytophtora* or another disease?[4] According to some agronomists in 1846, *phytophtora* was first observed in Europe near Hanover in 1832 and appeared in France some years later but it did not spread and did not catch attention (Decaisne, 1846: 89). The large enquiry about the potato disease launched by the Royal Society of Agriculture in 1846 wiped out such a possibility: 'there was no disease like this one within living memory'.[5] Actually, the harvest was good in 1843 and 1844, particularly in Alsace, even better than the average level.[6] The disease spread on a very wide scale and was violent only from 1845 onwards. In 1845,

---

[3] A.D.S.: Archives Départementales de la Sarthe; A.N.: Archives Nationales.
[4] See Bourke, 1964: 808; Rousselle and Crosnier, 1996:44.
[5] *Bulletin des séances*, 1846–47: 625
[6] A.D. Bas-Rhin, 11M and 63J. I am grateful to Jean-Michel Boehler for this data.

potato crops for the whole territory fell by about –20%: from about 103 million hectolitres in the previous years down to 78. The disease spread largely in 1846 and the shortage of potatoes immediately placed extra pressure on grain crops. That year climatic vagaries were responsible for disastrous grain crops. In 1846, production was down by about a quarter of average levels. In the Paris basin and more generally in the territory north of the Loire River, the rainy spring caused floods, then the drought of the summer desiccated cereals. The 1846 wheat harvest was about 61 million hectolitres, about 80% of the normal size (McPhee, 1992: 56–74).

Of course, the crisis varied from one place to another. Some harvests were good, such as maize, fodder crops, wine and madder. Cattle breeding suffered quite differently. Jura or Normandy where the earnings were good did not suffer at all, while in forested mountains the code forestier had dramatic consequences. The implementation of the forest law voted in 1827 aimed at evicting peasants and their animals from the forests, progressively restricting access to resources previously available such as wood gathering and stock-grazing. This progressive shortage in fodder drove peasants to sell their animals from 1840 onwards, and the hardship was severe in some mountain areas like the Pyrénées (Sahlins, 1994 and Soulet 1987, t.2: 149–171) and the Alps (Vivier, 1992).

Figure 11.5 Prices and wages in France, 1830–1870

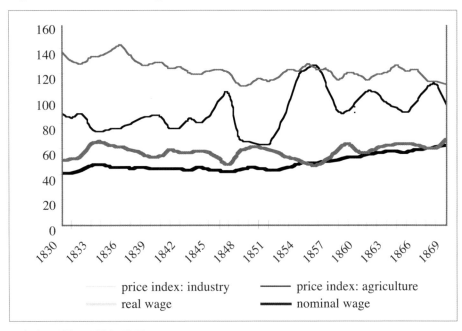

index 100 = 1908–1912
Source: Lévy-Leboyer and Bourguigon, 1985, 333–335.

The prices of cereals and bread climbed from mid-1846 to early 1847 and lowered again in May. The national average price of wheat increased from 24 Francs per hectoliter in June 1846 to 38 francs in March 1847, of potatoes from 1,94 Francs to 6 Francs per hectoliter in the same period. The trend of grain prices is given in Peter Solar's contribution (this volume). Díaz Marín (this volume) shows also that the sharpest rise in prices in Spain occurred between January and May. The French government bought important quantities of Russian wheat, imported via Marseille's harbour. Prices varied from one region to another, according to local production and the cost of transport. In the South East and Languedoc, prices rose moderately, never exceeding 32 F for an hectolitre of wheat. Thanks to the import of Russian wheat, there were sufficient supplies of cereals, the higher prices resulting from the cost of transport. The same situation existed in the South West where maize compensated for the loss of cereals. In contrast, Massif Central and the northern half of France had a disastrous harvest of wheat, rye and buckwheat, adding to the loss of potatoes. There, prices came 40% higher, and people went through a period of scarcity at the beginning of 1847. In the Sartre department, the price of rye soared from 14,90 F in June 1846 to 26,80F in January 1847. The crisis was even worse in the North-East where the potato disease was more severe (wheat cost 52 Francs in March 1847). As early as the beginning of 1846, anxiety about food prices turned into riots. During the winter 1846/47, a wave of direct actions by rural people broke out. They aimed at imposing price reductions, at confiscating the grain convoys passing through their villages, or at intimidating hoarders.

There is an important question about the role played by shortages and speculation in the high prices. Rightly or wrongly, people greatly feared speculation. Public opinion was far from the rational analysis of the Economist quoted by Peter Solar (this volume). The wheat harvest was about 80% of the normal size and prices doubled. Many regional studies emphasise speculation, on which administrative authorities focused.[7] Speculation was indulged in by the large producers (landowners and farmers) who did not want to sell during the winter of 1846, and preferred to wait for spring, with the hope of higher prices. Grain merchants also entered into speculation where they could. Pierre Lévêque showed how a rich merchant stocked grain, buying directly from farmers in Burgundy and then sending it to be sold in Jura and in Alsace (where the deficit was severe) when prices reached a peak (Lévêque, 1983: vol.3). As soon as May 1847, prices started to fall again, even though the new crop would not reach the market until November: the new harvest looked good and speculators could no longer sustain prices based on popular anxiety. This has led French historians to argue that the price increases were due far more to speculation than to shortages. The Spanish case was similar: the rioters of 1847 protested against people buying-up (Díaz Marín, this volume). It can be objected that prices were not only determined by the existing stocks, they reflected expectations of crops to come.[8]

---

[7] See for example, Desert, in Labrousse, 1956: 44–50; Bois in *Ibid.*: 286–288 and Lévêque, 1983: 3rd vol.

[8] A study made by Marcia J. Frost (2004) about prices in Bombay in 1824 shows how quickly prices responded to changes in growing conditions which affected expectations of future supplies to the market.

Regional studies have shown that the scarcity, although brief, had long-lasting bad consequences. Poor relief given by institutions or private charity was not sufficient. Small landowners, as well as the poor, became buyers of cereals, and thus poor people suffered from scarcity of food and were forced to ask for credit in order to buy cereals.

The harvest of cereals in 1847 was expected to be abundant and proved so. This eased the price crisis, and in September 1847 the price of wheat fell back to 22 F. By the end of 1847, the agricultural crisis was over. Nevertheless, the potato crisis continued, but the abundance of cereals concealed it. In the North-East, land devoted to potato production diminished. For example in the department of Doubs, the area cultivated with potatoes, 8,841 ha in 1836, was divided in half (around 4,000 ha) during the next twenty years or so; it was to return to the earlier levels in 1858 (8,302 ha, then 9,515 in 1862) (Suchet, 1870:18).

II.2.   A credit and industrial crisis

In addition to this traditional subsistence crisis there arose a credit crisis. Enthusiasm for railways had dried up all capital available for investment. This was due to an over-investment phenomenon: part of the capital that had been invested until then in short-term commercial operations was now injected in industrial or commercial businesses requiring recurrent new cash injections. The crisis came to a head on the day that liquidities were no longer available to factoring as well as to satisfy funding requirements of the railways companies. By the end of 1846, over-investment became obvious and the situation worsened with the agricultural crisis putting pressure on the State and individuals to rely on banks funding. In order to purchase Russian wheat, and to compensate for the reduced tax proceeds, the state issued Treasury bonds. The floating debt increased, the deficit amount was 257 millions of francs at the end of 1847. Unable to satisfy all these demands, banks and the companies they financed were having difficulties. In January 1847, the bank rate of the French Central Bank increased from 4% to 5% and stock prices dropped.

Businesses suffered from the decrease in purchasing power that resulted from the concomitant weakening of agricultural revenues and stock prices. This situation triggered an industrial crisis that first hit railway companies and related activities (mines and metallurgy), then spread to the textile and building sectors which suffered from mass unemployment. Bankruptcies reached the highest point in 1847. 20% of the workers were laid off in the coal mines, 35% in metallurgy and in textiles, and the railway works nearly ceased altogether. Small rural industries which had previous difficulties, suffered greatly: small ironworks in the East, hemp and flax in Dauphiné, French Flanders and Maine, etc. (see also Figure 11.1). The economic difficulties went hand in hand with social strain in 1846–1847. But in the summer of 1847, the cereal harvest was good, bread prices were reduced, and the strain lessened as a slight industrial recovery became discernible.

II.3.   February Revolution and mistrust

The revolution of February 1848 created a new crisis. The desire to establish a 'social republic' (*une république sociale*) led to the immediate voting of measures such as universal suffrage and the right to work, with the creation of a governmental commission for workers. This quickly worried the wealthy classes. Soon after the revolution, the workers in Paris, Lyon, or in the countryside stopped working, sometimes briefly to give expression to their joy; then by and large, they went on strike against bourgeoisie in March. The people with money became frightened, and took it out of the *Caisse d'Epargne* (Savings bank) or sold their stocks. Even those burgesses who willingly accepted the republic were conservative and prudent in regard to their own portfolios. Within a few days 'an unprecedented economic paralysis' spread across the country (Labrousse). It was first of all a monetary and banking crisis. The credit company created by Laffitte disappeared at the beginning of March. As soon as the Stock Exchange reopened on March 7th, share prices dropped. In order to fund their social measures, the government decided an exceptional tax for the year 1848, l'impôt des 45 centimes, i.e. an increase of 45% of the land tax. A letter received on 28th March 1848, by the commissaire de la Sarthe Trouvé Chauvel from his officer in La Flèche, exactly describes this general feeling of mistrust:

The paper is frightening and the presentation of bank notes at the cattle markets causes unfortunate dealings for the seller, who prefers to resign himself to a loss than to accept values he doesn't believe in. On the other side, the person who has money to invest, buries it in his garden, fearing to be refunded in bank notes in the long term. We have seen, in La Flèche, lenders refusing to sign prepared bonds and wishing to cancel the deal. Thus, cash value would be better for the countryside. Has the 45 cents tax been sufficiently meditated on? And will it produce the expected results?[9]

The lack of funds generated an industrial and commercial crisis which left lots of workers unemployed.[10] The Provisional Government responded by creating the National Workshops (Ateliers Nationaux).[11] But they were so expensive that the assembly decided on June, 21st, to close them down. Parisian workers reacted immediately. The insurrection of June, 22nd to 26th, les Journées de Juin, was aggressively put down by the army. General Cavaignac who directed these repressive tactics, became Home Secretary, the political elites were determined to reinforce social stability. A slight improvement began to emerge at the end of July, strengthened in October with the recovery of textile and banking, although metallurgy and building recovered more slowly. The economic recovery intensified during the year 1849, and commercial revival gave a boost to the harbours' activities and to most industries throughout the land.

II.4. The agricultural depression, 1848–51: overproduction and low prices

While industry and commerce became easier, a long lasting depression had struck agriculture as everywhere in Europe, but it seems that in France, difficulties were very severe, and production was significantly reduced. The inquiry decided by the parliament

---

[9] A.D.S., 1M175. *Commissaire* is the new name given to the *prefet*.

[10] The Minister of Finance started a revolution in the credit system with the decree of March, 7th. It permitted the creation of discount houses (*comptoirs d'escompte*) in order to advance money to the shops. The funds of those discount houses had to be provided by the municipality and private subscribers.

[11] The *ateliers nationaux*, like the temporary charity workshops of this period, offered earth works like digging. Unemployed men could earn 2 francs a day. From March, 9th, to June, 15th, 117,300 workers were registered.

and conducted in each canton during the second half of 1848 described a distressed situation, as can be seen from this answer by Vic, near Château-Salins, in the north-east of France.[12]

The agriculture suffers deeply. Independently from political events which have so quickly affected the credit, the confidence and the trade, the cause for the farmer is in the higher prices of leases demanded by the landowner, which the farmers are forced to accept considering the high numbers of competitors and also in the raise of the wage required by the rural workers. The abundant cereal crops in the past two years, the widespread death of trade, the lack of credit and the shortage of cash value, lowered the wheat price so that it became inferior to the price predicted in the lease. The crops' abundance that blocks markets do not compensate for the difference, the farmer is distressed and forced to contract expensive loans to honour his commitments. We have already brought to your notice that from an agricultural point of view, France can export cereals with benefits only to England…and this because of production costs are at least a third higher in France than in other countries.

Table 11.2 Production, prices and wages in French agriculture, 1844–1852

Agriculture	Total production (volume)	Price index	Wages index
1844	57.5	81	43.1
1845	54.3	86	45.7
1846	52.3	98	43.8
1847	62.2	104	42.9
1848	62	69	41.6
1849	60.6	66	43.4
1850	61.3	64	45
1851	59.8	64	44.7
1852	59.6	77	43.2

index 100 = 1908–1912
Source: Lévy-Leboyer and Bourguigon, 1985: 334.

Agriculture suffered from low prices, increased taxes and restrictions in credit. The harvests of 1848–1851 were exceptionally good and prices fell for wheat, rye, potatoes and fodder. Prices continued to fall until 1851 when they reached the lowest level in the century: 13 to 17 Francs per hectolitre of wheat (see Figure 11.5). The abundant harvests led to a glut in the markets, all the more severe because the commercial recovery was limited, because people had no faith in the future. While profits from the land diminished, the taxes increased. The general crisis in public and private credit continued, due to the general mistrust in this republican state governed by non-republicans. The countryside suffered from restrictions in credit, which had already been largely insufficient before 1846. There was simply not enough cash in circulation.

The consequences of this depression hit the various social groups in different ways. Small casual workers and servants did not suffer much because of the low food prices

---

[12] A.N., C959, canton de Vic, arrondissement de Château Salins, Meurthe.

and the employment given by the good harvests. The main victims of the depression were the landowners: large landowners saw their profits diminish, but more numerous and distressed were the small landowners who had to sell part of their crops to pay taxes and debts incurred during the July Monarchy (debts in order to modernise the farm in the years of prosperity, then debts to buy corn in 1846–1847). Many peasants became insolvent debtors and lost their farms, which were expropriated by the creditor. The parliamentary inquiry emphasized these difficulties, as for example in the canton of Tulle, in the western part of Massif Central : 'The mortgage debt on real estate property is immense'[13] as shown in the following figures.

Table 11.3 The mortgage debt in Tulle, 1824–1847

	1824	1836	1846	1847 first semester
Registrations	4,988 F	*NA*	9,755 F	4,917 F
Expropriations	*NA*	68	242	119

Those sales led to depreciation of the price of land, whereas it had increased in the years 1840–1846. The second consequence of the loss of benefits was a real slowdown in the progress and mechanisation in methods: neither fodder crops nor machinery (particularly winnowing machines) expanded. The second phase of the crisis (February 1848 – December 1851) during the Second Republic, can mainly be attributed to a loss of confidence in the political and economic environment. The economy stagnated until 1851 and Bonaparte's coup d'état, which suppressed political uncertainties and restored investors confidence. Shortly after the coup d'état, the Stock Exchange recovered. Thanks to several government measures in favour of capitalist initiative, many creations (banks, railways, public works) occurred in the first months of 1852, so producing a period of expansion.

The crisis of 1848–1851 appears as a crisis due to the adaptation of the economy. It was a turning point toward a kind of economic democratisation: democratisation of the government stock (la rente) and of the railways bonds. It was a turning point also in the period of the Second Republic when it began to think about the reconstruction of the liberal society. This was a turning point, at last, because it revealed the excess population of many regions.

---

[13] A.N., C949, canton de Tulle, Corrèze.

III. Demographic effects

III.1. Natality and mortality

The demographic evolution in the years 1830–1870 is presented by Chevet and O'Grada in this volume. It can be seen in their figures that 1846–1851 was a period of crisis, but not really more pronounced than others, and less than in periods of war (the Napoleonic wars in 1813, Crimean war in 1855 including deaths from cholera, and the French-Prussian war in 1870–1871). In 1846–1847, families adapted their behaviour: marriage and birth-rates dropped sharply. Marriages were postponed and conceptions avoided.

Table 11.4 Demography in France, 1841–1848

	1841–45 average number	1846	1847	1848
Marriages	282,300	(average 1846–50) 277,600		
Births	970,000		907,200	938,300
Mortality	796,715	831,400	856,000	844,000

Mortality increased slightly in 1846 (23.2‰) and 1847 (23.9‰) compared to the average rate of 22.7‰ for the years 1841–45. The scarcity of food worsened the health of poor people who suffered from insufficient nourishment and from malnutrition. The mortality rate increased for young children and old people. The scarcity of food certainly played a part in the spread of disease. In Avignon, it rose to 42.6‰ because of an outbreak of meningitis. But the period of highest mortality had no bearing on the scarcity of food: 27.4 ‰ in 1849 from a cholera disease (about a hundred thousand deaths)

It is obvious that cereals and bread prices always had an effect on mortality but not a determinant effect as in Ireland. This is the conclusion of the demographic studies about the 19th century presented by Jacques Dupâquier in 1988. The calculations show a high demographic crisis index:[14] 'Nearly all the mortalities [during the 19th century] came from diseases: scarcity, and particularly that in 1846–1847, could contribute to their aggravation, but no correlation can be established between the number of deaths and the price of cereals' (Dupâquier, 1995: 293).

III.2. Factors of mortality: subsistence and unemployment

One of the issues of Juglar's study of the French population was about the consequences of food scarcity and disease (Juglar, 1852: 378–379) and he highlighted precisely the factors of mortality:

---

[14] Calculus of a crisis index: $Ix = Dx-Mx$ / ? x (Dx= number of deaths in the year x; Mx= average number of deaths in the ten previous years; ? x= standard deviation during the ten years of reference). When the index is between 1 and 2, minor crisis, magnitude 1; index between 2 and 4, average crisis, magnitude 2; index between 4 and 8, important crisis, magnitude 3; index between 8 and 16, major crisis, magnitude 4. In 1847–1849, the crisis index is 6,38, magnitude 3.

'The period 1840–45 is the first one to show a decreasing mortality rate. A series of good harvests, abundant employment fairly paid, made an easier life for the masses. As a consequence, mortality decreased and natality increased. Unfortunately, prosperity is rarely long-lasting: after prosperity follows distress. The first three years of the 1845–50 period were deplorable. As early as 1846, the industrial crisis influenced the number of deaths that climbed to 831,400, i.e. 34,700 more than in the previous period. The effect of the food scarcity of 1847 was severely felt: 60,000 deaths in addition to the average level of mortality. In the years 1846 and 1848, the impact of mortality was less considerable. In fact, shortage of food during 1847 increased the number of deaths only by 30,000, whereas difficulties in both industry and commerce had increased deaths yet further by 34,000 in 1846. The high price of food worsened the existing crisis with its low wages and unemployment of workers. The urban or rural day labourer could usually feel the effects of starvation either from the drop in wages and no increase in the cereal price, or from an increase in the price of bread with no increase in wages. In the year 1848, the worker suffered starvation because of shortage of wages, when wheat price was normal; in 1846 and 1847, in addition to an already too slender income, the scarcity of food raised the level of distress to the highest pitch'

The main long-lasting demographic consequences of the crisis may have been the migrations from the countryside. As households were not able to afford sufficient food, some members had to go to the towns in search of work. 'Some joined the large number of beggars on the roads: in the Loiret, gendarmes were arresting 150–200 beggars monthly for the first half of 1847.' (McPhee, 1992: 62). In many regions, 1846 marked the time when the rural population reached its peak and declined afterwards.

IV. Government policy and social strategies

The economic difficulties naturally brought about social strain. Violent collective demonstrations occurred. To what extent should rural protest be seen as a traditional response to scarcity in a pre-industrial society, or as a more modern protest against the political economy, or even as a sign of mistrust of the July Monarchy? The small number of electors qualified by their tax assessment became controversial, particularly since a large number of people voted in rural council elections. The two moments of the crisis can be distinguished because of the different nature of the rural crisis, and because of the political change.

IV.1. 1846–1847, the liberal state versus popular demand for regulation

Even when facing a shortage of cereals, the liberal state considered that the market should be left free to find its own balance. The prominent economist Michel Chevalier (1847) championed a reform of the grain trade, for free trade. The State intervened only by manipulating customs tariffs in order to encourage imports and discourage exports, and to reduce transport charges for the movement of cereals (December 1846 and January 1847). It was also decided to buy large quantities of Russian wheat.

In contrast, the population at large wanted the grains to remain in the department and their price to be regulated. This disagreement was the cause of many riots. The violence rose to greater levels when grains were missing, or when a grain convoy was sent away.

Table 11.5   Cereals import in France, 1845–1850 (million Francs)

1845	1846	1847	1848	1849	1850	1851	1852
16	123	210	28	0.1	–	1.5	4.6

Some riots were turned against the notables of the area and houses and corn lofts were looted. The authorities exerted severe repression, and social fear spread widely. Among the notables, very few thought like George Sand that those poor people might have extenuating circumstances:

'All that is said should not be accepted as true (…) They are hungry people furious with the avaricious and the speculators. They show a rare discernment in their acts of revenge which, while having been very illegal, were nonetheless just' (Sand, 1964, vol. VII: 608).

A map was drawn by Rémi Gossez of the areas of unrest in 1846–47, based on the gendarmes' reports. The distribution of riots is not easy to interpret, as they are not a simple reflection of the severity of the crisis. Unrest was concentrated in the western part of the country, in the bocage areas. Historians used to see the reason for this in the fact that the dispersed inhabitants were unable to feel or exert internal community pressures. But if we compare to map 4, we can see that many riots occurred on the border of Brittany and Poitou, important areas for the production of cereals. Fearing shortage for themselves, people stopped grain convoys leaving the west for Paris. In the South, the lack of protest was due to the reasonable abundance of grains. In the North-East where the shortage was severe, there were troops in garrison and artillery units accompanied the grain convoys.

In order to reassure the population, many local councils felt compelled to take direct action. Frequently, the municipality decided to purchase cereals and to sell them locally without profit, or even at a loss. Sometimes, the council could fund such sales; in other cases, it needed to ask for the agreement of local notables and merchants on means of financing. The notables could alone also decide to fund the grain distribution: for example, Schneider in Le Creusot bought grains in Marseille and portioned out a daily 3000 kg of flour for the workers, who should reimburse from their salaries (Lévêque, 1983: 941 and Price, 1983a: 441). In extreme cases, some local councils passed a decree – annulled by the prefect but approved by the inhabitants – forbidding the exportation of grains out of the parish.

During the crisis, it became obvious that 'the established forms of relief and charity were simply inadequate'. The most common mechanism of providing poor relief in such circumstances was the bureau de bienfaisance, organised or at least recognised by the local administration and receiving limited state aid, but primarily financed and controlled by local notables (Price, 1983a: 429). The density of the network of bureaux de bienfaisance varied greatly and most of them were very poorly funded. In 1846 some municipalities levied a form of poor tax. Nevertheless, expenditure of bureaux de bienfaisance increased: from an annual average of about 10 to 11 millions francs between 1838 and 1843, it rose to 13 millions in 1845, 14 in 1846, 20,5 in 1847 and remained between 14 and 15 for 1848–52. 'The information on average value of help provided makes it clear that this offered an inadequate level of compensation for loss of earnings and the higher cost of living at the best times, but especially in a period of poor harvests and high bread prices as in 1846–47. Moreover, the large number of desperately poor

Figure 11.6 Map of the unrest due to high prices of grain, 1846–1847

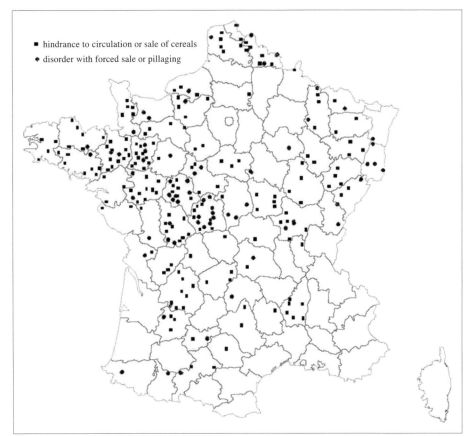

Source: Rémi Gossez, 1956.

people was simply not recognized as being in need of public assistance.' (Price, 1983a: 431–432). If 1 per 38,3 inhabitants (national average) were helped in 1846, the distribution of the bureaux was yet very unequal, with a contrast between towns and the poorest countryside. Municipalities, following the orders of government in November 1846, often established 'charity workshops' for public works, where the unemployed were given low-paid manual labour.

IV.2.   The Second Republic and the reconstruction of the society

In February 1848, workers and peasants' fury exploded. The belief in Fraternity leading to progress for everyone according to socialist ideology (the so called 'lyric illusion' of February and March 1848) did not overcome everywhere. 'This gives evidence of the misery and the bitterness towards economic transformation of the last decade, in town as well as in the countryside' (Vigier, 1967: 16). In the year 1847, the unrest of unemployed workers had increased: there were many cases of luddisme, machine breaking, in Reims, Armentières, etc. Soon after the Revolution a new outburst of dissension occurred: urban workers clashed with their employers, demanding better wages, breaking machines in Rouen. In forest areas, especially in the mountains, the violence was directed at the persons and institutions identified as threatening survival such as the Forest Administration, Eaux et Forêts (Figure 11.7). Peasants who wanted to control the use of forests took advantage of the revolution and the change in administrative personnel to send their animals graze in the woods ruled by the Forest authorities. Forest-rangers were molested and forced to flee. Social unrest, due entirely to the misery of poverty, was now clearly a claim of poor against rich, of the 'Small' against the 'Big' (les Petits contre les Gros) and a claim of the people against a mighty state.

Figure 11.7   Riots in the forests

Source: Vivier, 1992.

These upheavals occurred at a time when the new government of the Second Republic decided upon certain social measures. As early as February, 25th 1848 the right to work and the necessity to organize work were proclaimed.

The Provisional Government binds himself to insure the worker's subsistence by his work. It binds itself to insure work to every citizen. It acknowledges that workers must enter in partnership together in order to enjoy the rightful benefit of their work. (Décret du 25 février 1848)

The government tried to reorganize the labour market. The length of the work-day was limited to 10 hours in Paris, 11 in the provinces.[15] The Ateliers Nationaux were created: those workshops, very similar to the charity workshops, gave 2 francs a day to the unemployed workers.

For the first time there were edited laws about unemployment and the social regulation of work. During the years 1848–1851, parliament and government thought about the reconstruction of the liberal society, but they mainly thought of urban society and nearly never of the countryside where the large majority of the population lived. No institutional poor relief was created and only private charity could offer help. It can just be noted that urban hospitals were now obliged to receive people from rural areas (Law of 7 August 1851). The Republic gave nothing to the poor, and rural depopulation was the only solution that helped to lessen the social tensions and unrest in the following years.

V. Conclusion: statements about the 1845–47 crisis in France

French research on this issue was mainly influenced by the analyses of Marx who saw the origin of the revolution in the subsistence crisis of 1845–1846, and the crisis becoming less acute in the end of 1848 and ending in 1850 thanks to the inflow of gold from California (Marx, Die Klassenkämpfe in Frankreich, 1848 bis 1850). Such was the thesis of the historians' works around 1940s (Dautry, 1948). Since 1950, all the works have emphasised the long-lasting depression until the end of 1851. Debates continue about the importance and the meaning of this crisis. In 1976, Ernest Labrousse wrote a synthesis from the studies made on the price and the production movement, where he described a growth boost during the 1833–1865/74 period, interrupted by the 1846–1851 crisis.

The great crisis of 1847, announced by a few signs in the preceding year, considerably amplified by the political events of 1848 and by the social fear, (at the same time effect and cause), repeats in a worsened version the 1830s crisis and breaks the growth boost. A depression is outlined in the overall economic situation during the 1846–51 years. (Braudel & Labrousse, 1976: 983)

1846–1852 has been considered as a single economic period and is considered of major importance in French history. The crisis of 1846 was said to be the main cause of the revolution. Nevertheless, some historians qualified their opinion about the significance of the crisis. We can think of the statement of Philippe Vigier:

Without any doubt, the years 1846 and 1847 were very difficult for most people who earned their revenue from land (...) and yet, those agricultural difficulties did not give birth to a

---

[15] This measure will be abolished in 1849

revolutionary situation. (…) The agricultural crisis of 1846–47 appears more as the result of a previous evolution than as a rupture. It did not create new problems, it only made ancient problems more acute. (Vigier, 1963: 81–82)

From the 1980s, new research has often diminished the importance of the crisis. Lévy-Leboyer and Bourguignon, from their calculus, stated it was only a pause in the trend of growth (Lévy-Leboyer, 1985). Rowley goes even further when he argues that the 1846 crisis was overestimated: the textile crisis due to under-consumption of peasants was not so severe because, according to him, commercial banks could limit price increase. Neither the conditions nor the mechanisms of an ancien regime crisis existed and that is shown by the sudden outcome of the crisis between May and July 1847 (Rowley, 1985: 81–90).

If we now focus on the crisis of the years 1846–1847 only, in a renewed vision of our comparative study, we can put its importance in a general context. For writers of the 19th century it was considered as severe but not at all out of the ordinary. Major politicians and other actors in the 1840s, have written their memoirs: the prime minister Guizot, the leader of the dynastic opposition Odilon Barrot, the manager of the liberal newspaper *Le Constitutionnel*, Dr Louis Véron, the conservative royalists Comte de Falloux and La Bonninière, the liberal Charles de Rémusat, former Home secretary in 1840 and Alexis de Tocqueville, an historian who conferred great significance on economic factors. In those memoirs, we can find little reference to the economic difficulties: three lines in a long chapter of Odilon Barrot, none in the others, even Guizot, although a government leader, usually looks for extenuating circumstances. All of them saw the origin of the revolution in the political situation: the deeds of the opposition to Louis-Philippe and Guizot, especially from the republicans (Guizot, 1879: 740, Véron, 1854: 38) or socialists (De la Bonninière, 1857: 447); the denial by the king and Guizot of any reform (Barrot, 1875: 446–460; De Falloux, 1925: 239–240; De Tocqueville, 1893 : 83–86). Charles de Rémusat (1962: 93) stressed the important role of the movement of ideas in Europe:

'High prices of grains, nearly a dearth awkwardly denied by the Ministry of Trade, in addition to fire and flood, spread suffering and served malevolence: a financial crisis was to follow. But more over and above all, incidents happened across Europe that could have, and were to have heavy consequences, although hardly noticed by even the most careful observers.'

According to him, these incidents were, in 1846, the revolution and end of the Republic of Cracow, the election of Pius IX, a liberal at the time, and the economic reform of free-trade in England.

The economist Clément Juglar (1862: 25), comparing the crisis in England and in France, noticed large similarities. In both countries, the bad harvest emptied the banks' coffers. While the purchase of cereals required payment in cash, the needs of trade increased the amount of discount bills. This comparative analysis highlights two features: the addition of both effects led to a commercial crisis, but it did not determine the triggering of a revolution. Then, historians at the end of the 19th century and the beginning of the 20th century, pointed out the bad harvest but conferred it only a minor role in the break out of the revolution.[16]

---

[16] Among them Thureau-Dangin (1885) and Lavisse (1921).

The 1846–1847 crisis appears to have been overestimated. The subsistence crisis was severe but by no means exceptional, although it coincided with an industrial crisis and it worsened into a commercial crisis that triggered financing difficulties. It could not quite be counterbalanced with wheat imports as the means of transportation were insufficient. Later improvements in the banking and transportation systems would help compensate for the subsequent bad crops, such as those in 1855. No comparison is possible with Ireland. Unlike the Illustrated London News (Peter Gray, this volume), French journalists of this time who wrote during the winter 1846/47 the 'chronicle' in *La Revue des Deux Mondes* about the Irish famine could not find any common features. Nonetheless, the crisis, particularly emphasized by historians, became a memorable one, because of the ideological exhilaration of the times.

Bibliography

Agulhon, M. (1970) *La République au village. Les populations du Var de la Révolution à la Seconde République,* Paris.

Armengaud, A. (1961) *Les populations de l'Est aquitain au début de l'époque contemporaine* (vers 1845–1871), Paris.

Barrot, O. (1875) *Mémoires posthumes*, Vol. 1, 3ème ed., Paris.

Bourke, P.M. (1984) 'Emergence of 'potato blight', *Nature*, 203, pp. 805–808.

Braudel F. and Labrousse, E. (1976) *Histoire économique et sociale de la France*, Vol. 3, 1789–années 1880, Paris.

Bulletin des séances de la société royale d'agriculture (1846/7), 2.

Charon-Bordas, J. (1994) *Ouvriers et paysans au milieu du XIXe siècle. L'enquête de 1848 sur le travail,* Paris.

Chevalier, M. (1847) 'Des forces alimentaires des Etats et de la crise actuelle', *Revue des deux Mondes,* 17, pp. 397–429.

Clout, H. (1977) *Agriculture in France on the Eve of the Railway Age*, London.

Corbin, A. (1875) *Archaïsme et modernité en Limousin au XIXe siècle, 1845–1880*, Paris.

Dautry, J. (1948) *Histoire de la révolution de 1848 en France*, Paris, 1948.

Decaisne, J. (1846*) Histoire de la maladie des pommes de terre en 1845*, Paris.

De Falloux (1925) *Mémoires d'un royaliste*, Vol. 1, Paris.

De la Bonninière, E. (1857) *Histoire de mon temps*, Vol. 3, Paris

De Lavergne, L. (1857) *L'agriculture et la population*, Paris.

Démier, F. (1997) "Comment naissent les révolutions', cinquante ans après', in *Revue d'histoire du XIXe siècle*, 14, pp. 31–49.

Démier, F. (2000) *La France du XIXe siècle*, Paris.

De Rémusat, Ch. (1962) *Mémoires de ma vie, 1841–1851*, Paris, 1962.

Désert, G. (1955) 'La culture de la pomme de terre dans le Calvados au XIXe siècle', *Annales de Normandie*, vol. 5, pp. 216–270.

Désert G. (1975) *Une société rurale au XIXe siècle, les paysans du Calvados, 1815–1895*, Lille.

De Tocqueville, A. (1999) *Souvenirs*, written in 1850, first published in 1893, Paris.

Dowe, D., Haupt, H-G. and Langewiesche, D. (1998) *Europa 1848. Revolution and Reform*, Bonn.

Dupâquier, J. (1995) *Histoire de la population française*, tome 3, 1789–1914, P.U.F., 1988, éditions Quadrige, Paris.

Dupeux, G. (1962) *Aspects de l'histoire sociale et politique du Loir-et-Cher*, Paris.

Frost, M.J. (2004) 'Price responsive during scarcity in Bombay in 1824', Paper given at the Social Science History Association Meeting, Chicago.

Gossez, R. (1956) 'A propos de la carte des troubles de 1846–47', in E. Labrousse, *Aspects de la crise*, La Roche-sur-Yon, p. 47.

Guizot, F. (1879) *Mémoires pour servir à l'histoire de mon temps*, Vol. 8, Paris.

Heyberger, L. (2003) *Santé et développement économique en France au 19e siècle. Essai d'histoire anthropométrique*, Paris.

Juglar, C. (1852) De la population de la France de 1772 à nos jours', *Journal des économistes*, 128, 15 dec. 1851, pp. 367–380 and 129, pp. 75–80.

Juglar, C. (1862) *Des crises commerciales et de leur retour périodique*, Paris.

Labrousse, E. (1956) *Aspects de la crise et de la dépression de l'économie française au milieu du XIXe siècle, 1846–51.* Bibliothèque de la révolution de 1848, tome XIX, La Roche-sur-Yon. Includes studies by Agulhon, Bois, Chanut and alii, Désert, Deyon, Dreyfus, Dupeux, Gonnet, Gossez, Guiral, Perrot, Tudesq, Vidalenc.

Lavisse, E. (ed.) (1921) *Histoire de la France contemporaine*, Vol. 5, *La monarchie de Juillet* by Sébastien Charléty, Paris.

Le Roy Ladurie, E. (1973) 'Exploitation quantitative et cartographique des archives militaires françaises (1819–1826)', in *Le territoire de l'historien*, Paris, pp. 38–87.

Lévêque, P. (1983) *Une société provinciale, la Bourgogne sous la Monarchie de Juillet*, Paris.

Lévy-Leboyer, M. and Bourguigon, F. (1985) *L'économie française au XIXe siècle*. Analyse macro-économique, Paris.

McPhee, P. (1992) *The Politics of rural Life. Political Mobilization in the French Country-side*, 1846–1852, Oxford.

Meerten, M. van (1990) 'Développement économique et stature en France, XIXe–XXe siècles', *Annales E.S.C.*, 45, 755–777.

Price, R. (1975) *Revolution and reaction. 1848 and the Second French Republic*, Londres-New York. Includes the contributions of B. Moss, C. Johnson, P. Amann, P. O'Brien, Ch. Tilly, L. Lees, J. Merriman, R. Bezucha, T. Margadant, H. Machin, V. Wright.

Price, R. (1983a) 'Poor Relief and Social Crises in Mid-Nineteenth-century France', *European Studies Review,* 13, pp. 423–454.

Price, R. (1983b) *The modernization of Rural France*, London.

Rouselle, R. and Crosnier (eds) (1996) *La pomme de terre*, Paris.

Rowley, A. (1986) 'Deux crises économiques modernes: 1846 et 1848?' in *1848, révolutions et mutations au XIXe siècle,* 2, pp. 81–90.

Sahlins, P. (1994) *Forests rites*, Harvard.

Sand, G. (1964) *Correspondance*, Paris.

Soulet, J-F. (1987) *Les Pyrénées au XIXe siècle*, Toulouse, pp. 149–171.

Suchet, J.-M. (1870) *La pomme de terre en Franche-Comté*, Besançon.

Thureau-Dangin, P. (1885) *Histoire de la Monarchie de Juillet*, Paris.

Toutain, J. (1948) *La révolution de 1848 à Rouen*, Paris.

Verley, P. (1992) *L'industrialisation, 1830–1914, Nouvelle histoire économique de la France contemporaine,* Paris.

Véron, L. (1854) *Mémoires d'un bourgeois de Paris*, Vol. 4, Paris.

Vigier, P. (1963) *La Seconde République dans la région alpine. Etude politique et sociale*, Paris.

Vigier, P. (1996) *La Seconde République dans la région alpine. Etude politique et sociale,* 7th ed., Paris.

Vivier, N. (1992) *Le Briançonnais rural*, Paris.

12 Crisis: what crisis? Prices and mortality in mid-nineteenth century France

Jean-Michel Chevet, Institut National de la Recherche Agronomique-CORELA, Ivry-sur-Seine
Cormac Ó Gráda, University College Dublin

François-Marie Arouet (a.k.a. Voltaire) once quipped that if God did not exist, mankind would find the need to invent Him. The situation of French historiography and economic crisis in the mid-1840s is somewhat analagous. And for two reasons. First, a long tradition in French economic demography and historiography that can be traced back to Louis Messance and Jean-Baptiste de la Mithodière in the 1760s, and from them on to Jean Meuvret, Pierre Goubert, and other giants of the post-1945 French historical school, argues that high grain prices entail excess mortality: *la mercuriale secrète la mortalité*.[1] And the price of wheat in France did indeed rise considerably in 1846. Second, France and much of Europe experienced civil unrest and revolution in 1848.[2] An economic deterministic view of revolution, long popular in France, requires an economic crisis as the proximate cause of the construction of the barricades: in Alfred de Vigny's rendition, *c'est à la boulangerie que commencent les révolutions*. So what kind of crisis did France face in 1846–1847?

Our focus in this study is on the agricultural sector only. Historians agree that in the first half of the nineteenth century France escaped the terrible subsistence crises which, during the *ancien régime*, made life a precarious business for a considerable number of the very poor. In that earlier era, even though epidemics were also a threat, it is subsistence crises which were invoked as demographic regulators. Gradually, for a variety of reasons, these famines attenuated, though they could still cause mortality peaks. It was during the first half of the nineteenth century that the last of these crises occurred. In this view, the crisis of 1846 marked the final apparition of mortality of this kind.

But what is a crisis? In the absence of the kind of demographic data that become available only during the nineteenth century, historians have measured the effects of malnutrition or famine with the aid of a single measure, price: and perhaps they have relied too much on this measure. For price to offer a good picture of a crisis, there must be a strong correlation between harvests and prices on the one hand, and between harvests and mortality crises on the other. This approach has given rise to a long but productive controversy in French historiography.

In a brilliant exercise in political arithmetic published in 1766, Louis Messance was the first to posit a statistical association between wheat prices and mortality (Messance, 1766: 291–292, 309–330).[3] Messance's findings were recycled in the following century by others who posited a more systematic correlation between the two time series than

---

[1] The quote is due to G. Livet. It is cited in Cabourdin, 1988, who offers an excellent survey of the literature.
[2] For a panoramic overview of the revolutions of the 1840s see Dowe [et al.], 2001.
[3] Or, as seems more likely, his patron Jean-Baptiste François de la Michodière. See Chevet and Ó Gráda, forthcoming.

he did. It is this tradition that has influenced historical demographers and, particularly, Jean Meuvret, whose name is so closely linked to subsistence crises (Meuvret, 1946), and it is within this framework that 'modernist' French historians worked at first. Pierre Goubert, according to whom, 'the economic crisis of the traditional type gave rise to a demographic crisis of the traditional type', was followed by the likes of pioneering historical demographers Louis Henry and Étienne Gautier.

A reaction was inevitable. It began with René Baehrel who pointed out in his study of the rural economy of Basse-Provence that high prices and high mortality might well coincide, but that both could be driven or influenced by a third factor, the weather. A period of bad weather responsible for a particularly bad harvest was also bound to drive up mortality. Pierre Chaunu went further, denying any causation between high prices and high mortality, and emphasising the dominant role of disease rather than hunger *tout court*. For Chaunu there was a psychological explanation for this link between prices and deaths: 'the souvenir of ration cards obsessed Jean Meuvret, who was afraid of going hungry'.[4] Now, Jean Meuvret did not believe that all the excess mortality he encountered was the product of subsistence crises. After all, he warned us that 'a poor harvest entails a rise in burials, but the excess deaths could be due to either hunger or epidemic diseases'. The ensuing debate ignored this point and, certainly, the anti-Meuvret critique errs in seeking to minimize the role of poor harvests on mortality. Nonetheless, other factors, notably cholera (in the nineteenth century), plague, and dysentery have produced demographic crises that were not linked to harvest shortfalls (Chevet, 1993: 133). And panics and rumours impacted on markets, exacerbating the effect of a poor harvest, then one may easily imagine price increases that did not always lead to a rise in deaths.

Yet it was still possible to imagine that populations were still vulnerable to subsistence crises in the early nineteenth century. Thus in their classic on world population history Marcel Reinhard and André Armengaud claimed that 'economic crises are above all subsistence crises', and that early nineteenth-century France 'remains very close in the demographic sense to where it was in the second half of the eighteenth century' (Reinhard and Armengaud, 1961: 242). Labrousse's view of the first half of the nineteenth century was identical (Labrousse, 1976: 994).

However, André Armengaud (1976: 202, 244) introduced a discordant note in this concert in claiming that the era of the classic subsistence crisis had ended in France in the early eighteenth century, and that subsequent crises amounted to scarcities or dearths rather than true famines. That was not to deny that in times of scarcity malnutrition could not provoke a rise in the death rates of the young, the sick, and the elderly. With the impact of food deficits thus lessened, the primary role was left to epidemics, so much so that according to G. Caudelier, in the early nineteenth century 'the price of grain no longer had a decisive influence on mortality': the mercuriale was no longer the key to mortality.

For others, in the typology given to crises in the 1800–1870 period, that of 1847–1849 is deemed 'very serious' and should be placed in the context of 'the poor harvest of 1846, the economic crisis of 1847–1848, and above all the new cholera epidemic'. But here too cholera seems to dominate: according to historical demographer Alain Bideau (1988: 293), 'it will be noted that nearly all the mortality had an epidemic origin: subsistence crises – in particular that of 1846–1849 – might be an aggravating factor'.

---

[4] See Cabourdin, 1988: 178–180; Chaunu, 1991.

Against the background of the state-of-play just outlined, we propose to re-evaluate the nature of demographic crises in the first half of the nineteenth century: distinguishing those which are of purely epidemic origin and those, if they exist, which deserve to be called subsistence crises. For the reasons just cited, we will focus in particular on the crisis of 1847, which historians deem to be the only one to qualify under this rubric. That will lead us to an analysis of the impact of variations in the food supply on the price of wheat in this period.

We first analyse demographic variables – mortality, natality, nuptiality, population – with a view to identifying crises and their intensity in the 1820–1870 period (section 1). We then confront the crises that stand out with price and production data. We also take account of imports as a regulator of crisis. In section 2 each element in the analysis is refocused at the level of the region or *département*. This allows us to evaluate the role that substitutes for wheat production might play.[5] Section 3 concludes.

I.   Crises at the national level

I.1.   Timing and extent in the first half of the nineteenth century

Deaths, like population, rose between the 1800s and the 1860s (Figure 12.1). The trend, however, was subject to swings and to a number of peaks representing various crises. In order to measure the amplitude of the most important crises, we have also traced a nine-year moving average in Figure 12.1. Our yardstick for measuring crises – a deviation of ten per cent or more from the average – is not very stringent, and deliberately so. Compare Goubert, according to whom one can 'speak of a demographic crisis from the moment that the annual number of deaths doubles and when, at the same time, the number of conceptions falls in an indisputable manner, by at least one-third'. By our proposed measure, apart from the 1820s, the calender years that stand out are 1832, 1834, 1849, 1854, 1859. The 'demographic crisis' of 1847, with a deviation of only four per cent, is not on the list. Indeed it is placed only eighth, behind two peaks of five per cent in 1826 and 1837. If we focus on the post-imperial era, as Armengaud did, it is clear that the cholera epidemics of 1832, 1834, 1849, and 1854, were far more murderous than the crisis of 1847 because in those years excess mortality levels of twelve, ten, eighteen, and seventeen per cent were registered. And, of course, the toll in 1847 pales by comparison with those associated with mortality peaks in the eighteenth century (Armengaud, 1976; also Bourdelais and Raulot, 1987).[6] In effect, quite apart from the famine of 1693 and 1694 when mortality rose by 34 and 60 per cent respectively, or that of 1709 and 1710 when the rises were 22 and 29.5 per cent, there were mortality surges of over one-fifth in 1719, 1747, and 1779 (Chevet, 1993: 130; Lachiver, 1991). Applying the measure of moving averages to the same data, crises become more numerous. Seven out of fifty-one years experience deviations of more than ten per cent

---

[5] The results described here are set out in greater detail in Chevet and Ó Gráda, 2004.

[6] One might object that working with harvest years minimises the gravity of the crisis of 1847. That might be the case if one found a rise in deaths in 1846. That not being the case, taking account of the last six months of 1846 cannot augment the crisis of 1847.

in deaths, and eleven exceed five per cent. Not all of these crises were subsistence crises, of course, but the point is that when they were, their size dwarfed that of 1847. It would seem that over the long century between 1740 and 1850, there was a change, and scarcities became considerably milder or, indeed, disappeared.

As in the case of deaths, a tendency for the number of births to rise over time is apparent from Figure 12.1. However, the kind of 'cycle' that one sees here is much less marked and longer than those visible for deaths. One also detects in the curve a certain number of falls in births which at first sight are linked to crises. The most severe of these, amounting to just under six per cent, was in 1847, which offers support to partisans of a subsistence crisis. The other deficits are much less serious. We note those of 1831 (–4 per cent) and 1855 (–5 per cent); the rest are lower. Moreover, none of the declines in the number of births coincides with a significant rise in the number of deaths.[7]

Figure 12.1   The movement in the number of births and deaths, 1800–1870

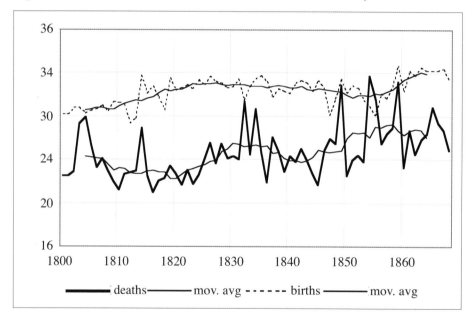

In times of crisis, the drop in the birth rate has a two-fold explanation. The first, mechanical, explanation is due to the deaths of mothers-to-be. If there are such deaths, the deficit in births occurs in the same year as the rise in deaths. Alternatively, as Emmanuel Le Roy Ladurie (1973) and others have argued, privation can induce famine amenhoerrea. In that case, the decline in births would occur with a lag after the rise in deaths. The disappearance of a husband or a wife could produce a similar outcome. The available annual data make it difficult to decide between these hypotheses. Note, however,

---

[7] Note that while it makes sense to think of harvest-induced crises in terms of harvest years, demographic data invariably (as here) refer to calender years.

that the demographic crisis supposedly following the poor harvest of 1846, was not followed in 1848 by a significant decline in births. The same holds for the other crises occurring in this period.

On the basis of the evidence so far we would argue that nineteenth-century crises were too far removed from the conditions defined by Goubert and Meuvret to qualify as subsistence crises. To this extent we agree with those historians who claim that the vigour of crises had lessened relative to the early eighteenth century. We would go a little further, however, and argue that in the nineteenth century crises did not resemble those of the later eighteenth century either, to the extent that they had attenuated so much that they had disappeared. This is what we are about to show.

A look at the annual variation in the number of marriages yields little of interest in this context. It rose modestly from 1825 on, tapering off in the mid-1840s and accelerating slightly in the mid-1850s. There were few significant breaks. The most important, a decline of 11 per cent, was in 1847. However, this may have had more to do with the industrial crisis of 1847 than with subsistence problems. Moreover, there was no correlation across *départements* between the changes in the marriage and mortality rates. The other declines, of less than seven per cent in 1832 and less than six per cent in 1854, were associated with cholera epidemics. Moreover, a look at French population trends during the nineteenth century suggests that it grew at a more or less regular pace (Chevet and Ó Gráda, 2004). The crisis of 1847 produced only a deceleration in population growth: hardly a surprise since there was no excess of deaths over births in that year. On the other hand, the impact of the cholera epidemic of 1849–1850, when deaths exceeded births, is more visible. The population curve, which refers to a constant geographic territory, shows that the effects of the war of 1870 were much more important; only on this occasion does one witness a break in the trend.

A comparison of this curve with that of the reconstituted population of eighteenth-century France reveals essential differences, the most important being that the latter contains several breaks, the most important being those associated with famines in 1693–1694 and 1709–1710. Later crises, though less intense, are nevertheless visible. Thus there were breaks in 1719, 1740, 1747, and 1779. Here again, it seems to us that the first half of the nineteenth century differs from the second half of the eighteenth.

I.2. Demographic crises, prices, and harvests

For the most part, historians of the *ancien régime* must do without harvest yield data; they rely on price movements as reflections of movements in output, a big rise in prices being taken to correspond to a a more or less proportionate deficit in output. Though harvest data are more plentiful for the nineteenth century, it is with prices that we first confront the crises identified above. We will pay particular attention to the price of wheat. We focus on wheat because cereals – wheat, meslin, rye – account for the bulk of production in this era. In the north of France, their cultivation represented nearly ninty-five per cent of the land surface devoted to human food, with wheat accounting for two-thirds of this.[8] In other regions, apart from the Southwest where they accounted for only

---

[8] Our calculation does not take account of oats and barley because they were produced almost exclusively for livestock consumption.

seventy per cent, cereals covered seventy-five to ninety per cent of land producing human food, with wheat's share being between sixty and seventy per cent. By contrast, the share of these cereals reached only two-fifths in the Centre and half in the South (see Figure 12.2).[9] If instead of analysing the area under cereal cultivation, one turns to their share in consumption, the landscape is modified due to high potato yields. In the North the share of cereal is reduced to about seventy-one per cent, and in the Southwest to 60.6 per cent. Three other regions, West, Centre, and South, with a consumption between fifty and sixty per cent, are next, and the remaining four (Northwest, Northeast, East and Southeast) with between forty and fifty per cent. In France as a whole, cereals and maize represent about fifty-five per cent of human consumption. And, since as elsewhere these crops are the main source of urban food, one can see how it makes sense to focus on grain as an indicator of price movements. Note that, as in the case of the demographic variables, we have calculated moving averages of nine years from an annual price series based on the harvest year.[10]

Figure 12.2 France's agricultural regions

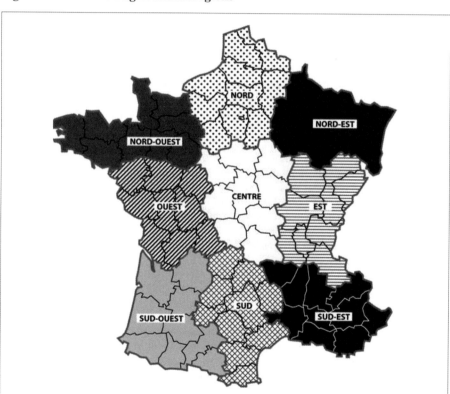

---

[9] Our thanks to Catherine Lefebvre for her skilful cartographic contributions.
[10] The prices used are those published in Labrousse, 1970.

Between 1820 and 1865, nine price rises of over ten per cent emerge. Among these that of almost fifty per cent in 1846 certainly stands out – see Table 12.1. Yet if this rise is compared to those in the years of famine towards the end of Louis XIV's reign, it is seen to be very modest. During 1693 and 1694 the price of wheat, relative to 1688–1691, rose by 147 and 228 per cent, respectively. In the wake of the '*grand hiver de 1709*' there was a rise of 285 per cent (Baulant, 1968: 539–540). These increases are out of all proportion to anything witnessed in the nineteenth century. Believers in a certain proportionality between harvest deficits and price rises must therefore concede that the crisis that followed the harvest of 1846 was on a very minor scale compared to those earlier famines.

Table 12.1 suggests that only one of the nine price rises, that of 1854, coincided with an increase in the number of deaths. Note that 1846 does not feature in the table because it produced only a very minor rise in deaths. The increase in the number of deaths of five per cent in that year does is in sharp contrast to the fifty per cent rise in the price of wheat.

Table 12.1 Years of demographic crisis, subsistence crises and high prices, 1820–1865

Year	Production deficit	Price increase	Increase in deaths
1820	12.5	Nil	Nil
1828	Nil	11.2	Nil
1830	15.5	Nil	Nil
1831	10.4	13.5	Nil
1832	Nil	Nil	12
1834	Nil	Nil	10
1839	Nil	16	Nil
1846	25.1	49.9	Nil
1849	Nil	Nil	18
1853	22.4	22.8	Nil
1854	Nil	11.7	17
1855	17	27.5	Nil
1856	Nil	21.2	Nil
1859	Nil	Nil	13
1861	23.2	25.3	Nil
1863	16.3	Nil	Nil
1864	16	Nil	Nil

We have also calculated deviations from a moving average of wheat yields. The average is an approximation, since substitutions between different food crops are likely to have taken place.[11] This produces deficits of over ten per cent in the 1820–1864 period. In six, the deficit was in the 10–20 per cent range. In the case of three harvests (those of 1853, 1861, and 1846), it exceeded twenty per cent, the deficit of one-quarter in 1846 being the biggest. Comparing these results with those concerning mortality

---

[11] The data on yields, area under cultivation, and production used in this paper come from Ministère de l'agriculture et du commerce, 1878.

opens up an important result: none of the deficits encountered in yields corresponds with an increase in the number of deaths. The crises occurring between 1820 and 1865 were therefore not subsistence crises. Setting aside those of 1832, 1849 and 1854, which were due to cholera, they must be due to epidemics that yet remain to be identified. The lack of a harvest deficit effect may arise from their mild character but, as we shall see later, it could also be due to compensating changes in other crops.[12]

Table 12.1 also shows that only five of the nine deficits (1830, 1846, 1853, 1855 and 1861) coincided with a rise in prices. Nor would there seem to be any proportionality between the rise in prices and the size of the harvest shortfalls. This suggests an initial conclusion which would seem, at least for the period considered here, to be of broader significance: price rises may be guides as indicators of deficits produced by poor harvests. This finding also suggests care insofar as the ancien regime is concerned, since some price increases could have been the products, not of poor harvests, but of political events.

I.3. Substitutes and Imports

We have seen that wheat, meslin, and rye were not the only items destined for human consumption. Depending on the region, they were supplemented by buckwheat, maize, and the potato. It is unlikely that all these crops were affected in the same way, with the result that some compensations between crops are likely to have occurred. Moreover, since these three crops were sown in April or May, or even June in the case of buckwheat, it was also possible that if the weather compromised the wheat and rye harvests, the area under these other crops was extended as a precautionary measure.

In 1846 the volume of the wheat harvest fell by 19 per cent relative to the 1842–1845 average, while those of meslin and rye fell by 25.3 and 29 per cent, respectively. The total cereal deficit came to 22 per cent, or a little less than indicated by the shortfall in yields. Against this, the buckwheat harvest rose by 29 per cent and the maize harvest by 26.5 per cent. The rise in these two items would have been sufficient to match the deficit in wheat and rye, were it not that the potato harvest was also a poor one. In aggregate the deficit in crops destined for human food was about 17.5 per cent, so that in this particular case, the wheat yield was a good indicator of the variation in output. However, the fact that the importance of buckwheat and maize across the country varied considerably suggests the need for a geographic analysis of regional disparities in harvest shortfalls. It also bears noting that in 1846 the area under buckwheat rose by 4.4 percent relative to 1842–1845, that under maize by 9.6 per cent, and that under potatoes by zero. It would seem therefore that farmers, in confronting the crisis that was unfolding, increased, where possible, the area under these crops. We need to see whether these rises occurred in those regions where the grain harvest deficits were greatest.[13]

---

[12] The years of scarcity have been identified from an annual average price series calculated from all *départements* between 1833 and 1860. Before and after these two dates, the average national price was based on only one third of the *départements*, which would seem to bias downwards a little the percentage rise in prices.

[13] In certain *départements*, barley and oats still accounted for a share, albeit small, of human diet in the mid-nineteenth century. It is quite likely that their share rose during scarcities.

Apart from these substitutes, economies at the beginning of the nineteenth century had another means of counteracting deficits: imports. Did they exploit it during the 1846 harvest year? That is what we are about to see. In 1846 France imported 4,910 thousand hl of wheat, either as grain or converted into flour. In 1847 she imported 10,100 thousand hl and in 1848, 1,250 million hl. The administrative practice of producing import statistics for the calender year force us to make a few assumptions, in order to evaluate the impact of imports on the 1846 harvest year. Since the 1845 harvest was an average one, we may assume that imports in 1846 are more likely to have been concentrated towards the end of the year, in other words, during the 1846 harvest year. As for imports in 1847, given a surplus harvest that year, the demand for foreign wheat is likely to have fallen, as was surely the case in 1848, another good year. The bulk of imports in 1847 are therefore likely to have been in response to the situation in 1846. So as not to stack the cards in favour of the case we are making, we will claim only the 10,100 thousand hl of wheat imported during 1846 for the 1846/7 harvest year. Even that reduces the wheat deficit from 14,150 thousand hl to 4,150 thousand hl, or only 5.5 per cent of wheat consumption. If these imports are included in the overall balance reached above, a deficit of 17.3 per cent is reduced to one of 13.4 per cent. This implies that there was no mortality crisis due to a lack of food in 1846. True, for imports to have had the impact described, they would have had to been present during the harvest year, and particularly during the second half of the year. As things stand, we cannot be certain about this, but the downward trend in prices from May 1847 on makes it more likely.

II.   Was the crisis of 1845/1847 a regional crisis?

Perhaps we should have ended this paper here on the basis that the mythical status of the crisis of 1846 would seem to be well established by now. We continue the analysis, however, since it is quite likely that marked regional disparities mask through cancelling out the existence of regional crises. For this reason, we move the analysis from the national to the regional and départemental level in search of possible regional crises. The strategy adopted is the same. Still, at the end of the day, the analysis of the substitute crops, buckwheat, maize, and potatoes will be more precise, since the importance of these crops varied considerably across France. To begin, we look at the extent of any mortality crises at *département* level.

II.1. Were there regional demographic crises in 1846/1847?

In seeking to identify crises, we proceed as before. The series at our disposal are long enough to generate deviations from seven-year moving averages for every département. An examination of the results reveals a certain number of *départements* with a rise in mortality in 1846; another group where the phenomenon is visible only in 1847; and a third where increases in mortality were insignificant. The outcome is summarised in Figures 12.3 and 12.4 below.

If we had information on mortality trends during the 1846/47 harvest year, the results might have been different, particularly if the mortality in *départements* that stand out in the 1846 map was restricted mainly to the second half of the calender year. To that extent, we may have underestimated the size of the 1847 crisis. However, lacking the number of deaths during the harvest year has one advantage. In effect, if we were dealing with a genuine subsistence crisis, the worst of the mortality would have been produced at the end of the harvest year, in other words in the first half of 1847 and not in the second half of 1846. That suggests two remarks. The first is that the spread of deaths argues in favour of deaths from infectious diseases than from the lack of food *tout court*.

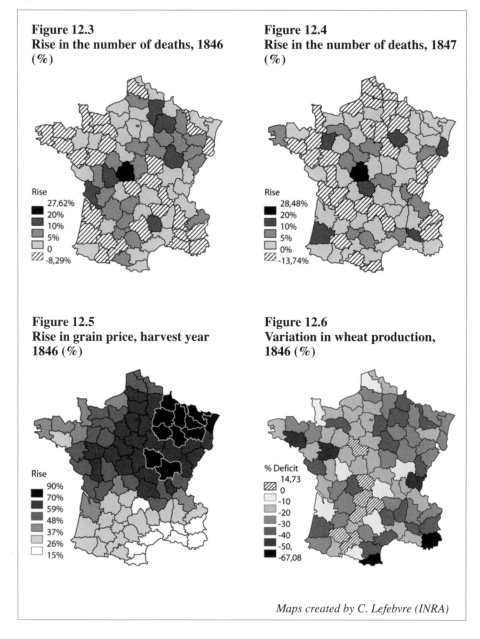

Figure 12.3
Rise in the number of deaths, 1846
(%)

Rise
27,62%
20%
10%
5%
0
-8,29%

Figure 12.4
Rise in the number of deaths, 1847
(%)

Rise
28,48%
20%
10%
5%
0%
-13,74%

Figure 12.5
Rise in grain price, harvest year
1846 (%)

Rise
90%
70%
59%
48%
37%
26%
15%

Figure 12.6
Variation in wheat production,
1846 (%)

% Deficit
14,73
0
-10
-20
-30
-40
-50,
-67,08

Maps created by C. Lefebvre (INRA)

The second is more general, and consists of a caution against reasoning based on annual data, be they harvest or calender years, without knowing their monthly breakdowns.

In 1846 twenty-eight *départements* out of eighty-six experienced an excess mortality of over ten per cent, and in ten of these it exceeded fifteen percent. The change in geographic scale thus offers another perspective on excess mortality, though this still remains very modest. The identification of the *départements* worst affected reveals an arbitrary distribution spread across France. It lacks any geographic coherence. The fifteen percent toll in Hautes-Alpes is isolated. And although Aisne and, to a lesser extent Aube, Oise and Marne, were hit, the Paris provisioning region remained untouched, an outcome far from characterising a real subsistence crisis. The Southwest was unevenly affected. Only the Centre seems to have been comprehensively hit. All in all, these excess mortalities, modest compared to those of the previous century, seem to have been of a local character. Perhaps they were epidemiological in origin, since a subsistence crisis would have affected a bigger region – one supplying the major cities, for example, or one sharing the same climatic or production mix characteristics. In addition, bearing in mind that there was no cereal deficit in that year, the case seems closed.

In 1847, forty *départements* had an excess mortality of over ten per cent (Figure 12.4), and in twenty the excess was over fifteen per cent. As in 1846, the change in geographic scale is telling. However, the increases in mortality were more or less the same in both years. This suggests some remarks. We have just seen than in 1846 some *départements* might register excess mortality above ten per cent, while at national level no crisis is visible. This finding can be extended to other years in this period, and even generalised. In 1839, for instance, a year in which mortality was a little below trend, no fewer than eleven *départements* suffered an excess mortality of ten per cent or more, and in Seine-Inférieure a level of twenty-nine per cent was reached. 1842 offers another example, when seven *départements* exceeded ten per cent. In these two years epidemics are the likely culprits for such local crises. A comparison between these two years, to which one might add 1846 and 1847, shows that a disparity in the number of *départements* touched by this excess mortality is the only difference between them, so much so that one may imagine that the excess mortality in these *départements* stems from local epidemics.

In 1847, as in 1846, the geographic spread of mortality by *département* lacks any of the spatial coherence expected from a subsistence crisis. It would be pointless to give a detailed description of this spread: enough to add that the affected *départements*, the Centre region apart, are spread throughout the whole of France. Which leads to the conclusion that in 1847 too the likely cause of the crisis was local epidemics, at best remotely linked to problems of subsistence. A comparative look at local output conditions adds further insight.

II.2. Demographic crises, price rises and harvest deficits at the regional level in 1847

If the supposed increase in deaths in 1847 resulted from insufficient food, the map that would show this ought to bear some resemblance to that of the rise in price. In order to verify this, we have calculated for harvest year 1846/47 the rise in price in each *département*, using a five-year moving average of the price of wheat. Figure 12.5 indicates the rise in prices was very significant. It was not uniform across the country, being greatest in the Northeast and least in the Southwest.

It is very difficult to establish a benchmark for a subsistence crisis, or even the existence of a crisis, on the basis of prices alone. Nevertheless, a close examination of the variations in price shows that rises of the order of twenty-five to thirty per cent were not unusual during the first half of this century, and that such rises were not associated with subsistence crises. That was even sometimes the case when the price rise was greater. We would therefore maintain, somewhat arbitrarily, it is true, that in cases where the price rise of wheat was less than fifty per cent, the existence of a crisis was dubious at the least. In this case, if wheat prices are used as a guide, the crisis held sway north of an imaginary Saint-Malo-Geneva line, though omitting Brittany and part of Normandy.

Yet comparing this map with that describing mortality, discussed above, suggests that there was no association between the two phenomena. The mortality crisis therefore would seem to bear little relation with subsistence crises or with the peaks noted in the price series. Thus if some *départements* in the Northeast and Centre affected by excess mortality experienced a significant rise in prices, others in the same zones did not. To be sure, one might claim that there was a subsistence crisis in the Northeast and the epidemics were at work where no increase in the price of wheat is observed. But this latter argument does not hold water since many *départements* saw prices rise without experiencing a mortality crisis.

Figure 12.7 shows price increases on the x-axis and changes in the death rate on the y-axis. The horizontal cloud of dots indicates that there is no relation between the two variables. For those in doubt, the correlation coefficient of 0.05 between the two confirms the conclusions drawn from comparing maps and from the graph.[14]

Figure 12.7 The influence of price change on deaths, 1846 (%)

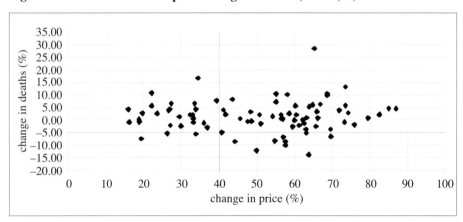

Next, we examine the relation between the rise in deaths and the variation in wheat output across *départements*, using the variation in the wheat yield as an index of output. We estimated this measure of the harvest deficit in each *département* relative to the

---

[14] Nor was there any correlation across *départements* between the marriage rate and the death rate in 1847.

average for 1843–1845. Figure 12.6 makes plain that the shortfall in grain yields was unevenly distributed across the country. There were considerable deficits in the northeast, along the Mediterranean coast and the Rhône corridor, along the Atlantic coast and in the north of Brittany. Elsewhere the declines were modest. Comparing figure 12.3 with that describing excess deaths in 1847 (Figure 12.4) suggests that both phenomena were relatively independent of each other. In the Northeast only a few *départements* with a sizeable harvest deficit show excess mortality. Nor does one find in the south a close correspondence between the two phenomena. As for the most *départements* in central France which saw increased mortality, they were not subject to food crises. In Figure 12.8 the change in wheat production in each *département* is plotted against the change in deaths. The resultant scatter of dots indicates that the two variables are independent of each other.

Figure 12.8 The influence of wheat production on mortality, 1846 (%)

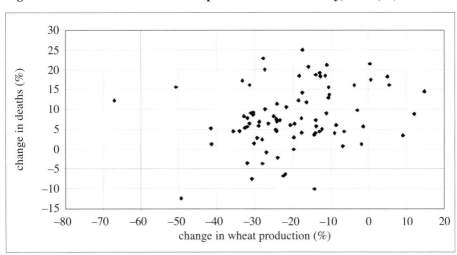

Clearly the map describing harvest deficits as defined above does not square easily with that describing the rise in prices (Figures 12.5 and 12.6). The correlation between price rises and harvest shortfalls is weak, and on that basis one would be hard put to argue that the price rises were due to harvest shortfalls (Chevet and Ó Gráda, 2004: 184–186). When we focus instead on the quantities sold on grain markets (i.e. apart from what is sold locally or consumed on the farm), however, and calculate the 1846 deficit relative to sales in 1844–1845, the outcome is as described in Figure 12.9. While the aggregate change in market sales was minimal, there was considerable variation across *départements*. As expected, the link between price and 'supply' is now stronger: the correlation between changes in quantities marketed (which include imports) and price is –0.55.[15]

---

[15] One must not ignore, however, the quantities of other grain crops sold on the market.

Figure 12.9 Changes in grain sold and price, 1846 (%)

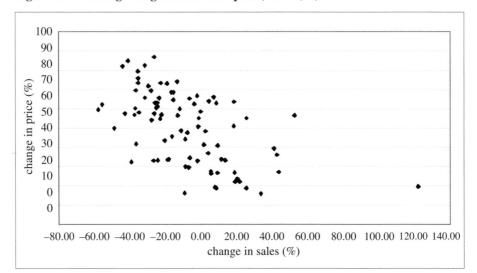

II.3. Did substitutes play a bigger role at the regional level?

Given the substitutability between crops and the likelihood that harvests are less than perfectly correlated, an approximate measure of the aggregate crop deficit is desirable. For this purpose, we rely on the nine-zone division used by the Ministry of Agriculture[16] (see Table 12.2). We first calculated the mean harvest for wheat, meslin, rye, buckwheat, maize, and potatoes in 1842–1845 for all zones, and then calculated the 1846 deficit as a percentage. For aggregation purposes we converted harvests expressed in hectolitres into quintals. Inevitably, this adds another element of approximation. The results of these calculations are given in Table 12.2.

First of all, Table 12.2 confirms that the deficit in the wheat harvest affected the whole country, apart from the Southwest. It was greatest in the North and East, and was by no means compensated by a rise in the output of meslin or rye. On the contrary, these two cereals registered even greater declines than wheat. At national level, taking all three cereals into account increases the deficit from 18.9 to 22 per cent. The outputs of other crops reinforce considerably the inequality in deficits. Buckwheat, though unimportant at national level, accounted for more than a quarter of output in the Northwest. Significantly, outside the North and Northeast the production of buckwheat rose in 1846, sometimes by a huge factor relative to the reference years. The same holds for other regions in the case of maize. Its production also increased in practically all regions. In the Southwest in particular, it helped compensate for the deficit in wheat, meslin, and rye, since maize accounted for about twenty-three per cent of production and its production rose by nearly one-fifth.

---

[16] In the text the zones are henceforth denoted by a capital letter, e.g. East, Centre.

Table 12.2 Harvest deficits of different crops destined for human consumption in 1846 (percentages by region)

	Wheat	Meslin	Rye	All Cereals	Buck-wheat	Maize	Potatoes	Total
Northwest	−19.9	−30.5	−37.6	−25.7	32.7	64.5	−53.0	−26.2
North	−16.3	−19.7	−36.6	−19.2	−21.8	−8.1	−6.9	−15.6
Northeast	−23.5	−26.6	−32.5	−25.5	−12.8	5.9	−20.4	−22.4
West	−20.0	−25.8	−37.8	−25.1	28.5	15.2	−28.9	−24.1
Centre	−16.1	−22.3	−37.2	−25.6	−1.5	−21.6	42.2	3.3
East	−22.4	−36.0	−24.1	−24.4	31.8	35.9	−42.0	−29.5
Southwest	−5.2	−16.8	−31.8	−11.5	64.8	19.7	−26.6	−6.3
South	−24.9	−20.5	−23.1	−23.9	19.2	47.0	10.4	−4.0
Southeast	−26.2	−50.2	27.8	−12.7	12.6	5.8	−6.8	−10.3
Total	−18.9	−25.3	−29.0	−22.1	29.2	26.5	−18.9	−17.4

The role of the potato is more varied. In the East, a huge shortfall in output in 1846 relative to 1842–1845 increased the overall food deficit from 24.4 per cent to 29.5 per cent. By contrast, in the Centre the potato helped greatly to compensate for the deficit in cereals. There, although the cereal shortfall amounted just over one-quarter, thanks to the potato the overall harvest was above normal. However, unlike buckwheat and maize, the potato did not help to reduce the overall food deficit – except in the Central and South regions. On the contrary it amplified it.[17]

Overall, four regions with losses of ten per cent or less – the Centre, Southwest, South and Southeast – seem to have escaped the 'crisis'. The North with a loss of 15.6 per cent occupied an intermediate position, whereas the other four regions saw aggregate output fall by between 22.5 and 29.5 per cent. Comparing the results in Table 12.2 to those in Figure 12.4, it is clear that *départements* experiencing an increase in mortality were mostly located in those regions where the production deficit was smallest. Only two of the eleven *départements* with a rise in deaths of over one-fifth were located in a zone with a deficit exceeding one-fifth. Another significant fact is that only two *départements* in the zone with the biggest deficit, the East, saw a rise in mortality, and a very weak one at that (for more detail see Chevet and Ó Gráda, 2004). In sum, the increase in the number of deaths cannot have been due to a subsistence crisis.

---

[17] In half a dozen *départements* in the west of France (the three Breton *départements* plus Ile-et-Vilaine, the Vendée, and Loire-Atlantique) the decline in the cultivated area under potatoes exceeded thirty per cent in 1847, and elsewhere in the west, south, and south-east the cultivated area also declined. Finisterre was the only *département* in France in which the area under potatoes exceeded that under either wheat or barley in 1845. Even given the considerable increase in the area under buckwheat, one might expect the failure of the potato to have caused some problems there. Yet there is little sign of this in Figures 12.3 and 12.4. On the other hand, in several *départements*, particularly in the north and east, there was an increase in the area under potatoes between 1846 and 1847. Such shifts were dwarfed by what was happening in Ireland and in the Low Countries.

III. Conclusion

This study suggests that the mid- and late 1840s harvest deficits were not severe enough to have resulted in a genuine subsistence crisis. While it is true that price rises were a fair guide to variations in the amount of wheat bought and sold on grain markets across the country, deficits in the wheat harvest, where they occurred, were uncorrelated with rises in mortality. Nor should the focus be so exclusively on the wheat harvest: buckwheat, maize and the potato, as well as imports, could – and did in places – compensate for a deficit in wheat. Moreover, because the potato was less affected by *phytophthera infestans,* it did not play the catastrophic role in France that it played in Ireland and Belgian Flanders (Solar, 1997). The total area under potatoes in France in 1845 was the same as in Ireland (abut one million hectares), and yields in France were considerably lower. As in Ireland the 1845 harvest was poor, but the shortfall in 1846 (as described above) was minor relative to the virtual destruction of the crop in Ireland. Besides, in France potato output in 1847 was back to its pre-1845 'norm', whereas in Ireland it was only a fraction of the tonnage achieved in the early 1840s.[18] This explains why the rise in prices was less and not as long-lasting in France. True, in some *départements* the increases in the price of potatoes at the peak in May 1847 were enormous, but on average they reached only 130 per cent above their pre-crisis level, to which they fell back thereafter. By way of comparison, the price of potatoes in Dublin, the Irish capital, reached four times the pre-famine average in late 1846 and again in the early summer of 1848. The rise in Belfast and elsewhere in the country was commensurate.[19]

All these changes mean that in France the first half of the nineteenth century marked a diametric break, as others have already noted, with earlier centuries and even with the second half of the eighteenth century. Why, then, has 1846 become a crisis year, when deaths in that year exceeded the moving average by only a few per cent and were dwarfed by the mortality peak due to the cholera epidemic of 1849? And why are the harvest shortfalls of 1853 and 1855, comparable in extent to 1846, largely ignored in the literature? Surely, in part, because the Revolution of 1848 required an economic basis: a long historiographical tradition links it with the economic distress of the previous two years, not least the poor harvest of 1846 (e.g. Labrousse, 1956; Tilly and Lees, 1975; Price, 1996: 11–12). Surely too, because contemporaries saw a food availability crisis in the undeniable rise in prices, a crisis which they linked too hastily with an excess mortality that was taken for granted. Armed with this conviction, why bother scrutinising a mortality curve when a graph showing prices is its spitting image, and when a price graph offers a photographic negative of output?

One caveat before concluding. This attempt at revising our understanding of the 1846–1848 period does not seek to deny that high prices on occasion resulted in genuine hardship. On the contrary: and, to make matters worse, in France the rise in grain prices in 1846 was followed by a fall in industrial output in 1847, which led to further hardship in 1848 (Chevalier, 1978; Tilly and Lees, 1975). If 'crisis' means privation, unemployment,

---

[18] These generalisations are based on official data (for France, and for Ireland in 1847) and on the estimates of Austin Bourke (1993: ch. 7).

[19] The underlying French data are in Archives Nationales, *Mercuriales de la France*, Série F11. The Irish data come from Ó Gráda, 2004.

panic, and disorder, then there is no denying that the 1846–1848 period represented such a crisis. Indeed, it is over a century since demographer Émile Levasseur pointed out the correlation between years of high food prices and peaks in criminality in nineteenth-century France, and the unrest in France in these years is well documented in Nadine Vivier's contribution to this volume (Levasseur, as cited by Sorokin, 1975: 228).

The link between resistance and famine is not a straightforward one. Individual violent acts, borne of desperation or shifting entitlements, should be distinguished from concerted action involving large groups of people. Food riots – as distinct from individual acts of thieving and cheating – are more likely to be the product of 'minor hunger and deprivation' rather than 'real starvation'. This was certainly the case in Ireland in the 1840s, where collaborative action in the early stages gave way to despair as the crisis became a catastrophe (compare Eiríksson, 1997). With reference to France in 1846/1847 and 1847/1948, the correspondence between popular unrest, on the one hand, and price rises and harvest deficits, on the other, was poor. Again, if we define 'crisis' by panic and unrest, France indeed went through a crisis; but our analyses of agricultural output and demographic data, and of the impact of substitute crops and imports on food availability, suggest that the reduction in food supplies in this period did not produce a 'crisis' in the historiographical – 'subsistence crisis' – sense of that term. As other chapters in this work show, in some other places in Europe it was a different matter.[20]

Bibliography

Armengaud, A. (1976) 'Le rôle de la démographie', in F. Braudel and E. Labrousse (eds), *Histoire économique et sociale de la France*, Paris, vol. 3., pp. 161–239.

Baulant, M. (1968) 'Le prix des grains à Paris de 1431 à 1788', *Annales E.S.C.*, 23, pp. 520–540.

Bideau, A. [et al.] (1988) 'La mortalité de 1800 à 1914', in J. Dupâquier (ed.), *Histoire de la population française*, Paris, vol. 3, pp. 279–299.

Bourdelais, P. et Raulot, J.-Y. (1987) *Une peur bleue: histoire du choléra en France, 1832–1854*, Paris.

Bourke, A. (1993) *The Visitation of God? The Potato and the Irish Famine*, Dublin.

Braudel, F. and Labrousse, E. (eds) (1976) *Histoire économique et sociale de la France*, Paris, vol. 3 (parts 1 and 2).

Cabourdin, G. (1988) 'Qu'est-ce qu'une crise?', in J. Dupâquier (ed.), *Histoire de la population française*, Paris, vol. 2, pp. 175–191.

Chaunu, P. (1991) 'Introduction to Sylvie Drame, Christian Gonfalone, Judith Miller, Bertrand Roehner', in *Un siècle de commercialisation du blé en France (1825–1913). Les fluctuations du champ des prix*, Paris, pp. vii–xi.

Chevalier, L. (1978) *Classes laborieuses et classes dangereuses*, Paris.

Chevet, J.-M. (1993) 'Les crises démographiques en France à la fin du XVIIème siècle et au XVIIIème: un essai de mesure', *Histoire et Mesure*, 8, pp. 117–144.

---

[20] See also Mokyr, 1979; Solar, 1997; Neal, 1997; Ó Gráda, 1999.

Chevet, J.-M. and Ó Gráda, C. (2004) 'Revisiting "Subsistence Crises": The characteristics of demographic crises in France in the first half of the 19th century', *Food and Foodways*, 12, pp. 165–195.

Chevet, J.-M. and Ó Gráda, C. (forthcoming) 'Grain prices and mortality: a note on La Michodière's Law', *European Journal of the History of Economic Thought*.

Dowe, D. [et al.] (2001) *Europe in 1848: Revolution and Reform*, Oxford.

Dupâquier, J. (1988) *Histoire de la population française. Vol. 2: de la Renaissance à 1789; Vol 3: de 1789 à 1914*, Paris.

Eiríksson, A. (1997) 'Food supply and food riots', in C. Ó Gráda (ed.), *Famine 150: Commemorative Lectures*, Dublin, pp. 67–93.

Labrousse, E. (1956) *Aspects de la crise et de la depression de l'économie française au milieu du 19e siècle*, Paris.

Labrousse, E. (1970) *Le prix du froment en France, 1726–1913*, Paris.

Labrousse, E. (1976) 'A livre ouvert sur les élans et les vicissitudes des croissances', in F. Braudel and E. Labrousse (eds), *Histoire économique et sociale de la France*, Paris, vol. 3.

Lachiver, M. (1991) *Les années de misère. La famine au temps du Grand Roi*, Paris.

Lebrun, F. (1983) 'Les crises démographiques en France aux XVIIIème et XVIIIème siècles', *Annales E.S.C.*, 38, pp. 205–234.

Le Roy Ladurie, E. (1973) 'L'aménorrhée de famine. (XVIII°–XX° siècle)', in *Le territoire de l'historien*, Paris, pp. 331–348.

Messance, L. (1766) *Recherches sur la population des généralités d'Auvergne, de Lyon, et de Rouen et de quelques provinces et villes du royaume*, Paris.

Meuvret, J. (1946) 'Les crises de subsistances et la démographie de la France d'Ancien régime', *Population*, 1, pp. 643–650. [repris dans *Etudes d'histoire économique*, Paris, pp. 271–278].

Ministère de l'agriculture et du commerce (1878) Bureau de l'agriculture, *Récoltes des céréales et des pommes de terre de 1815 à 1876*, Paris.

Mokyr, J. (1979) 'Industrialization and poverty in Ireland and the Netherlands: some notes towards a comparative case study', *Journal of Interdisciplinary History*, 10, pp. 429–459.

Neal, F. (1997) 'Black '47: Liverpool and the Irish famine', in E.M. Crawford (ed.), *The Hungry Stream: Essays on Emigration and Famine*, Belfast, pp. 123–136.

Ó Gráda, C. (ed.) (1997) *Famine 150: Commemorative Lectures*, Dublin.

Ó Gráda, C. (1999) *Black '47 and Beyond: the Great Irish Famine in History, Economy, and Memory*, Princeton.

Ó Gráda, C. (2004) 'The market for potatoes in Dublin during the Great Famine', http: // www.ucd.ie/economic/workingpapers/2004.htm.

Price, R. (1996) *Documents on the French Revolution of 1848*, London.

Rebaudo, D. (1979) 'Le mouvement annuel de la population française rurale de 1670 à 1740', *Population*, 34, pp. 589–606.

Reinhard, M. et Armengaud, A. (1961) *Histoire générale de la population mondiale*, Paris.

Solar, P. (1997) 'The potato famine in Europe', in C. Ó Gráda (ed.), *Famine 150: Commemorative Lectures*, Dublin, pp. 113–127.

Sorokin, P. A. (1975) *Hunger as a Factor in Human Affairs*, Gainesville. [The original Russian version was published in St. Petersburg in 1922].

Tilly, Ch. and Lees, L. (1975) 'The people of June, 1848', in R. Price (ed.), *Revolution and reaction: 1848 and the Second French Republic*, London, pp. 170–202.

13 Subsistence crisis and popular protest in Spain. The *motines* of 1847[1]

Pedro Díaz Marín, University of Alicante

I. Introduction

The progress of Spanish agriculture during the nineteenth century did not preclude the recurrence of subsistence crises, at roughly ten-yearly intervals and with serious repercussions for the least protected sections of the population (Sanchez-Albornoz, 1963: 8–9). The subsistence crisis of 1847 – the European dimensions of which were pointed out by Marx (1985: 109; see also Dowe, Haupt und Langewiesche, 1998) – although less intense than those of 1857 or 1868, struck the country hard[2] at an uncertain time. The social policy of the Moderates, who represented the interests of beneficiaries of earlier revolutionary upheavals, sought to guarantee the viability of a political system which, for all its image of solidity, could not hide a certain vulnerability. Political instability was marked from 1846 on, with the matrimonial problems of the monarchs threatening to become a national crisis, with conservative monarchism in the form of Carlism reappearing in strength and, on top of all this profound confusion, the subsistence crisis of 1847 provoking a serious social upheaval, complicating a conjuncture in which the same liberal regime saw itself at risk.

This study of the 1847 crisis consists of three parts. First, the market shortage of cereals and the factors which help explain it are analysed. Second, public actions to counter the food shortage – the restriction of exports and the authorization of imports – and the opposition of certain pressure groups, which complicated putting these into effect, are considered. In the final section, three questions are addressed: the unrest which affected the country during the first half of 1847; the means applied by the central and local authorities to contain them; and the connection between popular movements and the political crisis which affected the stability of the Moderate regime and impeded a major liberalisation.

II. Food scarcity and the deterioration of living standards

Despite the difficulties of measuring the evolution of agricultural production in Spain during the first half of the nineteenth century, there would seem to be a consensus that there was an increase, particularly in the yields of wheat, although estimates of the size

---

[1] Translated by Cormac O'Gráda. An earlier and slightly longer version of this chapter was published as Díaz Marín (2003). It forms part of Proyecto BHA 2002-01006 del Ministerio de Ciencia y Tecnología, and is supported by funding from FEDER. The comments of Professor Jesús Millán of the University of Valencia and of the editors of this book are gratefully acknowledged.
[2] According to Figuerola (1991: 115) the harvest shortfall of 1847 meant a food deficit of twenty-nine days for the Spanish population, and that of 1857, thirty-four days. Barquín (1999a: 189) indicates that the crises of 1825 and 1837 were less serious than that of 1847.

Figure 13.1 Map of Spain

of that increase vary (Tortella, 1985; Kondo, 1990; Gutiérrez Bringas, 1993; Prados, 1988; Simpson, 1989, 1997; Llopis, 1983). Not only was this increase sufficient to feed a population that rose from 10.5 million in 1800 to 18.6 million in 1900 (Pérez Moreda, 1985) – or at an average annual rate of 0.57% – but it left a surplus for export, such that wheat and flour increased their shares of foreign trade (Prados, 1982). Whereas the principal destination of the wheat was England and France, the principal overseas destination of the flour was the island of Cuba which, between 1825 and 1845, imported about 200 million kilos (*La Gaceta*, 16 May 1847).

Along with other factors such as amending legislation governing landed property, and the pressure of both internal and external demand, this may point to the role played in the expansion of agriculture because of governmental decisions which liberalised the wheat market from 1820, and other food products in 1834 (Garrabou and Sanz, 1985: 9–10).[3] These measures, which imposed a protectionist policy with respect to grain imports, reserving the home market for domestic producers, served as a spur to the

---

[3] Barquín (1997b: 27) analyses the relative importance of the protectionist legislation and the development of the internal market.

expansion and development of internal trade, but they did not eliminate scarcities such as that of 1847 (Gallego, 2001: 149–153).[4]

As seen in Figure 13.2, the prices of cereals were significantly higher in 1847 than in 1848.[5] The differences would be greater still if 1847 included the first four months of 1848, which was when prices reached their peak, before the government decided to permit the import of foreign grain.

Figure 13.2 Cereal prices, 1847–1848 (pts/hl)

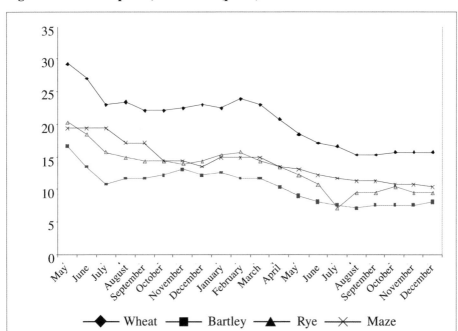

During the first half of the nineteenth century the trend in wheat prices was downwards. Prices fell 15% between 1842 and 1845. Then between 1846 and 1847 they rose about 60%, only to fall, with minor oscillations, by 23% until 1853, when the rise that culmi-

---

[4] Governments of different political hues applied this legislation. A Royal Decree of 5th August 1820 enacted the prohibition of grain imports, but another Decree of 8th September made it more flexible, fixing a wheat price limit above which imports were allowed. Wheat imports were banned below the price of 80 reales per fanega (1 fanega=26 kilos, approximately). Flour was affected by a similar policy, only if the price rose above 120 reales per quintal (100 pounds). During the so-called Ominous Decade [Década Ominosa] (1823–1833), this policy was maintained. It was not until the regency of Mary Christine that the Royal Decree of 24th January 1834 reduced the former import caps, both for wheat and flour. The latter was cut down to 70 reales per fanega, the former to 110 reales per quintal (Kondo, 1990: 110; Sánchez-Albornoz, 1963: 18–19).
[5] One potential problem with the prices in *La Gaceta* is that the averages are not weighted. Monthly prices by region for the four main crops are reported in Díaz Marín (2003).

nated in the crisis of 1857 began (Kondo, 1990: 77; Barquín, 2001: 182). The 1847 increase, which was particularly strong in the first months of the year, decreased from May on and between then and December 1847 the average price of wheat in Spain was 23.9 ptas/hl. However, prices in the cereal regions of the interior were considerably below the average. There prices were about 8% below the national average in 1800–1847, but between 1846 and 1847 they were 75% below the mean. In Andalucía the price level remained 9.5% above the national average. In western Andalucia the crisis of 1847 was the most acute of the century, and prices reached their peak, albeit briefly. The 1846 harvest had been poor, and prices began to rise in June. In some places the rise was marked; in Villafranca de Córdoba between May 1846 and May 1847 the price rose by 127%, and in Morón (Seville), in the same period, the rise was 228% (Bernal, 1979: 218–220). Other producing regions such as Aragón (Peiró, 1987: 230)[6] or Extremadura would see prices rocket.

Table 13.1 The evolution of prices between January and May/June 1847 (ptas/hl)

	January	May/June	Increase (%)
Alicante[*]	8.5	25.7	200
Jaén	14.8	32.9	121.3
Zamora	11.7	26.1	123
Badajoz	16.6/18	32	85
Ciudad Real	17.1/17.6	32	85
Sevilla	19.4/23.4	38	77.7
Málaga	25.2	34.7	37.7
Segovia	14.4/15.3	17.8	33.8
Palma de Mallorca	23.8	31.1	30.7
Guadalajara	20.3	26.6	31
Castellón	25.2/27	30	15
Coruña	27.2	30.2	11
Zaragoza	19.5	21.04	38.6

Source: La Gaceta, 1847–1848. The prices for January refer to 31 Jan. 1847 to 12 Feb. 1847. For Zaragoza, see Peiró (1987). Mountain wheat rose less, by 31%.
[*] Although the sources are silent on the issue, Alicante's outlier status might be due to differences in wheat quality.

What happened in the deficit and consuming regions of the periphery? Catalonia specialised in wine-growing. This limited the expansion of cereals, which were produced in the interior and supplied the coastal zone. The market was integrated. When harvests were short in the interior, the coastal area imported wheat, which it distributed inland (Vicedo, 1983: 168).[7] Its demographic growth – at an annual rate of 1.45% – was

[6] According to Peiró between May and December 1847 the mean price was 22.83 ptas/hl, 3.8% higher than in *La Gaceta*. In 1848 Peiró gives the mean price as 15.50 ptas/hl, 2.5% less than *La Gaceta*. According to Kondo (1990) price in the city of Zaragoza rose by 186% between 1842 and 1847. According to Peiró the rise was only 21%.
[7] In 1846 the prices of wheat in the coastal region went from 19.5 to 20 pesetas per hectolitre,

Table 13.2   Movements in the regional prices of cereals relative to the national average, 1847–1848

| | Wheat | | Barley | | Rye | | Maize |
	1847	1848	1847	1848	1847	1848	1848
Galicia	–4.65	10.08	20.59	47.06	–4.87	4.18	8.72
Cantabria	0.08	4.99	12.48	32.00	–4.48	15.83	4.19
Submeseta Norte	–21.13	–25.47	–6.90	–17.50	–19.48	–23.55	–24.35
SubmesetaSur	5.67	–10.29	–0.02	–16.67	7.63	–4.52	3.12
Alava-Navarre	–16.73	–14.13	–13.77	–6.36	–65.81	0.41	–17.56
Aragon	–3.63	–8.25	–14.65	–10.69	6.84	8.28	–26.16
Catalonia	21.13	28.15	3.39	26.14	37.29	46.34	9.32
Valencia Region and Murcia	9.06	11.66	–0.24	6.43	19.49	25.34	–0.80
Coastal Andalucia	11.46	9.72	4.72	4.98	11.47	30.27	21.25
Inland Andalucia	3.06	–7.04	–0.47	–19.36	–8.60	–3.53	6.75
Extremadura	–16.48	–20.54	–27.07	–24.10	–30.02	–23.22	–41.72
Baleares	12.12	–2.78	–6.45	–19.56	–30.81	-35.25	38.11

Source: La Gaceta, 1847–1848.

extraordinary (Kondo, 1990: 52). This made the country reliant on foreign markets for its supply of wheat, which translated into high prices, 22% greater than the average for 1840–1847, a difference that was practically maintained during the crisis. The rise of 1846–1847 entailed a break with the trend of Barcelona prices during the first half of the nineteenth century and sparked off a rising trend. The rise of 1846 relative to 1845 was double those of 1842 and 1844 relative to the preceding years (Segura, 1983: 185–186)[8] and in some markets it was really striking. In Balaguer the price of wheat rose by 29% between 1842 and 1845, but between 1845 and 1847 the rise was 97%, an increase much greater than the 28% experienced between 1855 and 1857 (Vicedo, 1983: 172). However, as Segura notes, Catalan food supplies were not endangered in the same way as other Spanish regions (Segura, 1983: 190). In effect, in 1846 more than 300,000 hl of wheat and about 23 million kilos of flour entered Catalan markets, as well as smaller quantities of barley, rye, and maize, significantly more than the quantities entered before the prohibition of 1820,[9] and in the first two months of 1847 the volume of grain and flour entering Catalonia continued to be plentiful. In fact, this region accounted for the major part of the cabotage traffic [or coastal trade] and was the main consumer market of the peninsula:

---

whereas in the interior they rose from 18.9 to 30.1 pesetas (Garrabou, Tello, and Roca, 1999: 450).

[8] Between 1845 and 1846 the price of wheat in the city of Barcelona rose by 8.9%, whereas the rises of 1841–1842 and 1843–1844 were of 3.9% and 3.5%, respectively.

[9] La *Gaceta*, 16 May 1847. Most of the wheat came from Alicante, whereas the flour was supplied by Santander (Moreno, 1995: 229). According to Fradera (1984), in the years just before the prohibition some 39 million kg of wheat entered Catalonia annually, which may be compared to the 57 million kg of wheat and of wheaten flour imported in 1847 (Garrabou and Sanz, 1985).

The exports of grain by cabotage have had the ports of Catalonia as an almost exclusive destination. These are the biggest and most secure with whom the grain-producing provinces trade. Without its help and that of Cuba, our agriculture would have stagnated. Since demand from foreign markets is unreliable, not only because of sustained competition in the face of cheaper grains and flour from other countries, but also because of lack and slowness of transport from the internal production centres to the ports, due to the lack of canals and good roads. (*La Gaceta*, 16 May 1847)

Table 13.3 Cereals and flour imported into Catalonia from other Spanish provinces in 1846, according to statistics of the Dirección General de Aduanas

Province	Wheat	Barley	Rye	Maize	Flour
Alicante	157,170	8,143	500	1,618	249,631
Almería	13,415				5,980
Cádiz	4,515				34,316
Castellón		781	279	3,213	10,626
La Coruña	12,873		5,128		135,355
Granada	180			1,269	
Huelva	2,800	78	873	1,522	
Lugo	832			389	
Málaga	3,081	794		455	
Murcia	35,066	7,814	3,471	115	2,760
Oviedo	9,081			438	258,428
Pontevedra	6,027		333	2,989	805
Santander	15,422	2,026			14.169,909
Sevilla	50,712	264		363	326,520
Valencia	2,659		3,892	161	7,570,220
Baleares	4,157	370			47,932
Canarias	278	111			
Total	318,270	20,380	14,475	12,531	22,812,481

Source: La Gaceta, 16 May 1847. Flour in kg, other products in hl.

In 1848 the mean price of wheat per hectolitre fell to 18.46 pesetas, or by 23%.[10] That of barley – which for many people, combined with rye, was a substitute for wheaten bread – fell from 12.7 ptas/hl in 1847 to 9.1 ptas/hl in 1848, or by 29%. Peripheral regions – Galicia, Cantabria, Catalonia, and coastal Andalucia – experienced the highest prices, a tendency which was accentuated in 1848.[11] As for rye, in 1847 its mean price

---

[10] The shortage caused distortions in the behaviour of prices. Between 1847 and 1848 the coefficient of variation rose from 0.1475 to 0.1893. The seasonal dispersion was 28.3% less in 1847 than in 1848. As Sánchez-Albornoz (1975: 35) has shown, in general the higher the national average, the lower the regional disparity.
[11] Sánchez-Albornoz (1975). Between 1847 and 1848 the coefficient of variation of prices went from 0.1680 to 0.2454, a rise of 46%. In 1857 this tendency was reversed, and the coefficient fell from 0.1806 to 0.1750 in 1858, a reduction of 6%.

was 15.8 ptas/hl, in 1848 it fell by 28% to 11.4 ptas/hl. Prices were highest in the periphery, in the Submeseta Sur and in Aragon. As for maize, the data are very fragmentary for 1847. The average price in that year was 16.8 ptas/hl. In 1848 it fell to 12.1 ptas/hl, a drop of 26%. Prices were lowest in the Submeseta Norte, Alava-Navarra, Aragon, and Extremadura (see Table 13.2).

A possible interpretation of the crisis would have to take account at a minimum of the following elements: the volume of the 1846 harvest, the importance of exports, and the conditions of commercialisation (Barquín, 1999b). We don't know the size of the harvest, although it would seem that there was a fall in output in some regions, as in Andalucía and in the east, where the harvest was poor (*El Heraldo*, 8 July 1846; Bernal, 1979: 218; Sánchez-Albornoz, 1975). Was it enough to feed the people? An answer would also require knowledge of consumption levels in the 1840s. There are no reliable data, but we can effect an approximation from information supplied by Simpson (1989).[12] In 1868 the government reckoned the annual consumption of wheat per head at 171.5 kilos, including provision for seed, or 141.7 kilos net of seed requirements. If we apply this level of consumption to the approximately 13.7 million inhabitants of Spain in 1847, it would have required 2,353 million kilos to cover the needs of the population, including allocation for seed. Tortella (1994: 13)[13] estimates the average annual production of wheat in the 1840s at 2,165 million kilos, which would have entailed a deficit of 187.9 million kilos, but the deficit would have been greater in 1846 because the harvest that year was below normal, whereas exports of wheat and flour increased. It might be concluded, therefore, that the harvest of 1846 failed, although we do not know to what extent, while the shipments to consuming areas from the periphery continued. That would have led to a rise in prices in the producing regions, which had few alternatives to wheat, and whose consumption was high and only at set periods were they able to substitute barley and rye, cereals which were also scarce in 1847 (Martínez Vara, 1997; Reher and Ballesteros, 1993; Serrano, 1999; Garrabou, Tello and Roca, 1999; Pérez Moreda, 1980: 411). The periphery could count on more varied substitute foods, such as beans, potatoes and figs in the Balearic Islands;[14] maize in Cantabria, the East, and Catalonia; or rice in in the Valencia region, a product of popular consumption, little extended to other classes, for 'only in times of increased daily wages would they tend to use this provision' (Archivo de la Diputación Provincial de Alicante, *Libro de Actas*, 16 Oct. 1847). Therefore, one must also take account of the rigidity of demand, which would explain how changes in supply had a significant impact on prices. Moreover, it must not be forgotten that the Spanish market was not sufficiently integrated, despite the steps in this direction that had been taken in the first half of the century (Martínez Vara, 1999:

---

[12] In 1840 Mariano Roca de Togores reckoned the amount of wheat needed to feed one person at 6 fanegas per year, that is to say, some 260 kilos. *Diario de Sesiones de las Cortes* (DSC), Congreso, 31 May 1840.

[13] Barquín (1999b: 300) estimates that c. 1860 a good harvest could reach 2.3 million kg and a very bad one 1.5 million kg.

[14] *DSC*, Congreso, 31 May 1840. The minister for finance indicated that there were provinces which 'did not produce enough for one-fourth of their population, and nonetheless exported their grain to other provinces, because they had other crops, other foods with which to make up for the lack of cereals'. Potato cultivation was slow to spread in the nineteenth century, but in the 1840s it was consolidating its position – yet not in a generalised way – becoming part of the popular diet in some places: see Kondo (1990: 89), Sáez (1995).

43–73; Barquín, 1997a: 54–64), above all with respect to wheat – and possibly other cereals – as is demonstrated by the approximation of price levels across the regions (Fontana, 1979; Barquín, 1997a, 1997b: 17–48; Kondo, 1990; Escrivá and Llopis, 1987).[15]

Another factor to be considered is the export of Spanish agricultural products to other European countries, a response to increased external demand, particularly from France and Britain.[16] If their volume does not seem large relative to output, it must not be forgotten that the Spanish market was closed to foreign cereals, possibly aggravating the problems entailed by a shortage. The foreign market also offered profitable opportunities, given the shortage of grain in Europe in 1846–1847. Between 1844 and 1845, wheat exports would rise by 496% and would rise by 225% in the following year (Kondo, 1990:142).[17] Such an increase, together with that of flour, is thought to have affected the internal market, which reacted with a price increase, although the danger of scarcity was not so evident. As seen in Table 13.4, whereas in 1846 more than four hundred thousand hectolitres of grain were exported to Europe, of which 80,8% was wheat, worth over six million pesetas at an average price of 14.41 ptas/hl, in the first six months of 1847 over six hundred thousand hl of grain, worth over 11 million pesetas, and at a mean price of 18.47 ptas/hl – 28% more – were exported, with a doubling in the price of rye, and a rise of 37% in that of wheat. As for flour (Table 13.5), between 1846 and the first half of 1847 over 38 million kilos were exported, of which 71% was for America and 29% for Europe. Whereas exports to America fell by 51% in the first half of 1847 compared to the previous year, the volume of flour destined for Europe rose by 169%. Exports to European countries were reactivated at the beginning of 1847. In January more than 111,000 hectolitres of wheat left through the ports of Alicante, Seville, and Galicia alone (*El Mensajero*, 18 February 1847).[18] This was destined mainly for France and Great Britain – which abandoned protectionism in 1846 with the repeal of the Corn Laws – where cereals realised considerably higher prices than on domestic markets.[19]

---

[15] In 1847 the city of Cáceres bought 949 fanegas [527 hectolitros] of wheat at 50 reales from Mérida, i.e. 47,450 reales, plus 7,344 reales for shipping, representing 13.4% of the total cost (Madrazo 1981: 67). Ringrose (1972) considered transport an obstacle to the formation of an integrated market. A report presented to the General Board of Agriculture by a commission in 1849 attributed the lack of competitiveness of Spanish grain to the cost of transport (Royal Commission, 1849).

[16] Garrabou and Sanz (1985: 33). The volume of wheat and wheat flour exported in 1846–1847 was 99,328,581 Kg, or 5% of the average harvest.

[17] According to Prados (1982: 242), the difference could have been even greater, for while in 1843 19,871 quintals [914,066 Kg] of wheat were exported, in 1846 exports rose to 260,476 quintals [11,981,896 Kg]. By these same dates flour rose from 136,470 to 211,923 quintals [6,227,620 Kg. to 9,748,458 Kg]. In any case, it was a sharper increase than that experimented with between 1854 and 1855, which was 11.1%, and fell by 73% in the following year (Sánchez-Albornoz, 1968: 74).

[18] Exports from the port of Alicante were 23,624 fanegas of wheat [13,111 hl]; 120,000 fanegas of wheat [66,600 hl] and 8,000 arrobas of flour [92,000 kg](1 arroba = 25 pounds, 11_ kilos) left Galician ports, and 51,793 wheat fanegas [28,745 hl] left Seville.

[19] *El Mensajero*, 25 February, 25 March 1847. In England wheat fetched between 70 and 84 reales per fanega, [31.5 Pts./hl and 37.8 pts./hl] whereas in Madrid it was worth 67 reales. [30.2 pts./hl]

In 1846 Spain exported merchandise to the value of 159 million reales to Great Britain and of the value of 150.6 million reales to France, which accounted for 31.5% and 29.8%, respectively, of total exports in that year. Wheat and flour accounted for a sizeable share of the exports, for both items accounted for in excess of 50.2 millions reales, entailing about one-tenth of the total (Prados, 1982: 242–243). Wheat sold in Great Britain in 1846 reached a value of £109,639 sterling, in 1847 the value dropped to £26.698 sterling, sums much greater than the £6,600 which the same country paid for the wheat imported in 1845 (Nadal, 1978: 351). The subsistence crisis was also affecting Europe, and French merchants travelled through the producing areas buying 'whatever grain was on offer'.[20] The spread of this kind of news no doubt contributed to the increase in prices.

Table 13.4 Exports of grain to Europe, 1846-1847

	1846 Hectolitres	First half of 1847 Hectolitres
Barley	20,663	919
Rye	40,827	9,927
Maize	20,384	361,885
Wheat	344,201	228,719
Total	426,075	601,450

Source: La Gaceta, 17 May 1848.

Table 13.5 Exports of flour to Europe and America, 1846–1847

	To Europe Kg	To America Kg
1846	2.999.108	18.189.527
1847: first half	8.059.902	9.000.038
Total	11.059.010	27.189.565

Source: La Gaceta, 17 May 1848.

Finally, reference must be made also to the distribution and commercialisation of cereals, handled by groups of traders who controlled transactions in a protected market, which favoured oligopolistic practices and allowed them to increase transaction costs (Hoyo, 1999: 278; Moreno, 1995).[21] In conditions of imperfect information, with rumours and signs of scarcity, traders took to hoarding and storing surplus stocks, contributing

---

[20] *El Mensajero* (1 April 1847) revealed that in Castilla la Vieja alone over seven million fanegas of wheat [3,885,000 hl] and two million arrobas of flour had been contracted for. [92 million kg.
[21] For an alternative view see Barquín (1997b: 44), who argues that transaction costs were low, and therefore the sector competitive. In Alicante the grain trade was in the hands of about twenty wholesale merchants, catering for a population of about 20,000 inhabitants. *Boletín Oficial de la Provincia de Alicante* (BOPA, 1852).

to speculation and to the rise in prices (Yun, 1991: 33), and provoking the anger of the population. There were 'pressure groups in whose interest it was to force up prices' (Garrabou and Sanz, 1985: 33–34.). All in all, everything points to the event of a bad harvest in 1846 coinciding with an unusual increase in exports, which continued to rise in 1847, although in that year the harvest was better. Expectations of gain and and rumours fomented speculative practices, which inevitably led to price increases.

The heavy rise in prices, together with strikes and low wages, contributed to a fall in the living standards of the average citizen. According to the agricultural inquiry requested by Bravo Murillo in 1849, the average wage of labourers in mid-century was about 4 reales per day, although it is important to bear in mind that monetary payment was not the only income, nor the most important in many cases (García Sanz, 1980; Del Moral, 1979; Garrabou, 1987). In general wages fell in 1847 (Bernal, 1979; Reher and Ballesteros, 1993; Serrano, 1999; Moreno, 2001; Garrabou, Tello and Roca, 1999) – although they increased in the case of some more specialised agricultural chores (Bernal, 1979; Calatayud, Millán and Romeo, 2000: 90; Garrabou, 1987) – and were insufficient 'to procure the most frugal sustenance for workers'[22] Misery extended 'to the extreme of forcing workers to beg for public charity'.[23] Some people died of hunger in Andalucia and robbery and insecurity extended to many parts of the country (*El Eco del Comercio*, 10, 12 March 1847). In effect, along with the labourers, many artisans and smallholders and tenants also lived in permanently precarious conditions (Millán, 1999: 147–173, 236–243) – burdened, moreover, with fiscal charges (Vallejo, 2001) – and their survival, as the count of Ripalda was informed by his administrator, 'is a miracle, since there are families who go for a week without tasting bread' (Calatayud et al., 1996: 93). Real wages fell and, taking account of the fact that more than half of peasant family income was spent on food, especially bread (García Sanz, 1980; Reher and Ballesteros, 1993; Serrano, 1993; Garrabou, Tello and Roca, 1999; Moreno, 2001), this fall increased pauperism[24] and 'affected both nutritional status and physical status' (Martínez Carrión, 2002: 51), which translated into an increase in mortality, particularly infant mortality (Sanz and Ramiro, 2002)[25], and a reduction in the mean height of unskilled day workers (Martínez Carrión and Pérez Castejón, 2002).[26] The inefficiency of the public granaries and the lack of a solvent credit system were other hindrances that accentuated the crisis for the farmers. On top of that was the incidence of the consumption tax. Although Santillán, minister for finance in the government of the Duke of Sotomayor, expressed in the Cortes the need to reform the fiscal system by seeking greater equity and less fiscal

---

[22] 'Contestación de la Junta de Agricultura de la provincia de Alicante al interrogatorio o encuesta agrícola de 1849', in Vidal (1986: 184–185). For Galicia and Asturias see Domínguez Martín (1997: 65).

[23] *El Heraldo*, 17 February 1847; *El Eco del Comercio*, 4 February 1847, 5 March 1847, In Aragon where as a consequence of the liberal reforms, 'the most characteristic type on the social landscape', was the small producer (Forcadell 1995: 508) the misery affected the greater part of the population. In Murcia drought prevented farmers from concluding the sowing.

[24] For example, The Casa de Misericordia de Palma, which normally housed between 900 and 1,000 poor, sheltered 1,600 in March; see *El Heraldo*, 18 March 1847.

[25] It rose by 7.3% in the 1845–1849 period relative to the previous quinquennium.

[26] The mean height of labourers born in the quinquennium 1846–1850 was 1.1 cm less than that of those born in the preceding five years. It was a different story for peasant proprietors, whose mean height rose.

pressure (Pirala, 1875–1879: 411), the levy on consumption, a tax which fell on necessities (Pan-Montojo, 1994), was an important source of revenue for the Treasury. It accounted for more than the 15% of the total in 1847, a fall of three percentage points relative to 1846. Nonetheless, the share of tax destined for provincial and municipal funds did not decline: in 1846 this part represented 21.2% of the total collected, in 1847 it represented 24.3% (Comín, 1990: 60, 61, 120). Therefore, the tax – the incidence of which was not limited to urban boundaries since it taxed both consumption and production, making agriculture subject to double taxation – was an essential source of revenue for the local authorities (Vallejo, 1996). As noted in the *Eco del Comercio (12-3-1847)*, the price of provisions had risen more than the wages of the working classes, raising the issue that 'it is one or the other: either the value of labour rises, or the price of food drops'. Both options were problematic. The lack of representation and bargaining power of the agricultural labourers exacerbated the situation facing the mass of the population (*Guía del Comercio, Agricultura y Artes*, 16 June 1847). In the Senate voices were raised, arguing for restrictions on the export of cereals and on the tax on bread. The government had to act, since 'when hunger arrives..., it is the state itself, it is society which is in danger' (*Eco del Comercio*, 30 March 1847). The panorama was complicated by a financial crisis that, according to Tortella, was the first of a clearly capitalist character, and resulted in the suspension of payments by public companies, bankruptcies, and the paralysis of railway construction (Tortella, 1975: 43).

III. The frustrated attempt to end the scarcity: Opposition from vested interests to the circular of 14th March.

In early March, the government founded an information unit to report, on the basis of data supplied from local authorities throughout the country, on the advisability of allowing free imports of both cereals and cotton textiles of foreign origin (*Boletín Oficial del Ministerio de Comercio, Instrucción y Obras Públicas*. Supplement to vol. I). On March 5th the Minister for Commerce accordingly wrote to the political representatives for information about the cultivable surface in each province, the number of flour mills, and productive capacity, making clear that this information would not result in the taxing of farmers or 'hindering them with duties'. Within two weeks data was available on the supply of cereals in the provinces, on exports abroad, and on the needs of other European countries. As in the crisis of 1857 (Garrabou, 1980), the data did not imply a situation that was beyond control, for it was believed that 'with the supplies available there cannot be a dangerous scarcity'. Nonetheless, special measures were taken in order to avoid a scarcity. Exports of cereals and potatoes were prohibited, imports of foreign cereals were permitted when the price of wheat reached 70 reales per fanega (31.5 ptas/hl). Declared grains and seed were to be free of city, county and national duties, and in order to avoid speculation in those markets, merchant societies were banned from trading in grains or other food-related goods, and retailers were not allowed to buy until after market hours (*BOPA*, 29 March 1847). These measures did not apply to ships either already loaded or about to load in the ports.

The publication of the official letter led to a heated debate in the Cortes that highlighted the controversy surrounding the measure and the clash of interests among the diverse pressure groups. On March 17th 1847, Moyano presented an appeal to the government.

He was promptly backed by various deputies, asking for an explanation of the letter of the 14th, which he considered damaging to the agricultural and trading interests of the country, besides being antiparliamentarian, for the issue of the provisions should not be the matter of a decree, but of a law approved by the Cortes. In addition, the measure was based on inaccurate information supplied by political officers after consulting the different lord mayors, and it was easy to imagine that they, 'afraid that the news asked was going to be used to increase the levies, were trying to lessen the inventories and increase the needs' (*DSC,* Congreso, 17 March 1847).[27] Finally, Moyano concluded that with this measure the government had alarmed the country in an unnecessary fashion, for there was a surplus of 20 million of wheat fanegas [11.1 million hl].[28] Modesto Lafuente expressed the uneasiness of the Malaguenian traders and proprietors, and did not believe in the justice of a measure that weakened the general rural interests. He rejected the idea that it was necessary to favour the poor by damaging the speculators, and added: 'And so my Lords, placed between the poor and speculator classes, is there not a yet more respectable class, the proprietary and productive class, that is being highly damaged with this letter?' Not even the likely alterations to the social order would justify the letter: 'It has been said that there are signs of unrest; and then I ask: these signs of turbulences, can they not be dealt with other than by means of these trade restrictive measures?' Identifying the general interests of the country with those of the propertied class, he concluded: 'Is it necesary to sacrifice the Spanish Nation interests to a handful of turbulent men?' (*DSC*, 17 March 1847). Peña Aguayo highlighted two aspects of the issue: the constitutional and the economic. The tariff legislation of July 9th 1841, allowing for the free export of food, had been infringed. The measure was also criticised for its implementation without consulting the Parliament, and for hurting foreign interests, whose governments had claimed for damages incurred by ships unable to load grain. Bertrán de Lis stressed the aforementioned; he highlighted the lack of prudence on the part of the government, for it raised an unnecessary panic that led to increased prices; and rejected the fact that only the extreme poor should be favoured, and not the producers. The Navy Minister, Oliván, justified the measure as temporary and useful as a means of controlling the prices of necessities. Madoz, who was politically connected to the parlamentary opposition yet also close to the protectionist interests of the Catalan producers, approved

---

[27] Sánchez-Albornoz (1975: 6–7) demonstrates that the government sought a fiscal objective when it proposed to produce data on prices throughout Spain. In fact, the *Instrucción para llevar a efecto las operaciones que han de dar por resultado el conocimiento de precios medios de frutos de cada provincia,* of 22nd April 1847, was promulgated by the Dirección General de Estadística de la Riqueza, an arm of the Ministery of Finance.

[28] Statistical ignorance and a blind faith in the agricultural potential of the peninsular soil sustained a bourgeois optimism which allowed Moyano to evaluate the production of wheat at 110 million fanegas [61,050,000 hl], a level which would not be reached until 1932 (Robledo, 1993: 70–71). Similarly, the commission of experts created by Royal Decree on March 4th 1847 betrayed no unease about the scarcity and reacted stubbornly to the introduction of foreign corn, given the agricultural potential of the country, to the point that it proposed raising the threshold above which grain imports should be authorized from 70 to 80 reales. This optimism was shared by the regional agricultural commissioner for the province of Alicante, Joaquín Roca de Togores (1849: 94), who estimated the average annual production of wheat at 120 million fanegas [66,600,000 hl], consumption accounting for some 100 million, [55,500,000 hl] and seed and exports for 20 million. [11,100,000 hl]

of the letter. He confessed to defending a 'popular and democratic cause' and accused Moyano and Lafuente of self-interestedly backing the interests of the wheat merchants. The minister of commerce, Mariano Roca de Togores, stressed the fact that it was not a political issue that was being debated, as supported by the fact that Madoz supported the Government's letter. He recalled that the Executive was not going to impede the coastal trade, and that the measure was a temporary one. In fact, Roca de Togores, an important crop-owner, was a convinced protectionist insofar as grain exports were concerned and it was his opinion that excessive red tape delayed exports.[29] Ponzoa – former professor of Political Economy and Statistics of the Central University, translator of Jean-Baptise Say and professor at the Sociedad Económica Matritense and at the Ateneo de Madrid (*El Español*, 6 July 1836; Martín, 2000) – defended the path taken by the government, forced by extraordinary circumstances into taking account of the general scarcity in Europe. Yet he suggested that it went against the general principles of political economy. To Ponzoa, the government measure protected the rights of property:

From the moment when producers, i.e. land owners, are granted an unlimited right to remove wheat that undoubtedly will be exported, the poor classes will perish of want, and from that moment the only basis that underpins the right to property will be lost. So how can the right to own land, seen by narrow-minded people as a monopoly at the expense of the population in general, be supported if it does not encompass the interests of all sections of society?... If the right to property is to be sustained, it must benefit all classes of the Nation. (*DSC*, Congreso, 17 March 1847)

Finally, a group of progressive deputies presented a proposition asking the Congress to de-authorise the conduct of the minister in the circular of 14th March. As Gómez de la Serna noted, in reality this amounted to a vote of censure against the government. At the urging of Bravo Murillo, minister of justice, who argued that up to that point the debate had been about economics, but that the intervention of Gómez de la Serna turned it into a political question, the proposition was put to a vote, and was rejected by 142 votes against and 42 in favour.

Yet the Government's letter not only sparked criticism in the Parliament, it was also rejected from other social and political instances, hence having a limited application. On the one hand, the free trade movement had gathered renewed strength since Cobden's tour of Spain in 1846 (Almenar and Velasco, 1987; Lluch, 1988), and many liberals associated free trade with the liberal party, whereas protection was associated with absolutism. On the other hand, the ban on exports might favour consumers, but it hurt harvesters and traders, who put pressure on the government not to apply the measure to its full extent. Due to these pressures, the *Gaceta* of 25th March published a Royal Order lifting in part the restrictions on exports. The ban would be put in place only when the price of wheat rose above 70 reales per fanega on the eastern Mediterranean coast, 60 reales on the south coast, 55 reales on the Cantabrian coast, 50 reales at the French frontier, and 45 reales at the Portuguese frontier. Moreover, the prohibition applied neither to the coastal trade nor to the Balearic Islands (*La Gaceta*, 25 March 1847).[30]

---

[29] In 1840 he criticized the complicated procedures entailed in exporting wheat in Congress (*DSC*, 31 May 1840).

[30] In the case of other basic products, the export prohibition came into action when the price of maize and rye reached 80% of that of wheat, that of barley 50%, and that of flour, when its price exceeded that of wheat by 50%.

For traders, the solution to the shortage was not to ban exports, but the elimination of restrictions on the expansion of the market. They emphasized the case for the suppression of monopolies, the abolition of prohibitions and fiscal reforms, especially of the port levies[31] which they blamed for reducing consumption and narrowing the market, but also for falling disproportionately on the poorest classes. Besides, ultimately, there were the local authorities who had to apply the governmental measure, and they often reflected the powerful agrarian and mercantile interests, because the municipal law of 1845, which regulated access to local power, restricted it to the major taxpayers, most likely to be big proprietors and traders.

IV. The subsistence riots and their repercussions

As a result of the considerations described above, the measures taken by the government were applied only in part and too late. Moreover, even when they slowed the export of cereals, they could not prevent an acute social reaction that affected practically the entire country in the form of popular protests. The latter frequently adopted the form of actual or threatened riots of varied intensity and gave the country a chaotic aspect, worrying the wealthy classes and the authorities, and had important political implications. Short-lived riots, in many cases of a day or two, were sparked off by a variety of factors. Even when the underlying cause was scarcity, other issues arose. There were strikes, complaints against grain monopolists and against middlemen for the fraudulent practices such as soaking grain in order to make it heavier and bulkier, against exports that continued despite the prohibition, against the authorities accused of permissive attitudes, if not of connivance with speculators, and against the hated consumption levies. Hunger was not only a consequence of scarcity, for, as E.P. Thompson (1995: 323) highlights, the market is not an isolated and abstract entity, working at the margin of the 'political, social and legal relations' in which it is situated. In addition, the fear of hunger, as much as hunger itself, sparked off riots. In many cases women played a leading role, being more alert to price fluctuations from being in direct contact with the market and subject to acute wage discrimination relative to men.[32]

In the País Valenciano, the disturbances began early, characterised by a strong anti-fiscal component, although less so than in 1854–56 in Old Castile (Moreno, 2002), and they were directed against consumption levies. In the province of Alicante, the communities of Jijona, Aspe, Elda, and Villena[33] were also affected by this kind of protest. In the Cantabrian cornice, there were protests during the winter and spring against the shipping of grain out of Llanes, Gijón, Castro Urdiales, and Avilés, where

---

[31] See *Diario del Comercio* of April–May; *Guía del Comercio y Boletín de Fomento*, 27 January, 3, 10, 17 February 1847; *Guía del Comercio, Agricultura y Artes*, 5 May, 16 June 1847

[32] In Palencia, the average salary earned by women in the 1840s was about 20% less than that earned by men (Moreno, 2001). In Navarre, the difference reached 36% (Lana, 2002).

[33] *BOPA*, 1, 3 March 1847; *El Heraldo*, 29 March 1847. In February a group of workers rioted and demanded that the Ayuntamento eliminate the two reales that burdened the consumption of flour and green beans. On February 24th others rioted in Aspe demanding the reduction of taxes on necessities. On the 28th a handbill distributed in Elda denounced the misery endured by workers and the lack of work and threatening an insurrection.

three people were killed and many wounded (*El Heraldo*, 1, 29 March, 5 April 1847; Ruiz, 1981: 45–46). In Galicia, the disturbances were at their most intense, and the discontent focused on the export of maize and rye. They began in mid-March in Vigo and spread to Redondela, Puente de Sampayo, Pontevedra (where labourers' wives destroyed sacks for carrying maize), Santiago, Coruña (where several were killed by military gunfire) (*El Heraldo*, 22, 24, 29 March 1847. *Eco del Comercio*, 26 March 1847), Rianxo, and Tuy (*Guía del Comercio, Agricultura y Artes*, 16 June 1847). In May, the unrest spread to Guipúzcoa.

In Catalonia, the anxiety was extreme for fear that the scarcity could fuel Carlism. The outbreak of rebellion in Rosas on March 20th (*El Heraldo*, 29 March 1847) alerted conservative public opinion, which considered Catalonia to be one of the most serious issues facing the government, because the 'paralysis of a major part of the textile sector, the scarcity of food, and the anguish caused by the rebels were producing panic in the country'. Repression was not enough, it was necessary to 'give jobs to the labourers', and with that Carlism would lose social support, for 'only hardship can drag the population to the ignominious life of robbery' (*El Heraldo*, 1, 13 and 24 May 1847).

The extension of the market was adversely affecting the general public. Some provincial authorities decided to paralyse grain extraction from the provinces under their control without backing from the Executive, which prompted a circular from Madrid, dated the 1st of May, ordering that this decision be revoked because of the grave and imminent risk of social confrontation (*La Gaceta*, 3 May 1847). Despite the measures taken by the government, exports continued, prices continued to rise,[34] and the protests became more acute in May, when they extended to Castille and Andalucia where they became very intense. In Leon, a multitude of women, joined by numerous groups of men and children, joined the protest in the early days of May. They insulted and stoned the authorities and the houses of merchants, smashed doors, and confronted troops, resulting in the imprisonment of many people (*El Heraldo*, 10, 12 May 1847, and 3 June 1847). According to *El Heraldo* (12 May 1847), the unrest might be eased if the local authorities announced that the price of wheat would be cut from 20 reales per hemina (18 litres) to 14; that out-shipments were prohibited, and that unemployed labourers were going to be given work; in addition to asking neighbours to contribute to the relief of those most in need. The paper's correspondent blamed the authorities:

'Such a sudden rise, setting aside its cause, deserves the immediate attention of the authorities. The previous harvest was abundant and there was no reason to fear the advent of this shortage; therefore, either this increase is fictitious and those who produce such results deserve to be punished; or it is the result of a large and rapid extraction against which one should make provision in advance, because it seems impossible to me that they do not know that bread is the only food, it might be said, in this country and that in the major part of it, there is no substitute for bread.'

There were also protests in Becerril and Fuentes de Nava (in Palencia province) and others that did not end peacefully in Valladolid, Burgos, Zamora and Ponferrada (*Eco del Comercio*, 28 March 1847; *El Heraldo*, 12 and 14 May, 1 and 12 June 1847).

In Andalucia, where a significant number of workers relied exclusively on their wages and access to relief was very limited (Florencio and López, 2000), the riots reached a

---

[34] In the second half of May wheat reached 45.4 ptas/hl. in Huelva, 47.7 ptas/hl in Cádiz, and between 50.4 and 54.4 ptas/hl in Algeciras (*La Gaceta*, 31 May 1847)

major intensity. In May, the situation was so critical that the executive authorized some southern provinces to import foreign grain, regardless of price. In the same way, it authorised the municipal governments to use local funds or ask for loans (*La Gaceta*, 9 May 1847), measures that did not prevent serious disturbances in the provinces of Granada and, above all, Seville. In mid-March, anxiety began to be noticeable among the Cordoban labourers who roamed around the city begging for money, and there was a riot in Montilla (*El Heraldo*, 19 March, 25 May 1847). In Granada, the conflict started on the 4th of May. The cause was unemployment. The authorities had promised work to a large number of labourers, but not all of them were given work. Feeling betrayed, they rebelled against the authorities, aiming their hatred at the political chief and traders. Even though troops were put on alert, a multitude, including a considerable presence of women, stoned the house of a merchant, who was at the time a provincial official, and plundered the bakeries. Riots continued during the afternoon, martial law was imposed, and there were four deaths. The situation repeated itself at the end of the month (*El Heraldo*, 10, 11 May 1847; *Eco del Comercio*, 2, 15 June 1847).

There were riots in Carmona on the 3rd of May, ending in one death.[35] Shortly afterwards the unrest spread to Seville where, even though there did not seem to be a shortage of wheat, speculation had raised the price from the beginning of the year on. A few days before the uprising the price of wheat in the grain exchange rose to 104 reales per fanega, [46.8 pts/hl] and bread reached 40 cuartos per three-pound loaf. The anxiety of the people grew, while the authorities vacillated. The recent events in Carmona offered a disturbing precedent. From early May handbills were appearing throughout the city inciting people to rebellion and the Municipal Government, fearing social upheaval, called on the biggest taxpayers to provide the population with food and proclaimed an edict for the intervention of the grain market and imposing a duty on bread. As a consequence of the edict, the bakers of Alcalá de Guadaira failed to appear at the Seville market on the 7th because, said the Mayor, 'they could not sell their bread without loss at the prices given'. At seven in the morning, there was no bread left. This prompted a riot, led by women who blamed the authorities for the situation. To shouts of 'bread, death to the authorities, death to the political elite' they headed for the tobacco factory, where some two thousand 'cigarreras' had gathered, whence they marched to Triana and to other neighbourhoods, as the number of protestors was swollen by workers who abandoned their duties on the public works, increasing the crowd to over ten thousand people. On their arrival at the town hall, windows were shattered, the political chief was injured and the authorities were insulted. The situation seemed out of control. The Captain General of Andalucía, Juan de la Pezuela, assumed total power and gave free rein to the army. He ordered out the troops, who began firing at the rebels, resulting in the death of a boy of twelve years and about twenty further injuries, several of them serious. The Ayuntamiento of Seville met urgently and decided to subsidize the price of bread,

---

[35] *El Heraldo*, 10 May 1847. From then on there was an air of increasing tension regarding increases in the price of bread. The local authorities promised a reduction that would place it at 18 or 20 cuartos per loaf, but on the 3rd the Ayuntamiento passed an edict announcing that the price adjustment could not be effected. The people felt deceived and formed themselves into numerous groups who attacked the mayor, municipal officials, and the police. The political leader promised to deal with the demands of the people, 'but without making any concession to the rioters'.

and asked the Captain General to allow the free trade of cereals, preventing monopolization of the trade. At the same time, relief groups were formed to activate public and private charity. From the 10th calm was restored, while wheat arrived from outer regions and cheap bread was distributed.[36] In the following week, the protests spread to Écija and toward the end of the month they extended to Utrera and El Arahal (*El Heraldo*, 14 May, 1 June 1847). Around the same dates in Guadalcanal (in the mountains north of Seville) labourers rose in protest against low wages.[37] In Cádiz, Jerez, and Málaga timely action by the authorities prevented the tension from escalating out of control, but there were riots in Ronda (Málaga), Úbeda, and Baeza (Jaén) (*El Heraldo*, 12 March, 12–14, 18, 25 May, 1 June 1847, Kondo, 1990: 111); *Eco del Comercio*, 18 May 1847). In many communities in Almería, where the pressure on agricultural resources had a knock-on effect on temporary migrants to Western Andalucía (Florencio and López, 2000), there was also tension. Countless destitute people roamed around the province, prompting an edgy government to provide them with barley bread (*Guía del Comercio y Boletín de Fomento*, 10 March 1847; *El Heraldo*, 12 June 1847).

There was unrest too in Extremadura and in the Meseta Sur. In Villanueva de la Serena, Don Benito, and Villafranca de los Barros (Badajoz) women protested their extradition to Portugal (*El Heraldo*, 24 May, 1 June 1847). In Calzada de Calatrava and Ballesteros (Ciudad de Real province), there was disorder when indigenous workers protested against the presence of outsiders, who were beaten and maltreated. The protestors threatened the mayor that they would set fire to the grain fields if he persisted in employing workers from elsewhere (*El Heraldo*, 26 May, 5 June 1847). Madrid, which suffered the most acute crisis of the reign of Isabel II, was the object of particular concern as the capital of the monarchy. The Ayuntamiento discussed the issue of subsistence at various sessions between January and March called specifically to analyse the shortage.[38] On 11th April, with bread prices on the rise, there was unrest in the city centre. During the Queen's promenade, Espartero and the National Army were shouted at, and the radical *Himno de Riego* was sung. Some politicians worried about the very viability of the Moderate regime, and one of its most qualified representatives, Pidal, warned that 'if panic increases, if these misbehaviours occur again... capital will flee' (cited in Comellas,

---

[36] On events in Seville, *El Heraldo*, 12, 18 March, 8, 11–15, 18, 20 May 1847. *Eco del Comercio*, 12, 13, 18 May 1847. The municipal law forced the warehousemen to inform the authorities within two days of quantities stored, where they were held, and daily transactions; hidden wheat would be confiscated and transported to the municipal warehouse where a third would be given to the party who informed the authorities, if such existed. The remaining two-thirds remained in the municipal warehouse. Bakers were obliged to make public at place of sale the prices directed by the commissions of the Ayuntamiento, and those same prices should operate in the ovens and grocery shops, where they should be displayed in public; any adulteration, whether in the quantity or quality of the bread, would be punished by disqualification and heavy fines. While the scarcity lasted bakers should bring all the bread they had on hand to the markets, and indeed the bakers of de Alcalá de Guadaira were being forced to bake less to prevent them from selling it in Seville.
[37] *El Heraldo*, 5 June 1847. Andalucian labourers did not receive a daily wage. They worked about two hundred days a year (Bernal, 1979: 414).
[38] Fernández (1986: 207). The Ayuntamiento estimated that a third of the population, about 75,000 persons, might be deemed poor and requiring assistance, but that the production of inexpensive bread, consisting of mixed grains, would cost more than one million reales fortnightly, which would exhaust municipal funds within two or three months.

1970: 249). Faced with the huge rise in bread prices, citizens voiced their complaints to the Municipal Government, which decided on 11the may to ask the government for help, in order to 'put an end to the monopoly... that is victimising Madrid as a whole'. The crisis mainly affected the poor, who blamed the authorities for the scarcity and for being lenient with speculators. Yet even though there were moments of unrest, harsh public order measures prevented street violence.

The disturbances ceased during the summer, although prices had not dropped much by June. Prices did drop from July in the areas where harvesting had started. On 26th July *La Gaceta* noted that 'prices follow the same irregular path even now', but in fact they were on a downward trend. By the end of July, the Government considered the danger over. On the 23rd it lifted the ban on cereal exports and taxes were restored to their pre-March levels (*BOPA*, 6 August 1847).

How did the authorities react to the popular protests? Not only did the goverment's measures regulating the grain trade fail to ease popular unrest, but in many cases, they exacerbated it for the want of action. No measure of a general nature was applied. Evasion, along with measures ranging from paternalist protectionism to harsh repression, was the norm. In any case, the municipalities ended up being the key players so that it was possible to mitigate the crisis and control the protests. Sometimes free trade in grain was prohibited, and traders were forced to set aside a specific amount of grain to meet popular needs (*El Heraldo*, 12, 14 May 1847, 1 June 1847; *Eco del Comercio*, 13 May 1847). The municipalities financed bread consumption, either distributing bread of a lower quality freely or selling it below cost price; and they controlled the production process so that the price of bread was adjusted to that of wheat (*El Heraldo*, 19 May 1847). Recourse to public works in the form of construction and road repairs in order to provide work was a frequent occurrence (*El Heraldo*, 9 March 1847; *Eco del Comercio*, 22 March 1847, 18 April 1847). Nonetheless, the municipalities were constrained by their limited monetary resources (Comín, 1996: 195; Sáiz Milanés, 1852: 475), which explains their willingness to encourage private charity, opening voluntary subscriptions among the inhabitants and ordering compulsory collections among the richer classes, the latter not always successful.[39] It was the institutional authority that frequently helped impose a variant of the 'Speenhamland' British system of the late 18th century, i.e. paupers were subsidised in the interest of public order. In Andalucía, labourers were allocated among farmers and landowners who paid them partly in kind, and partly in money (Bernal, 1979: 415–417). This suggests that landowners who, unlike traders, were safe from popular attacks, were in a position to bear this exceptional cost of excess labour.

---

[39] Many of these measures were applied during later protests (Arrier, 1984). The successes of Granada and Seville moved the authorities to take preventive measures through the importation of flour from Gibraltar, the operation of public works, and the voluntary subscriptions of local notables, which in the third week of May had already realized 118,850 reales (*El Heraldo*, 12 March, 13, 18, 25 May 1847). In Jerez the mayor called on proprietors to help ease the crisis. A subscription was raised, as in Cádiz, and in addition the Ayuntamiento financed the sale of bread at below the market price (*El Heraldo*, 12, 18 May 1847) In Málaga, the Ayuntamiento acquired between 5,000 and 6,000 fanegas [2,775 hl and 3,330 hl] of wheat for public use, paid for by a donation from the Chamber of Commerce (Kondo 1990: 111) The city's French consul hoped that these means would be enough 'pour calmer l'irritation que l'augmentation du prix du pain a causé depuis deux jours dans les faubourgs de cette ville' (cited by Sánchez Albornoz, 1963: 22).

All these measures involved, in one way or another, interfering with the market and amounted to deviations from liberal economic orthodoxy, but this was accepted in the interest of social order, deemed in liberal ideology a necessary condition for economic growth and both social and political stability. On top of this, the state had at its disposal an important instrument of persuasion against popular protests, viz. the Vagrancy Law, which treated the indigent like potential criminals and penalised beggars with confinement in designated places for up to three years (Díaz, 1998: 229). Furthermore, there always remained the armed forces to re-establish social stability, and their actions resulted in losses of life and the imprisonment of large numbers of people. It is significant that the number of arrests by the police in 1847 was greater than in the previous year: 21,701 versus 18,436 (Martínez, 1982: 205–206).

The crisis evolved against a complex political background, in which the Queen's marital problems risked unleashing a national crisis, and instability marked the period. Between February 1846 and September 1847, there were nine different governments, the so-called 'Ephemeral Governments' (Comellas, 1970: 213–251). At the zenith of the crisis during the first half of 1847, there were three different governments; those presided over by Istúriz, the Duque of Sotomayor, and Pacheco. These ministerial changes, usually accompanied by changes of political officials in the provinces, were bound to undermine the effectiveness of governmental measures. The crisis coincided with the rule of the 'puritans', who were ready to govern according to more liberal criteria, reinforcing the power of the civil administration and removing the army from a leading role (Ballbé, 1985: 154–159). Social unrest, however, contributed to the stalling of the reformist projects of the puritans, who had conceded amnesty and even begun to move closer to the progressives. The progressives, despite the electoral manipulation of moderate governments, were able to win forty parliamentary members in the elections of December 1846 (Santillán, 1996: 302). The Moderates' hard core, headed by Narváez, frowned on the inclinations of the progressive party, some of whose members showed a certain interest, falling short of enthusiasm, in Fourierism, which they would soon abandon (Elorza, 1970). In March 1847 *La Atracción* was published, edited by Fernando Garrido, 'whose mission was to defend and to spread social science...needed then more than ever, since *the terrible issue of subsistence in Europe...* had produced countless victims of the hardships of hunger and misery' (Garrido, 1868–69: 938–939). The *Eco de Comercio*, identified with the progressive movement, lent its pages in July to a Fourierist sympathiser, Francisco J. Moya, who published a text defending both the association and the universal suffrage within a new social order, 'in which, while acquired property is recognised, the humblest worker can participate by right...Only then will the unrest that leads to violence disappear' (Elorza, 1970: 148–154; Maluquer, 1977: 287; *Eco del Comercio*, 9 July 1847). Neither moderate politicians nor the oligarchies they represented could tolerate the spread of ideas that, even discreetly, criticised a property system that was the cornerstone of Moderate ideology. The wish of many proprietors for a rural police force that would protect property rights was realised in by-laws approved by the Government on 8th November 1849 (García Sanz, 1980; Díaz, 1998: 227). The propertied classes could not countenance either the projects of Patricio de la Escosura, aimed at containing the influence of the military on the administration. Perhaps social unrest helped to explain the abandonment of reform and the puritan platform. Despite the prospect of a good harvest, prices remained high in early 1848. Social unrest was palpable and a shadow was cast by the storms of events elsewhere. The executive opted for preemptive repression. In October 1847, Narváez was in power and on the 26th of November he circulated a letter to the municipalities ordering them to finance a secret police force, for Narváez was convinced that this was 'a sad need of modern societies' (cited in Salort, 1996: 354). One of his ministers, Sartorius, repealed the reforms of Escosura, substituting for them the creation of district administrators who increased the power of the executive on the municipalities and reinforced the social order mechanism (Díaz, 1998: 112). The Moderates were preparing for the convulsions of 1848.

V. Conclusions

In 1847 there was a food crisis which translated into a dramatic price rise, especially between January and May. Despite the lack of reliable data, it seems reasonable to suppose that different factors were acting in concert to produce a crisis: a decrease in cereal production, an increase in exports, and trading conditions which, amid rumours of scarcity, favoured speculation and cornering the market. The crisis was inscribed in a process of expansion of agrarian capitalism which, although in the long run improved the living conditions of the population, nonetheless in the short run, given unfavourable factors, could increase social inequality, and reduce living standards as well. The increase in grain prices reduced real wages.

In a context of political and social tension, the government, worried about threats to the social order, banned grain exports and allowed the introduction of foreign cereals from March on, in order to reduce prices. The decision, benefitting the poorer consumers but harming the interests of harvesters and traders, was taken at a time in which the free trade movement was on the ascendant, but did not command total acceptance, as illustrated by the parliamentary debate that ensued and the resistance it unleashed. Hence, the measure could not be applied systematically by some local authorities and municipalities who found themselves pressurised by proprietors and speculators, and trapped in the paradoxical situation of having to guarantee the grain supply to the people and foregoing any revenue that might normally accrue from the grain trade. The authorities were unable to prevent the sudden outbreak of mass protests throughout much of the country, protests that lay bare old grievances of the poor classes. The proximate cause of unrest varied according to region. Whereas in Andalucía, Extremadura and the Meseta Sur they seemed to stem from a desire for better working conditions, elsewhere the focus was on consumption or the tax burden. In any case, disturbances forced the intervention of the public authorities and helped redistribute basic resources using mechanisms that sidestepped the market.

The protests, even though lacking direct political content and directed towards those who cornered the food market rather than at the landed proprietors, coincided with a period of high ministerial instability and the re-appearance of Carlism, raising alarm among the Moderate leadership. The answer (although not the only one) was repression. As far as their wealthy supporters were concerned, privation was something unavoidable and inherent in the economic system, and only in extreme situations was it necessary to take measures, not to eradicate misery, but to soften it in order to avoid a questioning of the existing social order. The authorities therefore began to monitor the market, and forced both a subsidy on the price of bread, and the employment of the poor by farmer-proprietors. The latter was an extra cost that, for the moment, was considered bearable by the proprietors. At the same time, the Government relied on the municipalities to enact certain measures, particularly public works, but they were very constrained by their lack of resources.

Figure 13.3 Popular unrest and riots, 1847

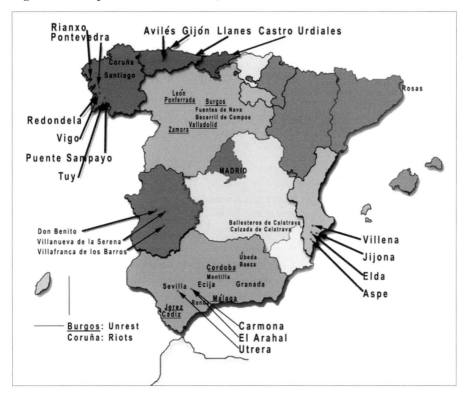

The development of the crisis coincided with the accession to power by the most liberal sector of the moderates, 'puritans' intent on turning the political system in a more liberal direction, and extending a hand to the progressives. The popular protests, nonetheless, alarmed the powerful, who constituted the social base of 'moderantismo', whose hard core frustrated the intention to make space in the centres of political decision-making for broader political and social centres. Military hegemony and centralisation, forces which the puritans had attempted to control, emerged, and were in fact strengthened by the crisis. The opening of the Estado and the strengthening of the liberal regime would now have to wait some more years.

Bibliography

Almenar, S. and Velasco, R. (1987) 'Una etapa en la consolidación del libre cambio en España: el viaje de Richard Cobden por Andalucía (1846)', in G. Ruiz (ed.) *Andalucía en el pensamiento económico*, Málaga, pp. 105–118.

Anes, G. (1970) *Las crisis agrarias en la España moderna*, Madrid.

Arriero, M.L. (1984) 'Los motines de subsistencias en España, 1895–1905', *Estudios de Historia Social*, 30, pp. 193–250.

Ballbé, M. (1985) *Orden público y militarismo en la España constitucional (1812–1983)*, Madrid.

Barquín, R. (1997a) 'La integración del mercado del trigo en el siglo XIX', in *VI Congreso de la Asociación de Historia Económica* (Gerona, 15–17 September 1997), pp. 55–64.

Barquín, R. (1997b) 'Transporte y precio del trigo en el siglo XIX. Creación y reordenación del mercado nacional', *Revista de Historia Económica*, 1, pp. 17–48.

Barquín, R. (1999a) 'El precio del trigo en España (1814–1833)', *Historia Agraria*, 17, pp. 177–218.

Barquín, R. (1999 b) 'El comercio de la harina entre Castilla y Santander y la crisis de subsistencia de 1856/57', in J. Torras and B. Yun (eds), *Consumo, condiciones de vida y comercialización. Cataluña y Castilla, siglos XVII–XIX*, Valladolid, pp. 293–309.

Barquín, R. (2001) *Precios del trigo e índices de consumo en España. 1765–1883*, Burgos.

Boletín Oficial del Ministerio de Comercio, Instrucción y Obras Públicas (1847), Madrid.

Calatayud, S., Millán, J. and Romeo, Mª.C. (1996) 'La noblesa propietaria en la societat valenciana del segle XIX. El comte de Ripalda i la gestió del seu patrimoni', *Recerques*, 33, pp. 79–101.

Calatayud, S., Millan, J. and Romeo, Mª.C. (2000) 'El rentismo nobiliario en la agricultura valenciana del siglo XIX', *Revista de Historia Económica*, 1, pp. 79–107.

Comellas, J.L. (1970) *Los moderados en el poder*, Madrid.

Comín, F. (1990) *Las cuentas de la hacienda preliberal en España (1800–1855)*, Madrid.

Comín, F. (1996) *Historia de la Hacienda Pública, II. España (1808–1995)*, Barcelona.

Del Moral, J. (1979) *La agricultura española a mediados del siglo XIX, 1850–1870. Resultados de una encuesta agraria de la época*, Madrid.

Díaz Marín, P. (1998) *Después de la revolución. Centralismo y burguesía en Alicante, 1844–1854*, Alicante.

Díaz Marín, P. (2000a) 'Oligarquía y fiscalidad. Los primeros pasos de la contribución de inmuebles, cultivo y ganadería en la provincia de Alicante', *Revista de Historia Económica*, 2, pp. 309–338.

Díaz Marín, P. (2000b) 'Antecedentes históricos del trasvase del Júcar: La utopía hidráulica de la burguesía alicantina en el siglo XIX', in *Congreso nacional. Gestión del agua en cuencas deficitarias* (Orihuela, 5–7 October 2000).

Díaz Marín, P. (2003). 'Crisis de subsistencia y protesta popular: los motines de 1847', *Historia Agraria*, 30, pp. 31–62.

'Dictamen que la sección de cereales somete a la aprobación de la junta general de información creada por Real decreto de 4 de marzo de 1847' (1979), in R. Garrabou (ed.), *Agricultura y Sociedad*, 10, pp. 339–375.

Domínguez Martín, R. (1997). 'Autoconsumo, mercado y niveles de vida en la España atlántica, 1750–1900', in *VIII Congreso de Historia Agraria*, Salamanca, pp. 57–72.

Dowe, D., Haupt, H-G. and Langewiesche, D. (eds) (1998) *Europa 1848. Revolution und Reform*, Bonn.

Elorza, A. (1970) *Socialismo utópico español*, Madrid.

Escrivá, J.L. and Llopis, E. (1987) 'La integración del mercado triguero en la Castilla la Vieja-León del Antiguo Régimen: avance y estancamiento, *Hacienda Pública*, 108–109, pp. 117–128.

Fernández, A. (1986) 'La crisis de subsistencias en el Madrid del siglo XIX', in A. Bahamonde and L.E. Otero (eds), *Madrid en la sociedad del siglo XIX*, Madrid, vol. 2, pp. 191–228.

Figuerola, L. (1991) *Escritos Económicos*, edición y estudio preliminar de Francisco Cabrillo, Madrid.

Florencio, A. and López, A.L. (2000) 'El trabajo asalariado en la agricultura de la Baja Andalucía. Siglos XVIII y XIX', *Historia Agraria*, 21, pp. 99–126.

Fontana, J. (1979) *La crisis del Antiguo régimen, 1808–1833*, Barcelona.

Forcadell, C. (1995) 'La difusión de la pequeña propiedad en Aragón durante el siglo XIX: estrategias campesinas hacia la proletarización', in J.Mª Donézar and M. Pérez Ledesma (eds) *Antiguo Régimen y liberalismo*, Madrid, vol. 2, pp. 507–517.

Fradera, J.Mª (1984) 'El comercio de cereales y la prohibición de 1820 (el caso del mercado catalán)', *Agricultura y Sociedad*, 30, pp. 137–167.

Gallego, D. (2001) 'Historia de un desarrollo pausado: integración mercantil y transformaciones productivas de la agricultura española (1880–1936)', in VV.AA., *El pozo de todos los males. Sobre el atraso en la agricultura española contemporánea*, Barcelona, pp. 147–214.

García Sanz, A. (1980) 'Jornales agrícolas y presupuesto familiar campesino en España a mediados del siglo XIX', *Anales de CUNEF*, pp. 49–71.

Garrabou, R. (1980) 'Un testimonio de la crisis de subsistencia de 1856–57: el expediente de la Dirección General de Comercio', *Agricultura y Sociedad*, 14, pp. 268–356.

Garrabou, R. (1987) 'Salarios y proletarización en la agricultura catalana de mediados del siglo XIX', *Hacienda Pública Española*, 108–109, pp. 343–359.

Garrabou, R. and Sanz, J. (1985) *Historia agraria de la España contemporánea. 2. Expansión y crisis (1850–1900)*, Barcelona.

Garrabou, R., Tello, E. and Roca, A. (1999) 'Preus del blat i salaris agrícoles a Catalunya (1720–1936), in *Doctor Jordi Nadal: La industrialització i el desenvolupament econòmic a Espanya*, Barcelona, vol. 1, pp. 422–460.

Garrido, F. (1868–1869) *Historia del reinado del último Borbón de España*, Barcelona.

Gutiérrez Bringas, M.A. (1993) 'La productividad de la tierra en España 1752–1930: tendencia a largo plazo', *Revista de Historia Económica*, 3, pp. 505–538.

Gutierrez Bringas, M.A. (1997) 'El intento de reconstruir una variante del nivel de vida del campesinado: los salarios agrícolas en España, 1765–1935', *VIII Congreso de Historia Agraria,* Salamanca, pp. 72–90.

Hoyo, A. (1999) 'Gestión comercial, precios y crisis de subsistencias en Castilla, 1820–1874', in J. Torras and B. Yun (eds) *Consumo, condiciones de vida y comercialización. Cataluña y Castilla, siglos XVII–XIX,* Valladolid, pp. 275–291.

Royal Commission (1849) *Informe presentado a las Juntas Generales de Agricultura de 1849 por su comisión novena, sobre las causas que contribuyen a que muchas de nuestras producciones agrícolas sean más caras que las de otras naciones. Y memoria sobre los remedios de estas causas, escrita por el Excmo. Sr. D. Mariano Miguel de Reinoso, Presidente de la misma comisión, y Comisario Regio para la inspección general de la Agricultura del Reino,* Madrid.

Kondo, A. Y. (1990) *La agricultura española del siglo XIX,* Madrid.

Lana Berasain, J.M. (2002) 'Jornales, salarios, ingresos. Aproximación a la evolución de los niveles de vida desde la Navarra rural, 1801–1935', in J.M. Martínez Carrión (ed.), *El nivel de vida en la España rural, siglos XVIII–XX,* Alicante, pp. 183–233.

Llopis, E. (1983) 'Algunas consideraciones acerca de la producción agraria castellana en los veinticinco últimos años del Antiguo Régimen', *Investigaciones Económicas,* 21, pp. 135–151.

Lluch, E. (1988) 'La 'gira triomfal' de Cobden per Espanya (1846)', *Recerques,* 21, pp. 71–90.

Madrazo, S. (1981) 'Precios del transporte y tráfico de mercancías en la España de finales del Antiguo Régimen', *Moneda y Crédito,* 159, pp. 39–71.

Maluquer, J. (1977) *El socialismo en España, 1833–1868,* Barcelona.

Martín, M. (2000) 'La enseñanza de la economía en España hasta la Ley Moyano', in E. Fuentes Quintana (ed.) *Economía y economistas españoles. La economía clásica,* pp. 593–619.

Martínez Carrión, J.M. (2002) 'El nivel de vida en la España rural, siglos XVIII–XX. Nuevos enfoques, nuevos resultados', in J.M. Martínez Carrión (ed.) *El nivel de vida en la España rural, siglos XVIII–XX,* Alicante, pp. 15–72.

Martínez Carrión, J.M. and Pérez Castejón, J.J. (2002) 'Creciendo con desigualdad. Niveles de vida biológicos en la España rural mediterránea desde 1840', in J.M. Martínez Carrión (ed.) *El nivel de vida en la España rural, siglos XVIII–XX,* Alicante, pp. 405–460.

Martínez Vara, T. (1997) 'Una estimación del coste de la vida en Santander, 1800–1860', *Revista de Historia Económica,* 1, pp. 87–125.

Martínez Vara, T. (1999) 'La integración del mercado del trigo en el Norte y la Castilla del Duero, 1800–1860. Algunas reflexiones', *Historia Agraria,* 19, pp. 43–73.

Marx, K. (1985) *Las luchas de clases en Francia de 1848 a 1850,* Madrid.

Millán, J. (1999) *El poder de la tierra. La sociedad agraria del Bajo Segura en la época del liberalismo, 1830–1890.*

Moreno, J. (1995) 'Protección arancelaria, distorsiones de mercado y beneficios extraordinarios: la producción de harinas en Castilla la Vieja, 1820–1841', *Revista de Historia Económica,* 2, pp. 227–250.

Moreno, J. (2001) 'Precios de las subsistencias, salarios nominales y niveles de vida en Castilla la Vieja. Palencia, 1751–1861, *Documento de trabajo de la AHE*, 0101, Madrid.

Moreno, J. (2002) 'Fiscalidad y revueltas populares en Castilla la Vieja y León durante el Bienio Progresista, 1854–1856', *Congreso internacional Orígenes del Liberalismo. Universidad, Política, Economía*, Salamanca.

Nadal Farreras, J. (1978) *Comercio exterior y subdesarrollo. España y Gran Bretaña de 1772 a 1914: Política económica y relaciones comerciales*, Madrid.

Pan-Montojo, J. (1994) 'Lógica legal y lógica social de la Contribución de Consumos y los Derechos de Puertas', *Hacienda Pública Española*, 1, pp. 17–229.

Paredes, F.J. (1991) *Pascual Madoz, 1805–1870, Libertad y Progreso en la monarquía isabelina*, Pamplona.

Peiró, A. (1987) 'El mercado de cereales y aceites aragoneses (siglos XVII–XX)', *Agricultura y Sociedad*, 43, pp. 213–279.

Pérez Moreda, V. (1980) *Las crisis de mortalidad en la España interior. Siglos XVI–XIX*, Madrid.

Pérez Moreda, V. (1985) 'La modernización demográfica, 1800–1930', in Sánchez-Albornoz (ed.) *La modernización económica de España*, Madrid, pp. 25–62.

Pirala, A. (1875–1879) *Historia contemporánea. Anales desde 1843 hasta la conclusión de la actual guerra civil*, Madrid.

Prados de la Escosura, L. (1982) 'Comercio exterior y cambio económico en España (1792–1849), in J. Fontana (ed.) *La economía española al final del Antiguo Régimen III. Comercio y colonias*, Madrid, pp. 171–249.

Prados de la Escosura, L. (1988) *De imperio a nación. Crecimiento y atraso económico en España (1780–1930)*, Madrid.

Reboredo, J.D. (1987) 'El motín del pan de 1856 en Castilla la Vieja', in VV.AA., *Crisis demográfica y tensiones sociales en la Castilla del siglo XIX*, Valladolid, pp. 117–204.

Reher, D. and Ballesteros, E. (1993) 'Precios y salarios en Castilla la Nueva: la construcción de un índice de salarios reales, 1501–1991', *Revista de Historia Económica*, 1, pp. 101–151.

Ringrose, D. (1972) *Los transportes y el estancamiento económico de España*, Madrid.

Robledo, R. (1993) *Economistas y reformadores españoles: La cuestión agraria (1760–1935)*, Madrid.

Roca de Togores, J. (1986) 'Memoria sobre el estado de la agricultura en la provincia de Alicante. 1849', in J. Vidal (ed.), *Materiales para la historia económica de Alicante, 1850–1900*, Alicante.

Ruiz, D. (1981) *Asturias Contemporánea*, Madrid.

Sáez, M.A. (1995) 'Aparición y difusión de la patata en Álava durante la primera mitad del siglo XIX', in J.M. Donézar and M. Pérez Ledesma (eds), *Antiguo Régimen y liberalismo. Homenaje a Miguel Artola. 2. Economía y Sociedad*, Madrid.

Sáiz Milanés, J. (1973) 'Origen e historia de los bienes de propios', in F. Estapé (ed.), *Textos olvidados*, Madrid, pp. 443–189.

Salort, S. (1996) *La Hacienda local en la España Contemporánea. La Hacienda municipal de Alicante*, Unpublished PhD Thesis, Universidad de Alicante.

Salort, S. (1997) *La Hacienda local en la España Contemporánea. La Hacienda municipal de Alacant*, Alicante.

Sánchez-Albornoz, N. (1963) *Las crisis de subsistencia de España en el siglo XIX*, Rosario.

Sánchez-Albornoz, N. (1975) *Los precios agrícolas durante la segunda mitad del siglo XIX*, vol. 1, Madrid.

Sánchez-Albornoz, N. (1977) 'La crisis de subsistencias de 1857', in *España hace un siglo: una economía dual*, Madrid, pp. 27–67.

Santillán, R. (1996) *Memorias, 1808–1856*, Madrid.

Sanz, G. and Ramiro, D. (2002) 'Infancia, mortalidad y niveles de vida en la España interior', in Martínez Carrión (ed.), pp. 359–404.

Segura, A. (1983) 'El mercat de cereals i llegums a Barcelona, 1814–1868', *Recerques*, 14, pp. 177–213.

Serrano, R. (1999) 'Los salarios reales en Valladolid, 1760–1875: resultados e interrogantes, in J. Torras and B. Yun (eds), *Consumo, condiciones de vida y comercialización. Cataluña y Castilla, siglos XVII–XIX*, Valladolid, pp. 245–271.

Simpson, J. (1989) 'La producción agraria y el consumo español en el siglo XIX', *Revista de Historia Económica*, 2, pp. 364–388.

Simpson, J. (1997) *La agricultura española (1765–1965) la larga siesta*, Madrid.

Thompson, E.P. (1995) *Costumbres en común*, Barcelona.

Tortella, G. (1975) *Los orígenes del capitalismo en España. Banca, industria y ferrocarriles en el siglo XIX*, Madrid.

Tortella, G. (1985) 'Producción y productividad agraria en España, 1830–1930', in N. Sánchez-Albornoz (ed.), *La modernización económica de España*, Madrid, pp. 63–88.

Tortella, G. (1994) *El desarrollo de la España contemporánea. Historia económica de los siglos XIX y XX*, Madrid.

Vallejo, R. (1990) 'Pervivencia de las formas tradicionales de protesta: los motines de 1892', *Historia social*, 8, pp. 3–27.

Vallejo, R. (1996) 'El impuesto de consumos y la resistencia antifiscal en la España de la segunda mitad del siglo XIX: un impuesto no exclusivamente urbano', *Revista de Historia Económica*, 2, pp. 339–370.

Vallejo, R. (2001) *Reforma tributaria y fiscalidad sobre la agricultura en la España liberal, 1845–1900*, Zaragoza.

Vicedo, E. (1983) 'Els preus dels cereals al mercat de Lleida durant la primera meitat del segle XIX', *Recerques*, 14, pp. 167–176.

Yun, B. (1991) 'Mercado de cereal y burguesía en Castilla, 1750–1868. (Sobre el papel de la agricultura en el crecimiento económico regional', in B. Yun (ed.), *Estudios sobre el capitalismo agrario, crédito e industria en Castilla (Siglos XIX y XX)*, pp. 47–76.

14 A disaster seen from the periphery. The case of Denmark

Ingrid HENRIKSEN, University of Copenhagen

This chapter demonstrates how the mid-19th century European subsistence crisis, while leaving its trace on the living conditions of the poorest part of the population, had no long lasting negative effects on Danish society.[1] In fact, the long term effects were favourable. First of all, the positive development in the terms of trade and the removal of the Corn Laws considerably increased the commercialisation of Danish agriculture. Second, the economic gain to agriculture in Denmark strengthened the bargaining power of the peasantry under the free constitution from 1849.[2] Thus the loss of many a European seems to have been the gain of the Danes.

I. The pre-crisis situation

I.1. The overall view

In a comment on the effects of rising grain prices a prominent 19th-century Danish economist neatly encapsulates the divergent effects of the mid-19th century crisis on this society.

Since Denmark is a predominantly agrarian country, a not inconsiderable part of the working classes will receive their pay in kind whereby they will care little about the price of food. Besides, the economic situation of the population as a whole may be improved substantially exactly because of high grain prices. It is well known in our case that even with ... a moderately good harvest high grain prices will bring wealth to the country and that this wealth, indirectly, will also benefit the urban working classes. (Falbe Hansen and Scharling, 1885: 509)

If this were true for the 1880s, it may be an even better description of the 1840s. At the time when the potato blight first hit the Danish crop in 1845, and before drought diminished the grain harvest in 1846, agriculture played a dominant role in the Danish economy. Furthermore, agriculture's share of total income in Denmark was higher than the European norm for countries at the same per capita income level (Crafts, 1985: chapter 3). Danish GDP per capita is estimated to have been 70 per cent of the United Kingdom's GDP per capita in 1820 and 72 per cent in 1850 (Maddison 1995 pp. 194–195). In his calculation Crafts (1985: 54) sets the 1840 level to 71 per cent of the UK level. These data suggest fairly high agrarian productivity at an early stage, which can mainly be explained by a relatively high land/man ratio.

---

[1] The author is grateful to the participants of the December 2003 Dublin workshop on the potato crisis for their comments, to Søren Rich for sharing the results of his thesis, to Hanne Sjuneson for IT-support and to Ole Hyldtoft and Margit Mogensen for their help.
[2] See below, Section IV.

Figure 14.1 Map of Denmark

What is important when looking at the effects of an agrarian crisis, of course, is how land was distributed. There is no precise and internationally comparable information on the structure of holdings at this time. Hansen (1984: 141) estimates the number of small holdings in Denmark in 1845 to be about 98,000, of which he says 42,000 were houses with so little land attached that they cannot be designated as agricultural holdings proper. Milthers (1934–45: 223) in an estimate for 1834 sets the number of persons living on small holdings to about 169,000 and the number of day labourers in the countryside to 118,000 out of a total population of 1.23 million that year. We will briefly try to estimate what percentage of the population had access to land and what percentage had to buy all or most of their food. The 1845 census shows a category of people who were definitely net buyers of food, namely the about 185,000 day labourers etc. (see Table 14.1 below). In a later publication from 1905 the members of this group were allocated to the occupation to which they were most likely to belong. This recalculation in Table 14.1 gives us an impression of the weight agriculture carried in the occupational structure.

Table 14.1 Population by occupation, 1845

Population by occupation	1845 census per cent	1845 census recalculated per cent
Agriculture	45.5	55.2
Fishing and shipping	2.7	2.7
Manufacturing	20.4	24.7
Trade	3.8	4.4
Day-labourers, unskilled labourers, domestic servants without permanent job	13.7	
Immaterial occupations	6.1	6.2
Renters	3.8	
On public support	3.0	
Unclassified	1.0	6.8
Total	100.0	100.0
Total population, absolute number	1,350,327	

Source: Statistisk Tabelværk, 1905: 160-162
Note: Both the figures by Milthers and the 1845 census figures include everybody being supported by an occupational group that is men, women and children, whether they were working or not.

In both classifications in Table 14.1, live in servants with a permanent job in agriculture (about 20 per cent of those occupied in agriculture) and in other occupational groups are included. Their living conditions were little influenced by the development in food prices since much of their remuneration, board and lodgings was in kind. People in 'immaterial occupations' were mostly better off towns people. Retired people in the countryside often got accommodation and support from the new owner of their farm, especially if the new owner was the son or another family member. Thus, they were little affected by price changes. The same goes for people on public support, at least in principle. Outdoor public relief would be handed out in, for example, oatmeal and firewood. Indoor relief that had become increasingly popular at the time,[3] entailed board and lodging in workhouses etc. We cannot exclude the possibility that the latter form of relief may have involved some stinginess during the later high price period. Thus a report from the public health authorities in Copenhagen records an abnormally high

[3] Towards the middle of the 19th century poorhouses had been built in most Danish towns. In the mid 1880s there were about 375 (Mossin, 2004: chap. 3, p. 21).

incidence of scurvy during the summer of 1846 in public institutions such as prisons and hospitals (*Det kongelige Sundhedskollegiums Forhandlinger,* 1848: 30).

We have no precise records on the share of people in manufacturing and trade etc who were employees in the 1840s. Danish urban occupations were still dominated by small craftsmen. Unmarried journeymen and apprentices stayed with the master and were mainly paid board and lodgings. The employers in manufacturing and trade are expected to have suffered from a deterioration of their terms of trade with agriculture. On the other hand, as the quotation above suggests, people in urban trades stood to benefit from a bigger volume of trade, that is, more demand for their goods, as a consequence of agriculture's gain.

Animal products, while less important in exports, made up 63 per cent of the total production value in agriculture in 1840 (Hansen, 1984: 144). The agricultural census in 1837 found that there were 682 pieces of cattle per 1,000 Danes (*Statistisk Tabelværk* V.C.4 1911: 106). This figure, according to Thomsen (1966: 142) was well below the Irish level but above the level later reached by most European nations, around 1880, although it must be kept in mind that the yield of beef and milk per animal was probably poorer than in some other regions of Europe. The number of pigs per 1,000 inhabitants was only 189. Animal production on smallholdings and small farms in the 1840s was typically for domestic use, one or two cows for milk and a pig to be slaughtered in November. Rural labourers with a small plot of land were often remunerated by some days of horsepower for ploughing etc, like the system in parts of Prussia (see Bass, this volume). While in many ways an exploitative system, it at least allowed poor families to have more production animals on their plot when they did not have to keep a horse. Besides the important income supplement coming from animal production, many small holders were not day labourers in agriculture but supplemented their income from other sources. They were part-time fishermen and sailors or they were craftsmen weaving, making clogs or working in the tile works. Although their real wage was bound to suffer under the crisis, their income base was broader than it would appear from the size of their holdings alone.

We suggest that the Danes were relatively well fed in the 1840s (see Johansen, 1998: 20–21 for a comparison with the other Nordic countries only). Unfortunately, we have no accounts of the calorific intake that could lend themselves to an international comparison. A very rough estimate of the share of the Danish population that was potentially vulnerable to an increase in food prices would be about 356,000 persons or a little more than one quarter of the population. That is, the small landholders[4] and the landless working in agriculture from Milters' 1834 estimate, plus the about 69,000 persons from the category of 'day labourers etc' who the 1845 census reallocates to manufacturing and trade. The extent to which these vulnerable people did indeed suffer during the mid 19th century subsistence crisis very much depended on their dependency on one crop, the potato. That is what the next section will try to examine.

---

[4] In Danish 19th century statistics a small landholder is defined as the owner or the tenant of a plot less than 1 *Tønde Hartkorn*. This was a measure of land quality that depended on local conditions and typically varied between 2 to 6 hectares in size.

I.2. How important were potatoes in Denmark around 1845?

I.2.1. Potatoes as a share of total agricultural production

There are no harvest statistics for Denmark between 1837 and 1875. Instead, we have to rely on the published statistics for cultivated land from 1861 and on estimates of production based on information about yields and prices. The most reliable estimates for potatoes sets the 1837 harvest to 1.6 million *tønder* = 160 million kilograms rising to 185.6 million kilograms in 1861, though according to the authors, the figures were no doubt higher during the (early) 1840s. Around 1880 production had risen to 250–300 million kilograms (Falbe Hansen & Scharling, 1887: 198–197 and 342). The same source estimates the yield of potatoes in 1837 to be about 6.4 (seed potatoes to harvest). The estimate for grain production in 1837 is loose, within a fairly large margin since the peasants, who feared a rise in taxation, apparently underreported the true size. It is assumed to have been between 900 million and 1100 million kilograms rising to 1200 million kilograms in the good harvest year of 1847.

Looking at the share of total arable land in 1861, potatoes were sown on 1.5 per cent of the land increasing to 1.8 per cent in 1881. If we compare this to the harvest figures quoted above the area used for potatoes was very likely smaller in 1837 but larger than 1.5 per cent in the mid 1840s. For the sake of comparison it should be mentioned that 46,6 per cent of the arable land in 1861 was used for grains and most of the remainder for grass, green fodder or fallow. The geographical distribution of potatoes, however, was highly unequal in the 1840s. To a certain extent the regions in which potato crops were most important coincided with the areas (the Danish Isles as opposed to the mainland) in which agrarian discontent was most pronounced in the 1840s. That is especially true in the case of the cottagers' movement, see Section IV below. It could be tempting to interpret this as proof of the potato crisis fuelling agrarian protest. There is, however, nothing in the written records to corroborate this.

To sum up, on the eve of the food crisis potato growing was increasing fairly rapidly in Denmark, though from a low starting point. The potato blight set back this movement for at least a decade and a half. Moreover, the increase in grain prices from the mid 1840s raised the opportunity costs of all other crops, besides potatoes these were rapeseed, hops and linen. (Bjørn 1988, p 147).

A brief look at potato exports may shed further light on the crop choice of Danish farmers. Whereas there seems to have been a small positive net export when we look at the *Statistisk Tabelværk* for the 1840s, according to Falbe Hansen and Scharling (1887: 342–343), in the 1880s Denmark had become a minor net importer.

I.2.2. Potatoes in the Danish diet

The most frequently quoted figure for annual potato consumption per head is a rough estimate for the period 1835–1875. Cohn (1957: 306) sets it to 92 kilograms (250 grams per day), which he thinks to be a bit on the high side for the beginning of the period. This is less than the figure from Rubin (1882) for Copenhagen, see below, but more than the figure from the official statistics net of potatoes used for distilling.

If we look at food consumption in Copenhagen, there is some statistical information about the development during the crisis years. This is of interest since city dwellers are net buyers of food. By the mid 1840s Copenhagen had about 125,000 inhabitants or about 10 per cent of the total population (excluding Schleswig-Holstein). The main source of data for consumption in Copenhagen at this time is the records of the *konsumen*, a duty on all goods carried through the city gates of Copenhagen and the major towns. The opening of the first railway line in 1847 made this duty obsolete and it was abolished in 1850. A fair amount of scepticism is called for regarding the *konsumen* as a source of information on the *absolute* level of consumption of various food items. First, we do not know to what extent it was circumvented. Second, even though the citizens of Copenhagen were net buyers of food there was still some food production, especially of meat of various sorts in the city itself. Third, when it comes to important items like grain and potatoes, we do not know how much was used for purposes other than food for humans; that is for distillation of spirits or for fodder. Finally, this source does not include foods shipped to Copenhagen from abroad, although this is probably a minor issue. Having said that the *konsumen* records of the 1840s will at least provide us with some idea of the *development* in consumption through the 1840s and thus of the possible effect of the food crisis. In 1882 the economist Marcus Rubin summarized the evidence for the years 1838–1849 and his results are replicated below using modern weights.

Table 14.2 Daily imports to Copenhagen of various food items, 1838–1849 (in kilograms per person)

Average of	1838–40	1841–43	1844–46	1847–49
Rye	0.24	0.23	0.25	0.22*
Wheat	0.09	0.10	0.12	0.12*
Barley	0.03	0.03	0.04	0.03
Potatoes	0.23	0.36	0.51	0.30
Beef	0.13	0.13	0.13	0.12
Pork	0.05	0.05	0.05	0.05
Butter	0.05	0.05	0.06	0.06

* Rubin estimates the true consumption of rye and wheat to be 0.46 kg/person.
Source: Rubin, 1882.

After examining the menus in various Copenhagen workhouses, a hospital and an orphanage, Rubin adjusted the consumption of the most important bread grains, rye and wheat, upwards to 0.46 kg per person, per day in the late 1840s. This leaves us with an impression of the proportion of potatoes in the basic diet in Danish towns. Potatoes were not even on the menu every day in these institutions but typically went with certain dishes such as split cod or stews.

While the Copenhagen figures are biased towards the groups in society that were, after all, less susceptible to a decline in the potato harvest, we lack quantitative evidence of the importance of potatoes to the rural poor in various regions. The district medical officer in *Viborg*, Mid Jutland observes in 1844 that

The poor moor land peasant lives on a diet inferior to that of dogs in the towns. Potatoes three times a day with salt or at most a bit of flour dipping, cheese and dry bread for dinner... mostly at summer a spoonful of cabbage boiled with leaf fat. (*Det kongelige Sundhedskollegiums Forhandlinger*, 1846: 49)

Admittedly the evidence on consumption is piecemeal but combined with the production figures of potatoes for 1837 and 1861, a daily intake of 200–300 grams per person is not unrealistic, allowing for non-human consumption and seed. The Copenhagen figures demonstrate that grain, mainly rye, was still by far the dominant basic food in Denmark.[5] This is obviously a major explanation of why the mid 19th century food crisis did not strike as hard in Denmark as in other European countries. The intake of potatoes was lower than that of most other European countries at the time, with the possible exception of France (see, Ó Gráda and Bass, this volume).

II.   The extent of failure

II.1.   The decline in the supply of potatoes

As mentioned already, there are no annual harvest statistics for Denmark for the years in question. A questionnaire was sent by the Danish government to all custom houses at the end of September 1845 asking about the spread of the disease, the estimated damage to the harvest, whether or not potatoes had been exported and whether or not potatoes had been bought for distilling. The answers concerning the harvest damage in 1845 showed large regional variation from next to nothing at that time on the island of *Bornholm* to between 50 and 80 per cent on the other Danish islands and 30 per cent in Eastern Jutland (Mogensen 2002: 62–64). The following years, of course, were to show higher losses all over the country.

It would seem from Table 14.2 that the consumption of potatoes per person in Copenhagen declined in response to the decline in production, which is not surprising. Moreover, the consumption of rye seems to have declined too. At the same time, however, consumption of more income elastic items such as wheat and butter increased a bit, whereas the consumption of beef and pork only went down a little. Possibly, most of the decline in supplies of potatoes (and grain) to Copenhagen was absorbed by an even larger decline in the use of these goods in the distilleries or as feed for animals. From 1841 there are statistical records of the quantity of potatoes used in the distillation of spirits. In 1847 this amounted to 9,480,600 kg out of the total of 19,323,868 kg of potatoes imported into Copenhagen, or 49 per cent. For Copenhagen and the major provincial towns taken together we find that the use of potatoes for spirits reached a temporary maximum of 55,971,200 kg in 1845 and had declined to 27,814,000 kg in 1847 (*Statistisk Tabelværk* 1848, p. 9). The distilling in Copenhagen and the major towns gives a rough picture of the total share of potatoes used for spirits. Unlike in Sweden, 'home distilling' was not widespread in Denmark.

II.2.   The grain supply during the crisis

As in other parts of Northern Europe the harvest of cereals in Denmark must have suffered because of drought in 1846. Solar (1997:118) mentions a decline in wheat production of 25 per cent and in rye of almost 40 per cent in the countries in which these crops were most relevant. Again, as with potatoes, we are left to guess about the effect

---

[5]   When converted into dry-matter the grain intake must be doubled compared to potatoes.

of drought in Denmark. The export of wheat (in tons) declined by 17 per cent whereas
the export of rye and barley declined by 18 per cent from 1846 to 1847, cf. Table 14.3.
These figures could, of course, conceal an even bigger decline in production that would
have left domestic consumers considerably worse off. A new calculation of export quotas
(Rich, 2004: A11) shows an increase in the share of rye, the most important food grain,
from 4.5 per cent in the 1830s to 9.2 per cent in the 1840s. We cannot, however, exclude
the possibility that the share of rye exported remained constant or maybe even declined
temporarily following the bad harvest year of 1846. By all accounts 1847 was a good
harvest year, as in many other parts of Europe. Consequently, 1848 saw a new record in
the export of the most important grains, notably wheat, which was in great demand on
the English market.

Table 14.3 Net exports and terms of trade, 1840–1860

Year	Export in 1,000 tons			Terms of trade index 1870=100
	Wheat	Rye	Barley	
1840	9.2	26.9	88.7	69
1841	12.1	19.2	73.5	73
1842	5.4	6.2	62.8	77
1843	7.5	20.2	74.8	77
1844	18.7	46.9	106.4	76
1845	22.0	41.8	107.5	79
1846	22.3	36.9	114.3	90
1847	18.6	30.4	93.2	103
1848	25.2	47.2	132.1	82
1849	32.8	56.9	163.3	75
1850	26.3	41.8	180.2	74
1851	27.5	28.5	136.6	83
1852	43.9	14.8	117.4	86
1853	30.7	31.9	112.9	94
1854	45.7	27.6	109.0	99
1855	38.5	67.2	129.8	103
1856	63.3	38.3	100.0	104
1857	44.4	27.6	107.3	88
1858	43.9	31.6	100.2	92
1859	51.7	32.2	126.2	91
1860	53.6	25.5	104.2	96

Source: Hansen, 1984: Appendix Tables for export of grain. From 1864 in financial
years beginning in May. For terms of trade: Appendix Table 17.

As for the use of grain for spirits, we find a marked decline in the use of wheat from
1846, while for rye there is only a temporary decline in the use for distilling. When the
rye price plummeted in 1848 it was, once again, widely used for distilling. The use of
other grains such as barley for distilling almost compensates for the decrease in the use
of bread grains during 1845–1848. The decline in the use of some bread grains for

distilling may have meant a decline in the average quality of grain used for human consumption. Thus, the district medical officer in *Aalborg*, Northern Jutland, in his accounts of the food situation in 1846, tells that,

The worse sort of grain which was formerly used for spirits is now used for bread and (this bread) mixed with ergot, corn cockle etc. by its (bad) quality and the large quantity in which it is consumed solely together with potatoes and undrinkable water contributes to the incidence of fevers, rachitis, dyspepsia etc. (*Det kongelige Sundhedskollegiums forhandlinger*, 1848: 34)

II.3.   The effects on prices at home and abroad – the integration with the English grain market

Only the potato price, on an annual basis, remained high in Denmark in the years after 1846 (Figure 14.1). The price, of course, mirrors consecutive years of harvest failures in most of Europe. The Copenhagen market prices of grains increased by 60 to 100 per cent during the first five months of 1847 following speculation by grain and others (Bitsch Christensen, 2002: 696). This development was halted by the anticipation of a good harvest later that year.

Figure 14.2   Price index for selected goods, 1830–1870

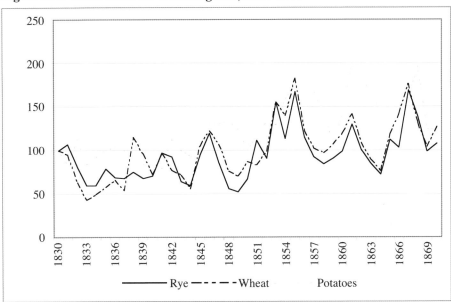

Source: Hansen, 1984: Appendix Table 15.

Looking at grain *exports* it appears that Danish wheat exports suffered a temporary set back in 1847 only to pick up again and to boom during the 1850s and early 1860s. The most interesting feature is the increase in the export of bread grains; wheat mainly going to Britain and rye destined for the Scandinavian market, mainly Norway, and for the Netherlands. This seems logical in the face of the 1840s food crisis and, later on, the crisis following the Crimean war in the late 1850s. In the case of wheat, moreover, the scaling down and subsequent removal of the duty on wheat imported to Britain played an important role.

Rich (2004) has analysed the integration of the Danish and British market for wheat in the 19th century. He generally finds that the markets were integrated early on in the sense that the price swings were parallel and the standard deviations followed each other. In relation to the 1840s in particular, Figure 14.3 shows the price difference between Danish wheat in London and best Danish quality wheat in Copenhagen (assuming that this quality was the most realistic for the sake of comparison). An important point is that only the repeal of the Corn Laws made wheat exports from Denmark profitable. This, of course, was the intention. The years from 1848 to the early 1860s are then an era of a high volume of trade and a price difference of close to 0 as theory on integration predicts.

Figure 14.3 Price difference between London and Copenhagen, net of transport and insurance costs and import duty (shillings per imperial quarter). Best Danish quality (the grey line below), 1845–1875

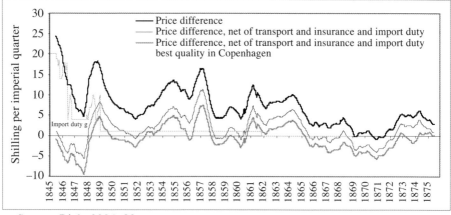

Source: Rich, 2004: 80.

Wheat prices are interesting in so far as wheat was the fastest growing exportable good from Denmark following the demise of the Corn Laws. From 1840 to 1850 wheat increased its share of total export value from 6.2 per cent to 12.6 per cent. The British market took 36 per cent of the Danish wheat exports in the 1830s, 57 per cent in the 1840s and 66 per cent in the 1850s. Moreover, the share of Danish wheat production exported increased from 14 per cent in the 1830s to 28 per cent in the 1840s and 43 per cent in the 1850s. Hence wheat was an important element in the Danish gain from the grain crisis. That said, wheat was still far less important than other grains in domestic production and consumption. The main bread grain was rye and the main grain for export remained barley, which made up 21–22 per cent of the total export value in the 1840s and 1850s.[6] Wheat was a regional product mainly grown in the southern part of The Danish Isles, that is South Zealand, Lolland-Falster and Funen.

---

[6] According to the 1861 census 56,200 hectares were sown with wheat, 189,400 with rye, 274,900

Figure 14.4 Regional price differences in Denmark, 1660–1902. Coefficients of variation for rye, barley and oats

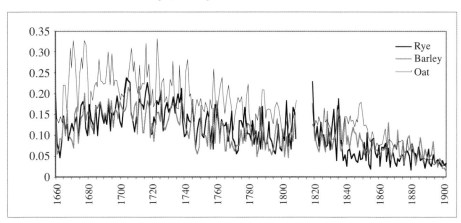

Source: Rich, 2004: 59.

The shipping of grain out of Denmark was not concentrated in a few ports only, it was spread geographically over most parts of the country. Rich (2004: 60) makes the point that the increase in grain exports from the late 1840s thus may have contributed to further integration of the domestic market for grain through growing market orientation and competition awareness. He tested the integration of the Danish grain market using what corresponds to county data[7] for rye, barley and oats. The traditional geographical concentration of wheat production meant that there were too few data for wheat. Figure 14.4 shows a decline in the coefficient of variation for rye in the 1840s and 1850s, which could confirm the possible effect on the integration of the domestic market. Obviously, the effect of local distress, whether it be caused by a decline in the supply of potatoes or grain, would have been lessened by the increased integration.

II.4.   The effect of the crisis on urban trades

Not surprisingly, in view of the previous section, Danish urban trade, by all accounts, was stimulated by the improvement in the terms of trade following the higher grain prices.[8] We find no records of a crisis in the cottage industry, in the crafts or in the small modern sector, which is in strong contrast to the crises found in France (see Vivier, this volume). An expert on the economic history of the Danish urban trades, Hyldtoft (1984: 74–77), characterises the 1840s as 'a time of prosperity'. He points to the effects of the agrarian income boom on the demand for consumer goods from domestic industry.

---

with barley and 27,700 with potatoes.
[7]   The average prices of grain collected for the assessment of tithes.
[8]   We suggest that a temporary decline in manufacturing GDP in 1848 and 1849 (Johansen, 1985: 395) was mainly a crowding out of private business caused by increased state expenditure during the period 1848–50. Thus the long rates of interest increased by 1 percentage point (*Kreditmarkedsstatistik* 1969: 148, 223–224 and 253).

Furthermore, the increased demand for investment goods in agriculture stimulated the growth of tile works and foundries in provincial towns. Perhaps more than anything else, transport and trade benefited from the increasing grain trade. Thus, the cargo carrying capacity of the Danish merchant fleet increased by 34 per cent from 1845 to 1852.

III. Prices, real wages and the demographic response

III.1. The macro level

The immediate impression from the price indices in Figure 14.2 on the most important foods is that the crisis of the mid 1840s was, on the one hand, serious, and on the other, that it was to be overshadowed by far by the crisis following the outbreak of the Crimean war. We look at a real wage index constructed on the basis of a new wage series for urban workers and two alternative estimates of the costs of living during 1830–1870 (Christensen, 1992: 107–109 and 132–133). An extract from the data used, showing 1840–1860, can be seen in Table 14.4 below. We find the ordinary 19th century pattern of relatively stable money wages. Perhaps the most interesting feature is the decline in money wages beyond the period of interest to this chapter, namely the decline in the late 1850s in the aftermath of the Crimean war. The result of the decline in wages was, it is believed, the creation of a Danish labour movement from the late 1860s.

Danish 19th century economists invariably used rye prices as a cost of living indicator. A recent calculation of the co-variation between relative fluctuations in demographic events (births, deaths and marriages) and rye prices 1840–1890 (Johansen, 2002: 124) shows that there was no impact from the price changes. We, however, have the option of deflating the wage index either by the consumer price index constructed by Svend Aage Hansen (1984) constructed on budget information from 1840 or by an index based on the budget of an unskilled worker in a Danish town 1879. The latter index shows the largest fluctuations. Using the first index, which provides information on 41 years, 1830 to 1870, two major declines can be identified, that of 1846–1847 and that of 1853–1856.

The question is whether we can establish a correlation between the development in real wages and some demographic variables. Looking at mortality figures for the 41 year period 1830–1870, some events should be noted. The high mortality in the early 1830s was due to repeated outbreaks of malaria according to Westergaard (1885: 430–436). The high death rates in 1853 were caused by cholera in Copenhagen and some major towns. Finally, the Second Schleswig War in 1864–1865 was the cause of many deaths. Westergaard only mentions harvest failure as a cause of excess mortality in the year 1846.

When we try to explain the year-by-year change in mortality by the change in real wage with a dummy variable for the cholera year the sign is right but the regression result is not significant (t-value = −1.16). This is perhaps not surprising in view of similar analyses for other European economies in the 19th century (see also Chevet and Ó Gráda in this volume). One interpretation is similar to that noted in Johansen (2002), that the Danes by then no longer lived at the margin of subsistence in which a temporary decline in the real wage would lead to deep distress and imminent death. If we narrow the dependent variable to the death rate of infants below the age of 1 year as percentage of live births for 1835–1870 (from Johansen, 1985: 112–113), the result is equally insigni-

Table 14.4 Death rate, birth rate and real wage, 1840–1860

Year	Deaths/10,000	Births/10,000	Realwage I 1870=100	Realwage II 1870=100
1840	224	318	80	70
1841	212	311	80	72
1842	215	314	75	69
1843	206	311	83	76
1844	207	317	89	78
1845	208	320	87	79
1846	228	314	75	73
1847	231	320	77	73
1848	225	320	93	82
1849	238	324	101	87
1850	206	329	109	90
1851	199	315	100	88
1852	212	348	92	88
1853	265	332	94	81
1854	200	342	78	75
1855	215	335	75	76
1856	202	339	86	85
1857	233	345	92	87
1858	247	347	97	90
1859	218	351	102	91
1860	215	339	94	89

Sources: Deaths and births are from Westergaard, 1885: 431-432 and 507. Deaths and births including stillborn children. The real wages are from Christensen, 1992: 107-109 and 132-133 and from Hansen, 1984: Appendix Table 16.

ficant (t-value = −1.37). Though infant mortality increased temporarily in 1846 there is no general tendency for changes in the real wage to explain changes in that variable.

We have no countrywide statistics of the causes of death going back to the 1840s with the exception of the statistics on suicides since 1835. Falbe Hansen and Scharling (1885: 638–653) points to three peak years, 1846, 1857 and 1868, in which economic conditions may be responsible for higher than average suicide rates. By adding suicides for all available years they are able to conclude that the highest rates were to be found among cottagers, labourers and pensioners. The most prominent Danish statistician in the 19th century believed that the unusually high suicide rate for Denmark compared to other countries was the result of 'disguised murders' particularly of old people.[9] If this were true, times of crisis, as well as driving poor people to suicide, may also provide some people with a greater incentive to kill their older relatives. Be that as it may a regression of real wage changes against suicide rates does not give any significant result

---

[9] It should be noted that according to the same source (Falbe Hansen and Scharling, 1885: 655) the Danish consumption of alcohol was also unusually high by international standards and that may have influenced the suicide rate as well.

(t-value = −1.06). As for the birth rate, there was no effect from the change in the real wage, cf. Table 14.4 above.

In Section I.1 we argued that the rural poor were the largest group of people vulnerable to an increase in food prices. The population in rural parishes increased by more than 114,000 during 1840–1849, 20,000 of which emigrated to Danish towns and to the capital. That corresponds to a rate of −1.9 per cent of mid-year population, compared to −2.0 per cent for the 1850s. (Johansen, 2002: 164). Gad (1956: 18) has estimated the annual decline in the agricultural population to be 1,000 for the years 1846–1855 compared to 2,700 for 1841–1845 and 2,600 for 1856–1860. Consequently, there is no evidence of any reaction in the form of higher migration rates to towns or overseas during the years of higher food prices. Nor is there evidence of the opposite migration, people fleeing the towns because of a worsening in the food situation. Net foreign migration from Denmark in the 1840s was roughly 0.0 and in the 1850s 0.6 (that is positive immigration).

III.2. The micro level.
Local accounts of disease and mortality during 1846–47[10]

The annual reports by the Danish district medical officers to The Public Health Authority (*Sundhedskollegiet*) on 'The possible shortage of food or the condition of food that may have influenced the health of the residents' with a few exceptions show little concern over the effect of the 1846–1847 crisis. The most reasonable explanation is that the time of high prices to the best of their knowledge did not create big problems. Perhaps some misunderstandings prevailed, however. A number of doctors dutifully record that nobody was found to be ill because of eating diseased potatoes. This was not really an issue since diseased potatoes were so foul smelling that even animals rejected them. The important issue was the effects of under nourishment or malnourishment due to lack of food or the supplement with poorer alternatives. Most doctors, for example, failed to make any connection between the food situation and the incidence of and mortality from typhoid fever. The mean number of deaths from all causes in Copenhagen for the 13 years leading up to 1846 was 3,403 but in 1846 the figure jumps to 4126 only to go down to 3,642 in 1847. According to the chief medical officer there was no single reason only 'a generally higher incidence of sickness'.[11] Typhoid fever alone claimed 160 lives in 1846 and the epidemic stretched into 1847. The same pattern was found in 1846–1847 in Northern Zealand, the island of Funen, and Viborg Mid-Jutland.

Not all reports disregard a possible connection between the higher incidence of some diseases and the worsening of the nutritional standard in these particular years. The district medical officers of Funen and of Aalborg in north Jutland do in fact lay the blame on the poor quality of grain and flour. Their colleague of in eastern Zealand finds that:

Scrofula seems to be in the increase and I most particularly blame the distress and lack of

---

[10] This section relies on a sample of the handwritten reports from the district medical officers on the island of Zealand for 1846 and 1847, kept in the Danish National Archive and on the published summary for the whole country in *Det Kongelige Sundhedskollegiums Forhandlinger* 1847–1894 (for 1845–1847).

[11] He suggests, though hesitantly, that the warm summer of 1846 may have had a bad effect on food quality, but says that earlier warm summers did not cause more deaths.

good nutrition that has been general here in the countryside. When children must survive the better part of the winter on poor quality rye bread or bread of mixed grains… they must count themselves lucky if they get away without large glandular tumours and the evils resulting from that.[12]

The district medical officer of Copenhagen mentions scurvy in both 1846 (2 deaths) and 1847 (4 deaths): 'Scurvy emerged in 1846 in an extraordinary number of patients just like in other countries such as England, where most writers explain it as a result of the failed potato harvest.'[13]

The relation between nutrition and disease during the crisis years is distorted somewhat by a relatively high incidence in some districts of diseases that are unrelated to the nutritional standard such as agues (malaria) in 1847 and measles. The latter caused many deaths in Southern Zealand and probably many miscarriages when caught by pregnant women, since the number of births declined markedly.

The main impression left from reading the printed summary as well as a sample of the original reports (from the island of Zealand including Copenhagen) is very far from that of a hunger crisis. At most, some of the medical experts expressed mild concern, as we have seen. It is, of course, questionable whether this relaxed attitude was justified.

IV. Crisis and revolution

Any attempt to analyse the effects of the food crisis, economically or politically, is hampered by the fact that the issue is closely interwoven with, or indeed overshadowed by, other important events in Denmark and abroad. These are the effects of the First Schleswig War (1848–50) and constitutional reform (1848) in Denmark and, of course, the phasing out of the Corn Laws between 1846 and 1849.

In a comprehensive study Berger and Spoerer (2001) explore the correlation between grain price shocks and revolution in 1848 for 21 European economies. They conclude (see p. 319) that the former is a powerful predictor of the latter: if and only if a country was subjected to a grain-price shock between 1845 and 1847, then it went on to undergo revolution in 1848. 'Among the six countries that escaped grain-price shocks, only Denmark experienced far-reaching, and in our sense revolutionary, constitutional reform.' This conclusion seems plausible. We also suggest that a marked improvement in the terms of trade of agricultural goods may have been among the forces that provoked political change. If this is correct, the relatively large and well-to-do class of farmers with middle sized farms supported reform from a position of strength. At the same time the poor and deteriorating living conditions of rural labourers and cottagers were used as leverage for democracy in the public debate. This class in rural Denmark, however, gained neither from high prices on agricultural goods, since they were net buyers of food, nor very much from democracy, as it turned out.

By the end of March 1848 the absolute monarch in Denmark bowed to the demand for a democratic constitution. The immediate background was the attempt of the duchies

---

[12] Modern medical science would probably put most of the blame for this disease on bad housing, which he also mentions.

[13] Scurvy is caused by vitamin C deficiency. Only newly harvested potatoes, however, contain any of this vitamin.

of Schleswig and Holstein to break away from the Danish monarchy in order to join the German League under a free constitution. The quest for separation clashed with growing nationalist sentiments in Denmark, particularly since a majority of the population in Schleswig was Danish speaking. The nationalists in Denmark joined forces with young liberal academics calling for a constitutional monarchy for Denmark as well as for the Duchies.[14] The monarch in his decision was, of course, not ignorant of the events in Paris in February 1848.

The demand for a free constitution was fuelled by the demand from the peasantry for various legislative measures to bolster the general emancipation of their social class. That is, equality with respect to land taxation, to the payment of tithes and to military service. Besides these issues of a general nature the peasants demanded that land remaining in leasehold should be sold to the tenants at their request and that lingering labour services paid by tenants were to be converted into monetary rents.[15] With a few exceptions the peasantry chose to let liberal urban academics represent their interests in the first parliament elected in 1849.[16] Most demands of a more general nature were given a favourable reception by the first democratic government within a relatively short time. As far as the more specific wishes were concerned, however, the results were disappointing. The idea of forcing landowners to sell their land to tenants and to abandon rent in labour services completely in favour of monetary rents were seen as conflicting with fundamental principles in the new constitution such as the inviolability of private property rights and the freedom of contracting.

Even more disappointing were the results of the demands from the poorest rural classes, the landless labourers and the small holders who did not own but rented their holdings. Their conditions were eagerly debated during the 1840s in the States General[17] as well as in the leading agricultural journals. It was generally held that they had experienced a relative deterioration in their situation compared to the farmers, who benefited from high food prices. Moreover, an estimate by Bjørn (1988: 114) based on a case study, suggests that their real wage had declined during the first half of the 1840s. Even before their problems were enhanced by the potato crisis and the high grain prices. The decline in the real wage, must to some extent, have been modified by remuneration in kind, as already mentioned. Many poor cottagers on rented plots were rewarded by the landowner-employer who sent his horses to work their plots a few days a year. Furthermore, cottagers working as day labourers normally got their meals on working days.

As mentioned already constitutional reform did not tackle the main problem of this disadvantaged group. The most urgent problem was the short term lease of the plots,

---

[14] The Schleswig-Holstein 'rebellion' sparked a military conflict that lasted until 1850. The military outcome was undecided. Denmark held the stronger position at sea and thanks to foreign intermediation kept supremacy over the Duchies. The constitutional conflict was, however, unresolved and the question was to haunt Danish politics for several decades ahead.

[15] For a majority of the peasants, about two thirds, these issues were no longer relevant. The great reform period 1784–1807 had left about 60–65 per cent as owner-occupiers. For most of the remaining tenants the system of rent payment had also found a satisfactory solution.

[16] The constitution finally agreed in 1849 to extend the franchise to males from 30 years with a household of their own, excluding servants and journeymen living with their master.

[17] The States General representing estate owners, large peasants, urban citizens and clergymen in the four main regions in Denmark was an advisory body during the last stage of absolutism, from 1835 to 1848.

sometimes down to 3 months. Most of the remaining tenant farmers usually held their leasehold for life or even as copyhold of inheritance. Demographic development in the countryside, however, worked against the poor and put the landowners in a strong bargaining position. The democratic government did not fundamentally change this, though the notice for discontinuing a leasehold was prolonged to 6 months from the first of May.[18] There is no mention in Danish historiography of a growing number of evictions of cottagers during 1846–1847. This may well be correct. The growing income of their employers-landowners caused by the increase in grain prices and a more moderate harvest decline in 1846 created less of a motive for evicting small tenants. The labourers with a small plot or with no land became poorer, especially if they relied heavily on potatoes, but their employment and tenancy were clearly less threatened than that of cottagers in Ireland and parts of Prussia (see, Ó Gráda and Bass in this volume).

To sum up, the 1848 revolution in Denmark was triggered by matters other than food prices. The group most affected by high prices did not have much voice. It is telling, however, that the poor did *not* vote with their feet during the food crisis.

V.   Government action

V.1.   Diagnosing the cause of the potato crisis

In the previous section we dealt with the main political events of the 1840s leading up to constitutional reform. The food crisis as such has been given little attention in Danish political historiography. One exception to that is a recent study by Margit Mogensen (2002) in which she characterises government reaction to the potato failure in Denmark during 1845–1847 as an example of 'successful crisis management'.

In late September 1845 the daily newspaper *Fædrelandet,* known for its liberal attitude towards and criticisms of the absolutist government called for action

…while governments and private citizens in other countries are concerned about, in time, to inform the public about the symptoms of the disease and the possible remedies against it in order to prevent or at least limit the dangerous effects of this scourge, and while the rumours in this country tells of accelerating spread of the disease, our government remains inactive…

As it turned out the government was just about to act upon the threat of crisis a few weeks later. One interesting feature was the government conclusion on exports. It was decided *not* to ban the modest export of potatoes from Denmark.[19] This may be an indication of how relatively moderate the crisis was regarded. Officially, the demand for an export ban had been countered by the usual argument for free trade from the Merchants' Guild. It was also argued that potato growers had a legitimate interest in getting rid of their product quickly.

Alongside the investigation by the custom authorities, see Section II.1, a potato commission was appointed in October 1845. It was to examine, in further detail, the cause

---

[18] Other improvements were the abolishment of corporal punishment (of day labourers) and the phasing out of labour services as rent in new contracts.
[19] Nor, apparently, did it ban distilling, which might have been more to the point. One explanation could be that is was possible to make spirits from diseased potatoes.

of the disease, possible remedies against it and also to what use, if any, the infected potatoes could be put, that is fodder, spirits or seed potatoes. The Danish commission was supported by its own investigations and by the findings of foreign researchers, able to establish that a mould fungus, later known as *Phytophthora infestans,* was the cause of the disease but like its foreign parallels it had no cure for it in the foreseeable future. Even so, Mogensen (2002: 70) states that a scientific explanation for the calamity had a certain reassuring effect on the public.

V.2. Dealing with the plight of the poor

The potato commission does not appear to have been overly concerned with the deteriorating living conditions of the poor. This question was, however, brought up by local reports to the commission from the regions in which the crisis had hit the hardest. The report from western Zealand said that potatoes were the essential food of the poorer classes and that landless labourers and artisans were already suffering from high grain prices.

The food situation in 1846–1847 initiated a kind of relief without distinction between the 'deserving' and the 'non-deserving' poor. This aid, however, was to flow *solely from private means.* Local authorities were, under no circumstances, allowed to raise taxes in order to bring relief to the hungry (Bitsch Christensen, 2001: 698–700) There was a widespread circulation of subscription lists in the parishes with appeals to the peasants to enter their names so that a possible grain surplus could be sold to those in need [at subsidized prices] (Banggaard, 2004: 124–125). Thus, the most detailed account of how poor relief policy was conducted in the 19th century gives scant information on the 1847 crisis. In the account of the concerns about the, much more serious, food crisis in 1853, it is mentioned that the 'time of dearth in 1847 had been weathered by private means' and more specifically that 'the wealthiest and most informed members of a municipality, such as happened in most places in 1847, would, by advances and gifts, enable the municipality to make lighter the burden of high grain prices on the impecunious part of the population [by buying grain to sell at a low price to cottagers and rural workers]' (Jørgensen, 1940: 99–100).

Events in the provincial town of *Kalundborg* are illustrative of how townspeople reacted. A private benevolent fund established by a group of large merchants in 1844 spent part of its means to assist in kind, 'under no circumstances in money', the poor who were deprived due to old age, sickness, accidents or a large family. In the winter of 1847/48, when reportedly a hunger crisis was imminent, it was this fund and not the state that relieved the worst of the emergency. During a few months it dispensed 2,000 dinners and 1000 loaves of bread (Nyberg and Riis, 1987: 85).

Was the lack of government action caused by the all pervasive liberalism of this era in Danish history an attitude shared by the democratic opposition, or was it caused by a (mis)perception of the food crisis of the 1840s as being mild and transitory? It speaks in favour of the latter explanation that, in the 1850s, when attitudes were much the same, the central government, nevertheless, on three occasions in 1853, 1855 and 1856 authorised local governments to dispense help to those hit by the high costs of living. Furthermore, assistance on these occasions was to be received without forfeit of civil rights.

VI. Conclusion

As suggested in the title of this chapter, a general finding is that the 1840s food crisis did not strike hard in Denmark. This is supported by an analysis of the Danish data on prices, trade and population changes 1830–1870. The main reason was, of course, that potatoes were not as important a food item in Denmark as they were in some other European economies. Added to that, as far as can be established, the grain crisis of 1846 didn't hit quite as hard in Denmark as in other countries. We, however, suggest two additional explanations of a more structural nature. The first one is the economic structure which was dominated by agriculture. Second, is the social structure which was still biased in favour of people who generally tended to gain from the rise in food prices or at least to be insulated against the worst of its impacts. They were either net producers of food (other than potatoes) or they were remunerated in kind. The power of a structural explanation, of course, hinges on an international comparison.

A new analysis of the Danish and English market for wheat shows that these markets became highly integrated in the 1840s. European grain price development had a full impact on Danish prices. Furthermore, the increase in the grain trade and the subsequent commercialisation of Danish agriculture following the demise of the Corn Laws are likely to have contributed to further integration of the Danish national market for grain.

Indirect proof of a relatively mild crisis in Denmark is the feeble reaction of the government. There was no ban on exports nor export duty, no ban on distilling nor any extra duty on spirits, and, most surprisingly perhaps, there was no government money spent on those who did indeed suffer during the crisis years. The food crises of the 1850s were to demonstrate that the government could act and would act if it deemed the situation serious enough.

Bibliography

Banggaard, G. (2004) *Befolkningsfremmende foranstaltninger og faldende børnedødelighed. Danmark ca. 1750–1850,* Odense.

Berger, H. and Spoerer, M. (2001) 'Economic Crisis and the European Revolutions of 1848', *Journal of Economic History,* 61, pp. 293–326.

Bitsch Christensen, S. (2001) *Monopol, marked og magasiner. Dansk kornhandel og kornpolitik 1730–1850 med vægt på reformårene,* Ph.d. Afhandling Århus Universitet.

Bjørn, C. (1988) *Det danske landbrugs historie 1810–1910,* Odense.

Bjørn, C. (1990) *Danmarks historie 1800–1850,* Copenhagen. (Danmarks historie; 10).

Crafts, N.F.R. (1985) *British Economic Growth during the Industrial Revolution,* Oxford.

Christensen, J.P. (1992) *Om lønudviklingen for byarbejdere i Danmark 1830–1870.* Institute of Economics, University of Copenhagen. Memo 188.

Falbe Hansen, V. and Scharling, W. (1885) *Danmarks Statistik,* vol. 1, Copenhagen.

Falbe Hansen, V. and Scharling, W. (1887) *Danmarks Statistik,* vol. 2, Copenhagen.

Gad, H. (1956) *Befolknings- og arbejdskraftproblemer i dansk landbrug,* Aarhus.

Hansen, S.A. (1984) *Økonomisk vækst i Danmark,* vol. I–II, Copenhagen.

Hyldtoft, O. (1984) *Københavns industrialisering 1840–1914*, Herning.

Johansen, H.C. (1985) *Dansk historisk statistik 1814–1980*, Copenhagen.

Johansen, H.C. (1998) 'Food Consumption in the Pre-industrial Nordic Societies', *Scandinavian Economic History Review*, 46, pp. 11–23.

Johansen, H.C. (2002) *Danish Population History 1600–1939*, Odense.

Jørgensen, H. (1940) *Studier over det offentlige Fattigvæsens historiske Udvikling i Danmark i det 19. Århundrede*, Copenhagen.

Det kongelige Sundhedskollegiums forhandlinger for Aarene 1844–1847, Copenhagen. Published annually 1846 to 1849.

Maddison, A. (1995) *Monitoring the World Economy 1820–1992*, Paris.

Medicinalindberetninger 1846–1847. The archive of Sundhedsstyrelsen. The Danish National Archive, 1252.

Milthers, A. (1934–45) in Otto Christensen, A. Milthers, and J.J. Hansen (eds), *Det danske Landbrugs Historie*, vol. 5, Copenhagen, pp. 191–299.

Mogensen, M. (2002) 'Kartoffelpesten i Danmark i 1840'erne – et spørgsmål om oplysning og forskning', in D.H. Andersen, C. Bjørn, T. Hessel and J. Mackintosh (eds), *Landbrug, Lokalhistorie og Langt fra Danmark. Festskrift til Erik Helmer Pedersen*, Odense, pp. 59–70.

Mossin, A. (2004) *Socialpolitikkens og velfærdssamfundets teori*. Institute of Economics, The University of Copenhagen www.econ.ku.dk/axelmossin, Axel Mossin's homepage.

Nyberg, T. and Riis T. (eds) (1987) *Kalundborgs historie. Bd. 2 Tiden 1830–1980*, Kalundborg.

Rich, S. (2004) *Integration af kornmarkeder i 1800-tallet – med Danmark og Storbritannien som eksempel*. Masters thesis, Institute of Economics, University of Copenhagen.

Rubin, M. (1882) *Konsumen i Kjøbenhavn, i alt væsentligt vedrørende Befolkningen Forbrug af de nødvendige Levnetsmidler*, Copenhagen.

Solar, P. (1997) 'The Potato Famine in Europe', in C. Ó Gráda (ed.), *Famine 150: Commemorative Lecture Series*, Dublin.

Statistiske Tabelværker 1845–52 udgivet af Tabelkommissionen og fra 1849 Finansministeriet, Copenhagen.

Statistisk Tabelværk (1905) 5.rk. A, 5. Befolkningsforholdene i det 19. Aarhundrede.

Statistisk Tabelværk (1911) 5. rk. C, 4. Landbrugsforholdene i Danmark siden midten af det 19. århundrede.

Statistiske Undersøgelser (1969) Kreditmarkedsstatistik. Danmarks Statistik, 24.

Thomsen, B.N. and Thomas B. (1966) *Dansk-engelsk samhandel – Et historisk rids*, Aarhus.

Westergaard, H. (1885) 'Fødselshyppighed og dødelighed', in V. Falbe Hansen and W. Scharling (eds), *Danmarks Statistik*, vol. 1, Copenhagen, pp. 430–475.

15 On the edge of a crisis: Sweden in the 1840s

Carl-Johan Gadd, Göteborg University

I.   Was there a Swedish crisis in the 1840s?

As far as Sweden as a whole is concerned the period 1845–1850 can hardly be considered a crisis period. Although it is true that mortality increased and the birth rate decreased for some years after 1845, these changes were not greater than those falling within the scope for normal variations for the period 1830–1860. Mortality was higher for several years during the 1830s and in the 'cholera year' of 1857. Much lower birth rates are noted as late as 1867–1868 (Figure 15.1; cf. Utterström, 1957: 700).

Figure 15.1   Wage for a farmhand deflated by the price of rye, mortality and fertility, 1830–1875

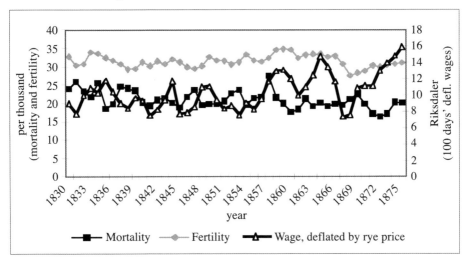

NB: Deflated wage = 100 day's wages divided by the price of a hectolitre of rye.
Sources: Statistics Sweden webpage; Jörberg, 1972a: 634–635; 712–713.

However, the period 1845–1847 is distinguished negatively by very low real wages for three years in succession; with the exception of the early 1850s such long periods of depressed wages never occurred between 1830 and 1875 (Figure 15.1).[1]

In the official report from the Government Enquiry on Emigration a comparison was made between Sweden and other parts of Western Europe for the 1840s. The report mentions the West-European crop failure in 1846, the potato blight, the Irish famine

---

[1] Cf. charts in Jörberg, (1972b: 337) and in Schön (2000: 65).

and the ravages of the cholera, altogether making '1847 and 1848 the worst years of suffering our continent has undergone since the great wars'. In addition, states the report, came the 'revolutionary orgies' of 1848. But, the report continues:

'There is probably no other European country which was so comparatively unaffected by all these as Sweden' (*Emigrationsutredningen*, 1913: 127–28)[2]

Nor in modern Swedish historical writing do the 1840s come out as years of general food supply crisis.[3] In the first half of the 19th century land reclamation in Sweden was much more rapid than population growth, resulting in an increasing agricultural production per capita. The 1840s do not seem to have differed much from this basic pattern (Söderberg, 1989; Schön, 2000: 69–73).[4]

If the period 1845–1848 is not mentioned as one of hunger in Swedish historical writing, this *is* the case with the years of crop failure 1867–1869, which are viewed as hard years especially in northern Sweden (and in Finland) as well as in the woodlands of southern Sweden.[5] The decrease in real wages during these years as well as the sharp decrease in fertility and rising mortality are visible in Figure 15.1. These 'last' years of hunger crisis gave rise to a first peak in Swedish emigration, which until then had been comparatively small-scale – and almost non-existent in the 1840s.

Nor in fiction have the 1840s been depicted as years of exceptional hardship, while this is, again, the case for the years 1867–1869. These years are remembered in the children's book and later film, *Barnen ifrån Frostmofjället*, by Laura Fitinghoff. This book, published in 1907, was later translated into most major West-European languages.[6]

So, is there anything to write on, in a book on the European crisis of 1845–1850? I think there is. In Sweden, the early and mid-1840s brought in their train bad, and in some regions disastrous, harvests. Even though crops in Sweden, taken as a whole, became better after 1845, the period of difficulties for large parts of the population was prolonged by the international rise in grain prices 1846–1847. Moreover, Sweden had its share of the

---

[2] Quotations translated by the author.

[3] See, e.g. the handbook on Swedish general history by Carlsson and Rosén (1970: 311–319). See also Utterström (1957: 243) and Schön (2000: 67–72).

[4] This comparatively optimistic view of the Swedish 1840s has been questioned by L. G. Sandberg and R. H. Steckel, who refer, among other things, to decreasing height among Swedish soldiers born during that decade (Sandberg and Steckel, 1980, 1987, 1988; Heintel, Sandberg and Steckel, 1998). However, generalizing from Swedish recruits to the male population as a whole produces some problems of interpretation (cf. Söderberg, 1989: 477). The soldiers studied were professionals and the labour market changed rapidly in the decades after 1850. If the profession of soldier became relatively less attractive in a widening labour market the recruitment authorities may have had to accept shorter recruits. In fact, the prescribed minimum height for soldiers was gradually lowered in the latter half of the 19th century in spite of a long-term increase in average stature of the population as a whole. The minimum height for a recruit in the late 18th century had been 168 cm, but it was 163 cm in 1895 (Kumm, 1949: 29). The average stature of Swedish 21-year olds by 1890 was 170 cm (Hultcrantz, 1896; Backman, 1919).

[5] On the famine of 1867–1869, see e.g. Lundsjö (1975: 126–127); Söderberg, (1978: 74); Ohlander and Norman (1984); Nelson (1988). The supply crisis of 1867–1869 is also mentioned in surveys such as Carlsson and Rosén (1970: 364–365); Gadd (2000: 365–366).

[6] Fitinghoff's book was translated to English as *The Children of the Frostmoor* in 1914, and later to Dutch, German and French, as well as to the other Nordic languages.

potato blight. In some regions the combined effects of all these led to symptoms of crisis similar to those found on the Continent. Some questions at issue in the present article are if and how these crises were dealt with by the authorities and the local communities.

On the whole, Sweden seems to have been stricken comparatively little by the potato blight. As I will be showing in this article the geographical distribution of this disease within Sweden gives a clue to why the country as a whole was affected so little.

II. Some geographical facts

Sweden is a vast country. The distance of 1,570 km from its northernmost to its southernmost point equals that from the coast of Scania to Rome, and the 400 km from Stockholm in the East to Gothenburg in the West the distance from London to Newcastle. With an area slightly more than 80 per cent of the size of France, Sweden in 1845 had a population of 3.3 million, which was less than a tenth of the population of France and a fifth of that of England and Wales. About 85 per cent of the Swedish population was to be found in the area south of the River Dalälven, which constituted 40 per cent of the total area. In other words, large parts of the North were extremely thinly populated. This applies especially to the inland of the counties of Västerbotten (ZA)[7] and Norrbotten (ZB) where few permanent settlements existed. Most of the population of the far North was concentrated in the coastal areas.

Sweden in the 1840s was still a largely rural country: 90 per cent of its population lived outside of the towns. Stockholm had a population of around 90,000, Gothenburg 25,000 and Karlskrona and Malmö each had 12–14,000 inhabitants. Other towns were, as a rule, much smaller and had an average population size of around 2,900 (*Historisk statistik*, 1955).

III. Harvests and grain prices

III.1. Harvest changes

Figure 15.2 shows the official yield estimates (*skördeomdömen*) for grain (excluding potatoes) for the period 1830–1860. These estimates are very approximate, but can be used as a rough indication of harvest variations.[8] In Figure 15.2 the series of weak or bad harvests between 1841 and 1845 is important. In these two years harvests were extremely bad in at least one of Sweden's foremost grain-producing provinces (Lundsjö, 1975: 94) and crops were below average in two of the three years in between.

In 1845 eastern and south-eastern Sweden were struck by severe drought. Three counties near Stockholm were hit the hardest. In close to 75 per cent[9] of the parishes of

---

[7] Letters after county names refer to designations on Figure 15.6.

[8] The *Tabellkommissionen*, predecessor of Statistics Sweden, produced these numerical crop summaries using a rather imperfect statistical method. For discussion concerning this source, see Hellstenius (1871); *Emigrationsutredningen* (1913: 58); Utterström (1957: 188–198).

[9] Percentages calculated from Lundjö (1975: 95). Total number of parishes in each county according to Nordisk familjebok.

Figure 15.2 Official yield assessments, Sweden 1830–1860. Annual observations and three years' moving averages

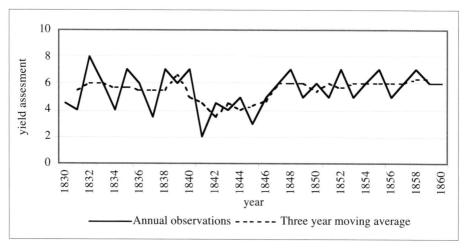

Source: Emigrationsutredningen, 1913: 58.
Explanation: 2–3 = poor harvest; 6 average harvest; 7–8 good harvest.

Stockholm (B), Uppsala (C) and Västmanland (U) counties food and seed shortages became serious. There was no question of general crop failure for the whole country, though. Crops in 1845 were more or less normal in the West and the South (Hellstenius, 1871: 93).

During the five years from 1846 to 1850 grain harvests were good, average or nearly average, as regards the country as a whole. Bad harvests were, however, reported both in 1845 and in 1846 in Kalmar (H), Kronoberg (G) and Blekinge (K) counties in the South-East (KB 1842–1847). During the 1850s and the larger part of the 1860s grain crops continued to be above the level for 1841–1845, until 1867, when the sparsely populated northern parts of the country were stricken by crop failure. During the next year, 1868, crops were poor in southern and central Sweden, especially Jönköpings (F), Kronoberg and Kalmar counties (Lundsjö, 1975: 125–126).

III.2.   Price fluctuations

In Figure 15.3 the monthly changes in rye prices during the period 1842–1859 are shown. Rye was the main cereal in Sweden during this period. A comparison between Figures 15.2 and 15.3 makes it clear that the prices of rye were only partially correlated with yields. Certainly, the bad harvest of 1841 is reflected in high prices at the beginning of 1842, and the bad harvest of 1845 in high prices from the autumn of the same year to the spring of the next year.[10] But in spite of a better harvest in 1846 prices peak in spring

[10] This interpretation is not undisputed, however. According to Nathorst (1846) even the prices of the crop-year 1845–46 were the result of international price-movements.

1847, and prices remain higher after the comparatively good harvest of 1848 than they had been after the weak harvest of 1844. In spite of fairly good crops during the 1850s rye prices stay at a relatively high level. A period of particularly high prices occurs in 1855–1856.

The explanation, as has been pointed out by academy secretary J.Th. Nathorst, the individual who compiled and published the data used in Figure 15.3, is that Swedish grain prices depended on domestic harvests only to a small degree. From the early 1840s onwards Sweden was a grain exporter and Swedish prices were mainly determined by international prices (Nathorst, 1845; 1846; 1850). The peak in prices from autumn 1846 to spring 1847 and the high level of prices in 1855–1856 was caused by high prices in the world market. The peak of 1846–1847 reflected poor harvests in 1845 and 1846 in Britain and large parts of the Continent (cf. Solar, this volume). The long period of high prices in 1855–1856 was due to the Crimean War.

Figure 15.3 Rye prices in Sweden, 1842–1859. Riksdaler rikgsgälds/riksmynt per hectolitre. Monthly averages for 18 of Sweden´s 24 counties

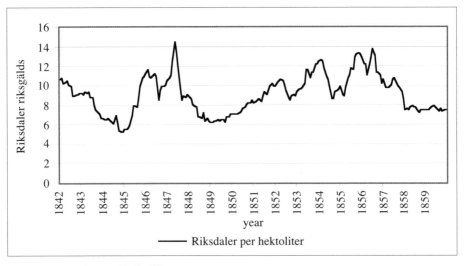

Source: Nathorst, 1842–59.

Figure 15.4 Prices of wheat, rye, barley and oats, 1842–59. Average prices for Sweden as measured in October each year (Riksdaler riksgälds/ riksmynt per hectolitre)

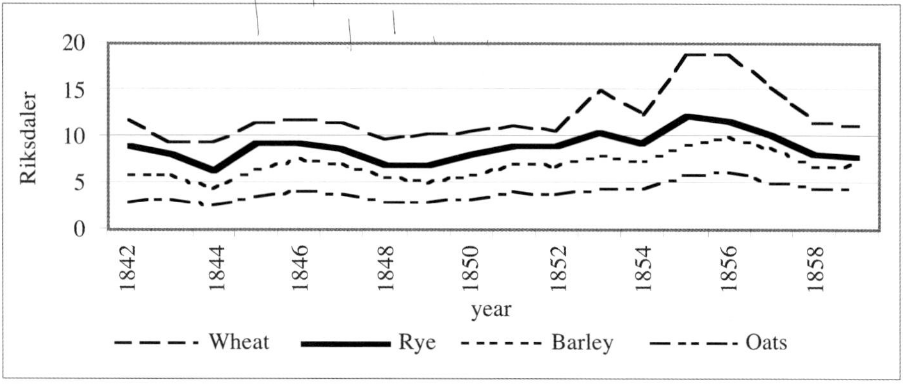

Source: Jörberg, 1972a: 634–635.

Figure 15.4 shows changes in prices for all four kinds of corn – wheat, rye, barley and oats – during 1842–1859, i.e. the same period as in Figure 15.3. The graph illustrates the fact that the prices of the four kinds of corn correlate. The source is the market-price scales (*markegångstaxor*), i.e. price data collected by the public authorities of that time (Jörberg, 1972). The trend-lines in Figure 15.4 appear different from the line in Figure 15.3 because the market-price scales refer to the prices each autumn. Consequently, a temporary peak in prices like that which took place from autumn 1846 to spring 1847 remains invisible in this material, since it occurred between two points of measurement.

IV. Grain export

Sweden had been a grain importer in the 18th and first decades of the 19th century. Equilibrium between import and export of grain was established around 1820, after a period of sharp increase in grain production (Utterström, 1957: 694–700; Schön, 1995: 45). When Sweden became a net exporter of grain in the 1840s, it was on a comparatively modest scale. However, even in 1845, when one of the most fertile provinces of the country was hit by crop failure, the country remained a net exporter (Utterström, 1957: 217–218).

IV.1. The export boom and the export ban

The international rise in the price of grain in late 1846 and early 1847 caused a boom in export (Figure 15.5), but also very strained conditions of food-supply among the poorer classes, as was pointed out by, inter alia, the governor of Blekinge county (KB 1843–1847). Governors in other parts of Sweden emphasize even more that the rising prices of grain were due to demand from other parts of Europe. For example, the governor of Kristianstad county wrote that

318

'in autumn 1846 and the beginning of 1847 grain exports were executed from the seaports of this county with such restless zeal, that although this year's crops were by no means weak, the want for bread in several parts of the county walked abreast with affluence in money' (KB 1843–1847: Kristianstad county: 6)

**Figure 15.5 Swedish exports of agricultural products, 1835–1865.
Million riksdaler, fixed prices**

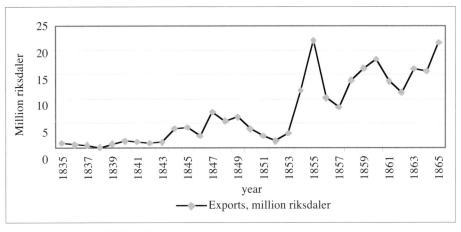

Source: Schön, 1995: 117.
NB: This chart shows both arable and animal exports. Comparatively small amounts of animal products were exported before ca 1870.

A measure taken by the government when prices rose in 1846–1847 was to put a ban on food exports: first on potatoes only and in May 1847 on all sorts of grain, potatoes and bread. The ban on grain exports lasted until August the same year. However, the export ban was a measure taken too late to have any effect. It proved unnecessary, since the boom in the international grain market ended in the spring of 1847, when food resources were found to be lasting longer and the grain crop turned out better than expected (Lundsjö, 1975: 97). After the withdrawal of the ban, exports were resumed on a comparatively high level in 1848 and 1849. Following a decline in the early 1850s, the next increase took place during the Crimean War, 1853–1856. In the last full year of war, 1855, the grain-export value was more than 8 times larger (in fixed prices) than the average for the years 1850–1853 (Schön, 1995: 117). Swedish grain exports were to reach a summit in the early 1870s, when grain (almost exclusively oats) constituted about 20 per cent of net exports (Krantz, 1987: 35; Morell, 2001: 99–100).

V.   The potato and the blight

V.1.   Potato cultivation up to the early 1840s

The potato had been cultivated sporadically in Sweden since at least the 1730s, and had its first breakthrough around 1770 when it found its way into the peasants' vegetable gardens in many parts of the country. A second, more important breakthrough came around 1800 when high grain prices forced people to rely on cheaper substitutes. In this period the cultivation of the potato spread to arable fields. The potato had also proven ideal for the ancient form of cultivation called swiddening (slash-and-burn), in which temporary plantation plots were created in the forests by means of axe and fire.

The potato gave as much nourishment as grain, measured in calories, for less than half the area. It thrived in light, sandy soils and consequently became important especially in the forest districts. As a result these parts of the country generally became self-supporting in food in the early 19th century, where previously some of their grain supply had been imported from the plains. The rapid growth of potato cultivation from the early 1800s is important for any explanation why the food situation in Sweden improved thereafter (Larsson, 1945: 17f; Gadd, 1998: 175f).

Table 15.1 shows proportions in total crop returns according to Swedish official statistics, 1802–1874. It is certainly well known that agricultural statistics from the early 19th century seriously underestimated the *quantities* sown and harvested (although these underestimations were levelled down in time), but the figures seem to give a fairly correct impression of the *proportions* of different sorts of crops (Gadd, 2000: 133–134, 331–332). This would suggest that these statistics give a tolerably realistic picture of the changes in relative importance of potato cultivation in Sweden.

As we see (column 7), the proportion of potatoes in crop returns (per cent of crop volume in hectolitres) increased from 8-10 per cent in the first years of the 19th century to nearly 40 per cent in the early 1840s. However, the nutritional content as well as the price of a hectolitre of potatoes was much lower than that of a hectolitre of cereal: the calorific content was about 25 per cent of that of a hectolitre of rye (Herlitz, 1988: 210–214). In column 9 the share of potatoes is recalculated according to the calorific content of the different crops. The proportion of potatoes is reduced to 3 per cent in 1802 and to 17 per cent in the early 1840s.

These statistics account only for what was produced on arable land. Of course potatoes were also grown in vegetable gardens. It also seems that they were cultivated in temporary plantations more often than most other crops mentioned in the statistics. Earlier research gives support for only very approximate estimates of the size of garden and temporary-plantation production. My guess would be that gardening increased potato production by roughly 8 per cent and temporary plantations by half as much, or 12 per cent altogether.[11] However, other vegetable foodstuffs were also produced in gardens, such as cabbage, turnips carrots, etc. In spite of their not being mentioned in the statistics

---

[11] In fact Schön (1995: 85, 111) gives figures indicating that gardening would increase the total value of agricultural production by 5–6 per cent. Here I make the assumption that the relative importance of potatoes in gardening was larger than of most other garden crops.

Table 15.1   Crop proportions in Swedish crop returns according to official statistics, 1802–1874. Percentages of crop volumes in hectolitres (columns 1–8) and potato crop calculated as percentages of calorie content of crop return (column 9)

Year/ period	Wheat	Rye	Barley	Oats	Mixed grain	Peas and beans	Potatoes	Total	Potatoes' proportion of calorie content
	1	2	3	4	5	6	7	8	9
1802	2	21	30	24	11	3	**8**	100	**3**
1805	2	24	27	23	11	3	**10**	100	**3**
1810	2	25	25	21	11	3	**13**	100	**5**
1815	2	21	28	19	10	3	**18**	100	**6**
1820	2	21	23	17	9	2	**25**	100	**9**
1818–22	2	21	21	16	8	4	**29**	100	**11**
1823–27	2	21	19	14	8	3	**34**	100	**13**
1828–32	2	21	18	14	7	3	**35**	100	**14**
1833–37	2	21	16	14	7	3	**37**	100	**15**
1838–42	2	18	16	14	7	3	**40**	100	**17**
1843–47	2	18	16	14	8	3	**38**	100	**16**
1848–50	2	19	16	15	8	3	**36**	100	**14**
1851–55	2	19	15	18	6	3	**36**	100	**15**
1856–60	2	18	13	22	6	2	**38**	100	**16**
1865–69	2	16	12	28	4	1	**37**	100	**16**
1870–74	3	15	11	29	4	1	**37**	100	**16**

Sources: 1802–1860, 1865–1870 according to Hellstenius, 1871: 106–107; 1861–1865 according to BiSOS series H; 1870–1874 according to BiSOS series N.
Calories per hectolitre according to Herlitz, 1988: 212 (here converted from 165-litre barrels). Herlitz gives no calorific value for peas and beans; the same values as for wheat have been used here.
NB 1: Crop return = net return, i.e. seed has been deducted.
NB 2: The following values have been used for converting grain and potatoes from hectolitres to calories (Column 9):

Crop:	Wheat	Rye	Barley	Oats	Mixd grain	Peas & beans	Potatoes
Cal./hl:	261,030	245,540	214,580	159,270	186,920	261,030	64,150

some of these vegetables in fact played a role in total food production and consumption which is not to be overlooked (Gadd, 1983: 109; Palm, 1997: 7, 61). So even if gardening and temporary plantations contributed to an increase in total potato production, it is more doubtful whether it significantly increased the proportion of potatoes in total arable production.

In Table 15.2 the two first columns show potatoes as a percentage of net crop (i. e. crop after deduction of seed) in Sweden's 24 counties, as stated in the county governors' reports for the period 1838–1842, i.e. when potato cultivation had reached an early maximum according to the figures in Table 15.1. Percentages show the proportion of potato in net crop in hectolitres (Column 1) and recalculated (the same way as in Table 15.1) to give a rough measure of calorie content (Column 2). The latter figures are mapped on Figure 15.6.

Table 15.2   Potatoes as a percentage of total harvest and as crop per capita in Swedish counties (excluding towns), 1838–1842

	County	Potatoes' proportion of crop return Per cent of unconverted volumes	Potatoes' proportion of crop calorie content. Per cent.	Potato crop per capita. Hectolitres
		1	2	3
B	Stockholm	37	14	3.17
C	Uppsala	26	9	2.41
D	Södermanland	37	14	2.41
E	Östergötland	37	15	2.65
F	Jönköping	41	18	2.28
G	Kronoberg	49	23	2.16
H	Kalmar	45	19	2.54
I	Gotland	42	17	3.35
K	Blekinge	61	31	4.78
L	Kristianstad	53	24	5.52
M	Malmöhus	29	11	2.85
N	Halland	43	20	3.15
O	Göteb. & Boh.	40	18	2.41
P	Älvsborg	55	30	3.64
R	Skaraborg	34	14	2.32
S	Värmland	34	15	1.38
T	Örebro	37	15	1.78
U	Västmanland	29	10	1.71
W	Kopparberg	20	8	1.07
X	Gävleborg	32	12	1.43
Y	Västernorrland	36	14	1.57
Z	Jämtland	45	20	1.30
ZA	Västerbotten	45	20	1.86
ZB	Norrbotten	25	9	0.66
	Sweden	40	17	2.54

Sources: KB 1838–1842; *Minnesskift*, 1949: 75–83.

NB 1: Crop return= net return (seed deducted).

NB 2: For conversion of hectolitres to calories, see Table 15.1.

NB 3: The figures in column 3 underestimate real quantities to a considerable degree and are given primarily with the purpose of facilitating comparisons between counties. To make a rough estimate of real quantities, multiply figures in column 3 by 1.45.

The variations between different counties were indeed considerable. While in some counties potatoes constituted almost a third of net crop calorie content, in others it provided less than a tenth. The counties where the potato was of greatest importance (esp. Blekinge (K), Älvsborg (R), Kronoberg (G) as well as large parts of Kristianstad county (L)) were usually characterized by low-pH moraine soils giving low grain yields. As was mentioned earlier the potato had proven ideal here, which helped to make these parts of the country self-sufficient in food after 1820. Plainsland counties where grain production was more important, such as Uppsala (C), Malmöhus (M) and Skaraborg (R) were all below average with respect to the potato proportion of crop calorie content.

Figure 15.6 Potatoes' proportion of calorie content of crop return in Swedish counties, 1838–1842 (per cent)

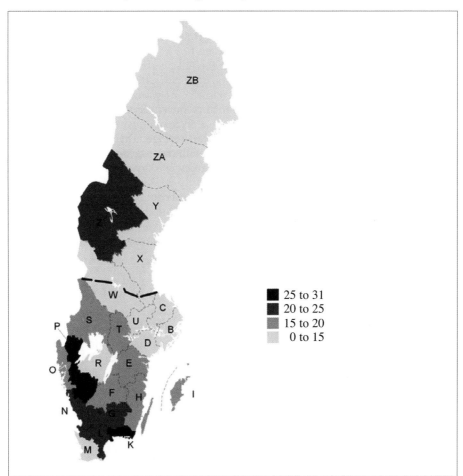

Source: Table 15.2, column 2.
NB: Broken line roughly delimits 'Northern' Sweden.

323

Table 15.2 also states net potato crop in hectolitres per capita (Column 3). The average for the whole country was, according to the statistics, 254 litres. However, as has been mentioned, these statistics are known to be affected by considerable underestimates. An increase by 45 per cent seems reasonable in order to reach realistic levels by 1840[12], which would give a production of about 368 l. of potatoes per capita. To this should be added the potatoes that were produced in vegetable gardens and temporary plantations. If the previously mentioned increase of 12 per cent is accepted, this would result in a per-capita production in the neighbourhood of 410 litres, or 290 kg (790 grams a day).[13] Not all potatoes produced in Sweden were consumed as solid food by humans, however. Some were used for animal feed and some for alcohol production. In fact the two uses were often combined, as the draff from alcohol production was used for animal feed. If we allow for a rough 30 per cent of the potatoes being used for distilling and fodder this would leave approximately 200 kg per capita, or 550 grams a day, for human consumption. This was a little lower than what was consumed in the Netherlands in the early 1840s, but on level with what was consumed in Belgium and Norway (see articles by Ó Gráda and Paping and Tassenaar in this volume).

V.2. Potatoes as the food of the poor

From the point of view of the poorest strata of the population, the potato had the advantage of calling for a comparatively small acreage per quantity of food produced, and only simple equipment for its cultivation and storage. The field work in potato cultivation could, if necessary, be accomplished with only the use of a spade or a hoe. Storage could be carried out by burying the potatoes in a dry, sandy slope. Moreover, children and immature workers could make a relatively greater contribution of productive work than they could in grain production (a small child could plant and lift potatoes but scarcely handle a plough, scythe or flail). All this was to the advantage of the poorer strata, who found in the potato an inexpensive food item, possible to produce on small plots. Probate inventories show that potatoes took a more prominent place in the seed of the landless than of the peasant farmers (Gadd, 2000: 256–257; Gadd, 1983: 93–95).

V.3. The potato blight

In Sweden the blight[14] devastated large parts of the potato crop in 1845 in the neighbourhood of Göteborg (Gothenburg) in the west, and in Scania in the very south. According to the reports of the county governors it also showed up in the counties of Skaraborg (R) and Värmland (S). Most of eastern Sweden was spared this year. In the following years, 1846 and 1847, the blight prevailed over more or less the whole of southern and central Sweden up to roughly the latitude of 150 km north of Stockholm (Juhlin Dannfelt, 1913: 320; KB 1843–47).

---

[12] Estimate based on study in progress by C.-J. Gadd.

[13] Weight of a barrel of potatoes according to *Minnesskrift* (1949: 182). A 'Swedish' barrel of 36 *kappar* (63 *kannor*) is estimated at 164.871 litres. Cf Forsell, 1833: 331; Morell, 1988: 40–44; BiSOS, ser. N.

[14] In 19th century Swedish the potato blight was usually called *torröta* ('dry rot') or simply *potatissjuka* (potato disease).

Only minor attacks of the blight were reported north of here, from the counties of Kopparberg (W), Gävleborg (X) and Västernorrland (Y). In the county of Gävleborg potato cultivation is said to have even increased during the period 1843–1847, and in Kopparberg during both 1843–1847 and 1848–1850. No blight at all is reported before 1850 from the two northernmost counties, Västerbotten (ZA) and Norrbotten (ZB), or from Jämtland (Z) county in the northern interior (KB 1843–1847; 1848–1850).

On the other hand, comparatively major attacks were reported for 1843–1847 by the governors of the two southernmost counties, Malmöhus (M) and Kristianstad (L). In their accounts for 1848–1850, however, both governors were much more optimistic. The potato disease was 'on the decrease and less extensive' (KB 1848–1850: Kristianstad county: 5).

Scholars agree that the effects of the potato blight were not as serious in Sweden as in Ireland and some other parts of Europe. Gustaf Utterström (1957: 700), a major Swedish agrarian historian, pointed out that:

1) The blight, when it appeared, did not cause as much damage to the potato crop as in some other parts of Europe.

2) The potato was not as important a part of the diet in Sweden as in e.g. Ireland.

A survey of the verbal comments by the county governors for the period 1843–1847 confirms that the effects of the blight were, as a rule, not considered alarming. In several cases the governors say that potato cultivation before the blight had been excessive. Some governors even seem to think that the decrease in potato crops might be for the good: Much liquor had been produced from potatoes, and the distillation of snaps was now expected to decline (see e.g. KB 1843–1847: Östergötland county: 11; Jönköping county: 6). The only report that expresses grave concern about the supply situation for parts of the population as a result of the blight is that written in Kristianstad county (L) in the very south, where a great many potatoes were cultivated in the woodlands (KB 1843–1847: Kristianstad county: 6–7).

Table 15.3 Net potato crop in Sweden according to official statistics, 1838–1855

	Lifted potatoes, hectolitres	Index
1838–42	7,838,051	100
1843–47	8,795,433	112
1848–50	8,056,819	103
1851–55	8,951,745	114

Source: Hellstenius, 1871: 107.

NB. 1: Seed potatoes have been deducted from crop results.

NB. 2: Barrels converted to hectolitres. 1 barrel − 1.64871 hl.

A problem with the Swedish official agricultural statistics 1818–1855, which applies especially to this study, is that figures are presented for five-year periods only (crop results as averages for each period), apart from the three-year period 1848–1850, when statistics were reorganized. As we have seen, one of these five-year periods covered the years 1843–1847, which makes it impossible to make detailed statistical comparisons of the situation just before and right after the spread of the blight. However, the figures available indicate that while the *relative* size of the potato crop had fallen by the end of the period 1843–1847 (see Table 15.1) the absolute size of potato production had increased from the previous five-year period (Table 15.3). For the next period, 1848–1850, the governors indicate an absolute decrease of 8 per cent from 1843–1847. This was followed by an increase of 11 per cent in 1851–1855. Even if the reader should not pay too much regard to the exact sizes of these changes (period-to-period comparisons tend to exaggerate increases and underrate decreases since the general underestimation inherent in these figures declines with time) this observation probably says something: There was a decrease in potato cultivation around 1845–1848, but it was modest in size and soon made up for.

The statistics allow us to calculate yield ratios (net crop result/seed, Figure 15.7). The yield ratio from potatoes had been on average 6.8 during the twenty-five-year-period 1818–1842. During the five-year period 1842–1847 the average yield ratio was reduced by 10 per cent to 6.1 and for the three-year period 1848–1850 by a further 5 per cent units to 5.8.[15] Until 1860 yield ratios for potatoes never attained the same levels as before the blight.

It should be pointed out that falling yield ratios were not a general phenomenon for all crops. For e.g. rye and barley there was a long-term increase, which is shown in Figure 15.7.

Figure 15.7 Net yield ratios for potatoes and for 1/2 rye, 1/2 barley according to official Swedish statistics, 1818/22–1856/60

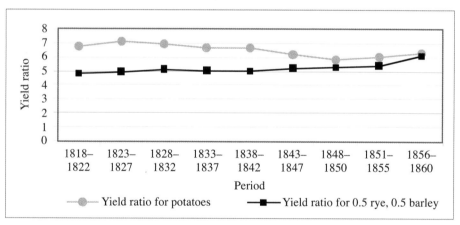

Source: Hellstenius, 1871: 106–107.
NB: Net ratios, i.e. seed has been deducted from crop results.

---

[15] These are net yield ratios, i.e. seed has been deducted from crop results.

Figure 15.8 Net yield ratios for potatoes in the Bysta property, central Sweden, 1818–1860

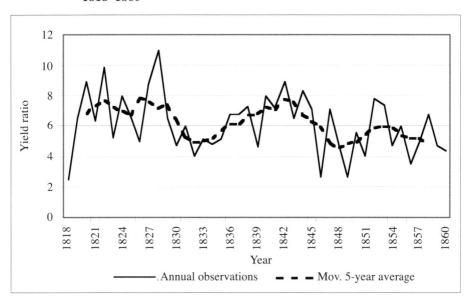

Source: Utterström, 1957: 203–204.

All in all, these statistics seem to confirm the verbal reports of the governors: The damage to potato crops caused by the blight was generally limited.

An example of annual yield ratios for potatoes originates from the Bysta property, Örebro county (T), central Sweden (Figure 15.8). The first attack of the blight seems to have come in 1846, when net crop return declined to 2.6, which was the lowest for 29 years. After a recovery in 1847 there was apparently a renewed attack in 1848. Yield ratios were also remarkably low in 1851 and 1856.

It is important to note that the potato crop of a region was seldom or never wholly stricken by blight. According to a survey in the *Proceedings* of the Swedish academy of Agriculture, published in 1847, the damage 'to the places worst hit amounted to half the crop, in other places to 1/4 or 1/5, but in general much less' (Fries and Wahlberg, 1847: 125).

What is more, not even the potatoes affected by the blight were considered completely useless. Damaged potatoes could be used as animal feed, for snaps distilling and for starch making (Fries and Wahlberg, 1847: 128; Arrhenius, 1862: 264; Lange, 2000: 151)

A considerable amount of all potatoes was used for distilling even before the blight, and at least some of them as animal feed.[16] Consequently, the effects of the blight on consumption may have been less dramatic than might have been expected, although it is possible that the proportion of potatoes used for cattle feed was raised, at least in some areas, as a result of the blight.

---

[16] Potatoes as cattle feed, see Arrhenius, 1862: 250.

V.4. Potato cultivation after the blight

In the course of time the attacks from *phytophthora infestans* subsided. The disease became endemic as in other European countries (Lange, 2000: 150–151; Arrhenius, 1862: 264).

If we look at the figures provided by the county governors (Table 15.1) potato cultivation constituted a lower percentage of the total crop than in 1838–1842, not only in 1843–1847, but also in 1848–1850 and 1851–1855. The *relative* importance of the potato, according to the statistics, never fully reached the level of 1842 before the mid-1870s. However, it should not be overlooked that there was a large overall increase in arable and crop size during the entire period investigated. Although the proportion of potatoes as a percentage of total crop remained largely unchanged, the physical quantity of the potato output increased considerably up to the beginning of the 20th century.

VI. Changes in the number of the poor

VI.1. The number of non-taxpayers

One way to investigate changes in poverty in a society is to estimate the number of people receiving poor relief, or to study variations in the total amount of poor relief, as done in articles on the Netherlands and France in this volume (see chapters by Paping and Tassenaar, and Vivier).

How did poverty develop in Sweden during the 1840s? In two studies by O. Lundsjö (1975) and J. Söderberg (1978) changes in the number of the poor as a percentage of total population are studied for the period 1826–1871. In these studies the 'poor' are defined as those individuals who were considered, by the official authorities, as unable to pay any tax because of destitution. Consequently, in these studies, 'the poor' includes both individuals who received poor relief and those who could narrowly support themselves with the bare necessities of life (Lundsjö, 1975: 38–46; Söderberg, 1978: 12–14).

Table 15.4 shows the percentage of the population, aged 18 and over, who are defined as 'poor', according to the criteria mentioned, every fifth year during the period 1826–1871. 14 of the 24 Swedish counties have been studied by Lundsjö and Söderberg for the whole 45-year period. These counties embraced almost exactly 2/3 of the population. It should be noted that the tax assessment for a certain year reflects the conditions at the end of the previous year. Thus the figure for e.g. the assessment year 1841 shows the situation at the end of 1840, the figure for the assessment year 1846 the situation in late 1845, etc.

On average and in the long run the poor amounted to some 20 per cent of the population, aged 18 and over, in the 14 counties for the whole period 1826–1871. The variations between the years studied are insignificant.

Looking particularly at the period 1845–1850 we find that the 'poverty quota' (the number of poor as a percentage of the entire population aged 18 and over) was, on average for the 14 counties, somewhat higher in the assessment year 1846 than it had been five or ten years earlier, although it was not exceptionally high. Judging from the subsequent measurements every fifth year, the level reached in 1846 did not change during the following 15 years.

Table 15.4   Non-taxpayers as a percentage of total population aged 18 and over. 14 counties, 1826–1871

County	1826	1831	1836	1841	1846	1851	1856	1861	1866	1871
Stockholm[1]	16.3	13.6	13.1	13.8	16.9	16.1	16.3	15.8	13.2	14.0
Uppsala	17.2	17.1	17.5	18.3	21.7	19.3	20.1	18.7	16.7	18.2
Södermanland	19.4	19.7	18.8	19.0	20.3	20.8	20.5	19.4	15.5	16.6
Östergötland	23.5	23.3	22.8	21.7	20.9	21.3	21.0	19.9	19.9	24.1
Blekinge	18.6	21.1	18.2	19.0	24.1	25.6	26.7	25.2	29.0	36.3
Kristianstad	18.2	16.9	19.0	18.4	16.2	16.0	17.1	18.5	18.5	21.0
Malmöhus	17.6	16.7	16.3	16.6	16.0	16.5	17.1	17.5	14.8	16.9
Hallands	21.7	25.6	20.2	20.8	18.6	19.4	20.0	19.5	16.6	20.2
Göteb. o. Bohus	27.9	32.1	25.9	26.1	25.2	25.4	23.9	24.8	21.6	23.6
Älvsborg	24.9	25.3	22.5	20.4	19.8	20.9	20.9	21.5	19.5	24.0
Skaraborg	23.6	25.3	21.5	23.2	23.1	22.7	22.3	21.0	18.4	22.4
Värmland	16.5	15.3	15.3	19.6	21.5	22.1	22.6	24.8	19.7	25.1
Örebro	18.8	18.5	17.3	17.8	17.4	19.6	18.6	18.1	16.7	19.5
Västmanland	22.8	20.3	18.7	20.5	22.2	20.7	19.1	16.8	15.9	17.1
Weighted average for 14 counties[2]	20.8	21.0	19.4	19.9	20.2	20.4	20.4	20.4	18.4	21.6

Sources: Blekinge, Kristianstad, Malmöhus and Halland counties according to Söderberg, 1978: 39. Other counties according to Lundsjö, 1975: 90, 103, 134. Population according to Historisk statistik, Table A5.
NB 1: Stockholm county excluding city of Stockholm
NB 2: Average for 14 counties weighted according to population size.

Six counties and two Scanian parishes have been studied annually with respect to poverty quotas by Lundsjö and Söderberg. On the whole, the period 1845–1850 does not stand out as one of poverty in these areas studied. It is true that there was a peak in poverty in the assessment year 1846 in the three eastern counties of Stockholm, Uppsala and Västmanland, and there is a peak in assessment year 1847 in a Scanian woodland parish studied. But poverty fell again subsequently, and in other areas studied it was largely unchanged or even fell in the five years after 1844 (Lundsjö, 1975: 101; Söderberg, 1978: 69). The governor of Uppsala county confirms this impression of a quick recovery in the eastern counties, saying in his report for the period 1843–1847 (probably written in 1848) that the need in 1845 and early 1846, which had been the worst in living memory, was now on the wane. The suffering during the previous years now seemed like 'a distant and dispersed gust of storm' (KB 1843–1847: Uppsala county: 5).

VI.2.   Strain on local poor relief

Söderberg has also studied the records of parish meetings to investigate when poor relief resources were particularly strained.[17] In the rich parish of Fleninge Söderberg found information only on one occasion indicating extra severe strain on poor relief. In the autumn of 1855 the parish decided to give an allowance of grain to the needy. This contribution would be paid for by the peasant farmers and landed proprietors (Söderberg, 1978: 73).

Nor in woodland parish of Loshult do the years 1845–1850 single out negatively in parish records, while e.g. the hard years some 20 years later do (Söderberg, 1978: 73–74).

To get a somewhat broader picture of local poor relief during the period 1845–1850, I have examined the chapters on the subject in a number of works on local history, i.e. mostly parish histories. These works were usually written by non-professional historians, which may make their scientific value questionable. However, their authors have ransacked parish records and the facts recorded are by no means randomly selected. Misfortunes and disasters have aroused interest. Poor relief – often discussed in parish meetings and therefore easily discernible in the sources – as a rule is given its own chapter.

How are the years 1845–1850 depicted in these books? As a matter of fact this period is hardly mentioned at all in the West-Swedish works (while the misfortunes of 1867–1869 often are).[18] The silence on the consequences of the blight seems somewhat surprising considering the role of the potato as the 'food of the poor'. If the blight deprived already poor people of an important foodstuff this might have been expected to strain poor-relief resources. A plausible explanation might be that the relative prosperity caused by high grain prices (the areas in question were not hit by grain-crop failure) created labour demand and thereby incomes to the poor that were large enough to compensate for the partial reduction in food production caused by the blight.

On the other hand, in the two parishes in my 'sample' from Uppsala and Västmanland counties the supply crisis of 1845–1846 is mentioned, and in a work from Kalmar county the more protracted crisis of 1845–1847. Some of the results will be discussed later. One striking feature is that failure of the grain crop is mentioned as more or less the sole cause of supply crisis; only in the parish in Kalmar county is the potato blight even mentioned, but merely in passing.[19]

VII. Crime statistics

There is one source in which the years 1846–1847 do stand out, and that is in national Swedish statistics on crimes against property. This was demonstrated as early as 1871 by the statistician J. Hellstenius, who also claimed that there was a correlation between

---

[17] Söderberg (1978) has gone through records from parish meetings 1820–1862.

[18] In Bergstrand (1955: 237–255) the difficulties of 1845 are reflected indirectly when peasant farmers decide to donate grain to the areas affected by crop-failure in eastern Sweden. In the nine other West-Swedish works on local history I checked, the period is not mentioned with the exception of a change in general poverty legislation in 1847: Andersson (1969); Bergstrand (1956); Bergstrand and Andersson (1967); Johansson (1971); Henningsson (1987); Johansson (1961); Bergstrand (1963); *Boken om Stenstorp* (1975); *Ytterby* (1957).

[19] Johansson, A (1940: 152–155); Madesjö (1961: 17–21); Tiscornia (1992: 108–111).

harvest results and such crimes. Hellstenius pointed out that the years 1846 and 1847 have the largest number of cases of thefts and pilfering during the whole period 1830–1868, and noted the connection with crop failure. Interestingly, the years of the Crimean war and the early 1860s show a low number of crimes (Figure 15.9) in spite of comparatively high grain prices.

Figure 15.9 Cases of theft and pilfering in Sweden per 100,000 inhabitants, 1830–1868

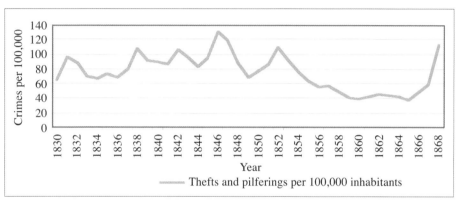

Source: Hellstenius, 1871: 101.

The low number of crimes against property during the Crimean War indicates that high food prices as such did not correlate strongly with this kind of crime. Crop failure correlated well with such crimes, however. This is demonstrated, apart from 1846–1847, by the high figure in 1868. The most probable reason why the number of cases of theft and pilfering was so high during and after years of crop failure is that in such years high food prices coincided with decreasing demand for wage labour. Fewer labourers were required in work such as threshing, and farmers had to make a general cut down on labour expenses (Utterström, 1957: 224, 229–230). The number of thefts during and after years of crop failure reflects the desperate situation of the un- and underemployed.

The quick return to a more or less normal crime ratio in 1848 supports the impression of a comparatively brief crisis, and the still lower ratios in 1849 and 1850 indicate even a small boom in the Swedish rural economy. The low crime ratios in the decade from the mid-50s to the mid-60s support the picture, given in earlier literature, of these years as a period of relative prosperity (Utterström, 1957: 703–704; Gadd, 2000: 348–349).

VIII. Government relief

VIII.1. 'Relief grain' and 'relief funds'

At least from the early 18th century the Swedish central powers tried to give temporary support to the needy when and where grain was scarce. Time after time, the Swedish government issued decrees to the county governors stating that they should find out about the stocks or shortages of grain in each district and inform the government in due time, so that areas struck by crop failure could be given support (Åmark, 1915: 220–229, 305–319). During the 18th century the advances of such 'relief grain' (*undsättnings-spannmål*) became gradually more common until they were 'a permanent object of the government's supervision' (Åmark, 1915: 230). A major reason for this policy was that the Government – extremely dependent on incomes from rural areas, considering the insignificance of towns – wanted to safeguard the long-term taxpaying capacity of the landed peasantry, and, indeed, the continued existence of this 'tax-paying estate' itself (cf Åmark, 1915: 229–230; Gadd, 1991: 214–215; Gadd, 2000: 49). The peasant proprietors (booth those who were actually landowners and those who were tenants of the Crown) were represented in the Diet and, of course, shared the objective of securing their own survival as a group. The political power of the peasants grew during the 18th and 19th centuries, and it is no bold hypothesis (although I have not studied the matter) that they supported and actively promoted Government-lending to areas struck by harvest-failure. Moreover, the Swedish government wanted to promote population increase and in every way counteract population losses, the landless poor being seen as an important labour resource.

The increasing frequency of relief grain and funds is evident from Table 15.5 (columns 1 and 2). In 46 out of 58 years 1719–1776 relief grain was delivered, but in each of the years 1830–1869. The relief funds were distributed in grain until 1798, in grain and money during the period 1799–1813, and mainly in money thereafter. At the local level the relief was organised by the governors with the assistance of the local clergy and county sheriffs (*kronobefallning*); in the 19th century agricultural societies (*hushållnings-sällskap*) and temporary parish-level relief committees also assisted (Åmark, 1915: 223; KB 1843–1847: Blekinge county: 9).

Table 15.5   **Relief grain and funds advanced, 1719–1798, 1830–1840 and 1845–1869 (all sums converted to hectolitres of rye)**

Period	Number of years, whole period	Number of years relief grain was delivered	Total quantity, hectolitres	Hectolitres per year, whole period	Hectolitres per year when grain was delivered
	1	2	3	4	5
1719–76	58	46	625,356	10,783	13,595
1777–98	22	21	516,401	23,473	24,591
1719–98	80	67	1,141,75	14,271	17,041
1830–40	11	11	444,578	40,416	40,416
1845–54	10	10	375,518	37,553	37,553
1855–64	10	10	177,764	17,776	17,776
1865–69	5	5	218,029	43,605	43,605
1830–40, 1845–69	*36*	*36*	*1,215,891*	*33,775*	*33,775*

Sources: Åmark, 1915: 221, 312; Utterström, 1957: 389; Jörberg, 1972: 633–634.

The advances were given as interest-free loans, to be repaid with the collection of taxes during the three following years (KB 1843–1847: Blekinge: 9; Johansson, 1940: 154). In principle, this would mean that those receiving support were those who could provide security, i.e. mainly landowning peasant farmers (Utterström, 1957: 338).

At least by the middle of the 19th century things seem to have worked somewhat differently in practice. During the crop-years 1845–1846 and 1846–1847, when several counties in eastern and south-eastern Sweden were hit by crop failures, the usual course of action seems to have been that the land-owning peasant farmers of the parish provided collective security for the loan, while some of the money borrowed was mediated to the poor through wage-work for these farmers. One gets the impression of a sort of relief work paid for by government loans and organized at the local level. As a rule, a special application to the governor from each parish was required, including a statement of the security that would be given, before relief funds were delivered (Tiscornia, 1992: 108–112; Johansson, 1940: 153–155; Madesjö, 1962: 17–21).

The variations between years were great with respect to the size of the funds advanced. This is shown for the periods 1830–1840 and 1845–1869 in Figure 15.10. While the average for the two periods was 304,000 riksdaler riksgälds per year (equivalent to roughly £18,500[20] or 33,000 hectolitres of rye), in 1831 1,342,000 riksdaler riksgälds was delivered; in the years 1845–1847 between one million and 580,000 riksdaler per year; in 1867 1,100,000 riksdaler and in 1869 840,000 riksdaler.

Figure 15.10 Annual delivery of relief funds, 1830–1840 and 1845–1869 (thousands of riksdaler)

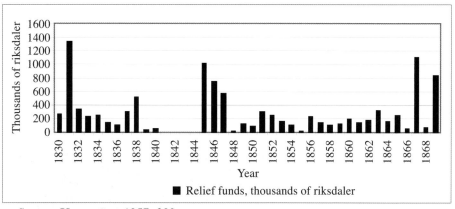

Source: Utterström, 1957: 389.

NB 1: Data is missing for the years 1841–1844; however, it is almost certain that funds were advanced for each of these four years.

NB 2: Annual sums, given in *rikdaler banko* by Utterström for the period 1830–1857, have been recalculated to *riksdaler riksgälds* to make them comparable with the *riksmynt* sums shown after 1858.

---

[20] From 1830 the official exchange rate was £1 = 10.94 riksdaler banko = 16.41 riksdaler riksgälds. Sveriges riksbank., vol. V: 159; Jörberg, 1972a: 81.

During the period 1750–1835 the Swedish population increased by 70 per cent. The relief funds increased by more: in the period 1719–1876 on average 10,800 hectolitres of rye per year were delivered and in the period 1830–1840 sums corresponding to slightly more than 40,000 hectolitres, which is nearly a fourfold increase. After c. 1830 the long-term increase ceased (Table 15.5).

On average a little more than seven counties per year received relief money during the 36 years investigated during the period 1830–1869. During the six years with the largest sums these were distributed roughly as follows:

In 1831 the three western counties of Göteborg & Bohus (O), Älvsborg (P) and Skaraborg (R) received almost 60 per cent of the money. In 1845–1847 comparatively large sums were distributed three years in succession. In 1845 the three counties of Stockholm (B), Uppsala (C) and Västmanland (U) in east-central Sweden got close to 90 per cent, and in 1846 Södermanland (D) and Östergötland (E) were added to make up 83 per cent. In 1847 eleven counties shared the money.

In 1867 almost 90 per cent of the money went to northern Sweden, from Kopparberg (W) and northwards with a heavy concentration towards Västernorrland (ZA), while in 1869 95 per cent of the sum went to four counties bordering on each other in the South and South-West: Älvsborg (P), Jönköping (F), Kronoberg (G) and Kalmar (H); the latter three form the province of Småland (Utterström, 1957: 389).

Figure 15.11 Social composition of agricultural population in Sweden, 1750–1870: Peasants (bönder) and landless + semi-landless (obesuttna). Male heads of households

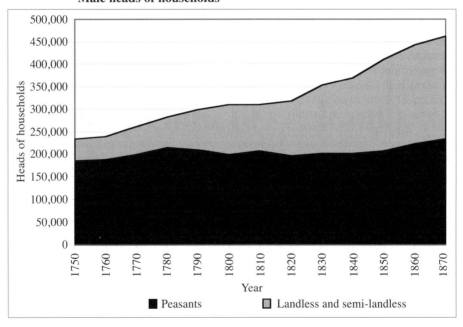

Source: Wohlin, 1909.

It may seem strange that the very high grain prices in the years 1855 and 1856 did not cause large payments of relief money. The reason is that the purpose of these funds was to reduce the effects of crop failures, but the crops these years were relatively good. Besides, the booming demand for grain these years created new job opportunities in agriculture (see above, Section VII).

After 1840, however, government funds found new ways into the Swedish countryside. During the years 1841–1859 46 million riksdaler were invested as government subsidies and loans in public work (*allmänna arbeten*) on railways, canals, dredging work, harbours, bridges and other road work, etc (Åmark, 1915: 319; Utterström, 1957: 392). While the stated reasons for these investments were mainly improvement in communications, they were to some degree also justified as relief work (KB 1842–1847: Uppsala county: 21, Stockholm county: 5). The evident reason for this development was the continued growth of a large, landless proletariat (Figure 15.11). The crofters and cottagers could offer no security for a loan, while their growing number called for a reorganisation of poor relief.

VIII.2. Did government aid matter?

Can the effect of relief funds be measured? Were they merely a drop in the ocean, or did they really make a difference? At least in a few cases the funds seem to have been of some importance. During the two years 1845 and 1846 1.3 million riksdaler riksgälds (£ 79,200) were delivered to the three counties of Stockholm, Uppsala and Västmanland in the proportions stated in Table 15.6. In 1845 the sum covered the purchase of 32 litres of rye per capita on average for the three counties (and in Uppsala county alone, 43 litres). The following year the average for the three counties was 19.5 litres per inhabitant. The quantities for especially 1845 are considerable. According to the standards of the time 410 hectolitres (2.5 barrels) of rye was considered the normal grain consumption for a man during a year. Consequently, 32 litres was about a month's grain consumption for a grown-up individual.

Table 15.6 Relief funds granted to three counties in 1845 and 1846

Year	County	Funds granted, rdr	Rye price/hl	Hectolitres of rye	Litres of rye per capita
1845	Stockholm	355,050	9.37	37,892	34.9
	Uppsala	322,500	"	34,418	42.9
	Västmanland	150,000	"	16,009	19.0
	3 counties	*827,550*		*88,319*	*32.4*
1846	Stockholm	150,000	9.19	16,322	15.0
	Uppsala	150,000	"	16,322	20.4
	Västmanland	189,600	"	20,631	24.5
	3 counties	*489,600*		*53,275*	*19.5*

Sources: Utterström, 1957: 388; Jörberg, 1972: 635; *Minnesskrift,* 1949: 75–83.
NB: The population in 1845, according to *Minnesskrift,* was 108,466 in the county of Stockholm, 80,198 in the county of Uppsala and 84,319 in the county of Västmanland.

The sums granted can also be compared to the value of all seed grain used in the three counties according to official agricultural and price statistics.[21] If the amounts of seed in agricultural statistics are increased by about 45 per cent in order to reach the probable real magnitude of seed grain volumes (see above, Section V.1) we get the following figures for the value of total seed: 1.2–1.4 million riksdaler riksgälds in Stockholm and Uppsala counties, and 0.9 million in Västmanland. Thus the sum of 0.83 million riksdaler, granted to the three counties in 1845, covered about 23 per cent of the value of all seed grain in the three counties.

What importance did the government relief policy have for the rapid recovery? Let us make a 'counterfactual' reformulation: What would have happened if the government relief funds had not existed? To answer such a question completely is probably impossible, since it presupposes the construction of hypothetical historical and institutional contexts entirely different from those that actually existed. However, without diving too deep into historical theorizing it can be argued as unlikely that 23 per cent of arable land (i.e. corresponding to the value of government relief funds) had been left unsown in the three counties, had the government funds not existed. More likely, the funds necessary would have been provided by private financiers or grain-traders, which would have implied interest charges and more exacting terms of repayment. This might have resulted in some debt-burdened peasants having to leave their farms The government loans, on the other hand, were interest-free (Åmark, 1915: 310; KB 1843–1847 Blekinge: 9; Johansson, 1940: 154; Madesjö, 1962:20), and were characterized by repayment conditions relatively favourable to the borrower. True, they were expected to be repaid within three years, but deferment was possible. Indeed, one of the purposes of the government relief policy was to maintain the continued existence of a landowning peasantry. With these conditions were associated the obligation to use some of the money to put the landless poor into wage-work, a type of restriction on the borrower hardly conceivable had the money been lent by private financiers.

IX. Why so little damage from potato blight?

The evidently quite limited effects of the potato blight in Sweden may seem surprising. This urges us to focus on the question 'why?'.

IX.1. Soil types?

A finding made both in Sweden and elsewhere was that the blight did not affect the potato crop to the same extent on all types of soils. For example, in the Netherlands, areas with sandy soils were affected less than areas with clay soils (Paping and Tassenaar, this volume). One reason why the consequences of the potato blight were never so serious in 19th-century Sweden as in many other countries may have been that a large proportion of Swedish potatoes were cultivated on sandy, water-permeable moraine soils.

---

[21] Volumes of seed (here recalculated from 1.65-hectolitre barrels) according to KB 1843–1847; prices for 1845 according to Jörberg, 1972a: 634–641, price of potatoes (not stated by Jörberg) estimated at 30 % of the price of rye (Herlitz, 1988: 212).

IX.2. Climatic factors

Evidently soil-types cannot give the full answer, however, because they don't seem to explain the characteristic geographical pattern of the spread of the blight within Sweden. The two southernmost counties were those worst affected by the blight, while the disease did not appear in the two northernmost counties before 1850. And although the blight did appear in other northern counties it never gained a footing strong enough to prevent potato cultivation from increasing there, even during the period 1845–1850.

In fact the difference between Sweden north and south of the broken line on figure 15.6 follows a familiar pattern. Biologists and ethnologists speak about a *limes norrlandicus*, i.e. a (notional) line running a little south of the broken line on the map. For climatic reasons this *limes* constitutes the northern limit for many plants and trees, e.g. oak and ash. Several crops are scarcely possible to cultivate north of the *limes*, e.g. wheat (the grain mostly grown in this region was barley).

From modern experience we know that the potato blight diffuses less easily the further north it goes. The reason, according to botanists, is that the demands on environmental conditions for the *phytophthora infestans* are in fact quite specific. The disease affects the tubers most effectively in day temperatures of about 20° C (while night temperatures may well be 5° lower), if these temperatures coincide with rainy weather.[22]

In northern Sweden these conditions – high temperature and rainfall – seldom occur together. Although day temperatures around 20° C are not unusual there in July, temperatures fall in rainy weather. Besides, summer weather is comparatively dry along the Swedish east coast, especially in the early summers (*National Atlas*: 80–81) – and it is along the coast of the Gulf of Bothnia that most of the northern population lives.

Another factor that would hamper the spread of potato blight in northern Sweden is the very cold winters with deep soil-frost. The latter prevents tubers left behind in the soil from surviving and becoming new plants the next summer.[23] Infected potatoes surviving the winters in the ground is an important source of infection in other regions.

A third factor that may have played some role is the long distances between potato plantations in a sparsely populated country such as Sweden, which is likely to have had a restraining effect on the diffusion of contamination.[24]

What applies to northern Sweden also applies, to some degree, to the central and southern parts of the country. Although temperatures favourable for the spread of *phytophthora* coincide with rainfall more often here than in the North, such conditions occur more seldom than on the Continent.

Evidently the Swedish weather in the summer of 1845 – the year the blight spread – had a double-edged effect with respect to the conditions for the diffusion of the blight. Temperatures as such may have been favourable for the *phytophthora* fungi. In Torup, situated in the woodlands of south-western Sweden, the average temperature for July and August has been estimated at 13,4 and 13,3° C respectively for the period 1758–1865, while the average for these months in 1845 was as high as 20,3 and 17,8. This was

---

[22] Personal information from Kjell Andersson, former senior lecturer, SLU; Lars Wiik, director of research, SLU; Hans Bång, agronomie licentiat, local manager, Svenskt Potatisutsäde AB. See also webpage of North Dakota State University, *Leaf Blight Diseases of Potato*.

[23] Personal information from K. Andersson, cf. note 22.

[24] Personal information from K. Andersson and H. Bång (cf. note 22).

a record for all July months and the second highest temperature for all August months during the 106 years investigated (Palm, 1997: 162–165). It seems as if hot weather prevailed all over Sweden during the summer of 1845. These high temperatures coincided with dry weather, especially in eastern Sweden. As we have seen, the drought in the East was so severe as to cause a major grain crop failure. These weather conditions probably explain why the potato blight diffused so little in the eastern and south-eastern areas of the country in 1845. The *phytophthora* fungi had to await the more normal weather conditions of the next two years to find a hold all over southern and central Sweden.

However, the long-term average temperatures mentioned go a long way to explain why the blight did comparatively little harm even in southern Sweden, and why it more or less disappeared during many summers.[25]

X. Summary

On the whole, the period 1845–1850 is not seen as one of deep crisis in Swedish history. Demographic and real-wage data give the impression of pretty normal circumstances. Certainly there had been a series of weak harvests in the first half of the 1840s and in 1845 a drought caused severe crop failure in the counties near Stockholm, which constituted one of Sweden's major granaries. In both 1845 and 1846 crops failed in the counties of south-eastern Sweden, less important as grain producers. These crop failures led to local crises that had, on the whole, been surmounted by late 1846 or (in the South-East) late 1847.

While crops in Sweden were generally normal or even good in the period 1846–1848, the high grain-price level caused by the East-Swedish crop failure of 1845 was prolonged by the international price-rise in the second half of 1846 and the first half of 1847. International prices proved more important than domestic harvests for the grain prices in Sweden, where incipient grain exports experienced their first boom.

The potato provided about 17 per cent of the calorie content of net crop by 1840. The production per capita – man, woman and child alike – by then seems to have been in the region of 790 grams a day. If we allow for roughly 30 per cent of the potatoes to be used for distilling and animal feed, this would leave 550 grams a day to be consumed by humans as solid food.

In 1845 the potato blight arrived. During that year southernmost and western Sweden were most affected. The probable reason why the disease penetrated so little into the eastern parts of the country was the severe drought of that year. In the next two years, 1846 and 1847, the new herbal disease diffused over all of southern and central Sweden. However, the blight gained little footing above the latitude of about 150 kilometres

---

[25] It should be observed that conditions for the diffusion of contamination were different in the 19th century than they are today. A major change occurred as late as in the 1970s when potatoes infested with new strains of contamination were imported into Europe. Before, the *phytophthora infestans* in Europe only propagated vegetatively, while it now propagates sexually (personal communication from Kjell Andersson; see note 22; See also information on webpage of SLU, Dept of Ecology and Crop Production Science on *Potatisbladmögel* (potato blight).

north of Stockholm, and by international standards the effects of the blight were mild even in the southern and central parts of Sweden.

Climatic factors seem to be the most important explanation why Sweden, and particularly its northern provinces, were stricken relatively lightly by the blight. Specific requirements with respect to temperature and rainfall must be fulfilled before the *phytophthora infestans* can propagate, and these conditions coincide less often the further north we go.

The regional supply crises of 1845–1846 in eastern, and in 1845–1847 in south-eastern Sweden were caused principally by grain-crop failure, and to a much smaller extent by the blight. One of the few regions where potato blight was mentioned as a prime reason for distress among the poor was the woodlands of Scania, an area of Sweden that was among those with the largest potato crops per capita.

Judging from data from 14 of Sweden's 24 counties the proportion of poor people in the population was somewhat higher in the mid 1840s than had been the case five or ten years earlier. However, the new level was by no means exceptional, and the period 1845–1847 was (judging from a smaller sample of counties and parishes) not characterized by a general increase in poverty. While there was an increase between 1844 and 1845/46 in the East, this was followed by a decrease in the years to come, and in the parts of the plainslands of western and southern Sweden reported poverty seems to have declined during the five-year period after 1844.

To some extent the impression of relative 'normality' given by demographic sources for the years 1845–1847 is invalidated by crime statistics: in 1846–1847 cases of theft and pilfering reached their highest level per thousand for the entire period 1830–1868. High rates of such crimes correlate with severe crop failures, but not with high grain prices as such. The probable reason is that in and after years of very poor harvests food prices rose while labour demand fell, both changes working to the detriment of the landless poor. When high prices were caused primarily by rising demand from abroad, as was the case during the Crimean war, rising wages seem to have compensated for the price-rise in food.

The Swedish Government had a long tradition of giving temporary support to regions subject to bad harvests. During the three years 1845–1847 2.3 million riksdaler riks-gälds, equivalent to the value of 290,000 hectolitres of rye, were distributed, generally as interest-free loans, from the Government to the parts of the country worst hit by harvest failure. In 1845 alone, the sums lent to the East-Swedish counties of Uppsala, Stockholm and Västmanland corresponded to 32 litres of rye per capita, or about 25 per cent of total seed-grain value in the three counties for one year. This was among the largest per-capita sums ever lent by the government to any region during the period 1830–1869. To some extent this was conducive to the quick recovery of the counties hit by crop failure in 1845 and 1846. An important effect was to make terms of repayment more lenient than would have been the case had the loans been provided by private financiers.

The most important reason why Sweden was affected so mildly by the European crisis of 1845–1850 was, in the end, that the failure of grain crops in 1845 and 1846 was regionally limited and that the potato blight never had the same penetration, for climatic reasons, as on the Continent or the British Isles.

Bibliography

Adamson, R. (1991) 'Statlig spannmålspolitik i övergången mellan merkantilism och liberalism 1810–25', in J. Myrdal (ed.), *Statens jordbrukspolitik under 200 år.* Stockholm, pp. 33–44.

Åmark, K. (1915) *Spannmålshandel och spannmålspolitik i Sverige 1719–1830,* Stockholm.

Arrhenius, J. (1862) *Handbok i svenska jordbruket.Vol. 2,* 2nd ed., Uppsala.

Backman, G. (1919) 'Om svenska värnpliktigas kroppslängd åren 1887–1894', *Svenska läkaresällskapets handlingar,* 45, pp. 494–521.

Bergstrand, C.M. (1955) *Essunga i svunnen tid,* Essunga.

Bergstrand, C.M. (1956) *Långareds krönika. 2. Tiden 1801–1860,* Alingsås.

Bergstrand, C.M. (ed.) (1963) *Kinnarumma sockens historia,* Viskafors.

Bergstrand, C.M. and Andersson B. (1967) *Stora Lundby, Bergum, Östad. Ur tre socknars krönika,* Gråbo.

BiSOS: *Bidrag till Sveriges officiella statistik,* Stockholm, 1857–1912.

Boken om Stenstorp. Bygden där bergen mötas (1975) Stenstorp.

Carlsson, S. and Rosén, J. (1970) *Svensk historia. Vol. 2,* Stockholm.

Emigrationsutredningen. Betänkande i utvandringsfrågan, Stockholm 1913.

Fitinghoff, L. (1907) *Barnen ifrån Frostmofjället. En barnberättelse för små och stora,* Stockholm.

Forssell, C. af (1833) *Statistik öfver Sverige, grundad på offentliga handlingar.* (Faksimile edition, Stockholm, 1978).

Fries, E. and Wahlberg, P.F. (1846) 'Utlåtande öfver potatoes-farsoten afgifvet till Kongl. Vetenskapsakademien', *Handlingar rörande landtbruket och dess binäringar,* 6:1, (pr. 1847), pp. 123–131.

Gadd, C.-J. (1983) *Järn och potatis. Jordbruk, teknik och social omvandling i Skaraborgs län 1750–1860,* Göteborg.

Gadd, C.-J. (1991) *Självhushåll eller arbetsdelning? Svenskt lant- och stadshantverk ca 1400–1860,* Göteborg.

Gadd, C.-J. (1998) 'Jordbruksteknisk förändring i Sverige under 1700- och 1800-talen. Regionala aspekter', in L. Palm, C.-J. Gadd and H. Nyström, *Ett föränderligt agrarsamhälle. Västsverige i jämförande belysning.* Göteborg, pp. 83–228.

Gadd, C.-J. (2000) *Den agrara revolutionen 1700–1870,* Stockholm. (Det svenska jordbrukets historia; Vol. 3).

Handlingar rörande landtbruket och dess binäringar, utgifne av Kongl. Svenska Landtbruksakademien, vol. 1–19 (1841–1859).

Heintel, M., Sandberg, L.G. and Steckel, R. (1998) 'Swedish historical heights revisited: New estimation techniques and results', in J. Komlos and J. Baten (eds), *The Biological Standard of Living in Comparative Perspective,* Stuttgart, pp. 449–458.

Hellstenius, J. (1871) 'Skördarna i Sverige och deras verkningar', *Statistisk tidskrift,* 20, pp. 77–120.

Henningsson, J. (1987) *Trökörna. En sockenbok,* Nossebro.

Herlitz, U. (1988) *Restadtegen i världsekonomin. Lokala studier av befolkningstillväxt, jordbruksproduktion och fördelning i Västsverige 1800–1860,* Göteborg.

Historisk statistik för Sverige. 1. Befolkning, Stockholm 1955.

Hultcrantz, J.V. (1896) 'Om svenskarnes kroppslängd. Ett bidrag till Sveriges antropologi', *Ymer,* 60, pp. 5–26.

Johansson, A. (1952) *Från 1800-talets Huddunge,* Sala.

Johansson, H. (1961) *Barne Åsaka förr och nu. En västgötasockens öde,* Vedum.

Johansson, H. (ed.) (1971) *Boken om Gudhem. Bygden mellan bergen invid Hornborgasjön,* Gudhem.

Jörberg, L. (1972 a-b) *A History of Prices in Sweden. 1–2,* Lund.

Juhlin Dannfelt, H. (1913) *Kungl. landtbruksakademien 1813–1912 samt svenska landthushållningen under nittonde århundradet,* Stockholm.

KB: *Kunglig Maj:ts befallningshafvandes femårsberättelser, 1818–55,* Stockholm.

Krantz, O. (1987) *Utrikeshandel, ekonomisk tillväxt och strukturförändring efter 1850,* Malmö.

Kumm, E. (1949) *Indelt soldat och rotebonde,* Stockholm.

Lange, U. (2000) *Experimentalfältet. Kungl. Lantbruksakademiens experiment- och försöksverksamhet på norra Djurgården i Stockholm 1816–1907,* Stockholm.

Larsson, T. (1945) *Reformen i brännvinslagstiftningen 1853–1854,* Stockholm.

Lundsjö, O. (1975) *Fattigdomen på den svenska landsbygden under 1800-talet,* Stockholm.

Madesjö sockens historia. Vol. 2 (1962) Madesjö.

Minnesskrift med anledning av den svenska befolkningsstatistikens 200-åriga bestånd (1949) Stockholm.

Morell, M. (1988) *Om mått- och viktsystemens utveckling i Sverige sedan 1500-talet. Vikt- och rymdmått fram till metersystemets införande,* Uppsala. (Uppsala Papers in Economic History. Research Report; 16).

Morell, M. (2001) *Jordbruket i industrisamhället 1870–1945,* Stockholm. (Det svenska jordbrukets historia; Vol. 4.).

National Atlas of Sweden. Climate, Lakes and Rivers (1995) Stockholm.

Nathorst, J. Th. (1842–59) 'Om spannmålsprisen 1842', 'Om spannmålsprisen 1843', '... 1844', etc. *Handlingar rörande landtbruket och dess binäringar...* Vol. 2–19.

Nelson, M.C. (1988) *Bitter Bread. The famine in Norrbotten 1867–1868,* Uppsala.

Nordisk familjebok. Konversationslexikon och realencyklopedi (1904–1923) Stockholm.

Ohlander, A.-S. and Norman, H. (1984) 'Kriser och katastrofer. Ett forskningsprojekt om effekterna av nöd, svält och epidemier i det förindustriella Sverige', *Historisk tidskrift,* 103, pp. 162–178.

Palm, L. (1997) *Gud bevare utsädet! Produktionen på en västsvensk ensädesgård: Djäknebol i Hallands skogsbygd 1760–1865,* Stockholm.

Sandberg, L.G. and Steckel, R.H. (1980) 'Soldier, soldier what made you grow so tall? A study of height, health an nutrition in Sweden, 1720–1881', *Economy and history,* 23, pp. 91–105.

Sandberg, L.G. and Steckel, R.H. (1987) 'Heights and economic history: The Swedish case', *Annals of Human Biology,* 14, pp. 101–110.

Sandberg, L.G. and Steckel, R.H. (1988) 'Overpopulation and malnutrition rediscovered: Hard times in 19th-century Sweden', *Explorations in Economic History,* 25, pp. 1–19.

Schön, L. (1995) *Jordbruk med binäringar 1800–1980,* Lund. (Historiska national-räkenskaper för Sverige).

Schön, L. (2000) *En modern svensk ekonomisk historia. Tillväxt och omvandling under två sekel,* Stockholm.

Söderberg, J. (1978) *Agrar fattigdom i Sydsverige under 1800-talet,* Stockholm.

Söderberg, J. (1989) 'Hard times in 19th-centuy Sweden: A comment', *Explorations in Economic History,* 26, pp. 477–491.

Sveriges riksbank 1668–1924. Bankens tillkomst och verksamhet. Vol. 5, Stockholm, 1931.

Tiscornia, A. (1992) *Statens, godsens eller böndernas socknar? Den sockenkommunala självstyrelsens utveckling i Västerfärnebo, Stora Malm och Jäder 1800–1880,* Uppsala.

Utterström, G. (1957) *Jordbrukets arbetare. Levnadsvillkor och arbetsliv på landsbygden från frihetstiden till mitten av 1800-talet. Vol. 1,* Stockholm. (Den svenska arbetarklassens historia).

Wohlin, N. (1909) *Den jordbruksidkande befolkningen i Sverige 1751–1900. Statistisk-demografisk studie på grundval av de svenska yrkesräkningarna,* Stockholm. (Emigrations-utredningen; Bilaga IX).

Ytterby förr och nu. En sockenskildring (1957) Göteborg and Ytterby.

Internet sources

North Dakota State University, NDSU Extension Service: http://www.ext.nodak.edu/extpubs/plantsci/hortcrop/pp1084w.htm, 2004-10-28

SLU, Dept of Ecology and Crop Production Science: http://www.tvs.slu.se/svensk/aktuellt/Potbladmogel/biologi.html, 2005-02-24

Statistics Sweden: http://www.scb.se/templates/Product_26046.asp, 2005-02-29